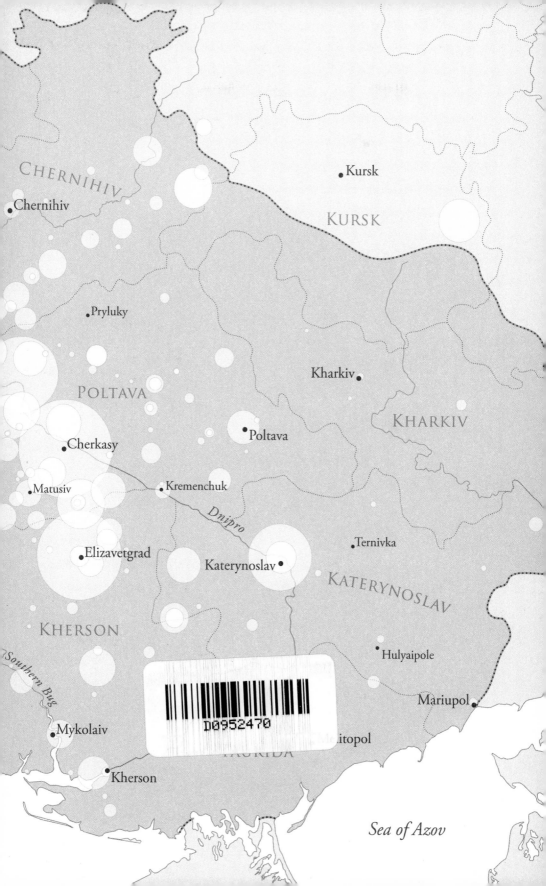

CHERNIHIV

• Chernihiv

KURSK

• Kursk

KURSK

• Pryluky

POLTAVA

• Kharkiv

KHARKIV

• Poltava

• Cherkasy

• Matusiv

Kremenchuk

Dnipro

• Elizavetgrad

Katerynoslav

• Ternivka

KATERYNOSLAV

KHERSON

Southern Bug

• Hulyaipole

• Mariupol

• Mykolaiv

D0952470

itopol

TAURIDA

• Kherson

Sea of Azov

IN THE MIDST OF
CIVILIZED EUROPE

IN THE MIDST OF CIVILIZED EUROPE

THE POGROMS OF 1918–1921 AND THE ONSET OF THE HOLOCAUST

JEFFREY VEIDLINGER

METROPOLITAN BOOKS

Henry Holt and Company   New York

Metropolitan Books
Henry Holt and Company
Publishers since 1866
120 Broadway
New York, New York 10271
www.henryholt.com

Metropolitan Books® and m® are registered trademarks of
Macmillan Publishing Group, LLC.

Library of Congress Cataloging-in-Publication data

Names: Veidlinger, Jeffrey, 1971– author.
Title: In the midst of civilized Europe : the pogroms of 1918–1921 and the
onset of the Holocaust / Jeffrey Veidlinger.
Other titles: Pogroms of 1918–1921 and the onset of the Holocaust
Description: First edition. | New York : Metropolitan Books, Henry Holt and
Company 2021. | Includes bibliographical references and index.
Identifiers: LCCN 2020054186 (print) | LCCN 2020054187 (ebook) | ISBN
9781250116253 (hardcover) | ISBN 9781250116260 (ebook)
Subjects: LCSH: Pogroms—Ukraine—History—20th century. |
Pogroms—Poland—History—20th century. |
Antisemitism—Ukraine—History—20th century. |
Antisemitism—Poland—History—20th century. |
Jews—Ukraine—History—20th century. | Jews—Poland—History—20th
century. | Ukraine—Ethnic relations. | Poland—Ethnic relations. |
Holocaust, Jewish (1939–1945)
Classification: LCC DK508.812 .V45 2021 (print) | LCC DK508.812 (ebook) |
DDC 305.892/4047709041—dc23
LC record available at https://lccn.loc.gov/2020054186
LC ebook record available at https://lccn.loc.gov/2020054187

Our books may be purchased in bulk for promotional, educational, or business use. Please
contact your local bookseller or the Macmillan Corporate and Premium Sales Department at
(800) 221-7945, extension 5442, or by e-mail at MacmillanSpecialMarkets@macmillan.com.

First Edition 2021

Designed by Kelly S. Too

Printed in the United States of America

1   3   5   7   9   10   8   6   4   2

In the very midst of civilized Europe, at the dawn of the new era for which the world awaits its charter of liberty and justice, the existence of a whole population is threatened. Such crimes dishonour not only the people that commit them, but outrage human reason and conscience.

ANATOLE FRANCE, 1919

CONTENTS

IN THE MIDST OF
CIVILIZED EUROPE

"Will a Slaughter of Jews
Be Next European Horror?"

In the years after the Holocaust, survivors around the globe began compiling memorial books, one for each city and town. These literary monuments to destroyed communities preserved local stories and documented the names of victims to keep memory alive. As a historian of eastern European Jewry, I have long appreciated the way these memorial books provide insight into the everyday rhythms of ordinary life. In them, contributors share anecdotes about the local schools, the fire brigade orchestra, the soccer club, the Zionist youth group. They paint portraits of local celebrities whose fame extended only as far as the wheat fields around the town: a favorite teacher, a respected rabbi, the town councilor, the water porter everybody knew. They document events small and large: the time a Jewish soldier returned home from the Russo-Japanese War, the time a traveling theater troupe from Odesa came to town, the time a fire burned down Yankl Friedman's inn, the day the Nazis arrived.

But such memorial books are not only histories of the prewar period; they are also prehistories of the war itself. Take, for instance, the memorial book from the town of Proskuriv, located in today's

Ukraine. The book's title, *Khurbn Proskurov*, captures the calamity the city endured. The Yiddish word *khurbn* ("destruction"), a term derived from the Hebrew *ḥurban*, denotes the destruction of the two biblical temples in the sixth century BCE and the first century CE—the ur-catastrophes of the Jewish people—and has since been used to describe an array of other disasters, from earthquakes to the sinking of the *Titanic*. After the Second World War, it became widely understood to refer to the fate of European Jewry under the Nazis.

As is typical of memorial books, *Khurbn Proskurov* begins with a dedication: "To the memory of the holy souls who perished during the terrible slaughter that befell the Jews of Proskuriv." The frontispiece depicts a common image in Holocaust art, a single memorial candle and a rosebush with thorny stems evoking barbed wire. A landscape of rolling fields beneath a city on a hill suggests the bucolic countryside around Proskuriv, with fields of flax and wheat and orchards of cherries and plums. As in many such memorial books, the text is in Yiddish and Hebrew and includes a foreword by a well-known townsman—in this case, the folklorist Avrom Rechtman. There are the usual tales of local personalities and municipal institutions. The book concludes with the names of the martyred, a list that extends to thirty pages.

What differentiates *Khurbn Proskurov*, though, is that it was written in 1924—nine years before Hitler's rise to power and fifteen years before the start of the Second World War.[1] It commemorates a different *khurbn*, a different holocaust. Or, perhaps, it is more accurate to say, the real beginning of the same Holocaust. The destruction of Proskuriv took place a year after the establishment of a Ukrainian state that promised broad freedoms and national autonomy to its Jewish minority, and three months after the armistice of November 11, 1918, that ended the Great War. Delegates from thirty-two nations had just gathered in Paris to work out the treaties that would formally cap what H. G. Wells called "the war that will end war."[2] Meanwhile, thirteen hundred miles to the east, on the afternoon of February 15, 1919, Ukrainian soldiers murdered over a thousand Jewish civilians in what was at the time possibly the single deadliest episode of violence to befall the Jewish people in their long history of oppression.

די ארויסגעבער פון דעם בוך, דער
פּראסקורראווער רעליעף פאראיין, דריקט
אויס זייער הארציגען דאנק צו מר. שלמה
נפתלי צבי המכונה אלטער גרייטער פאר
דעם ארטיקעל „דער פּראסקורראווער
חורבן", וועלכען ער האט צוזאמען מיט
מר. זוסיא וואהל פארפאסט. אויך פאר
דער רשימה פון די הרוגים וואס מר.
גרייטער האט צוזאמענגעשטעלט און אויך
פאר זיינע פילע לייסטונגען מעגליך צו
מאכן די ערשיינונג פון דעם בוך.

די הכנסה פון דעם בוך איז באשטימט
געווארען פאר די בתי יתומים און מושב
זקנים אין פּראסקורראוו.

די ארויסגעבער.

Frontispiece to *Khurbn Proskurov*

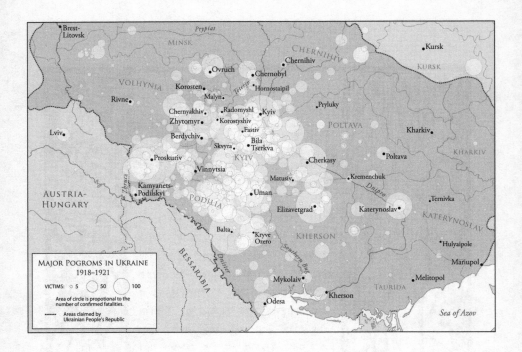

The massacre in Proskuriv was not an isolated event. Between November 1918 and March 1921, during the civil war that followed the Great War, over one thousand anti-Jewish riots and military actions—both of which were commonly referred to as pogroms—were documented in about five hundred different locales throughout what is now Ukraine, and which was at the time contested territory between Russian, Polish, Ukrainian, and multinational soviet successor states of the Russian and Austro-Hungarian empires.[3]

This was not the first wave of pogroms in the area, but its scope eclipsed previous bouts of violence in terms of the range of participants, the number of victims, and the depths of barbarity. Ukrainian peasants, Polish townsfolk, and Russian soldiers robbed their Jewish neighbors with impunity, stealing property they believed rightfully belonged to them. Armed militants, with the acquiescence and support of large segments of the population, tore out Jewish men's beards, ripped apart Torah scrolls, raped Jewish girls and women, and, in many cases, tortured Jewish townsfolk before gathering them in market squares, marching them to the outskirts of town, and shooting them. On at least one occasion, insurgent fighters barricaded Jews in a synagogue and burned down the building. The largest of the anti-Jewish massacres left over a thousand people dead, but the vast majority were much smaller affairs: more than half the incidents resulted only in property damage, injury, and at most a few fatalities. The numbers are contested, but a conservative estimate is that forty thousand Jews were killed during the riots and another seventy thousand subsequently perished from their wounds, or from disease, starvation, and exposure as a direct result of the attacks. Some observers counted closer to three hundred thousand victims. Although that higher figure is likely exaggerated, most historians today would agree that the total number of pogrom-related deaths within the Jewish community between 1918 and 1921 was well over one hundred thousand. The lives of many more were shattered. Approximately six hundred thousand Jewish refugees were forced to flee across international borders, and millions more were displaced internally. About two-thirds of all Jewish houses and over half of all Jewish businesses in the region were looted or destroyed. The pogroms traumatized the affected communities for at least a generation and set off alarms around the world.

I HAD ALWAYS thought that the Holocaust was simply inconceivable before it happened—that it was beyond the ability of humans to imagine, to predict, or to prepare for. My father, whose story of survival informed my early knowledge of the Holocaust, emphasized how "normal" everything seemed before. He lived an upper-middle-class life in Budapest, enjoying fencing lessons and family vacations at Lake Balaton, until the Nazi invasion of Hungary in March 1944. Likewise, the most famous victims of the Holocaust had their first encounters with genocidal antisemitism only several years into the war. Anne Frank went into hiding in July 1942, and the Gestapo discovered her secret annex in August 1944. Elie Wiesel reports that he first heard rumors of massacres as early as 1941, but it was not until May 1944 that he was deported to Auschwitz from the Sighetu Marmaţiei ghetto, which had been set up a few weeks earlier. Many popular portrayals of the

Holocaust similarly emphasize the suddenness and unexpectedness of what took place. When I bring my students to the Holocaust Memorial Center in Farmington Hills, Michigan, for instance, they enter the exhibition in a large open space filled with Jewish ritual objects and photos of everyday Jewish life in Europe, testifying to a vibrant, rooted existence. Then, turning a corner, they encounter a massive portrait of Adolf Hitler looming over a long hallway that descends into the next exhibit room. The impression is that Hitler appeared out of the blue, with no hint of the coming apocalypse.

But the evidence is clear that the murder of six million Jews in Europe was not only conceivable but feared as a distinct possibility for at least twenty years before it became a reality. On September 8, 1919, for instance, the *New York Times* reported on a convention held in Manhattan to protest the bloodshed then underway in eastern Europe. UKRAINIAN JEWS AIM TO STOP POGROMS, the headline read; MASS MEETING HEARS THAT 127,000 JEWS HAVE BEEN KILLED AND 6,000,000 ARE IN PERIL. The article concluded by quoting Joseph Seff, president of the Federation of Ukrainian Jews in America: "This fact that the population of 6,000,000 souls in Ukrainia and in Poland have received notice through action and by word that they are going to be completely exterminated—this fact stands before the whole world as the paramount issue of the present day."[4]

A few months before the *Times* warned of the extermination of the Jews of eastern Europe, the *Literary Digest* ran an article on the unrest in Russia, Poland, and Ukraine with the tagline WILL A SLAUGHTER OF JEWS BE NEXT EUROPEAN HORROR? These fears were enunciated in a comprehensive report by the Russian Red Cross that soberly concluded: "The task that the pogrom movement set itself was to rid Ukrainia of all Jews and to carry it out in many cases by the wholesale physical extermination of this race."[5] The American Jewish anarchist Emma Goldman, who spent much of 1920–1921 in the region, described a "literary investigator" she met in Odesa who had been collecting materials on the pogroms in seventy-two cities. "He believed that the atmosphere created by them intensified the anti-Jewish spirit and would someday break out in the wholesale slaughter of the Jews,"

UKRAINIAN JEWS AIM TO STOP POGROMS

Commission to Visit Europe and Prepare a Memorandum for President Wilson.

LANSING GIVES PERMISSION

Mass Meeting Hears That 127,000 Jews Have Been Killed and 6,000,000 Are in Peril.

The *New York Times* report on efforts to end pogroms in Ukraine, September 8, 1919

Goldman wrote.[6] The *Nation* titled a 1922 feature article on the pogroms in Ukraine THE MURDER OF A RACE, as though searching for a phrase to describe what would later be termed "genocide." Writing from Paris in 1923, the Russian Jewish historian Daniil Pasmanik warned that the violence unleashed by the civil war could lead to "the physical extermination of all Jews."[7] The Great War and the breakdown of social order had brutalized society, fostering a disposition toward barbarism and bloodshed.[8] The slaughter of over one hundred thousand Jews and the complete elimination of Jews from individual towns fostered the idea that the Jews as a whole could one day be annihilated.

During the interwar period, Jews not only spoke about the violence of the pogroms in cataclysmic terms, they also acted accordingly. They fled the threatened region by the millions, radically altering the demography of world Jewry. They established far-reaching self-help and philanthropic organizations. They lobbied the Great Powers, pressing the newly established states of Poland and Romania to accept clauses guaranteeing the rights of minorities in their constitutions. They colonized new lands, setting the groundwork for the establishment of a Jewish state in Palestine. They memorialized the pogroms in elegies and art. In the Soviet Union, one of the successor states to the ravaged region, they joined the civil service, government bureaucracy, and law enforcement expressly to prevent such atrocities from ever happening again and to bring the perpetrators to justice. And they acted, alone and in groups, to forestall what many adamantly believed was a coming catastrophe.

These actions cast suspicion on the Jews of Europe, whose desperate movements were seen as threatening what American president Woodrow Wilson had hoped would be a "just and secure peace." The hundreds of thousands of Jewish refugees arriving in Paris, Berlin, Vienna, Budapest, and Warsaw taxed the resources of these war-weary cities. Demagogic propagandists and pamphleteers stoked fears that the newcomers could be closet Bolsheviks, igniting a worldwide red scare and paving the way for the rise of right-wing political movements. Governments responded by issuing new border regulations; Romania, Hungary, Poland, Germany, the United States, Argentina, and British Palestine—the countries to which the largest numbers of

An ad for the *Literary Digest*'s special edition, "Will a Slaughter of Jews Be Next European Horror?"

Jewish refugees were fleeing—each revised their immigration policies to foreclose further Jewish immigration and to insulate themselves from the Bolshevik menace. The pogroms had rendered the Jews "the world's foremost problem," as Henry Ford's diatribe *The International Jew* put it in 1920.

DESPITE ALL THE alarms it raised at the time, the extermination of over one hundred thousand Jews in the aftermath of the Great War has largely been forgotten today, overwhelmed by the horrors of the Holocaust. Its absence from history textbooks, museums, and public memory of the Holocaust is startling. Yet the pogroms of 1918–1921 can help explain how that next wave of anti-Jewish violence became possible. Historians have sought explanations for the Holocaust in Christian theological anti-Judaism, nineteenth-century racial theories, social envy, economic conflict, totalitarian ideologies, governmental policies that stigmatized Jews, and power vacuums created by state collapse.[9] But rarely have they traced the roots of the Holocaust to the genocidal violence perpetrated against Jews in the very same region in which the "Final Solution" would begin only two decades later. The primary reason for this oversight has been a particular focus on the persecution of Jews in Germany, where anti-Jewish violence in the decades before Hitler's rise to power was relatively rare, and on the Nazi death camps in occupied Poland, where the German bureaucracy modernized and intensified its killing methods. Even the systematic shooting operations common in Ukraine were seen as categorically different from the type of localized frenzy of violence characteristic of pogroms. Pogroms, in short, seemed like relics of a bygone era.

But over the last several decades, historians have come to recognize that in the German-occupied regions of the Soviet Union, the killing was driven primarily by animosity toward Bolshevism and the perceived prominence of Jews in that movement, the same factors that had motivated the pogroms of 1918–1921.[10] Detailed examinations of the massacres that occurred in Ukraine and Poland in 1941 have also revealed the complex ways in which political instability, social and ethnic stratification, and group dynamics turned "ordinary men" and "neighbors" into killers.[11] These studies have expanded our allocation of culpability to include not just remote leaders like Hitler, abstract political philosophies like fascism, and large impersonal organizations like the Nazi Party, but also common people who made decisions on the local level. They have reminded us that about a third of the victims of the Holocaust were murdered at close range, near their homes, with the collaboration of people they knew, before most of the death camps even began functioning in 1942. Indeed, survivors of these massacres referred to them as "pogroms," linking their experiences to a familiar prototype. At the same time, a closer analysis of the pogroms of 1918–1921 shows them not only to be ethnic riots carried out by enraged townsfolk and peasants, but also military actions perpetrated by disciplined soldiers.

What happened to the Jews in Ukraine during the Second World War, then, has roots in what happened to the Jews in the same region only two decades earlier.[12] The pogroms established violence against Jews as an acceptable response to the excesses of Bolshevism: the Bolsheviks' forcible requisitioning of private property, their war on religion, and their arrest and execution of political enemies. The unremitting exposure to bloodshed during that formative period of conflict and state-building had inured the population to barbarism and brutality. When the Germans arrived, riled up with anti-Bolshevik hatred and antisemitic ideology, they found a decades-old killing ground where the mass murder of innocent Jews was seared into collective memory, where the unimaginable had already become reality. As the demographer Jacob Lestschinsky presciently noted on the eve of the German invasion of the Soviet Union, the "heritage of atrocities" left by the "Ukrainian horrors" of 1918–1921 had "still not fully healed."[13] The continued presence of Jews was a constant reminder of the trauma of that era, of the crimes that locals had perpetrated against them and their property, and of the terrible repercussions of those actions. The Nazi German genocide, with its unprecedented scale and horrifying death toll, offered the prospect of a type of absolution, the opportunity to remove the evidence of past atrocities and to relativize the sins of the previous generation, to allow the pogroms to be forgotten amid far greater villainy. As US president Bill Clinton put it during a visit to Kigali, where he acknowledged his failure to prevent the 1994 Rwandan genocide: "Each bloodletting hastens the next, as the value of human life is degraded and violence becomes tolerated, the unimaginable becomes more conceivable."[14]

MOST OF UKRAINE was once part of the historic Polish-Lithuanian Commonwealth, a multinational republic hailed as a "paradise for Jews." In the seventeenth and eighteenth centuries, though, this commonwealth was torn apart by neighboring powers. The lowland plains and vast steppes stretching eastward from the Zbrucz River across the Dnipro river basin to the Donets River, and from the Black Sea in the south to the Prypiat marshes in the north, were incorporated into tsarist Russia, becoming the provinces of Volhynia, Katerynoslav, Kyiv, Podilia, Poltava, and Chernyhiv. The area west of the Zbrucz, including the Carpathian foothills, became the Austrian province of Galicia.

In the early twentieth century, nearly three million Jews lived in these lands. Constituting about 12 percent of the overall population, they coexisted in a mutually beneficial, if fraught, relationship with Ukrainian peasants, Russian bureaucrats, and Polish nobility.[15] The Jews were an underclass, differentiated from their neighbors by their religious practice, language, clothing, names, occupations, and by hundreds of discriminatory legal edicts imposed upon them by a succession of tsars in the lands under Russian rule. The most notorious of these were the residency laws that restricted most Jews to the "Pale of Settlement" in the western provinces of the Russian Empire and to the Kingdom of Poland, which was also controlled by Russia.

In many of the cities and the small market towns, or shtetls, that overlooked the valleys and riverbanks, Jews made up more than a third of the total population and Yiddish was the most commonly spoken tongue.[16] Most of these Jews worked as artisans, shopkeepers, or petty merchants, eking out a living in one of Europe's poorest regions. But a small elite were making a mark in the growing metropolises. The port city of Odesa, the fourth-largest city in the Russian Empire at the turn of the twentieth century, attracted Zionist dreamers, Marxist revolutionaries, reform rabbis, Hebrew poets, and Yiddish playwrights. Kyiv, the medieval capital, only allowed Jews who met certain economic or educational criteria to settle in the city, but it, too, was acquiring a notable Jewish character, particularly around the booming sugar and grain industries. And Lviv, the largest city on the Austrian side of the border, drew, in addition to peddlers and traders, a growing number of Jewish entrepreneurs, who settled among the Polish upper crust that dominated the city.[17]

In the countryside, by contrast, Jews were a rarity, even a curiosity in the villages, where they typically made a living managing Polish noble estates or running roadside inns and taverns. Over 80 percent of the rural population spoke Ukrainian, a Slavic language that (despite a growing highbrow literature) was often disparaged as just a dialect; Russians called the language and the people who spoke it "Little Russian," while Austrians referred to them as "Ruthenian," a term derived from the same root as "Russian." The cities and the surrounding villages, in other words, spoke different languages, both literally and metaphorically. It is no coincidence that the Yiddish term *goy* can refer to a peasant as much as to a non-Jew, just as the Russian word for peasant, *krestianin*, is derived from the Russian word for Christian. For the most part, Ukrainians adhered to Orthodox Eastern-rite Christianity, which they inherited from Byzantium. In the eastern and central regions, the church was headed by a metropolitan; in the west, believers were in full communion with the pope in Rome and were therefore commonly known as Greek Catholics.

In literature, Ukrainian village life was often romanticized. The Ukrainian poet Taras Shevchenko idealized its authenticity along with the freedom-loving rebelliousness of the people. His 1841 epic poem *Haidamaks*, for instance, celebrated the revolt of peasant insurgents against the Polish overlords and their Jewish managers. In Austrian Galicia, the socialist writer Ivan Franko wrote popular stories about hardworking Ukrainian oil workers who are cheated by their Jewish

bosses. The image of indolent Jews exploiting the labor of the peasantry and mocking Christianity were tried-and-true tropes in Slavic
folklore. A popular myth told of Jews holding church keys or other
holy objects as pledges. Jewish estate managers and moneylenders
were accused of impoverishing the peasants by issuing them credit
they could never repay, and Jewish tavern keepers were blamed for
peasant drunkenness. But, most of all, Jews were simply baffling to
regular churchgoers, who wondered why they adhered to such bizarre
practices and why they obstinately rejected the truth of Gospel.[18]

Jewish folklore and literature, for its part, could also be cruel and
demeaning, often portraying Christian peasants as drunken simple-
tons. Sholem Rabinovich, the Yiddish writer better known as Sholem
Aleichem, whose stories are mostly set in these lands, portrayed the
pious Jews he wrote about as living separate lives in a hostile environment, satisfied that God had created Jews and Ukrainians differently.
As his most famous character, Tevye the Dairyman, puts it, "He created man in His likeness, but you had better remember that not every
likeness is alike."[19] In Sholem Aleichem's world, Jews prefer the third-
class cabin, where "you can feel like you are at home" and where "it
is only us brothers, the children of Israel."[20] In his stories, each community keeps largely to itself, interacting primarily in the highly controlled environment of the market, where money depersonalizes their
relations and "everything is mixed up together: *goyim*, horses, cows,
pigs, Gypsies, wagons, wheels, harnesses, and Jews of all kinds."[21]

Nevertheless, in ordinary times, relations between Jews and Christians were peaceable, sometimes even amicable. Peasant farmers would
ride their carts into town to have their wheat ground in a Jewish-owned
mill or to have the sugar extracted from their beets in a Jewish-owned
factory. They would sell the flour and their produce to Jewish traders
who brought it to market, and, while in town, would pick up some
dry goods from the Jewish shops, and perhaps stop by the Jewish
blacksmith to have their horse's hooves reshod or a kitchen implement repaired. The Jewish cobblers, tailors, coopers, glaziers, and
small-shop owners clustered around the market square and the
muddy streets leading into it, while Ukrainian townsfolk tended to

live farther out, closer to the fields, orchards, and pastures. In the east, Jews shared the urban space with Russian bureaucrats and military personnel garrisoned in town; in the west, they shared it with Polish nobles, many of whom were impoverished despite their distinguished ancestry. The growth of large factories in the first years of the new century also attracted growing numbers of Ukrainians to the cities; they labored there alongside their Jewish coworkers, then often returned to their villages in the summers to help with the seasonal farm labor.

Western Europeans tended to regard this part of Europe as economically backward. Barely industrialized, it was largely dependent upon the grain of the famed black-earth zone, which runs along southern Volhynia and Kyiv provinces eastward into Russia.[22] The forgiving land disincentivized agricultural innovation. It allowed the peasant farmers to maintain the old three-field system of crop rotation: to plow with oxen, reap with scythes, and thresh by hand.

However, the construction of railways and the development of soap, tallow, and leather factories transformed the crumbling market towns and regional administrative centers along the rails into bustling cities and created a new class of wealthy Jewish manufacturers. By the turn of the century, tobacco and sugar beet factories were emerging all around Kyiv Province, many of them named after their Jewish owners: Kogan, Rotenberg, Shishman. The growing disparity between town and country energized a revolutionary movement, which sprouted among the urban intellectuals and factory workers and quickly spread to the rural masses. The Great War intensified the growing unrest by destroying harvests, demoralizing villages, and destabilizing families. But it was the revolutionaries' promise of a postwar redistribution of the land from the predominantly Polish nobles who owned it to the Ukrainian peasants who farmed it that most excited the countryside.

As the great multinational empires collapsed in the waning days of the Great War, a Ukrainian People's Republic emerged, promising an equitable distribution of the land and autonomy for the region's national minorities, a commitment celebrated by Jews around the world. But the area quickly became embroiled in a bitter conflict, often called, somewhat simplistically, a civil war. Various proponents of Ukrainian statehood wrestled with anarchists, warlords, and independent militias, while fighting against a "White" army seeking the preservation of a united Russia, a "Red" army trying to establish a global Bolshevik empire, and a Polish army intent on recovering its historic borders. This war, from 1918 to 1921, led to the loss of about one million people in Ukraine through famine, disease, and military violence.[23] These casualties added to the six hundred thousand tsarist soldiers killed at the front during the Great War and more than two million soldiers and civilians across the Russian Empire who perished from disease.[24] Between 1914 and 1921, Ukraine lost nearly 20 percent of its total population.[25] The region's troubled history is reflected in the appellations that scholars have given it: "Bloodlands," "Shatterzone of Empires," "The Lands Between," "No Place."[26]

As is the nature of wars with no clear fronts, the enemy—whose identity could shift from week to week—could be anywhere and was often imagined to be in the rear, hiding among the civilian population. Accusations and rumors of collaboration ran rampant, encouraging individuals to stick closely to those most like themselves and to turn on those they perceived as different. Influenced by newspapers, broadsheets, and official proclamations, large segments of the population blamed the Jews for hoarding bread, importing hostile ideas, giving comfort to the enemy, and conspiring against the nation. At times, particularly in moments of regime change, these tensions were enacted in violence, often led by war veterans and deserters habituated to combat and unable to readjust to civilian life.[27]

The ensuing pogroms were public, participatory, and ritualized. They often took place in a carnivalesque atmosphere of drunken singing and dancing; crowds allowed for a diffusion of responsibility, drawing in otherwise upright citizens and ordinary people who in different circumstances might not have joined the proceedings. It was often the participation of these close acquaintances, trusted clients, and family friends that most galled the victims, instilling in them a feeling of powerlessness and alienation, a trauma that outlasted their physical wounds. Later in the conflict, the violence became more organized and methodical, carried out by military units acting on direct orders. These repeated attacks served no military purpose but rather expressed the sense that the Jewish civilian population was an existential threat to the new political, social, and economic order. To the distressed victims, who had expected the army to defend them and restore law and order, the attacks were a great betrayal.

Jews were not the only ethnic or religious minority targeted—Armenians, Mennonites, Muslim Crimean Tatars, as well as Ukrainians themselves, suffered heavily. But Jewish civilians alone were singled out for persecution by virtually everyone. The Bolsheviks despised them as bourgeois nationalists; the bourgeois nationalists branded them Bolsheviks; Ukrainians saw them as agents of Russia; Russians suspected them of being German sympathizers; and Poles doubted their loyalty to the newly founded Polish Republic. Dispersed in urban pockets and insufficiently concentrated in any one contiguous territory, Jews were unable to make a credible claim to sovereignty. They could be found on all sides of the conflict, allying with the group most likely to maintain stability and ensure the safety of the community. As a result, no party fully trusted them. Regardless of one's political inclination, there was always a Jew to blame.

THIS BOOK IS divided into five parts. The first provides background, focusing on the history of anti-Jewish violence in the Russian Empire and the impact of the Great War, including the treatment of Jews during the Russian occupation of Eastern Galicia and the mass expulsions of Jews from the war zone. It then looks at the revolutions of 1917 in Russia, the establishment of Ukrainian statehood (with its promise of autonomy for all national minorities), and the Bolsheviks' negotiations to end the war. It concludes with the collapse of the Austro-Hungarian empire in November 1918, when Ukrainian and Polish claims of statehood clashed in Lviv, and Polish military units capitalized on the chaotic situation to target Jewish civilians in what became the prototype of a new genre of pogrom.

The second part offers a detailed examination of some of the 167 documented pogroms that took place during the first three months of 1919 in the provinces of Volhynia and Podilia. In these pogroms, militias acting as part of the army of the Ukrainian People's Republic initiated or authorized attacks on Jewish civilians. The pretext for each episode was an allegation or rumors that the Jews were planning an uprising to install a Bolshevik government. But the military leaders were also motivated by a desire for loot, which they believed Jews were hoarding in their workplaces and homes. Once the veneer of public order was breached, ordinary citizens joined in the plunder and the city grew habituated to anti-Jewish violence. In the aftermath, Jewish aid workers initiated a campaign to document the violence for posterity, collecting testimonies in the hope of eventually prosecuting the guilty parties.

By April 1919, the Ukrainian People's Republic had mostly been defeated by the Bolshevik Red Army. However, large pockets of the region were controlled by insurgent warlords who moved into the power vacuum. Motivated by greed and the lust for power, they terrorized the Jewish populations in their midst. The third part of the book looks at some of the 307 documented pogroms unleashed by these warlords, as anti-Jewish violence spread throughout the region and peasants turned against their Jewish neighbors with pitchforks and machine guns. This section then draws upon memoir literature to look at the town of Slovechno, which produced its own local warlord who turned neighbor against neighbor. It concludes in Paris, where Poles, Ukrainians, and Jews debated the causes of the pogroms in their quest for international recognition.

The fourth part focuses on the Bolsheviks' triumph over their most formidable foes—the Whites' Volunteer Army and the military of the Polish Republic—as well as the last pockets of peasant resistance. In the late summer and fall of 1919, the White Army made significant inroads into Ukraine, briefly threatening the Bolshevik hold on the region and providing for the possibility of a restored Russian Empire. Made up of volunteers from the defunct tsarist army, the Whites had a die-hard hatred of the Bolsheviks and a fervent belief that the Jews were responsible for the revolution. They adopted scorched-earth tactics in the 213 documented pogroms they committed and left a legacy of anti-Jewish propaganda in their wake. But the defeat of the Whites did not end the turmoil. After years of intense violence in the town of Tetiiv, for instance, armed peasants forced the local Jews into the synagogue and burned it to the ground. In their final bid for military supremacy in the region, the Bolsheviks contended with a Polish invasion before battling their way back to the gates of Warsaw thanks in large part to the efforts of the famed Red Cavalry. Once again, this section demonstrates how the general tolerance for violence escalated with each episode, until the Bolsheviks were finally able to secure control over the region, gain a monopoly on the use of force, and put a stop to the pogroms.

The final part of the book looks at the global aftermath of the pogroms, arguing that the refugee crisis they created contributed to the rise of far-right politics in Europe, as global fears of Bolshevism became closely associated with Jewish migration. Collective memory of the pogroms further polarized relations between Jews and Ukrainians. In the newly established Soviet Union, revolutionary tribunals summarily shot peasant leaders on the charges of banditry and counter-revolutionary activity; urban zealots invaded the villages of Ukraine, wresting the land from the people and the churches from the faithful; and Soviet procurement brigades forcibly requisitioned grain and livestock from starving peasants. All this intensified animosity toward the new government and toward the Jews, who were blamed for its excesses. The concluding chapter examines the pogroms the Germans instigated when they invaded in June 1941, showing how the Nazis exploited local memory, drew upon existing patterns of violence, and capitalized on the popular association between Jews and Bolsheviks when they initiated a new and final round of slaughter.

A Note on Sources, Numbers, Dates, and Place-Names

We know about the pogroms thanks to the heroic efforts of aid workers, lawyers, and communal activists. As they rushed to provide medical assistance, resettle the refugees, care for the needy, and hold perpetrators responsible, they also recognized the historical implications of the violence taking place around them. "It must not be silenced!" declared the Central Committee for Relief of Pogrom Victims in a circular it distributed widely throughout Ukraine and to the Yiddish press. "You must tell and record everything. Every Jew who comes from a suffering city must report what they have seen so that the evidence will not be lost."[1] The Jewish population responded in force, producing tens of thousands of pages of testimony and reports in the days and years after the violence. Drawing extensively upon this material, this book not only tells the story of the pogroms but also honors the extraordinary work of those who documented them.

IN AUGUST 1914, a group of Russian Jewish industrialists and bankers established the Jewish Committee to Aid Victims of War, a voluntary relief association to coordinate the distribution of aid to Jewish war victims and to help resettle the refugees.[2] The committee, with funding from private philanthropy and the Russian government, acted as an umbrella organization, overseeing numerous prewar Jewish charities and local self-help societies. As the catastrophic impact of the war on Jewish communities along the border became increasingly evident, the committee expanded its scope. Under the directorship of the aid worker and socialist Zionist activist Nokhem Gergel, it eventually employed hundreds of medical personnel, teachers, lawyers, and other aid workers, who were stationed in 325 localities around the Russian Empire.[3]

In January 1919, as pogroms began to replace the war as the most immediate concern of relief agencies, Gergel and other aid workers established the Central Committee for Relief of Pogrom Victims in Kyiv to distribute aid to the "thousands of orphans, hundreds of widows, decimated cities and towns, and violated women."[4] The committee relied for the most part on private philanthropy: "Let every community organize its own committee to collect money and let them send what they have collected to the Central Committee," its circular declared. "Every Jew is obligated to give and nobody should refuse."[5]

As the political situation in the region deteriorated during the early spring of 1919, infighting among the Jewish organizations and parties that supported the committee hampered its work. In May, the Bolsheviks forbade the Central Committee to function in areas under their control and instead directed relief work to their own Committee to Aid Victims of the Counter-Revolution. The Russian Red Cross also established a Relief Committee for Victims of Pogroms.

Gergel's Central Committee, which continued to function in regions where the Bolsheviks had not established control, turned primarily toward documenting evidence of the pogroms. Under its auspices, the historian Elye Tsherikover, the Yiddish philologist Nokhem Shtif, and the demographer Jacob Lestschinsky—all of whom had previously been active in Jewish socialist and Zionist politics—established an Editorial Committee to Collect and Publish Material About the Pogroms in Ukraine.[6] The committee collected firsthand testimonies from victims and witnesses, protocols from various commissions, memoirs, official declarations, military orders, press clippings, lists of victims, and photographs. It also sent out questionnaires to local officials—rabbis, burial societies, and aid organizations—asking for biographical details of those who could be confirmed dead and statements from those who survived.[7] Responses ranged from scribbled notes of a few lines describing a personal experience to detailed typewritten reports spanning dozens of pages and incorporating multiple perspectives and witness accounts. Written in the immediate aftermath of traumatic events, some display raw emotions or are phrased to maximize impassioned reactions; others are presented matter-of-factly and with cold precision. Many draw upon well-worn tropes and familiar imagery. Some respondents sent meticulous typed lists offering the names not only of those murdered but also of the injured and of women and girls who had been raped; others only jotted down first names on scraps of paper. Some victims were identified in full ("Yitshok Vaynberg, age 60"); others only by last name ("Dubinsky, age 45"); and still others only by description ("itinerant, name unknown, 65 years old"; "three young men from Piotrkow").[8] Whatever information was available, local do-gooders forwarded on to the committee in Kyiv. As can be expected, details are sometimes misremembered and cannot always be corroborated, but the similarities in testimonies taken by different people at different times and in different places lend credence to the overall narrative.

Further, in addition to calling upon the goodwill of the public, the committee also dispatched lawyers to the sites of pogroms to take testimonies, collect photographic and documentary evidence, and issue reports. Iosif Braudo conducted investigations in Kyiv and Podilia provinces, Ilya Tsifrinovich worked in Volhynia and Podilia provinces, and, most important, Arnold Hillerson investigated the Proskuriv and Ovruch pogroms. During the tsarist period, Hillerson had established himself as a defender of Jews, famously representing victims of a 1906 pogrom in Białystok during an influential civil trial. On account of his courtroom speech at that trial, in which he condemned antisemitic groups tied to the government and exposed the tsarist military troops who provoked the violence, Hillerson was charged with inciting rebellion, treason, and the overthrow of the existing social order. The case against Hillerson became a cause célèbre and a test case for the still relatively new Russian judicial system. For calling the perpetrators of the Białystok pogrom to justice, Hillerson was sentenced to one year in prison. The comprehensive reports he authored about the 1919 pogroms were widely distributed and subsequently published in multiple languages.

In 1921–1922, Gergel, Tsherikover, Shtif, and Lestschinksy fled Bolshevik rule and settled in Germany, bringing with them tens of thousands of pages of documents they had collected, which they were able to smuggle out of the Soviet Union with the help of the Lithuanian ambassador Jurgis Baltrušaitis. In Berlin, they converted the Editorial Committee's materials into the Eastern Jewish Historical Archive and planned the publication of a seven-volume series on the pogroms.[9] At the same time, Tsherikover and Shtif helped establish the Yiddish Scientific Institute (YIVO) to serve as an institutional base for eastern European Jewish scholarship.[10] Following the Nazi seizure of power in Germany, YIVO set up its headquarters in Vilnius, taking part of the Eastern Jewish Historical Archive with it, while Tsherikover took other parts with him to Paris. After the war, activists affiliated with YIVO shipped and smuggled some of the remaining materials from Vilnius and Paris to New York, where YIVO had been reestablished.[11] While much of the archive was lost in Vilnius, 753 folders containing 63,168 numbered pages are available for consultation at YIVO's archives in the Center for Jewish History, and 606 folders from the Paris collection are available at the Central Archives for the History of the Jewish People in Jerusalem.

Alongside these efforts, numerous amateur writers chronicled individual pogroms they witnessed, either in single-author memoirs or as part of larger memorial book projects.[12] The most prolific of these private investigators was Eliezer David Rosenthal, a Jewish teacher from Bessarabia, who embarked upon a personal mission to collect information on pogroms in every town in which they had occurred. With the support of the Hebrew writer and publisher Hayyim Nahman Bialik, Rosenthal eventually published three volumes of documentation.[13]

А К Т.   34832

1919 года _____ 25 дня. Члены Проскуровской Городской регистраціонной Комиссіи учрежденной Думой с цѣлью установленія факта событія насильственной смерти лиц, убитыхъ и умершихъ отъ ранъ в г. Проскуровѣ, в дни 15—18 февраля с. г. опрашивали сего числа, нижепоименовн. свидѣтелей, которые удостовѣрили, что ___ февраля с. г. по _____ ул. в домѣ _____ былъ убитъ/раненъ слѣдующ. лица.:

№№ по пор.	Имя, отчество, фамилія, званіе и мѣсто приписки	Возраст
1	_Хана Кельмановна Ройш_	40
2	_Уина Срулевна Ройш_	23
3	_Эстира Срулевна Ройш_	15
4	_Энкель Срулевна Ройш_	12
5	_Злата Срулевна Ройш_	9

Об изложенном постановили: Заключить настоящій актъ, который передать названной регистраціонной комиссіи на дальнѣйшее распоряженіе.

Подписи свидѣтелей [signatures]

Члены комиссіи [signatures]

[YIVO INSTITUTE FOR JEWISH RESEARCH]

A form signed by S. Roysh stating that five people in his household were killed during the Proskuriv pogrom, February 15–18, 1919. The victims range in age from nine to forty years old. The Eastern Jewish Historical Archives contain 485 such forms from the Proskuriv pogrom.

As the Bolsheviks secured their hold over much of Ukraine in the summer of 1920, they consolidated the existing Jewish relief institutions into the Moscow-based Jewish Public Committee. The Kyiv branch's archive, which was declassified in 1991, includes over thirty-three thousand pages of victim lists, testimonies, and administrative material.[14] Tribunals and trials from later in the decade generated additional documents, testimonies, and reports, many of which were incorporated into the YIVO archives and the collections of the Central State Historical Archives of Ukraine.

Finally, the American Jewish Joint Distribution Committee, a relief agency established in November 1914 to provide aid to Jewish communities affected by the war, recorded testimonies from refugees who had fled the chaos of the war zone to Warsaw. Later, when the committee was able to send representatives to Ukraine, it issued reports based on firsthand observation, all of which fill in additional details on the pogroms and their aftermath.

EACH OF THESE organizations also attempted to calculate the number of victims, achieving totals ranging from forty thousand fatalities to three hundred thousand. Even the counts of individual pogroms vary, often by a factor of three or more. Some organizations counted bodies in mass graves or cemeteries, while others surveyed the population for the names of the deceased. Some organizations carefully estimated the number of excess deaths based on statistical sampling, whereas others hastily broadcast exaggerated figures to raise global alarms. Each mode of reckoning resulted in a different number of victims and survivors.

The Soviet Jewish Public Committee estimated that 180,000 to 200,000 Jews were murdered in 1,520 pogroms in Ukraine and Belarus between 1917 and 1921, leaving some 300,000 orphans and directly impacting the lives of 700,000 people.[15] Jacob Lestschinsky, the demographer and aid worker, estimated the total number of immediate victims at 75,000, to which he added another 125,000 who subsequently died of disease and malnutrition. Lestschinksy set the total number of those whose lives were affected by the pogroms at 600,000, including refugees, orphans, and widows.[16] Nokhem Gergel, on the other hand, estimated the total death toll at 50,000 to 60,000 victims, a figure he arrived at by counting 31,071 documented deaths and calculating an average death toll of 45.5 people per pogrom. He then used this average to project fatalities for pogroms for which no precise figures were available. Finally, he added another 16,000 to 26,000 to the total in order to account for those he assumed subsequently died of their wounds and were not included in initial necrologies.[17]

In 1921, the Jewish Section of the Soviet Commissariat of National Affairs, an official branch of the Soviet government, counted 33,398 names in the lists collected by the relief committees. In towns and cities for which more detailed information was available, the Jewish Section found that only about a third of the fatalities had been counted, mostly because the lists neglected those who perished of hunger and disease or died of their wounds as a direct result of the pogroms. For instance, in Borshchahivka, a small town of 4,000 people, 18 people were killed in the pogrom of June 1919, but another 31 subsequently died of their wounds. In Yustingrad, 143 Jews were killed in a mass execution in August 1919, but by 1920 the impact of the violence had led to about 800 Jewish deaths.[18] Thus, the Jewish Section concluded that the total number of deaths was three times the number of names included in the necrologies, and set the official fatality rate at 100,194, exactly tripling the 33,398 figure.[19]

Due to the chaotic situation on the ground, the massive movement of people, and differing interpretations of how to count and whom to count, we will likely never arrive at a precise tally of victims. It is safe to say, though, that taken as a whole, the pogroms of 1918–1921 were the largest catastrophe to befall the Jewish people to date. They were also only the beginning.

THE BOLSHEVIKS NOT only transformed the political landscape of Eurasia but also changed the way the calendar was rendered under their rule. Prior to February 1918, Russia and its former empire counted the days in accordance with the Julian calendar, which was thirteen days behind the Gregorian calendar used in the rest of Europe. Thus, the 1917 storming of the Winter Palace—the "October Revolution," which took place on October 25, according to the Julian calendar—was celebrated in the Soviet Union on November 7, its Gregorian date. The change, though, was not universal, as some opponents of the Bolsheviks continued to adhere to the "old style," as did the Orthodox Church. To ease confusion, I have chosen to use the Julian calendar when referring to events that took place within the orbit of the Russian Empire prior to the Bolshevik Revolution, and the Gregorian calendar for all subsequent dates.

A note on place-names. In an irony of history, Proskuriv, where one of the worst pogroms of the era took place, was renamed

Khmelnytskyi in 1954 to commemorate the three hundredth anniversary of the 1648–1657 uprising led by Bohdan Khmelnytskyi. Khmelnytskyi, whose statue still stands in one of Kyiv's major squares and whose image graces the five-hryvnia banknote, is a figure lionized by Ukrainians as one of the fathers of their nation for his role in fighting against Polish oppression. But he is loathed by Jews who remember instead the massive wave of anti-Jewish violence he unleashed. The uprising he led resulted in what was possibly the deadliest attack on Jews worldwide before the pogroms and is memorialized in countless Jewish dirges and martyrologies.[20]

This single example is just one demonstration of how contentious the naming of places can be. Even in 1919, when the Proskuriv pogrom took place, the spelling and pronunciation of the city's name varied. The seventeen thousand Jews and five thousand Russians in the city generally referred to it as Proskurov, whereas the eight thousand Poles called it Płoskirów, and the five thousand Ukrainians pronounced it Proskuriv. Many place-names in this region have similar histories, posing quandaries for those who choose to write about them.

In cases in which there are numerous variations of the same name (Lemberg, Lviv, Lwów) I have chosen to use a transliteration of the current official name. In most locations, this means I use the Ukrainian variant. However, in order to avoid anachronisms, when there has been an actual name change—Proskuriv to Khmelnytskyi, for instance—I have maintained the name of the city as it was known at the time in the linguistic variant of the country in which it is currently located, with the current name in parentheses at first mention. I have included Kishinev in this category, which may not be recognizable to English readers in its official Moldovan variant of Chişinău. The repeated name changes throughout the region remind us of the ever-changing climate in which the subjects of this book lived and died.

PART I

WAR AND REVOLUTION

MARCH 1881–DECEMBER 1918

The Last Years of the Russian Empire

The word "pogrom," derived from the Russian *gromit'*, to smash or destroy, and related to the Russian word for thunder, entered the international lexicon in the 1880s. By the early 1920s, it had become so familiar that a champion racehorse in Britain was named Pogrom; it won the 1922 Epsom Oaks and the Coronation Stakes.

In the *Times* of London, the word first appeared on March 17, 1882, defined in parentheses as "riots against the Jews."[1] The riots to which the paper was referring first broke out in a tavern in Elizavetgrad (now Kropyvnytskyi, Ukraine) during Easter week of 1881. Easter had long been a perilous time for Jews: reminded of the myth that Jews were responsible for killing Christ and offended by the continued Jewish presence in their midst, churchgoers would often feel emboldened to assault their Jewish neighbors. But this time the unrest was precipitated by the assassination of Tsar Alexander II, who had been killed a month earlier by revolutionary terrorists, at least one of whom was revealed to have had a Jewish background.[2] Similar riots soon took place in Kyiv, and the following summer they spread to over two hundred communities throughout the southwestern provinces of the Russian Empire, as impoverished peasants, demobilized soldiers, railway workers, and laborers attacked Jewish-run shops, canteens, mills, and banks. Accompanied by occasional instances of physical violence, the riots, which continued sporadically for over a year, resulted in an estimated twenty-five to forty Jewish fatalities.

Right-wing Russian newspapers encouraged the attacks by blaming the Jews for the murder of the holy tsar. Left-wing activists, meanwhile, saw the riots as the first stage of a wider revolution: the Jews, they believed, were merely the weakest link in the moribund imperialist system. Jews themselves blamed the pogroms on the new tsar, Alexander III, whom they accused of scapegoating the Jews in order to divert popular economic, political, and social unrest away from those in power.[3] In reality, the wave of riots was likely motivated less by the political agendas of the elites than by the economic resentment of the masses against those Jews who were becoming more visible in the urban marketplace. The unrest spread not as a result of some deliberate governmental conspiracy but rather because the understaffed local police were unable to effectively put it down.[4] The pogroms of 1881–1882 were seen as a major turning point in Jewish history long after the violence ran its course, stimulating mass migration to the Americas, the origins of the Zionist movement, and the radicalization of Jewish students and intellectuals throughout the Russian Empire.

Twenty-one years later, during the 1903 Easter week, anti-Jewish riots broke out again, this time in Kishinev (now Chișinău, Moldova). A cosmopolitan metropolis of over one hundred thousand people, nearly half of whom were Jewish, Kishinev was located in the Russian province of Bessarabia, bordering Romania. The local paper had been circulating spurious stories that a Christian child found dead in the neighboring town of Dubosary had been the victim of a Jewish ritual murder; the "blood libel," the medieval myth that Jewish law requires the use of Christian blood for ritualistic purposes, continued to resonate in Russia long after it had been debunked in western Europe. Enflamed by the paper's hatemongering, hundreds of rioters attacked Jewish residents, first in the marketplace and then around the city. Within two days, forty-nine Jews were murdered and many more assaulted, robbed, and raped.[5]

The publicity that surrounded the Kishinev pogrom, as well as the failure of the tsarist government to punish the perpetrators, was likely a factor in a similar episode that took place in September 1903 in Gomel, a mixed Jewish-Christian city of forty thousand in Mogilev Province (in today's Belarus). Spurred again by rumors of a missing child, Christian townsfolk attacked Jews and charged them with having murdered the child for ritual purposes. This time they were met with resistance: in the aftermath of the Kishinev pogrom, Zionist youth and Jewish socialist activists had concluded that passivity in the face of violence invited further violence. A Jewish self-defense committee in Gomel fought back against the assailants; the riot ended with ten Jews and eight Christians killed, as well as extensive property damage and numerous injuries.

The mass mobilization for Russia's war with Japan in February 1904 brought more attacks. Peasant recruits ransacked Jewish-owned taverns to enjoy a last night of drunken debauchery before heading into battle, and minor altercations between Jews and Christians in marketplaces around the region led to wide-scale looting and violence.[6] When word spread that the American Jewish banker Jacob Schiff had provided loans to the Japanese government to finance its war effort, the right-wing press accused the Jews of aiding the enemy, inciting yet more anti-Jewish violence. In total, dozens of Jews were killed in some forty episodes of rioting and looting that year.

As news of Russian military defeats at the front circulated back home, general unrest threatened the very foundations of the tsarist empire. Beginning in January 1905, worker strikes, military mutinies, and peasant uprisings paralyzed the economy. Several illegal Marxist-inspired political parties that had formed clandestinely in the last years of the nineteenth century each aspired to direct the popular discontent into a political revolution. The Socialist Revolutionaries tried to rouse the peasantry with promises of seizing nobles' land and delivering it into the hands of those who toiled on it; Vladimir Lenin's Bolsheviks, meanwhile, focused their attention on organizing the urban proletariat. As it turned out, the sectors of the population most receptive to such revolutionary calls were ethnic minorities who had been oppressed by the tsar, the Jews most of all. The largest of the revolutionary parties, in fact, was the General Union of Jewish Workers in Lithuania, Poland, and Russia, better known as the Bund, which advocated both for a socialist redistribution of resources and for national minority rights, particularly the right to use the Yiddish language for education and cultural development.[7] Jewish intellectuals were also prominent in the leadership of other leftist political parties: many hoped to shed their ethnic and religious difference—what they regarded as the stigma of Jewishness—within a united community of international workers. The historian Isaac Deutscher famously called this type of revolutionary a "non-Jewish Jew," a "Jewish heretic who transcends Jewry" yet still "belongs to a Jewish tradition."[8]

On the other side of the political spectrum, the Union of the Russian People, a monarchist party that championed Russian national identity based on Orthodox Christianity, blamed the empire's Jews for the growth of the revolutionary movement and the political instability of the time. It had the support of the Black Hundreds, paramilitary forces made up mostly of petty government officials and veterans of the Russo-Japanese War, who spread antisemitic conspiracy theories and engaged in anti-Jewish thuggery.[9] The Black Hundreds were responsible for inciting many of the violent clashes with Jews that punctuated the politicized and chaotic atmosphere of the summer of 1905. Some of these episodes were perpetrated by tsarist loyalists riled up by the right-wing and antisemitic press; others by traveling thugs, intent on roughing up their targets and making off with stolen booze and valuables; still others by disaffected workers simply lashing out against war shortages and acting in the heat of the moment. They were manifestations of popular discontent, premodern ethnic riots fused with criminality. The state tolerated a limited amount of bloodshed as a means of releasing pent-up frustrations, but when the riots got out of hand the police would intervene to put them down and restore equilibrium.

One of the worst of these confrontations took place in Zhytomyr, the capital of the province of Volhynia, about one hundred miles west of Kyiv.[10] Zhytomyr had been selected in the 1840s as one of only two cities in the empire (along with Vilnius) to host a state-run rabbinical school, intended to train future leaders in secular subjects as well as religious matters. Over the decades, the school had attracted a number of upwardly mobile young intellectuals, but Zhytomyr never fully blossomed into the type of illustrious intellectual center the school's founders had hoped to fashion; instead, it remained primarily an administrative seat, and a largely provincial city. Its architecture was dominated by the large neoclassical and neo-Byzantine buildings of the provincial government: the Treasury, the Main Administration building, the Military Services Offices, the State Bank, the Office of Trade and Industry, and the Ministry of Justice. Interspersed among these official edifices were the predominantly Jewish-owned shops and stores that catered to the governmental clerks, bureaucrats, and ordinary petitioners seeking their services. Most of the thirty thousand Jews in the city—one-third of its total population—were poor artisans and shopkeepers, struggling to make a living in the wartime economy. At the turn of the century, locals would purchase their rubber galoshes at Vaysman's store, their medicines and cosmetic supplies at Shvartsman's, their watches and clocks at Pomerants's, their brushes at Gitman's, and their "surgical supplies and bicycles" at Zilbert's metal workshop.[11] Jews and Christians shopped together, traded with each other, and cordially shared the city streets, parks, and public spaces, even as they tended to maintain separate social circles and communal institutions.

The vast majority of Jews in the city looked to their rabbis rather than revolutionaries for answers to their questions. But a small number of Jewish students, eager to show that "Zhytomyr is not Kishinev," established self-defense brigades affiliated with the Bund or with the Socialist Revolutionaries. Alarmed by the growing number of armed Jews, some Christians worried that "the Jews intend to retaliate against the Christians" for the Kishinev pogrom and "massacre the Christians." Black Hundreds sympathizers printed leaflets blaming the revolutionary movement on the Jews, urging the Christians to boycott Jewish shops and the Jews to emigrate to "China, Japan, or Palestine."[12]

On Saturday, April 23, 1905, during the feast of Saint George's Day, a group of peasants from a nearby village started throwing rocks at some young Jewish men spending their Sabbath boating on the Teteriv River. It was good old-fashioned fun for the teens to taunt the Jews. The boaters, though, were all members of the city's Jewish self-defense brigade; they were armed with revolvers, and convinced that if Jews were to avoid becoming victims they needed to defend themselves with force. They fired warning shots into the air, sending the peasant boys running into town shouting that Jews were shooting at them. Alarmed residents spilled out of their homes with clubs and axes and attacked their Jewish neighbors. The next day, word of the incident spread, leading to further marketplace riots, gunfights that pitted the self-defense brigade against the police and the military, and the death of twenty-one Jews. "Zhytomyr looked like a graveyard after the pogrom," according to one account.[13]

News of the unrest reached the nearby town of Chudniv, where a Jewish self-defense brigade mobilized and marched toward Zhytomyr. As the brigade reached Troyaniv, a neighboring village, Christian residents—stunned by the unusual sight of armed Jews marching through the countryside—sounded the church bells in alarm and came out in force to defend themselves against the invaders. The small Jewish community of Troyaniv intervened, begging the armed Jews to give up their weapons lest the townspeople turn on the innocent members of the community. The self-defense brigade acquiesced to their coreligionists' anxieties. But as soon as they disarmed, the townsfolk fell upon them with swords, axes, and clubs. Seven members of the brigade were killed in the melee, while a pair managed to hide in the synagogue. The next day, a crowd of peasants broke into the synagogue and found the two Jews—one in the attic, the other in the Torah ark. Neither survived the angry mob.[14]

Zhytomyr was just one site of strife. Across the Russian Empire, dissatisfied students, alienated clergy, oppressed minorities, and ordinary workers and peasants organized massive demonstrations in the fall of 1905 that eventually compelled the tsar to issue his October Manifesto, granting some civil liberties and establishing a parliament.

The concessions did little, though, to quash the demands of revolutionaries for more radical reforms. In the tense atmosphere following the release of the October Manifesto, antisemitic baiting by the press, the Black Hundreds, and individuals within the tsarist police incited over six hundred pogroms in two months, resulting in extensive property damage and up to three thousand fatalities. As terrifying and devastating as these pogroms were, though, their scope was circumscribed: the military remained on the side of law and order, curtailing the disorder when possible and zealously guarding its monopoly on violence. Still, the pogroms of 1903–1906 helped model behavioral patterns that were further refined with each wave of unrest.[15]

The deadliest of these incidents took place in Odesa. On October 18, patriotic demonstrators carrying icons and portraits of the tsar clashed with a procession of radical students, leading to a breakdown of authority in the city. The next day, laborers, dockworkers, and other rioters spilled into the seedy Moldavanka district that the writer Isaac Babel would make famous in his *Odesa Stories*. Encouraged by the inaction and even participation of the local police, they destroyed Jewish property and killed an estimated eight hundred people in four days of rioting. Many were motivated by their resentment against Jewish prominence in the grain trade or by rumors of Jewish disloyalty. Student militias and Jewish self-defense brigades tried to fight off the rioters but were overwhelmed and ultimately proved ineffective.[16]

In the fall of 1906, the tsarist police finally cracked down on the unrest and put an end to the pogroms. At the same time, the government enacted further reforms that alleviated some restrictions on the press, political party formation, public gatherings, and the rights of ethnic minorities. A flowering of Jewish culture followed. Yiddish drama circles emerged out of amateur gatherings to entertain eager audiences in theaters, fire halls, and barns; Jewish writers narrated the times in Hebrew, Yiddish, Polish, Russian, and even Ukrainian; Jewish fiddlers, cimbalonists, and clarinetists performed at weddings and celebrations, often alongside Gypsy, Hungarian, or Romanian musicians; and countless social, educational, and leisure clubs brought together like-minded people.[17] But the tsar continued to restrict Jewish residency to the Pale of Settlement and to limit Jewish access to higher education, the civil service, and the military.[18]

Many officials in the Russian bureaucracy scorned the Jews as the enemies of Christendom or viewed them as an alien group of ruthless competitors in the economic marketplace. Still others believed they were part of a global conspiracy. The notorious forgery *The Protocols of the Elders of Zion*—first circulated by the Black Hundreds publisher Pavel Krushevan in 1903 and widely disseminated among Russian ultranationalists—denigrated the free press, liberalism, democratic elections, and countless other aspects of modernity as Jewish plots to dominate the world. The *Protocols* seemed to confirm what many in the Russian government had long suspected: that Jews were devious agents controlling world markets and manipulating kings and parliaments to the detriment of innocent Christians.[19] The extent to which agents of the Russian state were willing to believe the most absurd accusations against their Jewish subjects became clear in 1913, when prosecutors pursued a highly publicized case against Mendl Beilis, the Jewish superintendent of a Kyiv brick factory, who was wrongly accused of murdering twelve-year-old Andrei Yushchinsky in order to use his blood for ritual purposes.[20] It was in this frame of mind that the Russian Empire would enter the Great War.

IN RESPONSE TO a Serbian nationalist's assassination of Archduke Franz Ferdinand, the heir presumptive to the Austrian throne, on June 28, 1914, the Russian General Staff, viewing Serbia as a "vital Russian interest," placed its forces on a war footing. Prewar military alliances were triggered in rapid succession, and the Triple Entente of Russia, France, and Britain found itself at war with the Central Powers of Austria-Hungary, Germany, and the Ottoman Empire.[21] People of all nationalities greeted the mobilization of forces with patriotic demonstrations. In Russia's Ukrainian provinces, peasants holding icons and pictures of the tsar assembled in front of churches, while Jews carried Torah scrolls in processions through town squares. Many Jews in the Russian Empire hoped that the tsar's alliance with Britain and France would introduce liberal ideas to Russia and result in the removal of residency restrictions and quotas.

The four hundred thousand Jews serving in the tsarist army at the beginning of the war welcomed the opportunity to prove their worth. They were aware that the commanders were watching them closely, skeptical of their ability to fight. Indeed, many officers and members of the General Staff distrusted Jewish servicemen, a suspicion they passed on to their troops. The officer corps, a conservative group drawn from the old imperial elites, tended to associate Jews with the economic modernization threatening the status of the landed nobility, and with the revolutionary movement endangering their hold on power. "The presence of Jews in combat units is certainly undesirable," wrote one commander to his superiors. "They are poorly developed physically, they are barely able to endure the difficulty of infantry life, they often get sick, they are very sensitive, and their nervousness is detrimental to others."[22] Jewish soldiers, another top commander asserted, "are not only useless, they are harmful."[23]

In the fall of 1914, during the first months of the war, the Russian army advanced rapidly into Austrian Galicia, home to about nine hundred thousand Jews who had been granted full citizenship and legal rights by the Austrians. The prominent Jewish presence in the conquered region unnerved the Russian soldiers. They were mistrustful of their own Jewish comrades, whose knowledge of Yiddish made them easy conversation partners for the Galician Jews; unit commanders complained that their Jewish infantrymen seemed to have more in common with the Galicians than with their fellow soldiers. The military brass worried about Jews fraternizing with the enemy, deserting their units, and betraying Russian military secrets. Because Yiddish and German are closely related, Jewish soldiers in the Russian army were often tapped as interpreters. Their officers and fellow soldiers wondered if they were in league with the enemy.

Rumors about Jewish betrayal of Russia and secret loyalty to Germany ran rampant. As the ethnographer and aid worker S. An-sky wrote in his wartime diary: "It all began with whispered accusations, secret allegations, and libels, with the purpose of depicting the Jews as betrayers of Russia [. . .] Jews served the enemy as spies, they communicated with him through secret telephones, conveyed the best-kept secrets through light signals or bonfires, sent him millions of rubles in gold, etc."[24] An-sky recounted ludicrous stories of elderly Jews smuggling Germans hidden in sacks across bridges and of Jews sneezing to signal passing airplanes. The folklorist Avrom Rechtman shared that in Proskuriv, which was near the front during much of the war, there were rumors that Jews were smuggling money to the enemy by hiding the riches in pine caskets and disguising the transfer as a funeral procession. Another rumor had it that a Jew was caught communicating with the enemy with a telephone hidden under his beard.[25] Peasants claimed to have seen a German airplane filled with gold land in the Hornosteipel Rebbe's courtyard.[26] The historian and economist Nikolai Poletika recalled hearing military officers in Kyiv in September 1914 boast that "first we will deal with the Germans, and then with the Jewish traitors."[27]

During their advance, the military commandeered Jewish homes and broke into Jewish-owned taverns and wine cellars, often beating and robbing the occupants. Officers gave free rein to their troops in Jewish neighborhoods, permitting them to plunder as a reward for their conquests. Soldiers torched the largely Jewish market towns along the border, on the false pretext that Jews were aiding the enemy and shooting from their windows at the Russian soldiers. In 1914 alone, Russian troops killed eighteen Jews in Lviv, eighteen Jews in Brody, and more than one hundred and fifty Jews in Jarosław. These atrocities were committed in the hours after the Russians secured military control, not in the heat of battle.[28] According to a concerned Russian foreign ministry official, the war, "which could have been holy and honorable, has instead become a raid of some wild horde, a mockery of all law and honor."[29] Jews were also legally discriminated against: those who had held administrative positions under the Austrians were promptly dismissed by the occupying army, Yiddish cultural organizations were closed down, Jews were prohibited from traveling from one district to another, and Jewish landowners were dispossessed. "They ruined them, down to the last penny, seized their horses and cattle, grain, and machines," wrote An-sky.[30] Some two hundred thousand Jews fled Russian-occupied Eastern Galicia to safety in Vienna.

Fearing Jewish treachery, units of the Russian military forcibly removed Jews from towns along the front lines. Such measures were part of a new policy to deport suspect individuals from zones of combat. Although the policy was originally intended only to be applied to individuals, local commanders immediately used it to deport entire populations—Germans, Turks, Armenians, Bulgarians, as well as Jews. The deportations became more systematic in January 1915, when, upon hearing rumors that Jews had been rejoicing at Russian defeats, the imperial commander in chief, Nikolai Yanushkevich, circulated an order authorizing the expulsion of "all Jews" in zones where the military was active, a region that included almost the entire Pale of Settlement.[31] Some thirty thousand Jews were deported to Warsaw from the smaller towns in the vicinity. The three thousand Jews of Grodzisk, twenty-five miles southwest of Warsaw, were given only three hours to gather their belongings, as crowds of locals shouted: "Go to Palestine!"[32]

In April and May 1915, Austria launched a major counteroffensive, driving the Russians out of Galicia. The Russian army adopted a scorched-earth policy, ransacking and burning down towns as it hastily departed, and took 50,000 Jews as prisoners.[33] It also issued a new round of deportation orders, now targeting the northwest provinces of the Pale of Settlement; this time, approximately 190,000 Jews from the Baltic provinces of Kovno and Courland were packed into cattle cars and deported hundreds of miles to the east, far from the front.[34] In other instances, the military took hostages from among the Jewish population, detaining about 5,000 rabbis, communal leaders, and wealthy businessmen and threatening to murder them if the Jewish community misbehaved. One witness described the Jews of Panevėžys (in today's Lithuania), north of Vilnius, being driven toward the train station, "their belongings in hastily formed sacks, table cloths, baskets, chests, all falling down in heaps. Children losing their parents, parents rushing about looking for their children. Children crying, the sick groaning, clamoring, screaming."[35] Jews were often told to bring their valuables to a central point, where their possessions were auctioned off to local residents before their former owners were forced into trains.

In the trains, deportees suffering from scarlet fever and diphtheria were crowded in together with the healthy. Food and medical care were scarce; local Jewish communities were overwhelmed and unable to provide assistance. In Kyiv Province, a report issued by the Jewish Committee to Aid Victims of War noted that "thousands of women, the elderly, and children—hungry, naked, exhausted, suffering—are existing between heaven and earth, not knowing when the end of their torment and wandering will be."[36] At major railroad stations, like Korosten and Sarny, where trainloads of refugees were passing daily, officials refused to allow local aid workers to feed the starving Jews, convinced that the Jewish aid committee was "the main leader of the Jewish revolutionary movement in Russia."[37] "The slow-moving trains were not allowed to stop at stations where food could be supplied to the poor wretches," wrote one correspondent. "The trains could stop only at a distance of at least one kilometer from any station. But the poor stricken people who were carted away in these trains were perhaps not much worse off than the thousands upon thousands for whom the trains had no accommodation, but who had to leave nonetheless."[38]

The overflow of deportees forced the government to loosen Jewish residency restrictions and allow for the settlement of some Jews outside of the Pale of Settlement. Christian residents of war-torn towns greeted the unwanted arrival of downtrodden and destitute Jewish newcomers with dismay; they feared the refugees would burden local social services and viewed them as a threat to the public order. Many associated the Jews with the German enemy or blamed them for fomenting the revolutionary movement. Small communities also feared that Jewish newcomers would import the troubles of the big cities. But perhaps most important, they were wary of the epidemics that traveled in the unsanitary freight cars with the passengers. Scarlet fever, measles, diphtheria, typhus, dysentery, and even cholera killed thousands and made no distinction between Jew and Christian.

By July 1915, Russia had not only retreated from its newly acquired territories in Galicia but had also lost its Baltic possessions and the Kingdom of Poland. Emboldened by the prospect of redrawing borders in a postwar world, Ukrainians and Poles began planning for eventual statehood in overlapping territories. Polish nationalists envisioned a republic that would replicate the historic borders of the Polish-Lithuanian Commonwealth by reuniting the Kingdom of Poland with Austrian Galicia and the western provinces of the Russian Empire that made up the Pale of Settlement. Ukrainians, meanwhile, dreamed of a state that would encompass the large Ukrainian-speaking populations of Eastern Galicia as well as Russia's southwestern provinces, encompassing most of the southern half of the Pale of Settlement. The Germans, for their part, plotted to undermine Russian rule from within: they promised the Ukrainians support for statehood and secretly channeled funds to revolutionaries who sought to overthrow the tsar. The French, on the other hand, permitted Polish legionnaires to train in France in expectation of eventual Polish statehood, which would serve as a bulwark against

German expansionism. Within this contested region lived the largest Jewish community in the world, divided in its political loyalties between those who placed their faith in Bolshevik internationalism, Russian constitutional democracy, Polish freedom, Ukrainian autonomy, German culture, Austrian tolerance, French liberty, Zionist sovereignty, and the God of Abraham, Isaac, and Jacob.

—— 2 ——

The Revolutions of 1917

"We, the intelligentsia, hardly knew the people among whom we lived," lamented the Jewish lawyer Arnold Margolin soon after his final departure from Ukraine.[1] Margolin had spent the summer of 1917 campaigning as a liberal candidate for a seat in the inaugural All-Russian Constituent Assembly. It was the first general election in Russia since wide-scale demonstrations in February had forced Tsar Nicholas II—grandson of the assassinated Alexander II and son of Alexander III—to abdicate the throne. "I traveled in locomotives, tenders, the corridors of passenger cars, and in freight cars," Margolin recalled.[2] He was preaching the new gospel: that the February Revolution heralded a modern age of interreligious understanding and cooperation, that Jews, Russians, Poles, and Ukrainians could flourish in an autonomous Ukraine as part of a federated socialist republic. In some towns, he would stand on a table in the market square and lecture massive assemblies of three thousand soldiers and peasants on the concepts of national autonomy, federal government, and land use indemnification, as his audience cheered in approval, grumbled their dissent, or just nibbled on sunflower seeds.

It still seemed inconceivable to Margolin that the tsar had been overthrown. As the son of a wealthy sugar baron, industrialist, and philanthropist, Margolin had been spared most of the restrictions that affected the Jews of Russia. Still, he knew their sufferings, having first made his mark as an attorney for Jewish plaintiffs affected by the pogroms of 1903–1906. In 1913, while Nicholas II was celebrating the tercentenary of Romanov rule with a gala performance of Mikhail Glinka's *A Life for the Tsar* and gifts of Fabergé brooches, Margolin had been working as a defense lawyer on the ritual murder trial of Mendl Beilis.[3] Now, four years later, the deposed monarch was being held in captivity in Siberia and Margolin was running for government in Kyiv.

Margolin was committed to the type of moderate social democracy represented by the revolutionary leader Alexander Kerensky and his provisional government, a cabinet that ruled in place of the tsar until elections could be held. He was encouraged by its immediate revocation of all legal restrictions on the Jewish population, including the abolition of the Pale of Settlement, and ardently believed that the provisional government would usher in an era of liberal rule. But he bemoaned the fact that the soldiers he encountered that summer were more enthusiastic about the Bolsheviks, who had promised an immediate end to the war. The Marxist radicals were winning over the soviets, or councils, that represented the workers, peasants, and soldiers, and that vied for power with the provisional government. The soviet in Petrograd (today's St. Petersburg), under Bolshevik control, had issued "Order Number 1," calling upon military units to elect committees in place of commissioned officers and instructing soldiers to do away with formal titles when addressing their superiors. The order led to the breakdown of military authority and discipline, reducing the entire army to what one observer called a "mob of debating circles."[4]

Margolin was also concerned by the ease with which the soldiers he met blamed the Jews for all their woes. They "cursed Kerensky horribly, asserting that he and 'all his twelve ministers' were Yids. . . . When I tried to tell them that Kerensky and his 'twelve ministers' were not Jews, they did not believe me, and often said that I too was a Yid and therefore stood up for Yids."[5] False rumors that Kerensky

Ukrainian election poster from 1917 reads: "Vote for the United Jewish Social-ist Workers' Party"

was Jewish were rampant throughout the empire, yet many soldiers seemed willing—at least for the moment—to overlook the fact that the most visible representative of the Bolsheviks was Leon Trotsky, whose pen name, fine suits, goatee, and deep blue eyes did little to conceal the inconvenient fact that he was born Lev Davidovich Bronstein. Indeed, a piece of graffiti seen in 1917 proclaimed: DOWN WITH THE JEW KER-ENSKY! LONG LIVE TROTSKY![6]

To many soldiers and peasants the world felt so upside down that they were willing to believe anything. The idea that there would soon be democratic elections for a Constituent Assembly throughout Russia would have seemed a utopian dream only one year earlier. Was it really possible that Kerensky was Jewish and all his cabinet as well? It seemed absurd that a Jew could be running the government; before the revolution, Jews were not even permitted to serve as postmasters. But then again, here was the well-known Jewish lawyer Arnold Margolin running for office, campaigning from a makeshift podium in the market square.

Margolin had been confident, he bitterly recalled years later, that with "the overthrow of tsarist absolutism, pogroms would become impossible."[7] He had believed that the pogroms of the tsarist era were all orchestrated by the state, and he was certain that once a benevolent

[ABBUS ACASTRA / ALAMY STOCK PHOTO]

Arnold Margolin

government was installed and the legal restrictions on Jewish political and cultural rights were removed, Jews would flourish.[8] He certainly didn't expect that in less than a year, he would hitch a ride aboard one of the last steamers out of Ukraine, having resigned his post as deputy minister of foreign affairs of the Ukrainian People's Republic on account of the "tragic fact of the unending Jewish pogroms."[9]

UKRAINIAN NATIONALISM, ONCE derided by Rosa Luxemburg as "a mere whim, a folly of a few dozen petty-bourgeois intellectuals" and as "a ridiculous pose of a few university professors and students," had been gaining strength since the 1905–1906 reforms on censorship and public assembly.[10] Underground groups of intellectuals had skirted the remaining tsarist restrictions to organize socialist political parties, advocating for the right to use the Ukrainian language, the creation of Ukrainian schools, the organization of Ukrainian military units, and the institution of Ukrainian electoral curia. The revolution provided the opportunity for these nationalists to move from the university to the state house. Two weeks after the tsar was deposed, the Ukrainian socialist parties formed a governing entity, the Central Rada (council)—modeled on the soviets—to serve as a coordinating body for Ukrainian workers, peasants, and soldiers. Within a month, the Rada organized an All-Ukrainian National Congress of 1,500 delegates, who elected 150 members to serve in the Central Rada. The eminent historian Mykhailo Hrushevsky was elected its leader, and the writer Volodymyr Vynnychenko, who became his second in command, was tasked with the crucial job of negotiating with the Russian provisional government.[11]

A handsome man with a long, thick beard, bold horseshoe mustache, and oval pince-nez, Hrushevsky was an iconic symbol of Ukrainian identity, even though his own mother was of Polish nationality. He had taught Ukrainian history at the University of Lviv, where his lectures inspired hundreds of young students to embrace their heritage. His monumental ten-volume *History of Ukraine-Rus'*, which documented a continuous Ukrainian culture and way of life, energized the Ukrainian national movement. Vynnychenko, for his part, projected a European air, with a tightly trimmed beard and mustache, slicked-back hair, and perfectly tailored suits worn over crisp shirts with tall, rounded collars and cuff links. A member of the Ukrainian Social Democratic Workers' Party, he had emerged from a peasant background to become a prominent author of Ukrainian short stories and plays, many of which feature forceful and idealistic protagonists who become immobilized by internal doubts as they seek moderation and compromise in an age of extremes. One colleague commented on how the writer himself was "the model for one of the lead characters in a Vynnychenko drama."[12] He was, in the words of one observer, "a characterless person without a strong will, a writer and a bit of a dreamer, a man with a greater connection to the world of ideas than to realpolitik."[13] Vynnychenko's wife, a French Jewish doctor, may have inspired some of his stories about the difficulties of Jewish life in Russia. Both Hrushevsky and Vynnychenko had spent time in tsarist prisons for their involvement in revolutionary movements, a rite of passage for most liberal and freethinking writers of the era. Politically, they shared a strong commitment to the multinational character of the region and advocated for legal equality and special protections to preserve the distinct cultures of the national minorities—Jews, Poles, and Germans. Each of these, they believed, should have the right to use their own language, worship according to their own faith, educate their children in their own schools, and receive proportional representation in national political bodies.

But the provisional government in Petrograd balked at the prospect of granting autonomy to the Ukrainians. This led the Central Rada to unilaterally issue its "First Universal" in June 1917, a manifesto calling for Ukrainian autonomy within a democratic and federated Russian republic. It later asserted the right to use the Ukrainian language in schools, courts, public institutions, and the church, and the right to establish Ukrainian military units within the Russian army.

To prepare for governing, the Central Rada established a general secretariat headed by Vynnychenko. The position of secretary of military affairs went to the journalist Symon Petliura. Born into a modest peasant family—his father was a coachman—and educated in an Orthodox preparatory school to become a priest, Petliura was an odd choice for the job of military commander. After abandoning the religious path, he had joined the Ukrainian Social Democratic Workers' Party and moved around as an itinerant intellectual: to Tiflis (today's Tbilisi), Ekaterinodar (Krasnodar), St. Petersburg, Lviv, and Moscow, taking various office jobs and editing newspapers. In Moscow, while working at a bank, he began publishing the journal *Ukrainskaya zhizn* ("Ukrainian Life"), a Russian-language review of Ukrainian affairs. In 1916, he volunteered to distribute supplies to the ill-equipped soldiers at the front, where he proved to be an effective organizer, developing a rapport with the troops. But he still had little military experience when the Central Rada tapped him to establish a Ukrainian national army by bringing together ethnic Ukrainians who had served in the tsar's army. Vynnychenko remarked that Petliura "was entrusted with this position only as a result of compromises and agreements between different political parties and not because he had any more knowledge of military affairs than anybody else."[14] "If I were asked how I assess Petliura as a person," echoed another colleague, "I would have to say that he is mediocre in all ways: mediocre in intellect, mediocre in education, mediocre in ability. . . . The only extraordinary thing about him may be his stubborn will."[15] Others were even less generous. "He was elected military representative . . . because he happened to be the only member of that body who had a uniform," wrote a correspondent for the London *Times*.[16] But Petliura was a man of action—some would call him a firebrand—whereas Vynnychenko, mild-mannered and elegant, was prone to excessive deliberation. And during a revolution, no one has time to think.[17]

Although Petliura had no actual battle experience, he appreciated the power of political rituals and understood the military way of life. His critics would claim that he was mainly attracted by the uniforms and decorative metal trinkets that came with the job. "He organized military parades, religious services in public places, issued circulars and grandiose manifestos that had no real force," wrote Vynnychenko.[18] But he was able to inspire the soldiers in a way that the

[TsDKFFA]

Symon Petliura, August 1919

more reserved intellectuals could not. Units representing hundreds of thousands of Ukrainian soldiers serving in the former tsarist army declared their loyalty to him, an achievement all the more impressive since the majority of Ukrainians were serving far from Ukraine. The socialists in the Rada opposed the notion of a conscripted army, which they saw as a glorification of imperialist militarism, and preferred to raise a volunteer force. As a result, Petliura was compelled to rely in large part upon makeshift brigades of "Free Cossacks"—former tsarist soldiers, Ukrainian peasants, and townsfolk who had bonded together to establish local guard units to defend themselves from bandits on the prowl.[19]

Petliura skillfully deployed the "Cossack" myth—the idea that modern Ukrainians were descendants of the freedom-loving horsemen of the steppe who had overthrown the Polish magnates in the seventeenth century and established their own independent state, known as the Hetmanate. This state ultimately merged with the Russian Empire, and the Cossacks themselves were recruited into the tsar's service, where they were recognized as among the most lethal forces in the Russian military. Petliura dressed his peasant soldiers in the *papakha*, the fur Astrakhan hat of the Cossacks, and named his military units after Cossack bands or historical heroes. He adopted the Cossack title *otaman* (also seen as *ataman* or *hetman*) as a military rank, called his soldiers "Haidamaks" after the eighteenth-century Cossack insurgents, and would later crown himself the "Chief Otaman."

Petliura quickly emerged as a symbol of the Ukrainian national movement. His name "leapt from the walls, from the dreary wire communiqués," wrote Mikhail Bulgakov in *White Guard*, a fictional account of the civil war in Ukraine. "It dripped into your morning coffee from the pages of your newspapers, quickly transforming the divine tropical beverage in your mouth into the most revolting slops. It roamed over people's tongues and was tapped out in Morse code by telegraph operators' fingers."[20]

After the Central Rada's declaration of the First Universal, the provisional government in Petrograd reluctantly recognized Vynnychenko's government, and in July 1917 dispatched Kerensky to Kyiv to negotiate with it. Trotsky, having little faith in Kerensky's diplomatic skills and observing from the sidelines, scoffed that Vynnychenko "was distinguished from Kerensky only as a mediocre novelist from a mediocre lawyer."[21] Certainly the war had not been going well for Kerensky. In early July, the "mediocre lawyer" had suffered heavy losses in a misguided offensive against Austria-Hungary and Germany. Kerensky urgently needed an agreement with the Ukrainians to dissuade them from turning to the Central Powers for support instead.

When negotiations ended at an impasse, the Rada issued its Second Universal, declaring its aspiration to become the "sole supreme body of revolutionary democracy in Ukraine" in coordination with all the nationalities living in its territory. While the First Universal had been addressed to "the Ukrainian People," the Second Universal was addressed to "citizens of the Ukrainian Land," expressly recognizing Ukraine as a multinational territory. The Central Rada agreed to expand from 150 to more than 800 seats, to reserve nearly a third of those seats for representatives from the national minorities (Russians, Jews, and Poles), and to create new vice secretariats for each nationality within the cabinet. (The position would eventually be upgraded to general secretary, and in January 1918 renamed to minister.) These moves were meant not only to gain the political loyalty of the minorities but also to reflect the genuinely tolerant ethos of the Ukrainian socialist leadership. "Without them," Vynnychenko declared of the national minorities, "we could not consider ourselves the government of the whole population."[22] Avrom Revutsky, who would become minister of Jewish affairs, agreed: "Jewish autonomy was not simply an enticement offered by 'cunning Cossack politicians' as certain skeptics now think," he wrote from Berlin in 1924. Rather, he continued, "it was fundamental to the overall Ukrainian approach to government."[23]

As the Great War dragged on and the revolution failed to bring an immediate peace, massive social destabilization and economic collapse spread through the countryside and into the towns. The war had displaced an immense number of civilians: throughout the Russian Empire, about five to seven million refugees, including three hundred thousand to five hundred thousand Jews, were in need of assistance in the summer of 1917. Over ten million men were serving in the army, leaving their families without breadwinners and their fields untilled.[24] Demoralized soldiers deserted their units, attacked liquor stores, raided towns, raped women, and carried out "self-requisitions" of grain from farmsteads.[25] Orders to shoot deserters on the spot did little to quell the violence. One former officer described the situation in the fall of 1917: "The soldiers had lost all military semblance, strutted in crowds through the streets and unceremoniously broke up stores, entered private residences, and robbed the inhabitants of their property. Bazaars were established in the city squares where the soldiers sold their loot for next to nothing."[26] Faced with food shortages, many interpreted the revolution as an open invitation to take what they believed was rightfully theirs.

In Ukraine, the Jewish role in the economy, combined with widespread rumors that the Jews were stockpiling grain and speculating in currency, gave the unrest antisemitic overtones. Striking workers looted the largely Jewish-owned sugar beet and tobacco factories; peasants seized the mills, also mostly Jewish-owned; and in the towns, the urban poor looted Jewish shops and the homes of wealthy Jewish merchants. Peasants also confiscated the nobles' land, burning down Polish-owned manors and attacking the Jews who managed them. By late fall, many cities had run out of bread. Crowds clashed with guards outside provincial storage facilities, plundering them of cotton, cloth, and produce.[27]

Following the economic and military failures of the summer, popular support for the provisional government collapsed. The Bolsheviks gained a majority in the Petrograd Soviet, and on the morning of November 7, Lenin issued a manifesto announcing the overthrow of the provisional government and the transfer of power to the Petrograd Soviet. An hour later, Kerensky slipped out of the capital in a Renault borrowed from the American embassy. Later that day, Trotsky, already the dominant voice of the coup, famously decried those who opposed it as "miserable bankrupts" destined for the "dust heap of history." In the early hours of November 8, a Military Revolutionary Committee, led by Trotsky's close associate Vladimir Antonov-Ovseyenko, entered the Winter Palace, where the rest of the provisional government was sheltering, and detained the ministers.[28]

With victory in his hands, Lenin promised a "democratic peace to all nations and an immediate armistice on all fronts" and proclaimed "the right of self-determination" for "all nationalities inhabiting Russia." Elections to the Constituent Assembly, he continued, would proceed as planned in January. The Bolsheviks had succeeded in securing power in the Russian capital and immediately set about exporting their revolution to the rest of the former Russian Empire. This meant, first, encouraging workers, peasants, and soldiers to establish soviets and assume power in their own regions; and second, raising a Red Army to conquer by force those territories that resisted.

In Kyiv, the Central Rada refused to recognize the undemocratic Bolshevik coup and responded on November 20 with its Third Universal, proclaiming the establishment of a Ukrainian People's Republic still within a "democratic" and "federated" Russia. The new republic claimed for the Rada all power to establish order and promulgate laws within the Ukrainian provinces until the promised convocation of the Constituent Assembly. The proclamation adopted many aspects of the Bolshevik program—it declared all land the property of the working class and the peasants, introduced the eight-hour workday, declared the nationalization of industry, and promised an end to the war—but sought to implement them through a democratic process rather than dictatorial fiat. It accused the Bolsheviks of hurling the country into an "internecine and bloody struggle" and of spreading "chaos, disorder, and ruin." Issued in Ukrainian, Russian, Polish, and Yiddish, the Universal also reaffirmed the Rada's commitment to multinationalism, announcing that "Russian, Jewish, Polish and other nations in Ukraine are granted autonomy to guarantee their own self-government in all matters of their national life." The secretary of national affairs was charged with the immediate task of drafting legislation to guarantee these rights.[29]

The Bolsheviks did not react well to the Central Rada's appropriation of its program or to its defiance in declaring autonomy. Joseph Stalin, then Lenin's commissar of nationalities, responded with an article in the party newspaper *Pravda*, accusing the Rada of aiming to destroy the revolution. The Rada, he declared, is "a government of traitors to socialism" and a "bourgeois government" that "is fighting to prevent peace."[30] The Bolsheviks immediately sought to overthrow the Central Rada and began to cultivate Ukrainian workers, peasants, and soldiers through their respective soviets. They failed in their attempt to gain control of a Ukrainian-wide congress of soviets that met in Kyiv on December 17, but they did manage to gain a majority in the industrial city of Kharkiv, in Ukraine's northeast. With the support of university students and workers from the massive railway yards and the Kharkiv locomotive factory, on December 24 the Kharkiv soviet declared the establishment of a Ukrainian Soviet Republic allied with Bolshevik Russia. The two rival governments—the Ukrainian People's Republic based in Kyiv and the Ukrainian Soviet Republic based in Kharkiv— claimed sovereignty over much of the same territory and competed for the allegiance of Ukrainians, national minorities, and the soldiers on Ukrainian soil. Where they differed was in their attitude toward the Bolshevik party and its extralegal seizure of power. The Ukrainian socialist leadership, aspiring to build a republic based on multinational tolerance and the consent of the governed, did not trust the disorderly and pugnacious methods of the Bolsheviks. Parliamentarians and peaceful citizens hoped that the conflict could be resolved the following month at the highly anticipated Constituent Assembly.

"A SOLEMNLY HOPEFUL spirit pervaded Petrograd on the memorable morning of January 18, 1918," wrote Margolin of the day the Constituent Assembly opened. Although he had lost his election, Margolin was among the thousands who gathered in the city to welcome the arrival of the delegates. The four hundred men and ten women who arrived as newly elected parliamentarians represented a cross section of the former empire: Russians, Ukrainians, Jews, Armenians, Georgians, Latvians, and Muslims; radicals, liberals, conservatives, and socialists. Vynnychenko and Petliura won seats. So did Trotsky and Lenin. But the Bolsheviks as a whole had failed in their bid to gain an electoral majority, losing decisively to the Socialist Revolutionaries.[31] Nevertheless, Lenin and his clique, who retained control of the powerful Petrograd Soviet, resolved not to let that stand in their way and "to crush by guns and bayonets the will of the majority," as Margolin bitterly put it.[32] Trotsky, who was not in Petrograd at the time, recalled years later that many delegates brought food and candles with them, expecting that the Bolsheviks would cut off electricity to the building. "That was how democracy marched into battle against dictatorship," he scoffed, "fully armed with candles and sandwiches."

As processions of onlookers ushered the newly elected delegates

[TsDKFFA]

Workers in Ukraine greet Red Guards

into the Tauride Palace, machine guns installed by the Bolsheviks on the roofs and in the garrets fired on the crowds in a show of force. Inside the palace, the Bolshevik delegates urged the assembly to ratify the authority of the soviets, thereby invalidating the election and dissolving the Constituent Assembly itself. When they lost the vote, the Bolsheviks walked out of the hall. They were joined by a leftist faction of the Socialist Revolutionaries, known as the Left SRs, who became close allies of the Bolsheviks. The remaining delegates returned the next day to find that the Bolsheviks, under the authority of the soviets, had sealed the building and unilaterally dissolved the assembly. Russia's first experiment with democracy was over. The people, Trotsky wrote, "did not even give a thought to defending those who considered themselves the nation's representatives, but were, in fact, only faint shadows of an outworn period of the revolution."[33]

Watching from Kyiv, a disillusioned Central Rada issued its Fourth Universal on January 22, declaring that "henceforth the Ukrainian People's Republic forms an independent and free sovereign State of the Ukrainian people." The Bolsheviks' cynical power play offended the democratic sensibilities of the Central Rada and convinced Vynny-chenko that, as he put it years later, "the Bolsheviks were, in essence, the same Russian chauvinists and imperialists" as the Black Hundreds had been.[34] Days later, tens of thousands of Russian soldiers together with "Red Guard" units of Bolshevik paramilitaries from the Ukrainian Soviet Republic moved toward Kyiv. The Bolsheviks were now at war with the Ukrainian People's Republic. The civil war that was already tearing apart the former Russian Empire had come to Ukraine.

The Central Rada of Ukraine

Frustrated by the debacle of the Constituent Assembly, Arnold Margolin left the Russian capital for Kyiv. "It was my belief," he wrote, "that as a native of the Ukraine I should take some part in the constructive work that had already been going on."[1] Elected by the Central Rada to the Supreme Appellate Court, he began to work on behalf of the Ukrainian People's Republic, which he believed "displayed remarkable liberalism in regard to the cultural rights of Russian, Jewish, Polish, and other minorities."[2]

The Law on National Autonomy, passed in January 1918, was the clearest expression of Ukraine's tolerance. The law defined nationality on the basis of one's personal declaration rather than on the basis of religious membership—a victory for Jewish socialists intent on breaking free of the rabbinical leaders who had dominated Jewish communal institutions in the past. According to the statute, elected representatives of Jewish communities would be responsible for keeping records of births, deaths, and marriages; maintaining cemeteries; organizing loan associations; providing representatives to state and local governments; and supporting Jewish schools, hospitals, nursing homes, orphanages, and other educational, welfare, and health institutions. All of this would be funded through taxation by the city's general treasury. Another law declared Yiddish one of the official languages of Ukraine. As a public symbol of Jewish inclusion, the Rada introduced a new banknote, the 100 karbovanets, which included inscriptions in Yiddish as well as Ukrainian, Russian, and Polish.[3]

Young militant Jews expressed their support for the new Ukrainian state by establishing self-defense brigades, which they hoped Petliura would incorporate into his army as Jewish regiments. Many were inspired by Joseph Trumpeldor, a Jewish tsarist officer who had helped create the Zion Mule Corps, an all-Jewish unit that fought for the British at Gallipoli. Joseph Schechtman, a follower of Trumpeldor who was serving in the Ukrainian Central Rada as a Zionist delegate, proposed that "Jewish soldiers be allowed to organize special all-voluntary defense units to protect their fathers, mothers, and sisters."[4] Some of the most active self-defense units came from Odesa, which, as a modern metropolis, attracted the young and adventurous. Many grew out of Jewish sports organizations, Zionist youth movements, and Jewish soldiers' unions.[5] Semen Leibovich, a champion of Jewish self-defense, explained: "We are a people of great creative strength, of strong spirit, who have given the world many significant scholars, yet we have lived

[ART HERITAGE / ALAMY STOCK PHOTO]

The 100 karbovanets banknote designed by Hryhoriy Narbut for the Central Rada government, featuring the denomination and currency name in Russian, Yiddish, and Polish. The obverse side was in Ukrainian.

for centuries under the yoke of slavery and inequality. . . . Patiently and without complaint we waited for the hour of liberation, waited and hoped, that we too, tired and frozen, would be warmed by the rays of the shining sun. . . . If we had our own regiment, which could when necessary stand in the defense of our brethren, then, without doubt, the pogroms would disappear spontaneously."[6] In February 1918, a Jewish infantry battalion of three hundred volunteers was formed. They wore white and blue bunting with a Star of David, and were armed with Maxim machine guns and Mosin–Nagant rifles from the Odesa armory.[7] It was a powerful symbol of Jewish-Ukrainian cooperation.

The Law on National Autonomy was greeted with elation around the world. In New York, the Yiddish paper *Der tog* ("The Day") wrote: "For the first time in all Jewish history the Jewish people will be recognized by a government as an equal part of the general population, not only in a civil and political sense, but in a national sense. . . . The government of Ukraine isn't just recognizing 'assimilated Israelites,'

[YIVO INSTITUTE FOR JEWISH RESEARCH]

Jewish self-defense brigade in Odesa

or a 'cosmopolitan' community; rather it is recognizing the Jews as a people, as a nation that deserves all the rights of every other people, including national autonomy."[8] In Moscow, the Russian-language *Evreiskaia nedelia* ("Jewish Week") echoed these sentiments. "Our Ukraine is a happy oasis," it proclaimed. "We stand on the threshold of a social revolution unprecedented in the history of humanity." The paper celebrated, in particular, Ukraine's "full constitutional guarantees, which recognize that 'national minorities' possess the right to national self-determination as well as personal autonomy."[9] Vynnychenko, too, remembered this period as "one of the best moments of mutual existence for the various nationalities in Ukraine" and recalled that "there was a friendly will to live and work together for the general good."[10]

Other Jewish voices, though, expressed reservations about the Ukrainian People's Republic's separation from Russia. Moyshe Litvakov of the United Jewish Socialist Workers' Party argued that it was "tearing the living body of Russia to pieces."[11] Jewish religious leaders and Jewish nationalists also had reason to fear the proclamation of an independent Ukraine. The breakup of the Russian Empire, which had housed the world's largest Jewish population, threatened to cut off Ukrainian Jews from their coreligionists in Russia and Poland, potentially severing ties between rabbinical leaders and their followers and erecting borders between communities. Finally, upwardly mobile Jews had long viewed Russian fluency as a path toward career advancement and valued access to Russian markets. Many saw their fortunes better served living within a large multinational empire than as a minority within a nation-state, regardless of how tolerant it claimed to be.

IN LATE NOVEMBER, the Bolshevik government of Russia agreed to meet representatives of the Central Powers for peace talks at German headquarters near the burned-down fortress town of Brest-Litovsk. "This is a curious place—melancholy, yet with a beauty of its own," Ottokar Czernin, the Austrian delegate to the negotiations, wrote in his diary. "An endless flat, with just a slight swelling of the ground, like an ocean set fast, wave behind wave as far as the eye can see. And all things grey, dead grey, to where this dead sea meets the grey horizon."[12]

The Russian delegation arrived on the morning of December 2, 1917. It was chaired by Adolph Joffe, and included Lev Kamenev and Grigori Sokolnikov among its members. All had been close associates of Trotsky's in exile (Kamenev was married to his sister), and all had some type of Jewish heritage. It was the first meeting between the old world's nobility and the new era's radical revolutionaries. Everybody dressed the part. A photo of the Russian delegation arriving at the station shows the Russians in their long fur coats and black fur hats greeting the German diplomats in their gray greatcoats and spiked helmets. The Austrians wore imperial mustaches; the Russians wore goatees (Joffe alone had a full beard). Walking behind Joffe, Kamenev, and Sokolnikov is another member of the Russian delegation, the only woman in the photo: Anastasia Bitsenko, the Left SR terrorist famous

[ART WORLD / ALAMY STOCK PHOTO]

Russian delegation arriving in Brest-Litovsk

for having assassinated Russian minister of war Viktor Sakharov in 1905. The veteran old guards of the ancien régime with their high military ranks and lengthy noble titles (Czernin's full name was Count Ottokar Theobald Otto Maria Graf Czernin von und zu Chudenitz) sat down at the long, cramped negotiating table across from the bespectacled eastern European Jewish intellectuals who were giving their debut performance on the world stage. They shared pens, ink, and ashtrays distributed along the length of the table. "Their leaders are almost all of them Jews with altogether fantastic ideas," Czernin wrote, "and I do not envy the country that is governed by them."[13]

Czernin described his first meal with the Russians: "We then went to dinner, all together, including the whole staff of nearly one hundred persons. The dinner presented one of the most remarkable pictures ever seen. The Prince of Bavaria presided. Next to the Prince sat the leader of the Russian delegation, a Jew called Joffe, recently liberated from Siberia; then came the generals and other delegates. Apart from this Joffe, the most striking personality in the delegation is the brother-in-law of the Russian Foreign Minister, Trotsky, a man named Kamenev, who, likewise liberated from prison during the revolution, now plays a prominent part."[14] After dinner, Czernin had his first conversation with Joffe about the revolution and the Bolsheviks' goals. The conversation ended, Czernin recalled, when "in a kindly, almost imploring tone that I shall never forget, he said: 'Still, I hope we may yet be able to raise the revolution in your country, too.'"[15]

The revolutionaries' comportment was epitomized by the well-known agitator Karl Radek, who arrived in late January with a pipe emerging from his toothless grin—his front teeth had been knocked out by German police during a protest five years earlier. He relished the reversal of fortunes as he sauntered past the professional German diplomats with their arms stiffly outstretched and instead warmly grasped the hands of their attendants, engaging the porters in amicable discussion and addressing them as "comrade."[16]

The Bolsheviks demanded that proceedings of the negotiations be made public in the hopes of inspiring revolution abroad. They repeatedly frustrated their Austrian and German counterparts with long speeches directed more toward the factory workers of Austrian Linz and Wiener Neustadt than the diplomats sitting across the table. Not much had been accomplished when they decided to take a break so the Germans could return home for their Christmas. Russia's Orthodox Christmas would not arrive for another thirteen days, but the Bolsheviks had little interest in that anyway. They would soon abolish the Julian calendar that had marked the Orthodox life cycle for centuries, and synchronize Russia's calendar with the Gregorian calendar used in most of the rest of Europe.

While the Bolshevik diplomats negotiated in Brest-Litovsk, a new group—commonly known as the Whites, in contrast to the Bolshevik Reds—emerged in the Don Basin, in the south of Russia. Several former tsarist generals who had been involved in an August coup attempt against Kerensky had escaped there, and now established the Army of South Russia, a volunteer force of former tsarist officers and military cadets, aiming to restore a united Russia and reinstitute elements of the old regime. Their talk of law and order appealed not only to conservatives and reactionaries but also to many liberals who feared the radicalism of the Bolsheviks. They even garnered the financial support of wealthy Jewish elites, who saw them as the surest guardians of private property rights. The White officers in charge of the Volunteer Army, as the Army of South Russia came to be known, were so confident of success that they refused to build alliances with any of the more liberal political parties; instead, they sought support from the Entente Powers, the tsar's former allies of Britain and France, with whom they formed close partnerships. Hoping that the Whites would stave off the Bolsheviks, the Entente eagerly supplied them with arms.

The Whites' promise of preserving the old order did not do much to excite the peasants and the lower classes. In the words of the former Volunteer Army officer Prince Andrei Lobanov-Rostovsky, "The White movement was not the promise of a new day, which it might have become if any constructive program had been put forward—say along lines similar to what later became Fascism in Western Europe, or some other new creed alternative to Communism which might have rallied the masses; instead it was the mere afterglow of a dead era."[17] But it would become a potent military force in the struggle for control of the vestiges of the Russian Empire and remained a constant threat to both the Ukrainian independence movement and the Bolshevik advance.

ON JANUARY 4, 1918, the Central Powers returned to Brest-Litovsk after their holiday break. While they waited to see who else would show up—they had hoped to bring France and Britain into the negotiations but were not even sure if the Russians were still on board—the Austrians went hunting. The forested area nearby was pristine, having just been blanketed by a snowstorm, and the air was crisp and cool. They returned with a pig and two hares.[18]

A few days later, there was a new group at the table: a delegation representing the Ukrainian People's Republic, hoping to gain international recognition of Ukrainian independence. The Central Powers saw the Ukrainians as a viable alternative to the Bolsheviks and were confident they could do business with them. "The Ukrainians are very different from the Russian delegates," wrote Czernin. "Far less revolutionary, and with far more interest in their own country, less in the progress of Socialism generally."[19]

On January 7, the Russians arrived, now with a delegation headed by Trotsky, who was then serving as commissar for foreign affairs. France and Britain, who were now backing the Whites, had declined to participate, leaving the Bolsheviks to go it alone with the goal of securing a separate peace. Trotsky shattered the delicate rapport that had been established between the negotiating teams. He immediately announced that the Russian delegation would no longer dine with the rest of the group or socialize outside of the negotiating table. "I decided to put an immediate stop to the familiarity that had quite imperceptibly been established during the early stages," he explained in his autobiography.[20] A few days later, after Radek got into a tussle with his German chauffeur, Trotsky grounded the Russian delegation, forbidding them to even leave the grounds of the estate. As the Hohenzollern and Habsburg diplomats spent the quiet time between sessions bonding on hunting expeditions, Trotsky holed up in his quarters and began writing what would become his monumental *History of the Russian Revolution*. "Trotsky is undoubtedly an interesting, clever fellow, and a very dangerous adversary," wrote Czernin. "He is quite exceptionally gifted as a speaker, with a swiftness and adroitness in retort which I have rarely seen, and has, moreover, all the insolent boldness of his race."[21]

The Ukrainian question dominated the second session of the negotiations. Trotsky affirmed his party's support for the principle of self-determination of all peoples but refused to negotiate borders. Although he claimed it was because borders should be decided by popular plebiscites, he knew full well that the Red Army was at that very moment advancing toward Kyiv and that final borders would be determined on the battlefield, not at the conference table.

Realizing that the Bolshevik declaration of support for national self-determination meant little in practice, the Ukrainians turned to the Central Powers for support. Both needed a deal. The war had exhausted the Austrian and German home fronts, leaving their cities hungry and demoralized. The Austrians knew that only a fresh food supply would forestall the growing revolutionary movement at home. In exchange for black earth grain, they were willing to support Ukrainian independence in the former Russian provinces so long as it didn't excite the Ukrainians in Austrian Galicia. Meanwhile, with the Reds in control of Kharkiv and approaching Kyiv, the Ukrainian Central Rada was facing an existential threat they could only survive with the help of the Central Powers. Trotsky's goal, on the other hand, was to stall for as long as possible—waiting for Bolshevik soldiers to take Kyiv and the revolution to take Vienna.

As the Ukrainian and Bolshevik leaders faced off in Brest-Litovsk, their soldiers met on the battlefield. Both Trotsky's Red Army and Petliura's Haidamaks, though, still resembled insurgent bands more than modern armies. Neither force was even a year old; both of them lacked clear command structures, provisions, adequate arms, and esprit de corps. They spent nearly as much time securing armaments, food, and clothing from the civilian population as they did fighting the enemy. Jewish merchants and traders, who tended to travel by rail, carrying cash and merchandise as they made the rounds of regional fairs, were easy targets for military supply raids from both sides.

Already in January there were reports of Ukrainian soldiers targeting Jews at the bustling Bakhmach station, a major node along the Kyiv–Voronezh line, holding them up for money or preventing them from getting on the trains to reserve space for military personnel. Along the entire Kyiv–Poltava line, Haidamak soldiers with the infamous braided whips favored by Cossack horsemen were flogging Jewish passengers, stealing their wallets, and throwing them off the moving trains.[22] In the first days of April, six corpses of Jews were found along the lines in Chernihiv Province. A report also mentioned that in a train carriage at the Baryshevka station, "five dead bodies were found of Jews who had been strangled with ropes and leather belts."[23] That same month, Ukrainian soldiers flogged several Jews at the Romodan station on the suspicion that they were Bolsheviks because they had been heard using the word "comrade." "The population is terror-stricken, and the stations Romodan and Grebenka are 'danger zones' which Jews dare not approach," declared another report.[24] Children sang a popular ditty: "The train is coming; from its chimney smoke is rising; through its windows Jews are flying."[25]

Red Army soldiers were just as likely as their Ukrainian counterparts to attack Jews, believing them to be wealthy members of the bourgeoisie who were hoarding supplies. In March 1918, Bolshevik recruits in Chernihiv Province killed twenty-five Jews in Seredyna-Buda and eighty-eight in Novhorod-Siverskyi. In nearby Hlukhiv, according to one report, the Roslavlsky Detachment "slaughtered all the bourgeoisie and the Yids,"[26] killing about a hundred people as Bolshevik soldiers yelled, "We were ordered to kill all the Yids."[27] The problem of Red Army soldiers attacking Jews was becoming such a troubling issue to the Bolshevik leadership in Moscow that in the spring of 1918 it formed a Commission for the Struggle Against Antisemitism and Pogroms, with the goal of coordinating educational projects to fight antisemitism in the Red Army.[28]

One of the worst incidents took place in Kyiv, where the fate of Ukraine was being decided. There, over seven hundred armed workers supported by Red Army detachments had assembled at the Kyiv Arsenal, the largest military factory in Ukraine, to carry out an insurrection. Ukrainian military authorities declared martial law in the capital and ordered all residents who had settled there during the war to leave. Although the decree was soon rescinded, it spread fear among the Jewish community, most of whom had recently arrived in the city either as wartime deportees from the front or as refugees after the abolition of the Pale of Settlement.[29] In late January 1918, a group of Free Cossacks under the command of the engineer Mykhailo Kovenko, acting as part of Petliura's army, stormed the Arsenal and defeated the Bolshevik uprising.[30] In short order, Kovenko's troops executed dozens of captured Bolsheviks. Viewing the Jews as likely Bolshevik supporters, they also attacked the Jewish quarter of Podil, chanting "We will slaughter all the Yids" as they marched through the streets. Twenty-two Jews were killed, including Yona Gogol, the leader of the Union of Jewish Warriors, an organization that had advocated the formation of Jewish self-defense brigades. Gogol's death galvanized Jewish nationalists and renewed a debate on whether Jewish self-defense was an effective means of defense or a provocation.[31]

Kovenko held the capital for only a week before being forced out again by the Reds. The Bolsheviks, in turn, carried out brutal reprisals against the symbols of the old regime, chiefly the remnants of the tsarist army and the church. The former tsarist officer A. E. Shiller, meanwhile, was staying at an inn occupied entirely by officers when the city came under attack. "A hail of bullets rained into the windows" as he and the others began to search for an escape route. They tied together sheets and towels, rappelled from a third-floor window into the backyard, then crawled into neighboring cellars. In these cramped quarters, Shiller managed to convince a soldier who was also in hiding to exchange coats and caps. Shiller justified his action: "My officer's uniform could do him no harm, as his face was so unintelligent that even a blind man could detect the peasant in him." Shiller was captured and held for two days in a school room; periodically, the Red Guards would take groups of officers and shoot them in the yard. He survived by identifying himself as a released prisoner rather than an officer.[32] A few days later, Bolshevik soldiers barged into the sacred Kyiv-Pechersk Lavra monastery and assassinated Metropolitan Vladimir Bogoyavlensky, the head of the Russian Orthodox Church in the region, reportedly strangling him using the chain from the cross around his neck.

The ministers of the Central Rada were forced to flee the city for Zhytomyr. One of Mykhailo Hrushevsky's apartments was struck by Bolshevik artillery, destroying his library, and his mother died during the bombardment, likely as a result of a heart attack. The loss the ministers felt as they abandoned their capital was palpable. Some supporters of the Rada blamed their setbacks on the Jews, who they claimed had handed Kyiv over to the Bolsheviks.

AT BREST-LITOVSK, TROTSKY now questioned the Central Rada's right to speak on behalf of Ukraine. The Rada, he pointed out, controlled neither Kyiv, Kharkiv, nor Odesa, Ukraine's three largest cities, and could not even define the borders of its own territory. To further complicate matters, at the end of January a second Ukrainian delegation showed up, this time claiming to represent the Ukrainian Soviet Republic, based in Kharkiv and backed by the Bolsheviks. Mykola Liubynsky, speaking for the delegation from the Central Rada, vehemently protested what he characterized as Trotsky's meddling in the internal affairs of the Ukrainian state. "The Bolshevik Government," he charged, "only proclaimed the principle of national self-determination in order to resolutely combat its practical application."[33] The session ended with Germany reaffirming its recognition of the Ukrainian People's Republic as "an independent, free, and sovereign state," and Austria, wary of Ukrainian national claims in Galicia, reluctantly following along. Trotsky, watching the movements of his Red Army, scoffed that the so-called Ukrainian People's Republic would soon consist of little more than the delegation at Brest-Litovsk.[34]

At two o'clock in the morning on February 10, with Kyiv in Bolshevik hands, the delegates representing the Ukrainian Central Rada, eager for international recognition and support, signed the first peace treaty of the war, formally ending hostilities between the Central Powers and the Ukrainian People's Republic. The Central Powers agreed to recognize the Rada and to provide it with manufactured goods and military assistance in exchange for a Ukrainian commitment to supply the Central Powers with grain and to allow German and Austro-Hungarian troops on its soil. An optimistic president of the Ukrainian Delegation declared: "From today, the Ukrainian People's Republic is born to a new life; it enters as an independent state into the circle of nations, and ends the war on its front. It will see to it that all the powers which in it lie will rise to new life and flourish."[35]

On February 18, in accordance with the terms of the treaty, six German divisions, their steel scuttle-shaped helmets rusted from years of fighting, moved into Ukraine. Together with Free Cossacks under Petliura's command they retook Kyiv from the Bolsheviks and restored the Central Rada to power. The hardened soldiers of the Central Powers were shocked at the disorder they encountered among their Bolshevik antagonists. "The enemy we were fighting against," wrote a German commander, "included representatives of different groups. They were mainly Bolshevik bands and the Red Guard of the Russian government sent to Ukraine. Among them were Russian ex-service men, sailors, factory workers, the unemployed, and peasantry with no farmland of their own, who had nothing to lose and were looking forward to high pay and the right to rob."[36]

Over the coming weeks and months, the starving peasants of Ukraine watched as the German occupiers looted their land. German trains carried grain, bacon, and American-made Packards that had belonged to the Russian imperial army out of the country. They even took thousands of carloads of precious black earth topsoil, literally stealing the land itself. Peasants, workers, and soldiers were outraged by the German requisition orders and felt betrayed by their government, which had promised the land to them. "The people, specifically the peasants and workers, are not well disposed and are even hostile. They are afraid that the German invasion will imperil the achievements of the revolution," noted one German report.[37] Many soldiers who had thrown in their lot with Petliura now abandoned him. Entire units went over to the Bolsheviks; others evaporated into the country-side. The Rada's influence disintegrated. "No central authority exists to control a considerable territory," wrote the popular German travel writer Colin Ross. "From time to time individual political adventurers, dictators, or bandits control the situation. One can encounter villages surrounded by lines of trenches and engaged in an endless battle with a neighboring community for the land of an expropriated estate."[38]

Trotsky, still at Brest-Litovsk, was furious that the Central Rada had concluded a deal without him. In his memoirs, he mocked the Ukrainians for displaying "frantic self-humiliation . . . before vain aristocrats who only despised them," and dismissed them as "over-zealous flunkies" of the Austrians and Germans.[39] But Trotsky, too, needed peace with the Central Powers to consolidate his revolution and to deal with the growing threat from the White Army. The Central Powers, for their part, had gotten what they wanted from Ukraine and had little incentive to make concessions to Trotsky. The terms they offered required the Bolshevik government to relinquish its claim to nearly five hundred thousand square miles of territory in the western

UKRAINE AFTER THE
TREATY OF BREST-LITOVSK
MARCH–OCTOBER 1918

and southern borderlands of the former Russian Empire, inhabited by over fifty million people. The Bolsheviks would be compelled to formally cede Lithuania and the former Kingdom of Poland, to recognize the independence of Finland and Ukraine, and to remove their military from all Ukrainian territory. Having little choice, on March 3 the Bolshevik delegation at Brest-Litovsk signed the humiliating peace treaty—according to Trotsky, "without even reading it."[40]

From the Hetmanate to the Directory

On April 24, 1918, Abraham Dobry, the Jewish director of the Kyiv branch of the Russian Foreign Trading Bank, was kidnapped from his nine-room apartment in one of Kyiv's most ornate residences. Dobry's kidnappers drove the banker by automobile to the railway station and placed him under guard on a train heading to Kharkiv. There he was held at the Grand Hotel for four days, until he was able to bribe his guards and secure his release.

Dobry had made his personal fortune dealing in sugar, one of the region's most lucrative resources. The area around Kyiv was blessed with dry and sunny weather that yielded beetroot with the high saccharine content valued by dealers, and after Russia joined the Brussels Sugar Convention in 1907 the sugar industry took off, stimulated by the reduction in tariffs. But the market was risky, as early frosts or wet summers could decimate the delicate harvest, and the cost of maintaining technologically advanced refineries and transporting the goods was high. Individual proprietors were heavily mortgaged, and after the poor harvest of 1912 a small coterie of predominantly Jewish "sugar barons" began buying up factories and refineries with loans from foreign banks. Soon they had a controlling stake in the industry.[1] When war conditions sent the price of sugar skyrocketing in 1916, the press accused the Jewish sugar barons of war profiteering. Dobry, whose bank was heavily involved in the industry and who himself received financing from Deutsche Bank, was arrested at one point on charges of price speculation and illegal monopolistic practices. He was able to shake off the accusations and returned to his philanthropic and business pursuits.

Several years later, when it came time to negotiate the finer points of financial and commercial relations between Ukraine and Germany in accordance with the Treaty of Brest-Litovsk, the Ukrainian government called upon Dobry to assist.[2] For his role in those negotiations, Dobry was widely derided as having sold out Ukraine to foreign powers. As German military authorities ordered the Ukrainian peasants to fulfill grain quotas for export, Dobry became a symbol of the Central Rada's bad deal.

It turned out that Dobry's kidnapping had actually been coordinated by several of the Ukrainian government's own ministers. On discovering the plot, Field Marshal Hermann von Eichhorn, commander in chief of German troops in Ukraine, was outraged. "Irresponsible individuals and groups are attempting to terrorize the population," he proclaimed. "In violation of law and justice they are making arrests, with the object of frightening those who, in the interests of the country and of the newly born state, are ready to work hand in hand with Germany."[3] Citing specifically the disappearance of Dobry, Eichhorn declared martial law. He had been receiving reports for weeks that the Central Rada was incompetent—"the people who are at present unsuccessfully trying to rule Ukraine are like children," one German general had written—and he relished the opportunity to assume direct control.[4] Since the Rada had failed to maintain security, he announced, the German military would take it upon itself to do so.

On the afternoon of April 28, the Central Rada held a stormy session to determine its response. Accusations of collaboration with the Germans were flying, and many members questioned the decision to have signed the peace treaty altogether. Moyshe Rafes, a representative of the Jewish socialist Bund who had advocated a closer relationship with Bolshevik Russia, had just begun to speak when a German lieutenant barged into the chamber and announced that the entire government was under arrest. German soldiers had surrounded the building and were streaming into the Rada chambers. The lieutenant ordered the members of the government to hand over their weapons on pain of death. One after another, the parliamentarians solemnly walked up to the front of the chamber and placed their revolvers on the presidium table. German soldiers questioned every member of parliament and detained those they suspected of involvement in the Dobry kidnapping plot.[5]

The next morning, hundreds of landlords, officers, and bankers—the elites of the former tsarist regime—met under the dim electric lights of the Kyiv Circus, Europe's largest indoor hippodrome, to protest the socialist land policy of the Central Rada and to reaffirm the sanctity of private property. The congress had been organized by Ivan Poltavets-Ostrianytsia, a Free Cossack commander. The illustrious crowd, which filled the huge hall to the outer stands, applauded when speaker after speaker called for the restoration of a strong authority and the appointment of a new chief of Ukraine. "We need a strong power, we need a dictator, we need a Hetman in accordance with our old custom," they declared, using a variation of the traditional Cossack honorific.[6]

At around three o'clock, Pavlo Skoropadskyi—a distinguished nobleman, decorated tsarist officer, close associate of Poltavets-Ostrianytsia, and one of the top leaders of the Free Cossack movement—made a dramatic entrance, arriving in the hall with an entourage of officers to the applause of the affluent crowd. He had heard some of the speeches from the corridor and felt stirred to action, recognizing that his nation was calling him. As he described it, "The next speaker said the same thing as the previous one. When he called my name and demanded that I be proclaimed Hetman, the entire circus stood as one and started screaming loudly to acknowledge their agreement. . . . Already in the morning I knew that I must say something and had prepared a speech. But I had not expected that my proclamation as Hetman would happen as it did."[7]

Later that same afternoon, the assembly reconvened in the square in front of Kyiv's eleventh-century St. Sophia Cathedral, forming a massive circle in the plaza. Inside, beneath the magnificent central cupola, the Metropolitan of the Russian Orthodox Church anointed Skoropadskyi the Hetman of Ukraine, establishing a new government that would become known as the Hetmanate. Poltavets-Ostrianytsia—whom Skoropadskyi described as "a great Ukrainian enthusiast" and a man "of extraordinary ambition, an adventurer in the fullest sense of the word"—became the head of his personal chancellery.[8]

Skoropadskyi announced the end of the Ukrainian People's Republic and the dissolution of the Central Rada. He ordered the arrest of many activists within the former Rada government, including, in July, Petliura himself. It was a harsh rebuke to the workers and peasants who had supported the Rada's socialist policies, to the Jewish intellectuals whose hard-won national autonomy was now threatened, and to the Ukrainian nationalists who had been resisting foreign intervention. "We owe our salvation to the mighty support of the Central Powers," Skoropadskyi declared in his first speech as the new Hetman. "The right of private property, which is the basis of civilization and culture, is hereby fully restored."[9] Old Russian elites were to resume their ancestral power.

Fritz August Thiel, German consul general in Kyiv at the time, reported that Skoropadskyi's government was "politically so hopelessly impractical" that it demanded extensive German guidance.[10] Most Ukrainians, for their part, saw Skoropadskyi as a counterrevolutionary German stooge whose only positive achievement was to reintroduce imperial vodka—unavailable since the start of the war—into the stores. Workers and peasants responded to the return of the tsarist-era landlords and factory owners and to the Germans' forcible requisition of foodstuffs with uprisings, prison revolts, terrorist attacks, and work stoppages, the most destabilizing of which was a general railroad strike to protest German control of the railways. They set fire to the manors, mills, and factories that employed them and attacked German positions. Thousands of German soldiers were killed.

[TsDKFFA]

Pavlo Skoropadskyi

The Germans blamed the Jews, whom they accused of fomenting revolution and profiting from the unrest. They put up signs in train stations warning travelers to beware of "Jewish moneychangers" and accused the Jews of "carrying on a shameful propaganda" against the German occupation.[11] The Germans made it clear that as a result of "the solidarity of all Jewry," they must "hold responsible the whole of Jewry" for the "doings of individuals."[12] Their Austrian allies similarly accused the Jews of working with France and England to undermine the Central Powers.[13] Skoropadskyi himself issued pamphlets blaming the Jews for the scourge of communism and warning German troops to stay away from Jews lest they become infected with Bolshevism. In July, he formally repudiated the Law on National Autonomy, so cherished by the Jewish community.

German suspicion of Jewish revolutionaries grew after July 6, when Yakov Bliumkin, a Jewish orphan from Odesa who belonged to the Bolshevik-allied Left SR party, assassinated Count Wilhelm von Mirbach, the German ambassador in Moscow. Bliumkin managed to flee in a waiting car, but he left behind his cap, bags, and forged credentials. The daring terrorist act was just the first of a series of high-profile attacks that struck fear into the authorities.[14] A few weeks later, on July 29, an unknown gunman jumped into a car carrying Skoropadskyi's minister of transportation, Boris Butenko, and tried to shoot the minister in the head. The gun failed to discharge; as the driver put his foot on the gas, the assailant escaped. The governor of Volhynia responded with mass arrests and, without any information on the identity of the attacker, threatened to "drown the city in Jewish blood."[15] The next day, Boris Donskoy, an ethnic Russian and another Left SR, threw a bomb at the carriage carrying Field Marshal Hermann von Eichhorn, killing the commander in chief of German troops in Ukraine.

While the occupying forces and the Hetmanate denounced Jews as Bolshevik sympathizers, the Bolsheviks were accusing Jews of being members of the bourgeois class and collaborating with the Germans. In the town of Surazh, a Bolshevik cavalry unit carried out a pogrom on the grounds that the Jewish population had welcomed the Germans.[16] Some pointed to Skoropadskyi's first minister of trade, Sergei Gutnik— born Izrail Mikhelov to a family of Jewish bankers—as evidence that the new government was being controlled by the Jews and would continue the policies of Dobry. In reality, Skoropadskyi was accommodating to Jewish concerns only insofar as they intersected with the interests of the old tsarist elites. The wealthiest sugar barons, bankers, and railroad magnates benefited from his conservative pro-business positions, but the vast majority of Jews, the urban working poor, suffered from the requisitions as much as their peasant neighbors.

The spate of terror attacks continued the next month in Moscow and Petrograd, now aimed at the Bolsheviks. Once again, many blamed the Jews for the unrest, an accusation made tenable by the prominence of several individual Jews in separate incidents. On August 30, 1918, twenty-eight-year-old Fanny Kaplan fired three poison-tipped bullets at Lenin as he was leaving a Moscow factory; one bullet passed cleanly through his coat, the others lodged themselves in his shoulder and collarbone. The Bolshevik leader, she asserted during her interrogation, had been a "traitor to the revolution." The same day, the anti-Bolshevik activist Leonid Kannegisser successfully assassinated the head of the secret police in Petrograd, Moisei Uritsky, shooting him in the head before fleeing on a bicycle. Kaplan acted because she thought the revolution had not gone far enough; Kannegisser, a defender of the provisional government and son of a wealthy shipyard owner, had been opposed to the revolution from the beginning. Although the two terrorists were motivated by very different political perspectives, many observers noted that both were born in Ukraine to Jewish families. Ironically, Uritsky, the assassinated secret police chief, shared this background as well.

The Bolsheviks responded immediately to the assassination of Uritsky and the attempt on Lenin's life by expanding their own brand of terror. In the early days after the October Revolution, the Bolsheviks had established the Extraordinary Commission for Combating Counterrevolution, Profiteering, and Corruption, a secret police force known colloquially as the Cheka, from the Russian acronym for "extraordinary commission."[17] "Terror is an absolute necessity during times of revolution," declared Felix Dzerzhinsky, its first director.[18] Yakov Sverdlov, chairman of the Bolshevik Central Executive Committee, called for "merciless mass terror" and supported the arrest or execution of anybody suspected of counterrevolutionary activity.[19] The Cheka publicized its activities as a warning to others. The point, according to a future director of the Ukrainian Cheka, was to make "such an impression on the people that the mere mention of its name will quell the desire to sabotage and plot."[20] The party newspaper *Izvestiia* trumpeted Cheka killings; for six weeks in the fall of 1918 the Cheka even experimented with publishing its own newsletter, *Ezhenedel'nik VChK* ("Cheka Weekly"), which advertised the organization's extrajudicial executions.[21]

The Cheka grew rapidly, with branches established in almost every province, district, canton, village, and military unit. There were even railway Chekas and factory Chekas. Cheka units followed the Red Army into conquered areas to root out potential opposition through the use of torture and terror. They functioned in collaboration with revolutionary tribunals, which were entrusted with "investigating matters of counterrevolutionary activity" and were authorized to shoot "on the spot" all "enemy agents, profiteers, marauders, hooligans, and counterrevolutionary agitators."[22] At the height of the civil war, there were some two hundred tribunals trying two hundred thousand cases per year throughout Bolshevik-controlled areas. Often, the tribunals were mobile, dispatching "troikas" of three judges to patrol the countryside.[23] The conviction rates were staggering, between 85 and 90 percent, suggesting the near inevitability of a guilty verdict for those who found themselves on trial.[24]

The Bolsheviks' most dramatic foray into terror had come on July 17, when Cheka death squad leader Yakov Yurovsky—a former Talmud student—forced the deposed tsar Nicholas II into the basement of the house where he was being held in Ekaterinburg and executed him together with his wife, son, and four daughters. It was a shocking escalation, intended to signal to Russia and the world that the Bolsheviks were irreversibly committed to their revolution. The order had been approved in Moscow by Yakov Sverdlov.

Both Yakovs were born into Jewish families, an inconvenient coincidence that gave fodder to the Bolsheviks' enemies, who had already noted that many of the most prominent leaders in the Bolshevik movement were Jewish. These numbers, though, were grossly exaggerated by the tsar's supporters and by the Whites, who publicized the percentage of Jews in Bolshevik brigades, detachments, and leadership positions in order to discredit the enemy, dissuade potential Red Army recruits, and stoke ethnic strife.[25] This policy of "unmasking" Jews in power gave credence to the myth of Jewish dominance and was a powerful means of raising suspicion of the new regime in the eyes of the Christian population. The accusation that one was a secret Jew was a slander that could be attached to any opponent, particularly those who wore a pince-nez. Indeed, in the imagination of some Russian conspiracy-mongers, even US president Woodrow Wilson was a clandestine Jew.[26]

Many Jewish opponents of the revolutionary movement were also disturbed by the significant Jewish presence in the Bolshevik leadership. Solomon Goldelman, who had represented the socialist Zionist party Poale Tsiyon ("Workers of Zion") in the Central Rada, had nothing but disdain for what he called "these Jewish proselytes of Bolshevism." He maintained they "were responsible in no small measure for poisoning the friendly mutual relations which were created during the first period of the revolution between the Ukrainian and the Jewish camps."[27] Across the ocean, the *American Jewish Chronicle* also chastised "the political meddling of our radicals and ultra-radicals in Russia," who, the *Chronicle* contended, "were greatly responsible for the growth of anti-Semitism in Russia." The editorial urged the majority of Russian Jews to "declare to all those interested that these destructive elements are not representative of the Jews and do not express Jewish sentiments and Jewish opinions."[28]

THE WORLD REVOLUTION HAS BEGUN! screamed the headlines of the Bolshevik daily *Pravda* on November 1, 1918.[29] Trotsky's dreams of the spread of revolution to Europe seemed to be coming true. Two days later, German sailors mutinied in Kiel, launching a wider uprising throughout Germany. On November 7—the first anniversary of the Bolshevik Revolution—the Jewish journalist, theater critic, and activist Kurt Eisner led thousands of marchers through the streets of Munich to demand the abdication of the monarch, the establishment of a democratic state, an end to the war, and the introduction of an eight-hour workday. By November 9, the unrest had spread to Hamburg, Cologne, Bremen, and Berlin, and the dynastic rulers of the German states, from the Habsburgs to the Hohenzollerns, were forced to abdicate the thrones their families had held for generations. On November 10, the German emperor, Kaiser Wilhelm II, fled to Holland; he would formally abdicate the throne two weeks later. *Pravda* again heralded world revolution: ALL OF NORTHERN GERMANY IS IN THE HANDS OF REBELLIOUS WORKERS, SAILORS, AND SOLDIERS. SOVIETS OF WORKER AND SOLDIER DEPUTIES ARE IN ALL THE CITIES. THE CROWN OF WIL-HELM HAS FALLEN IN MUD. THE FOURTH IN A ROW! LONG LIVE THE GERMAN PROLETARIAT, LONG LIVE THE WORLD REVOLUTION![30] On November 11, Karl I, the emperor of the Austro-Hungarian Empire, announced he was relinquishing participation in the administration of the state. On the same day, in the forest of Compiègne, seven hundred miles to the west, the Allies signed an armistice with Germany, the last remaining belligerent party among the Central Powers, ending four years of armed conflict and ushering in what they imagined would be a new era of peace.

In a stunning development, the imperial structures that had ruled central Europe for generations had crumbled in just a few days. Many noted the prominence of Jews among those who had led the masses in bringing the old order down. Most famously, a young Gefreiter (private first class) in the Bavarian army named Adolf Hitler read about the unrest from a hospital bed in Pomerania, where he was recovering from a gas attack that left him temporarily blinded. He would later describe the Munich revolution as "the greatest villainy of the century" and blame it on "a few Jewish youths."[31] The notion that the European revolutionary movement was a tool of the Jews was by no means restricted to right-wing radicals. Ellis Loring Dresel, the chief of the US Special Mission in Germany, spoke for many when he disparaged the uprisings as having been "led by radical fanatics, who are, with few exceptions, foreigners or Jews."[32]

With the fall of the German and Austro-Hungarian empires, the soldiers of the Central Powers stationed in Ukraine prepared to go home. Exhausted and demoralized, many tore off their epaulettes, sold their weapons to locals, and merged into the civilian population. Others, buoyed by revolutionary excitement, rushed home, leaving their equipment behind. As Bulgakov wrote, "The Germans, the iron Germans with basins on their heads, appeared in Kyiv with Field Marshal Eichhorn and a splendid, tightly drawn-up string of wagons. They left without the field marshal, without the wagons and even without machine guns. The infuriated peasants took everything from them."[33]

Abandoned by the Germans, Skoropadskyi, who had failed to attract sufficient numbers of Ukrainians to his cause, searched for new alliances among the Whites and other conservative forces. Finding no friends anywhere, on December 14 he disguised himself as a wounded German officer, sewed his wedding ring and Saint George's Cross into his sleeves, and fled to Germany in a medical transport.[34]

WITH THE HETMANATE in disarray, an opportunity emerged for Ukrainians in Lviv to challenge Kyiv's title as the birthplace of a Ukrainian state and to declare sovereignty without the taint of the Rada's socialist politics or Skoropadskyi's German backing. The capital of Austrian Galicia, Lviv had been transformed by the oil boom of the fin de siècle from a provincial administrative center into a metropolitan hub; the grand neoclassical "Habsburg yellow" government buildings around the Renaissance market square and amid the baroque churches reflected the city's growing political importance. Lviv drew comparisons with Vienna for its broad avenues and clean, modern urban center. The people, as well, had come to value Habsburg orderliness. More organized than their counterparts in Kyiv and with disciplined Austrian-trained soldiers behind them, Ukrainians in Galicia were convinced that a government in Lviv would succeed in defending Ukrainian sovereignty where the Central Rada and the Hetmanate had failed.

But Lviv figured into Polish dreams of statehood as well. When President Wilson, in his momentous "Fourteen Points" speech to Congress in January 1918, declared an independent Polish state to be part of his plan for an enduring peace, he had suggested that it should include "the territories inhabited by indisputably Polish populations." In large part, Lviv fit the bill: although it was surrounded by a largely Ukrainian countryside, its population of two hundred thousand was half Polish, 28 percent Jewish, and 13 percent Ukrainian.[35] For Józef Piłsudski, the military hero and head of the newly established Polish Republic, Lviv was the linchpin of the multinational state he envisioned within the historic borders of the Polish-Lithuanian Commonwealth.

The Ukrainian minority, though, made the first move, proclaiming the establishment of the West Ukrainian People's Republic on November 1. Ukrainian soldiers who had been part of the Austrian garrison in the city raised the blue and yellow Ukrainian flag over the 260-foot-high tower of City Hall and occupied the train station and major government buildings. The next day, as thousands of Ukrainians celebrated outside Saint George's Cathedral, the city council declared its allegiance to Poland instead. "When we beheld the Ukrainian flag on the city hall, inconceivable feelings shocked us to the core. How dare they!" remembered Janina Chomówna, a Polish resident.[36]

The Ukrainians took control of the Ringplatz in the center of the city, but within days the Polish neighborhoods to the west, by the train station, fell to groups of Polish nationalists—or what one joint British and American investigative report apologetically called "a few hundred Polish boys, combined with numerous volunteers of doubtful character."[37] Skirmishes between former Austrian soldiers of Ukrainian and Polish nationality over the next three weeks left nearly two hundred fighters dead. Many of the "volunteers of doubtful character"—criminals who had been released from the prisons and military deserters—raided the town center, where they pillaged Jewish-owned shops. A self-defense brigade formed by Jewish soldiers who had been in the Austrian army responded with force. Although the leaders of the Jewish community had publicly declared their neutrality in the dispute between Ukrainian and Polish claims to the city, many Poles saw the Jewish brigade's resort to arms as an endorsement of the Ukrainian side. It was an impression reinforced by Ukrainian bulletins that celebrated the Jewish brigade as an ally and mischaracterized the official Jewish position as pro-Ukrainian.[38]

On Saturday, November 22, Polish reinforcements arrived from Kraków, forced the Ukrainian soldiers out, and attacked Jewish civilians with a barbarity that outraged the world. The British Jewish writer Israel Cohen described the scene in a report he wrote as a special commissioner of the World Zionist Organization:

The first act of the Polish troops was to disarm the Jewish Militia, officers and men, and imprison them. Then a military cordon was drawn round the Jewish quarter, machine-guns were posted at the top of each street, and systematic looting began. One shop after another was forcibly entered, the iron shutters were broken open by means of guns or hand-grenades, and the windows were smashed. Only Jewish shops were looted: the premises of Poles and Ukrainians were spared. Private dwellings were also raided by armed bands of civilians and soldiers, often led by officers. All who resisted were brutally assaulted or shot, and many women and girls were outraged.[39]

According to another witness, "women had to disrobe and stand naked, to the crude mob's delight. Lawyers' wives were treated like whores, university attendees grossly besmirched, their womanly dignity shamelessly trampled on."[40] Later in the day, Polish cars carrying petroleum and benzene were driven into Jewish neighborhoods. Polish soldiers doused houses and set them aflame as firefighters stood idly by. Locals could be seen running through the smoke, carrying fur coats and other valuables looted from the burning homes. "I observed that all were watching the Jewish houses burning with pleasure and laughter," one witness recalled.[41]

The soldiers then turned their attention to the synagogues, tearing apart Torah scrolls, destroying antiquities stored in the basements, and setting the buildings on fire, killing several Jews who had barricaded themselves inside. Jews were targeted on the pretext of shooting at Polish soldiers, importing Bolshevism, concealing weapons, speculating in currency and sugar, and generally exploiting innocent Poles. "You Jews robbed long enough, now it's time you were plundered," one victim reported being told by a military commander.[42] Polish soldiers even stopped pallbearers on their way to the cemetery, opening the caskets to search for arms and loot. The violence continued for three days, during which 73 Jews were confirmed killed and 443 wounded, although a reported 108 bodies were found in a mass grave. Sixty twelve-year-old girls were said to be recovering in the hospital from the "brutal mishandling of Polish hooligans."[43] On November 25, the day after the pogrom ended, the city council met to celebrate the return of Lviv to Polish rule and gave a standing ovation in honor of the "heroism of our young people" who had fought for Poland.[44]

Aside from a few little-known instances of Bolshevik atrocities in the heart of the war zone, Jewish observers could find no precedent for such destructive and organized violence. In contrast to previous waves of pogroms with which they were familiar, the Lviv pogrom was instigated by armed soldiers in the line of duty rather than by roaming gangs of ruffians or local discontents. The soldiers deliberately targeted Jews in their homes and places of business with no apparent military objective. They were joined by ordinary townspeople, who took advantage of the situation to loot from their Jewish neighbors. The entire scene was marked by public displays of power, often manifesting themselves through sexual humiliation and rape.

Many feared it heralded a new type of pogrom. The number of casualties in Lviv, they noted, was far greater than in previous known incidents; even in the midst of the brutality of the Great War, targeted massacres on this scale were unheard-of. The shock was compounded by the fact that the massacre had taken place not during the three-week conflict between Polish and Ukrainian forces over control of Lviv but rather after Polish soldiers had secured the city. The murdered Jews were not collateral damage during a battle; they were deliberately slaughtered by organized soldiers, who were encouraged by a supportive population that included not only antisemitic ruffians but also members of high society—"women wearing fur coats and gloves," in the words of one witness.[45] The participation of their neighbors destroyed the sense of security Jews had felt in the city. The humiliated survivors were dehumanized by the mocking, carnivalesque scenes, which seared into the minds of onlookers images of the Jews as creatures devoid of human dignity.

The Lviv pogrom was accompanied by a string of anti-Jewish riots and marauding in 130 other locales throughout Galicia and Poland, as local residents and soldiers celebrated Polish independence by ransacking Jewish shops and houses and assaulting Jewish civilians. In Eastern Galicia, Jews were targeted on the fabricated grounds that they had sided with the Ukrainians, leading Polish military authorities to forcibly disarm Jewish militias and self-defense brigades. But even in Warsaw, where Jews had little sympathy for Ukrainian nationalism, Cohen described how soldiers "repeatedly raided houses and shops in the Jewish quarter on the pretext of searching for weapons, and 'requisitioned' money, valuables, and anything useful."[46] Although most of the violence outside of Lviv was confined to looting, desecration of cemeteries, arson, and minor assaults, fifty-nine fatalities were recorded.[47]

Within days, word of the pogroms had spread around the globe. At a Zionist rally in Berlin on November 25, Nahum Goldmann, then an activist working for Jewish interests as part of the German Foreign Office (and later the president of the World Jewish Congress), called for "the entire civilized world and the democracy of Poland to put an end to these crimes, and to acknowledge and realize the rights of Polish Jews to civil and national equality."[48] Using the German name of the city and, without evidence, placing blame on the central Polish government and an imagined Polish tradition of intolerance, Prussian deputy minister of justice Oskar Cohn told the American legation that "the pogroms against the Jews in Lemberg and many other places were an actual fact, and had been instigated by the Polish authorities themselves. They proved the correctness of the old assertion that the Poles were less tolerant of national minorities than any other civilized nation on earth."[49] In Washington, DC, US secretary of state Robert Lansing took the accusations seriously, ordering that "any Americans sent to Poland should carefully investigate and report this matter" and began to assemble an official American investigative commission.[50]

Poles and their sympathizers, on the other hand, complained that the press was "spreading false reports about an anti-Jewish movement in Poland" and that "only through an entire lack of good faith" could the government be blamed for what many Poles insisted were spontaneous riots provoked by the Jewish betrayal of Poland for the promise of autonomy in Ukraine.[51] The real victim, they maintained, was Poland, which the Jews were discrediting in order to reduce the newly proclaimed republic's territorial integrity and force it to grant them privileged status.

DEFEATED BY THE Poles in Lviv, the West Ukrainian People's Republic still managed to retain control of much of Eastern Galicia, including the oil fields. But the Galician dream of spearheading a large Ukrainian state was in tatters. In Kyiv, on the other hand, where the Hetmanate formally remained in power, but without the German backing that had sustained it, left-leaning Ukrainian nationalists saw renewed opportunities for statehood. Under the leadership of Volodymyr Vynnychenko, in November 1918 the remnants of the Central Rada regrouped in the town of Bila Tserkva, south of Kyiv, and formed a Directory—a name borrowed from the committee that governed France during its revolution—in order to restore the Ukrainian People's Republic. Bulgakov mocked them as "men possessing the talent of turning up at the right time."[52] Certainly they were an unlikely group, poorly equipped to play the monumental role they were about to step into. But Petliura, who had been released from detention, managed to persuade the remnants of the Free Cossacks to remain loyal to him, giving military backing to the Directory's ambitions.

On December 12, the members of the Directory boarded a train to Kyiv. At every stop along the way, the ministers were greeted by crowds of cheering people, patriotic music, and laudatory speeches celebrating their return. In Kyiv, posters on lampposts announced the restoration of the Ukrainian People's Republic and ordered all public signs in the predominantly Russian-speaking city to be in Ukrainian. Ladders appeared along the main streets as shopkeepers replaced their shingles—sometimes just taping paper signs in Ukrainian over the Russian-language metal letters, under the assumption that the new government would be short-lived.[53] "No one knew who would be arrested tomorrow, whose portrait it was best to hang on the wall and whose to hide, which currency to accept and which to try to pass on to some simpleton," wrote the novelist Ilya Ehrenburg, who lived in Kyiv at the time.[54]

The Directory

The Directory received enthusiastic support from many Jewish quarters, based on its promise to usher in a new era of peace and stability
grounded in socialist principles and a renewed pledge to restore national
autonomy and minority rights. "The Jewish nation that stands today on
the verge of a new life in the Diaspora," declared a socialist Zionist
activist in Ukraine, "has always been attached to the Ukrainian liberation movement with full hearts, seeing in the movement a clear model
of national self-determination."[55] Avrom Revutsky, who would become
minister of Jewish affairs, envisioned a massive investment in the Jewish community: new Yiddish-language schools, cultural institutions, a
Jewish university, Jewish hospitals, funding for Yiddish literature and
the publication of Yiddish textbooks. His optimism was reflected in one
of the first statements he issued as minister: "The waves of the stormy
national calamity have eroded the government of the Hetman and made
an end to the reactionary domination of the nobility and capitalists. The
working classes of Ukraine have power again in their hands and they
will use it to create a new society, to definitively tear the chains that
enslave the working people. Together with the Ukrainian revolution,
Jewish revolutionary democracy has come to power."[56]

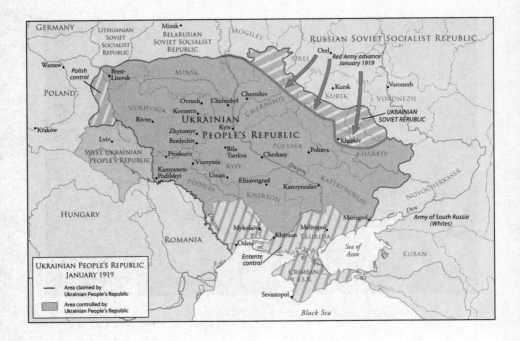

Arnold Margolin, who was appointed deputy minister of foreign affairs, was more guarded. "It was premature to concentrate on domestic reforms," he later wrote. The existence of the new state was "jeopardized from two sides": the Red Army from the north and the growing Volunteer Army—the Whites—from the east and south.[57] Indeed, on January 3, 1919, the Red Army retook Kharkiv, and Lenin appointed the prominent Bolshevik diplomat Christian Rakovsky as head of a new Ukrainian Soviet government. Margolin quickly realized that the process of rebuilding would be a long one. Surveying the remnants of the Russian Empire, he wrote: "When a great edifice has been torn apart it cannot be restored by spreading over it a new roof; the foundations must be rebuilt, the floors and walls relaid."[58]

PART II

THE UKRAINIAN PEOPLE'S REPUBLIC

DECEMBER 1918–MARCH 1919

The Ovruch Pogrom

In the winter of 1918, boots were hard to come by in Ukraine. A good pair of winter boots took an expert craftsman fourteen to sixteen hours to make and used about three times as much leather as an ordinary shoe. The best ones came from the Ukrainian north: unlike in warmer climates, where insects would bore their way into the hides, producing a pitted leather, the hides in the cold north made for a smoother-grained leather that could easily hold a stain.[1]

In an interview just before his hundredth birthday, in 2003, Veniamin Feldman recalled how the fur had to be worked into the soft leather around the vamp and quarter of the insole and how the outer sole had to be hammered onto the boot. Feldman, who was born in the village of Yanova Rudnya, about twelve miles from the town of Ovruch, in northern Volhynia, explained that in his youth a cobbler would come to his village to sew boots for anybody who provided their own leather and fur.

Ovruch had been near the front lines for much of the war; the various soldiers who paraded through the forests and swamps of the region always requisitioned supplies from the townsfolk. It was common practice to make such demands of local artisans and shops when a battalion moved through a town. The troops fed themselves by slaughtering the geese and chickens they found in the yards, forcing the homeowners to cook the birds for their consumption. If residents tried to hide their carts, their leather, or other goods under haystacks or in the cellars, the soldiers who discovered the hidden possessions would punish them severely for "expropriating the people's property."

Military officers repeatedly note in their memoirs the challenges of supplying their men and nonchalantly describe commandeering supplies from the civilian population. "Local shoemakers received orders for 200 pairs of boots," writes Commander Pavlo Shandruk of his unit's arrival in Lubny, for instance.[2] But he is silent on how the shoemakers were persuaded to deliver the boots and how they were supposed to obtain the leather. Forcible requisitions gave license to soldiers to terrorize the predominantly Jewish artisans and shopkeepers, and often resulted in violence.

One day in the winter of 1919, Feldman continued, a man who had been a warrant officer in the tsarist army and now led a local band of anti-Bolshevik fighters showed up at his house and demanded leather for boots. Feldman's father sent the officer away, retorting that he didn't even have enough leather to make boots for his own family, let alone any to spare. That evening, Feldman recalls, the warrant officer returned along with other men. "They dressed my father in a winter coat with boots and all, took him into the woods and killed him. They took away his boots and left."[3] A week later Feldman found his father's frozen, barefoot body in the woods.

Feldman's father was probably a victim of the Ovruch pogrom, a three-week reign of terror that lasted from late December 1918 through mid-January 1919 and resulted in the deaths of an estimated fifty-eight to eighty Jews and the pillaging of over twelve hundred houses.[4] But it was not numbers that made Ovruch so notable—more Jews had been murdered in several pogroms in 1905, and Bolshevik soldiers had killed a larger number in Hlukhiv just a few months earlier. What differentiated the Ovruch pogrom was that unlike those earlier ones, it was not a spontaneous spree committed in the heat of battle by unruly soldiers rampaging through civilian neighborhoods. Rather, it took place during a protracted reign of terror led by an officer acting under the authority of the state military. It was perpetrated at the very moment that the Directory was reestablishing the Ukrainian People's Republic and by forces representing it—the same government that only a year earlier had been the first in the world to grant national rights to the Jewish people; the same government that only days before the pogrom was being hailed as the harbinger of a new age for Jews in the Diaspora; the same government that had promised to usher in a new era of peace and security for Ukraine. It was a watershed moment, demonstrating to the Jews of Ukraine and to the world that even a government established on the principle of minority rights and national autonomy could not protect Jews from violence. In the following two months alone, at least eighty-five attacks on Jewish life and property would take place in Ukraine, more than double the total number of such incidents documented in the prior twelve months. And most would be carried out by military officers acting in their official capacities as part of the army of the Ukrainian People's Republic.

Thanks to detailed reports produced by investigative committees that collected evidence and testimonies, we are able to reconstruct four of these pogroms in detail. All used real threats of Bolshevik uprisings as pretexts to attack the Jews, but each also had its own distinct character. The first, in Ovruch, occurred just as the Hetmanate was falling and the Directory was establishing control. It was perpetrated by a single military detachment led by a sadistic officer in a region cut off from Directory headquarters. The second, which occurred in Zhytomyr at the same time the Ovruch pogrom was raging to the north, began with military incitement but quickly drew in broad segments of the population who took advantage of the chaotic period of regime change to loot from their Jewish neighbors. The third episode, in Proskuriv, was perpetrated by a military division with genocidal ambitions. The most lethal of the period, it took place over just four hours on Saturday, February 15. And the fourth, again in Zhytomyr, followed the Directory's rout after the January pogrom and two months of Bolshevik rule in the city. Ukrainian military authorities were convinced that the Jews had supported the Bolsheviks and punished the

Jewish population accordingly. Thanks to precedents established by the pogrom in the city two months earlier, the military encountered little resistance.[5] In all four pogroms, troops affiliated with the army of the Ukrainian People's Republic attacked Jews for their alleged support of the Bolsheviks, betraying the trust that Jews had placed in the Directory's promise of restoring Jewish national autonomy in a multinational Ukrainian state.

OVRUCH WAS IN many ways a microcosm of Ukraine as a whole. Its 1917 population of eleven thousand included three thousand Jews.[6] Most of the city's merchants were Jewish; they traded in mushrooms, furs, honey, and grain, transporting their goods by oxcart to neighboring villages. Some owned shops and stores around the market square, selling dry goods and crafts. Others worked in the cottage tanning industry, fashioning shoes, boots, and saddles from wrought leather, steeping the hides in vats on the street, and kneading and greasing them at home. Although the industry still lagged behind Berdychiv and Kyiv, where large tanneries had been established in the mid-to-late nineteenth century, Ovruch boasted six smaller plants. A railroad line was completed in 1913 linking the city to the larger station of Korosten, about thirty miles to the south.[7]

The rural villages around the town were overwhelmingly Ukrainian.[8] As one aid worker noted in 1919: "Poles are landlords, Russians are bureaucrats, Ukrainians are peasants, and the remaining population are Jews."[9] The demographic segregation between city and country was exacerbated by a typhus epidemic that had swept through the town: Ukrainian laborers fled back to their familial villages, leaving Jews, Poles, and Russians, who had no roots in the countryside to which they could return, in the city. As prices for basic goods rose due to wartime scarcity, many blamed the Jewish shop owners for profiteering. When soldiers from the Russian imperial army quartered in the city were demobilized in December 1917, they looted the Jewish-owned shops. The Jewish community responded by raising a self-defense brigade.

During the mass rebellion against Skoropadskyi's Hetmanate in the summer of 1918, socialist agitators had circulated among the peasants in the villages, urging them to seize the noble estates that the Central Rada had once promised them. When the 150 German soldiers stationed in the region abandoned their posts in November, the local peasants took up arms against their Polish landowners and seized control of Ovruch. They released the political prisoners who had been held by Skoropadskyi's government, and appointed two of them as their leaders: a Ukrainian named Dmitriuk became city commissar, and a member of the Jewish Bund, Scholem Freedman, was appointed his deputy. United by socialist democratic principles, they welcomed news of the Directory's entry into Kyiv.

But the new government was not able to hold on to power for long. Within weeks, a Bolshevik faction supported by Red Army units from a nearby town managed to gain control of the city by force. Many residents noticed that there were several Jews among the Bolshevik leaders and that the Bolsheviks had executed the Ukrainian commissar, Dmitriuk, while his Jewish deputy managed to escape. There were widespread rumors that the Bolsheviks were planning to close down the churches and that they had compiled a list of civic leaders—exclusively Christians—they were planning on executing.[10] The Jews seemed to be protecting their own.[11] To the south, though, the forces of the Directory were achieving moderate success, as the former tsarist soldiers stationed in Korosten declared their support for Petliura. As opposition to the Bolsheviks mounted in Ovruch, the Ukrainian peasant leadership sent word to Korosten that they were in need of military assistance.[12]

A paramilitary "partisan" detachment of three hundred men armed with rifles responded. It was led by otaman Oleksii Kozyr-Zirka, who had served in a dragoon regiment during the Great War and was an early recruit to Petliura's army.[13] He was, by all accounts, a sadistic drunkard. But with highly developed oratorical skills he was able to carve out a power base amid the lawlessness. Even Arnold Hillerson, who led an investigative committee that excoriated Kozyr-Zirka, could not help but compliment the warlord as "a handsome young fellow, a fiery brunet of gypsy type with good manners."[14] One of the officers who served with him recalled Kozyr-Zirka as "a very handsome man who was as dangerous as a cat and as cowardly as a hare." He was the type of man who would feign illness before a battle in order to remain in the barracks: "He didn't like the sound of bullets." He was caught on several occasions stealing from the division's treasury to fund his drinking, and would eventually sell his horse and arms for the bottle. "Even though he was cowardly, he was also very blood-thirsty; he got pleasure from killing unarmed people." Later, according to the same officer, Kozyr-Zirka joined the Bolsheviks—his former enemies—and got a job working for the Cheka. "That's how he found what he was always looking for: the opportunity to kill and rob unarmed people with impunity."[15]

FROM THEIR FIRST entry into town on December 25, 1918, Kozyr-Zirka and his men interpreted their mission to root out Bolsheviks as a license to terrorize the Jewish population: they "took the Bolsheviks and the Jews to mean the same thing," wrote an aid worker, despite the fact that many of the Jews in town were supportive of the Directory and one had even served as the deputy of the government ousted by the Bolsheviks.[16] On December 26, Kozyr-Zirka summoned the town rabbi to his military headquarters and announced: "I know that you are a Bolshevik, that all your kin are Bolsheviks and that all the Yids are Bolsheviks. Know that I will exterminate all the Jews in the city. Gather them in the synagogue and let them know."[17] The rabbi retorted that even if some of the Bolshevik ringleaders were Jewish, the Jews as a whole could not be blamed for the misdeeds of the few.[18] But Kozyr-Zirka wasn't interested in the rabbi's wisdom or ethical exhortations. When a Jew from nearby Kalinkavichy happened to be passing through Ovruch, for example, Kozyr-Zirka's men arrested him and brought him to their commander. He declared him a Bolshevik and ordered him shot.

More attacks followed. According to Hillerson's report:

There were also arrested two Jews passing through from the hamlet Narodychi; they were peddlers of cheap tobacco and matches. They were declared profiteers and brought to the Otaman. There they were stripped naked, scourged with whips, and made to dance. . . . Kozyr-Zirka himself stood with raised revolver and threatened to shoot them if they stopped dancing. Afterwards they made them beat each other and kiss the spot beaten. They also compelled them to cross themselves, etc. After amusing themselves with them as much as they liked they drove them out naked on the street, and then threw their clothes out after them.[19]

The peasants and workers of the region realized that Kozyr-Zirka had come to amuse and enrich himself and had little sympathy for the concerns of the common folk. On December 27, some of Kozyr-Zirka's partisans traveled to Narodychi to requisition supplies from the Jewish leatherworkers in the town. On the way back, they were ambushed by a group of peasants who had turned against him. Four of Kozyr-Zirka's men were killed. Upon hearing of this affront to his authority, Kozyr-Zirka retreated to Korosten to muster reinforcements. In his absence, the peasant socialists seized control of Ovruch again and attacked the wealthy landowners in the city, many of whom were of Polish heritage and were accused of having aligned themselves with Kozyr-Zirka. A few days later, Kozyr-Zirka, now armed with machine guns and accompanied by reinforcements of regular troops loyal to the Directory, started to make his way back to Ovruch, terrorizing and robbing Jews in the villages he passed along the way.[20] In Potapovichi, where a few Jewish artisans lived with their families, Kozyr-Zirka's men fatally shot the blacksmith, his father-in-law, and his nephew. (In this particular case, they claimed that the killing was in retaliation for a Bolshevik operation to sabotage the railway tracks; the blacksmith was an obvious suspect for his skill in ironworking.)[21] They also shot two other Jews in the village, one fatally.

The same day in the nearby settlement of Hoshiv, Kozyr-Zirka's troops encountered two elderly Jews—a deaf teacher and a butcher. They seized both of them and strung them up from the high branches of a tree, "one by a telegraph wire, the other by a strap." They left the two corpses hanging and placed a placard warning that anybody who

removed the bodies would be killed.[22] This episode was widely circulated in the foreign press as an example of the brutality of the pogrom,
often with exaggerated details that conflicted with the official report.
The New York Yiddish paper *Der morgen zhurnal* ("The Morning Journal"), for instance, reported that an elderly butcher in a small town
near Ovruch was tortured and hanged after he refused to kiss a cross
that "hooligans" put to his mouth. The report continued that the "hooligans," together with soldiers assisting them, tried to hang the butcher,
but the gallows collapsed. So they tore out his tongue and whipped
him to death.[23] A handwritten report to the Jewish Committee to Aid
Victims of War also reported on this incident, saying that the butcher
was hanged "and when the rope snapped, they cut out his tongue and
killed him."[24]

Kozyr-Zirka and his troops reconquered Ovruch on the afternoon
of December 31. He set up his headquarters at the railway station,
from where he could dictate orders and be prepared for a quick escape
if necessary.

The town's Jews collected money to offer in exchange for their
lives, while Kozyr-Zirka's troops roamed the streets searching houses
for cash and goods. In the marketplace, they seized ten Jewish girls,
dragged them into an inn, and raped them. In one house, the men
found a father and three sons sitting at a table; "they led all four out
into the yard and shot them one after another."[25] When Kozyr-Zirka's
troops arrived at the house of a lawyer named Glossman, "they took
him and his elderly father out in the street, then decided to free the
old man and told him to go. But he refused to abandon his son, and
the Cossacks began to beat the old man with whips, in the course of
which they struck out his only eye (he had long before lost his other
eye); and they shot the younger Glossman on the spot."[26] Not only
was Kozyr-Zirka himself present at this shooting, but several sources
report that the town mayor also happened to be walking by when
this slaughter occurred. Glossman spotted the mayor, whom he knew
well, and appealed to him to come to his defense, but the mayor "went
on, pretending not to hear the entreaty." In the first two days of the
pogrom, seventeen Jews were killed.[27]

On January 2, Kozyr-Zirka's forces gathered all the Jewish men of the city in the synagogue courtyard and "threatened those gathered that they would be burned in the synagogue," according to a desperate letter sent to the minister of Jewish affairs. As the crowd was assembled, Kozyr-Zirka drove up in an automobile and announced that he would allow the Jews to live for now, but he warned them that if he found a single Bolshevik spy among them, he would massacre the entire Jewish community. The Jews responded by pledging allegiance to him and offering tribute.[28]

OVER THE NEXT two weeks, Kozyr-Zirka ruled the town through terror. He ordered all the Jewish tailors and cobblers to work for him, outfitting his troops with clothing and fabrics stolen from the Jewish population. Other Jews were selected to clean the railroad station and the railway cars. Jewish musicians were forced to form an orchestra to play for the drunken banquets the troops enjoyed and to perform as background during public floggings and executions of suspected Bolsheviks. Kozyr-Zirka's troops selected some of the community's most distinguished Jewish residents, as well as random Jewish citizens, to bring to his encampment. There, as he lay sprawled in bed, his assistants stripped the prisoners, dressed them in ladies' hats and outlandish costumes, forced them to sing Yiddish songs and dance, and flayed them with whips. Kozyr-Zirka convulsed with laughter.[29]

In mid-January, Bolshevik forces of the Sixth Grodno Regiment massed to the north of the city. Kozyr-Zirka recognized that he was outnumbered and that his violent spree was over. As his farewell, on January 15, he ordered his troops to round up Jewish men and bring them to the station.[30] The militants gathered about fifty victims in the center of town, telling them they were being recruited to gather firewood. Lashing their captives with whips, they ordered the Jews to sing and dance the *mayufes*—a Sabbath table song that Polish noblemen had traditionally forced Jews to sing for their amusement—as they marched them in a grim carnival parade toward the station.[31] Forced dancing as a form of anti-Jewish humiliation was a familiar motif, appearing, for instance, in "The Jew in the Thorns" by the Brothers Grimm (1815) and in many Polish fables. The carnival atmosphere it induced facilitated the type of "joyful abandon" that often preceded outbreaks of violence.[32] When the procession arrived, additional militants were waiting with sabers and revolvers; they killed thirty-four Jews that day, before fleeing the city by rail. As the train departed, Kozyr-Zirka surveyed the scene and congratulated his men on their fight against the Bolshevik enemy.[33] Residents of the city would remember well how the surviving Jews rejoiced as the Bolsheviks moved in, greeting them as "our liberators."[34]

The Directory government was ignorant of events in the city until refugees started flooding into neighboring towns. The first news about the incidents was not received in Kyiv until after Kozyr-Zirka had left, and when officials did get word of the pogrom, they assumed it was of the same genre as the sporadic outbursts that had been occurring over the past year: unruly soldiers and peasants looting Jewish shops or robbing Jewish travelers. Such looting and robberies had occasionally resulted in fatalities, but they were few and far between. While the Red Army had massacred dozens of Jews in its fight against the bourgeois class and Polish troops had committed atrocities in the battle for Galicia, nobody in the multinational Ukrainian government imagined that one of their own would be terrorizing and killing innocent citizens under the banner of the Directory.

The problem was that although Kozyr-Zirka and his forces were nominally fighting on behalf of the Directory, in reality the government had little control over events in Ovruch, leaving the otaman to behave with impunity. Revutsky, who was in the process of negotiating his appointment to minister of Jewish affairs at the time, wrote: "The Ovruch pogrom did not make as strong an impression in Kyiv as did later pogroms, such as those in Berdychiv and Zhytomyr. It occurred in a remote location at the front, where the authority of the regime existed mostly in name only. The 'hero' of the pogrom, Otaman Kozyr-Zirka, was a shady person; people weren't even sure in which military he served."[35] Margolin echoed Revutsky: "It was impossible even to find out whether the government's orders were obeyed in

Jews killed by the Petliurites in Ovruch

places farther than a few miles from the seat of the government."[36] In *White Guard*, Bulgakov likewise portrays the situation on the ground as murky and unsettled, both during Skoropadskyi's rule and in the early weeks of the Directory. "The problem was that the City [of Kyiv] was the City and it had its police, a ministry, even an army, and newspapers of various names, but what was going on around them, in the real Ukraine, which was bigger than France and had tens of millions of people in it—no one knew that. They didn't know, they didn't know anything, not just about remote places but even—and this will sound ridiculous—about villages fifty miles from the City itself."[37]

Once word of what had happened in Ovruch did break out, it reverberated around Ukraine and the world. Some saw Kozyr-Zirka's cruelty and sadism as the acts of a lone madman gone amok. Others saw Kozyr-Zirka as an extension of Petliura, and, without evidence, blamed the Directory leadership for fomenting Jew-hatred. Hillerson's interpretation was perhaps the most pessimistic. "In this case, the pogrom took place under the slogan 'beat the Jews because they are Bolsheviks,'" he concluded. "But the attitude of the masses in Ukraine toward the Jews is such that any other slogan would be suitable for a pogrom as well."[38] Yet despite Hillerson's warning, the anti-Jewish rhetoric and violence was restricted for the most part to the occupying military authorities and did not spread to the masses. Indeed, the peasants who led the initial rebellion against the Hetmanate had selected a Jewish socialist as their deputy leader, and the reports make little reference to local peasants as anti-Jewish agitators or participants in the pogrom. By most accounts, although their lives were not being threatened, the peasants were terrorized by Kozyr-Zirka as well.

In reality, the problem was that the high-minded ideals of the Directory cabinet and the intellectual elites who supported it were not shared by the rest of the military leadership. Instead, the officers and soldiers, many of whom had been poisoned by the antisemitic rhetoric of the imperial Russian army they had previously served and by prejudices they had learned in their villages, continued to view the Jews as speculators stealing the wealth of Ukraine, as enemies of the church, and as the agents of Bolshevism. It was a belief system that resonated far beyond Ovruch.

The Zhytomyr Pogrom

In December 1918, as German forces were evacuating Kyiv and Petli-ura was assembling an army to retake the city from the Hetmanate, Konstantine Vozny—a thirty-two-year-old commander in the army of the Ukrainian People's Republic—was appointed commandant of Zhy-tomyr, the capital of Volhynia Province, and placed in charge of the three regiments garrisoned in the city. Zhytomyr's population of ninety thousand, including thirty-eight thousand Jews, had been devastated by the war and the Germans' hard-nosed requisitioning of foodstuffs and clothing. In the hopes of staving off further destruction in the wake of the Germans' departure, the newspapers had just called for the for-mation of self-defense brigades.

Having learned little from the experience of the Rada, the Direc-tory continued to resist a nationwide military draft. Although it had been possible in the early days of the revolution to maintain some sem-blance of military discipline, over the course of 1918 all sense of order had been lost. Even those soldiers who had remained to fight during the summer had been motivated primarily by the desire to end German requisitions. After the German retreat, the army largely disintegrated, as the peasant fighters lost their incentive. With no military leadership to follow, soldiers joined a dizzying array of divisions and regiments, seemingly desperate for some type of direction, not to mention some authority to provide them with food, clothing, and shelter. Many still wore the same overcoats the tsarist military had issued them years earlier, with new insignia and epaulets drawn on by hand. They were armed with rusted bayonets and sheepskin boots too worn to keep out the frostbite. With little military training and resources, they billeted in private homes and used their greatcoats as blankets.

When Vozny arrived in the Volhynian capital on December 4, he found a chaotic situation. "There was no command structure, no prepared provisions, not even suitable barracks," he recalled.[1] Vozny's deputy, Ivan Vykidanets, agreed. He explained that the situation for the troops was "very dire. The garrison was comprised of a significant number of armed peasants from the area who had gathered in the city. They had no provisions or clothing, and the barracks were for the most part unserviceable and dilapidated. On account of these conditions, there was growing discontent."[2] The peasants had signed up to fight for Petliura and the Central Rada earlier in the year, only to see their commanders replaced with the old elites of the Hetmanate. Some had gone along with the new regime, others had joined in the uprising against it, and still others had wandered off to their villages, where they were once again corralled into service with the promise of a restoration of the Ukrainian People's Republic and the return of the land to the peasants.

Freshly armed with equipment foraged from the retreating Germans, forces from this disorganized local garrison now had the run of the town.[3] These peasant soldiers had only the vaguest notions of what they were fighting for: some called themselves Revolutionaries instead of Republicans, not fully understanding the difference, but latching on to whatever slogan they had last heard. Many were inspired by the Bolshevik slogan of "peace, land, bread," but also understood from their officers that the Bolsheviks were the enemy. Bolshevik ideas were fine, some believed, but the Bolsheviks themselves were Jewish traitors. The soldiers displayed a similar contempt toward the municipal government and professional civil service, disdaining them as antiquated members of the old regime. They mocked the civilian police force of about 160 lightly armed guards as "hirelings of the bourgeoisie" and touted the vast superiority of their own weaponry.[4] They saw themselves as a bulwark against Bolshevism, which one high-ranking official called the "unchecked agitation of the Russian and Jewish-Cosmopolitan party."[5]

VOZNY HOPED TO stave off violence by disarming the civilian population. He dispatched soldiers to conduct door-to-door searches; they confiscated weapons along with any valuables they found. At the same time, his staff worked quickly to establish an administration that would work with existing municipal institutions in order to gain the trust of all residents. Vozny assigned thirty-three-year-old Nikolai Gladky to the task. Gladky immediately proceeded to make contact with the local soviets, which he believed could be co-opted to support the Directory. "I saw nothing wrong with the workers forming a workers' soviet," he explained.[6] Gladky himself even served in the peasants' soviet.

Pleased with this progress, Vozny sent a telegram to Petliura's general staff in Kyiv, requesting permission to allow the establishment of a soldiers' soviet in the city. The general staff, likely wary of the potential of the soviet to become radicalized, refused the request. But it was too late. The soldiers had already established a soviet of their own, and now—lacking official approval—were forced into an oppositional stance. The soldiers also turned against the existing city council and institutions of government, accusing them of being relics of the old tsarist order, controlled by a hostile bourgeoisie. They adopted the Bolshevik slogan: "All power to the soviets."

On Friday, January 3, delegates to a united soviet of workers', soldiers', and peasants' deputies in Zhytomyr met with revolution on their minds. Members affiliated with the Bolsheviks and Left SRs proposed the establishment of a Military Revolutionary Committee to take control of the whole province of Volhynia in the name of the soviets, on the model of the 1917 October Revolution in Petrograd. Most of the peasants and moderate socialists stayed away from the meeting, believing that the Bolsheviks could not be trusted because, as Gladky put it, "the majority were Jews."[7] "I have to say," Gladky continued, "that among the simple people, like the Cossacks and others, there was a hostile attitude toward the entire Jewish nation."[8] Nine of the thirty-five delegates who attended the meeting of the soviet that day were Jewish—an underrepresentation, in fact, since Jews made up nearly half the city's population. But all nine of the Jewish delegates were worker delegates, those most supportive of the revolution. As Gladky explained, "This didn't surprise me because I already knew that the majority of organized workers in Zhytomyr were Jews."[9]

Abram Gilinsky, the chair of the united soviet, led the call for revolution, pointing to the peasant and worker unrest that had shaken Ukraine throughout the summer as evidence that the time was ripe.[10] Others within the soviet protested that revolution was premature: it would be disastrous to make a power play in the city before the Red Army had secured military control of the region as a whole, they said. Zhytomyr could not stand alone.[11] Ultimately, Comrade Abram, as Gilinsky was known, prevailed. Soldiers in the local garrisons sprang into action, abandoning the Directory for the Bolsheviks.

At ten o'clock in the morning of Sunday, January 5, a group of armed soldiers from two of the garrisons Vozny had just taken command of arrived at the provincial printing house and announced that they were requisitioning the press. They ordered the typesetters to print a manifesto from the soviet addressed to the population of Volhynia. Other soldiers took over the train station, sealed the banks, cut the telegraph and telephone lines, and halted tram service.[12] By nightfall the city was cut off from the world. The only news came from the manifestos that plastered the city, announcing that the soviet had seized power.

As soon as he saw the first manifesto on January 5, Vozny knew he was in trouble. He fled the city to Berdychiv, where he tendered his resignation. Vozny's train was packed with government officials, well-to-do members of Zhytomyr society, and many Jews, all of whom feared the Red Terror and the Bolsheviks' threats to nationalize private property. As soon as the echelon arrived in Berdychiv, Petliura's soldiers, suspicious of Jewish Bolsheviks, demanded to know whether there were any Jews among the refugees. Vozny assured the soldiers that the entire party was of Ukrainian nationality, saving his Jewish travel companions from potential trouble.

THE FEARS OF those who fled were not misplaced. On the afternoon of January 7, Christmas Day according to the Orthodox liturgy, soldiers from the local garrison who had gone over to the Bolsheviks arrested several of the wealthier members of the Jewish community: Shmul Vaynshteyn, who owned an iron-casting factory; Ia. A. Shpilberg, a member of the Zhytomyr city council; a dentist by the name of Grinboym; and Avram Bregman, Duvid Brusilovsky, and Noyekh Bezymensky. Bezymensky reported that he was sitting at home in his apartment when two soldiers barged into the room and shouted at him to put up his hands. "They told me that I was under arrest by authority of the Military Revolutionary Committee."[13] The same fate befell the other luminaries. Bolshevik soldiers took the civic leaders and wealthy businessmen to the provincial government headquarters. Also being held there was a Christian German nail factory owner by the name of Tayberg, who may have been mistaken for a Jew, as well as some Russians and three unruly regiment soldiers who had been arrested for looting—a total of sixteen people.[14]

At about ten in the evening, the prisoners heard a commotion among the soldiers guarding them; they watched their guards put on their coats and abandon their posts. A couple of hours later, a new soldier arrived wearing a white *papakha*, the high cylindrical fur hat made of karakul sheepskin recognizable as part of the Cossack uniform. The soldier in the hat introduced himself as the new otaman and told the prisoners that Directory reinforcements—about six hundred of them, cavalry and infantry—had retaken the city. They were determined to crush the Bolshevik uprising, which, he said, "had been prepared by the Jews and the landowners, who now needed to be massacred completely."[15] The soldier released the Russian prisoners, telling them: "You are Russians. Fine. We will slaughter all the Jews."[16]

He turned to the rest of the prisoners and continued: "Tomorrow, for you Jews, I am going to arrange a bloodbath."[17]

At four a.m., two Directory soldiers appeared in the building, led the prisoners out into the street, and ordered them to stand in two rows. "They told us that we were going to be shot," Bezymensky reported.[18] The soldiers marched the group down Bolshaya Berdichevskaya Street. As the convoy passed through the city, the soldiers beat and humiliated the prisoners, forcing them to chant slogans like "Glory to Ukraine" and "Long Live the Directory."[19] They finally arrived at the Directory government's headquarters, where an officer searched them: "They took my gold chain, black watch, and 50 rubles in cash," recalled Bezymensky.[20] Tayberg, the German factory owner, was released, but the rest of the prisoners were kept under guard. According to Bregman, "The whole time the soldiers were talking to each other about the 'Jews' as the eternal enemies of Ukraine."[21]

Brusilovsky remembered that one of the guards, a young man in an iron helmet who introduced himself as an assistant to the new commandant, told them that "as Jews we have a relationship with the soviet government and as enemies of the republic we will be mercilessly exterminated." The captives "pointed out to him that we were not Bolsheviks; quite the contrary, it was the Bolsheviks who had initially arrested us as their enemies."[22] The young guard promised to investigate their case. When he returned later that day, he indicated he would secure their release from City Hall but told them it was not safe for them to leave: a pogrom was raging in the city. He would continue to detain them for their own safety. For three days, the prisoners watched as soldiers brought loot—some of which may have come from their own apartments—to the offices of the otaman: shoes, sugar, jam, silver. Like pirates, the soldiers divided the booty among themselves.[23]

UNAWARE OF THE arrests that had taken place that day, Ivan Vykidanets was driving through the city on January 7. A light snow was falling. Vykidanets was one of the few officials who had remained behind when Vozny and the rest of the city government fled to Berdychiv.

Vykidanets had become active in socialist circles during his studies at the Zhytomyr Geological Institute, then had taken up arms against the German occupation in the summer of 1918, before offering his services to Vozny. In Vozny's absence and with the support of the local Left SRs, he took over the role of commandant.[24] As he passed through Sobornaya Square, the plaza in front of the Orthodox Transfiguration Cathedral, where cabbies with their horse-drawn carriages congregated to await their fares, he noticed what he later identified as the first signs of unrest: a small crowd was watching a group of soldiers from the local garrisons pry open trunks and chests that had clearly been stolen.

When he arrived at his office, he learned that a phone call had summoned him to the train station. There he was greeted by a Ukrainian officer who introduced himself as part of a forward detachment of the army of the Directory, which had been dispatched by Petliura to take charge and put down the soviet's rebellion. Vykidanets described the unrest in the city and asked the officer to provide soldiers for a night watch. The officer refused on the grounds that it was too dangerous: Bolshevik troops might be waiting in ambush, he said.[25] In reality, as soon as Petliura's reinforcements had appeared, the local soldiers who went over to the Bolsheviks had abandoned the revolt, either returning to their home villages or staying around only to ransack the city. The workers who led the uprising proved to be more capable of issuing manifestos than corralling an army. Vykidanets returned to his office, issued an order for the remaining soldiers from the local garrisons to guard the city overnight, and went home to sleep.

That same night, Efim Eliasberg, an auditor at the Azov-Don Bank and a member of the city council, was accosted by a group of soldiers. "You are a Jew?" they demanded in a half question, half statement. "Indeed, a Jew," he replied. He heard a shout: "Beat him!" When a passerby intervened on Eliasberg's behalf, one of the soldiers urged the others to let him go. Eliasberg escaped.[26] Another Jewish member of the council, a man named Goldfeld, was attacked as he left City Hall. Breaking loose from his assailants, he left behind his coat and his galoshes. Both Eliasberg and Goldfeld understood that it was no longer safe to be a Jew in Zhytomyr, at least not a wealthy Jew.[27]

AT ABOUT SIX in the morning on Wednesday, January 8, City Councilor Konstantin Novikov received a phone call from Deputy Mayor S. I. Ivantsky, summoning him immediately to City Hall. On his way he noticed that many stores on Gogolskaya, Mikhailovskaya, and Bolshaya Berdichevskaya streets had been ransacked. The unruly local soldiers that Vykidanets had observed the night before were still there. They had been looting all night. "There were a number of soldiers hanging around the emptied stores," Novikov remembered. "There were also a number of women townsfolk with them, often carrying handbags or baskets. The thieves appeared to be very calm, and took their time picking out the goods they intended to steal. Several of them even took the time to try on hats."[28]

As soon as Novikov arrived at City Hall, he learned that the army of the Directory had placed the city under military control and had ordered all the councilors to appear at the train station. Most of them were not around at that early hour, but it was clear that the order was urgent, so Novikov and Ivantsky went to the station by themselves, taking back roads to avoid the gunfire that broke the silence of the cold January morning. On one street corner, they noticed a group of soldiers wearing *papakha* hats with a red silk ribbon flowing off the back. Novikov had not seen this type of headgear in town before. He knew immediately that these were not soldiers from the local garrison but the troops dispatched by the Directory to put down the rebellion.

Novikov and Ivantsky were greeted at the railway station by a Directory officer who boasted that his forces had seized the station and already murdered the "Bolshevik-Jew" who had been the station head.[29] He offered to show his esteemed guests the body; they politely declined. During their conversation, other civilian and military officials, including Vykidanets, began to arrive. At around ten, there was a tumult at the station: a slender young colonel, a real dandy, wearing a blue

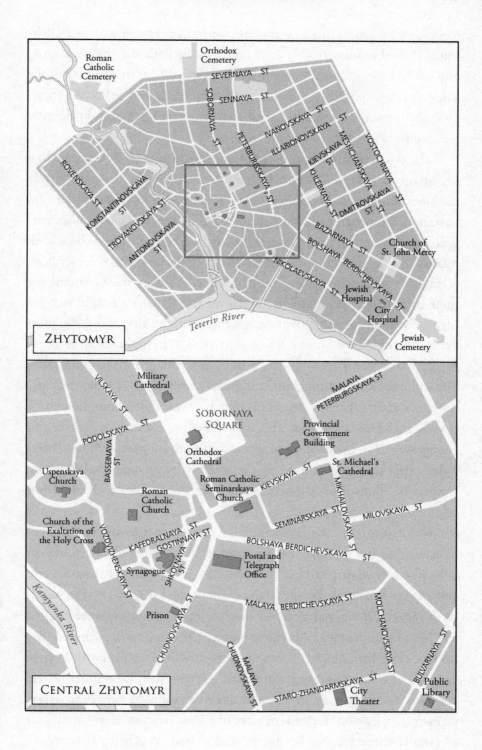

ZHYTOMYR

CENTRAL ZHYTOMYR

Cossack's overcoat, made a dramatic entrance. The newcomer, Oleksandr Palienko, immediately exchanged kisses with the city councilors
and wished them season's greetings. He invited them to join him in the
station's telegraph office, which he had commandeered as his headquarters, and presented himself as the commander of a battalion fighting
with Petliura's Northern Group.[30]

Palienko had earned a reputation for boldness after taking part in a
prison uprising in Kyiv, where he had been held by the Hetmanate over
the summer. In mid-December 1918, he had become commander of a
battalion composed primarily of former tsarist soldiers and volunteers
who had joined the Free Cossacks. It was he who outfitted them with
papakhas topped with red ribbons. Many of his men had recently been
released from prison, where they had been held by the Germans for
their role in the anti-Hetmanate insurgency. Palienko fought not for
ideals but rather for the love of the fight. His specialty, and the highest
value he cultivated among his troops, was the application of brute
force. Vozny compared him to a bull, describing him as "intellectu-
ally immature, dimwitted, and completely incapable of independently
understanding official instructions that are even a little complicated."[31]
Another official wrote that "his detachment is useless for fighting an
enemy who is in the least bit organized" and that Palienko himself was
"absolutely ignorant of military tactics."[32] Gladky described Palienko
simply as "a suspicious individual."[33] He was neither well liked nor
admired, but he was feared.

Addressing the city councilors in the telegraph office, Palienko
insisted that his interest was in fighting the Bolsheviks. Ukraine, he
continued, was surrounded by enemies—Jews, Poles, Russians, and
Bolsheviks—and the Bolshevik movement, he said, was in the hands
of the Jews. "It was understood that he was inciting violence against
the Jews in Zhytomyr," Novikov noted.[34] The colonel continued that
he had only brought his battalion into town to quell the Bolshevik
uprising; he promised that he would get the job done quickly and
soon be on his way again. He had done the same in Berdychiv a few
days earlier, he said. Indeed, rumors of Palienko's January 4 slaughter
of twenty-three Jews in Berdychiv had already reached Zhytomyr.[35]

Palienko concluded his speech by ordering Deputy Mayor Ivantsky to dismiss all Jews and Poles from the city council. When Novikov objected, Palienko expressed surprise that he would "stick up for the Jews."[36] He then ordered the arrest of Vykidanets, whom he considered a lackey of the Left SRs, and appointed one of his own men as commandant in Vykidanets's place. Detained in the Hotel Rome, Vozny's deputy was able to watch the pogrom unfold from his window.[37]

BACK DOWNTOWN, ON Sobornaya Square, a military truck appeared at about ten o'clock that same morning, Wednesday, January 8. Soldiers wearing *papakha*s with the red ribbons of Palienko's detachment fired machine-gun volleys from the flatbed of the truck to disperse the crowd of looters and onlookers. As the marauding soldiers scattered in various directions, witnesses felt a palpable sense of relief that order was being restored.[38]

But it quickly became apparent that Palienko's men only wanted to get rid of the competition. Yulii Shulkhin, who spent the day peering out the window of his apartment across from the Petrograd Hotel on Bolshaya Berdichevskaya Street, reported seeing a car pull up and two men emerge who immediately took control. One was wearing a military uniform and began to shout orders while the other one directed the looters, placing handfuls of goods in his car. Soon, more men wearing *papakha*s with red ribbons arrived on horseback and took over. The leader of the new group watched menacingly from the middle of Sobornaya Square as the looting spread around him. At one point a soldier brought him a bottle of pilfered booze, which he downed on the spot.[39]

Zelman Gorlovsky, who lived on the ground floor of an apartment building on Kafedralnaya Street, reported that he went with his children to his brother-in-law's apartment on a higher floor of the same building, where he thought he would be safer. At around eleven in the morning, he heard a commotion below. He looked out the window, which faced the old market square, and saw a crowd robbing shops as six mounted soldiers in uniform stood by. A young boy in the street glanced up and caught Gorlovsky's eye. The boy broke off from the crowd and ran to one of the soldiers, pointing up at the window. Before Gorlovsky realized what was going on, he heard a shot and felt as if something had hit him in the head. He took off his hat and saw that the bullet had gone right through it. His scalp was untouched. A few minutes later, six soldiers armed with rifles, revolvers, and bayonets were at the apartment door. They falsely claimed that a sniper had fired at them from the window, searched the apartment, stole cash and half a pound of tea, and left with a warning: if anybody should dare to step foot out of the apartment in the next two days, they would be shot. When Gorlovsky told his story to an investigator with the Legal Bureau of the Committee for Relief of Pogrom Victims, he brought along the bullet-pierced hat as evidence.[40]

Once they had taken control, Palienko's soldiers systematically set out to pillage what was left in the stores adjacent to Sobornaya Square. They were joined by reinforcements, differentiated from Palienko's soldiers by their helmets. Groups of five to ten soldiers in their military overcoats proceeded in an orderly fashion, street by street—breaking shop windows with the butts of their rifles, smashing storefronts with their axes, and occasionally tossing grenades into stubborn doors they couldn't otherwise pry open. Trucks full of soldiers shooting their rifles at upper-level windows rolled down Bolshaya Berdichevskaya Street.[41]

Many witnesses noted that only Jewish-owned stores were robbed. Christian merchants knew to draw white crosses on their walls, display their icons, or simply attach notes to their doors indicating that the owners were Christian. Some Jews had a similar idea, saving their stores by drawing crosses on them.[42] Isaac Giterman, an aid worker who visited the town in the days after the pogrom, noted that "in the entire city, you will hardly find two dozen small Jewish shops that have by some miracle not been robbed, and if you do come across one open store among those that have been torn apart and destroyed, you will soon notice a big white cross to indicate that the place belongs to a Russian or a Pole."[43] Palienko's men were guarding Christian-owned stores, like the high-end clothiers Jacques and Gentlemen, to protect them from looters.[44]

Soldiers filled their trucks and carts with pilfered goods and took them in convoys to the station. What they didn't want for themselves they sold to the highest bidder or just tossed into the street for others to scavenge. The first civilians to take to the streets were local women who scooped up the goods left behind. Soon, crowds gathered around to wait their turn. Excited children ran alongside the soldiers, who playfully tossed them stolen treats. As the day turned into a festive free-for-all, ordinary city folk, including even members of the civil service and polite society, joined in. Novikov commented that some of the looters even looked to be Jewish.[45]

Witnesses described seeing soldiers and women carrying furs, leather, clothing, and other goods in handfuls—or in baskets, bundles, satchels, sacks, boxes, and trunks—as they helped themselves to the property of their fellow townsfolk under the watchful eyes of Palienko's men. They looted Elia-Aron Zamd's fish store, Pesia Segal's pottery shop, Shama Nudel's grocery store, and Hirsh Gaetsky's shoe store.[46] Nudel provided a detailed accounting of the groceries armed men stole from her: nine hundred pounds of jam, one thousand pounds of preserves, a barrel of honey, a barrel of grapes, a barrel of herring, seven hundred pounds of apples, one hundred pounds of pears, thirty-five pounds of mushrooms, ten thousand Salve cigarettes, ten boxes of chocolate candy, and one hundred pounds of nuts. It was enough food to feed an army.[47]

As the day progressed, peasants came into town with carts to carry off loads of stolen goods, returning to their villages with cloths and quilts slung over their backs. Then they came back to take a second helping. Some brought rifles with them. There were checkpoints everywhere, but the soldiers manning them seemed to have no compunction about allowing peasants into the city with empty carts and leaving with carts overflowing with goods. One observer reported seeing a looter calmly leaving a ransacked house wearing a woman's pelisse and a pink coverlet.[48]

[YIVO INSTITUTE FOR JEWISH RESEARCH]

Interior of a store vandalized during the January 1919 pogrom in Zhytomyr

AROUND SUNSET, SOLDIERS, peasants, and townsfolk streamed out of the depleted city center, expanding their scavenging into the private residences along the grand boulevards leading into Sobornaya Square: Mikhailovskaya, Bolshaya Berdichevskaya, and Kievskaya streets. Children pointed out the Jewish apartments in the elegant baroque and rococo buildings that lined the upscale avenues.[49]

The first residences the mob ransacked belonged to the wealthy, the type of people with evening gowns in their wardrobes, jewels in their cupboards, and china in their pantries. Kiva-Khayim Azhorsky had hidden his valuables inside his piano. Although pianos had been sold in Zhytomyr since at least 1879, when Ottokar Appel opened his store on Moskovskaya Street, a piano in a private home was still a rarity, an indication of Azhorsky's wealth. The piano also made for what Azhorsky considered to be a perfect hiding spot. But he had assumed that any intruders would be drunken delinquents; he didn't count on being robbed by refined officers. At six in the evening, seven or eight armed men appeared at his apartment, claiming to have heard the sound of sniper fire coming from the window. They rummaged through his home in search of weapons to no avail. (Azhorsky had already turned over his revolver in accordance with Vozny's directive to disarm the civilian population.) When the search was finished, one of the men sat down at the piano "and played a few chords." The musician noticed that the notes were dull, as though something was dampening the hammers. He lifted the lid and found a silver-embroidered bag with diamond earrings, a gold watch, a gold bracelet, diamond rings, a silver wallet, and cash.[50]

Many residences in town doubled as small businesses and were located in buildings arranged around square courtyards, with a single gate leading to the street. Each courtyard had a groundskeeper, or *dvornik*, who cared for the gardens, maintained the buildings, and served as a guard, porter, and custodian. It was a position of great trust and intimacy.[51] That's why the involvement of the *dvornik*s in many break-ins was so galling to the victims.

Shlem-Avrum Liberov Filtser told an investigator that the tavern he ran was robbed twice by soldiers. The second time, at around two p.m. on January 9, the soldiers set the establishment on fire when they left. His neighbors, who witnessed the ordeal, revealed that his *dvornik*, Serhy Astafev, was among the culprits; so was a boy Filtser knew, who apprenticed with a carpenter a few doors down.[52] Isaac Melamed, meanwhile, reported that when robbers began to shoot up his laundry business on the evening of Thursday, January 9, he hid in a neighbor's apartment with his family. When he returned, his entire store was destroyed. A neighbor told Melamed that he saw another neighbor's *dvornik* going in and out of the building taking pillows and other items.[53] Shlem Pressman also reported that a *dvornik* pointed out Jewish apartments to the soldiers.[54]

It wasn't just *dvornik*s who took part in the looting. Anyone who knew the secret hiding places, had keys to the storehouses, or had simply eyed some valuables while performing their duties got in on the action, robbing from their employers with abandon. Many wealthy members of the largely Jewish bourgeoisie in town employed domestics and laborers from the villages, some of whom resented the economic differential they observed between town and country, Jew and Christian. Even the less affluent often relied upon a "Shabbes goy," a Christian helper, to perform many of the menial duties religious Jews refrained from on the Sabbath. Class conflict fueled the riot, as Christian servants felt they were finally getting their due from their Jewish employers.

Moisei Vinokur, who had already been robbed on the first day of the pogrom, stated that on January 9, his milklady led a group of twenty soldiers to his apartment, where they broke down the front door and loaded everything—his furniture, his pillows, even his undergarments—into a waiting cart.[55] The men who broke into Genia Psakhis's home in the middle of the night tried to hide their identity by forcing Psakhis and her family into a dark room while they rummaged through the house in search of valuables. But Psakhis, the wife of a merchant, recognized the voice of her employee Grigorii Nesteruk. When the bandits returned later, Psakhis also suspected that the man they were calling Timoshak was, in fact, Timofei Gorbunov, a mason she had employed to help build her house.[56] Srul Fefer's cook, a peasant woman named Kharitina Shumskaya, was detained after the pogrom with forty rubles and a basketful of goods stolen from Fefer.[57] Elye-Yitskhok Slepak, whose grocery store was ransacked, testified that when he visited his laundress's house in the village of Berki after the pogrom to pick up his clothes, he was surprised to see one of the men who had robbed him sitting in her living room drinking vodka.[58]

When later questioned about their activity during the pogrom, few of those caught in possession of stolen goods displayed any remorse or fear of prosecution. Most justified their actions nonchalantly. Aneliya Volynchuk protested against being singled out for doing what everybody else was doing. Ekaterina Korchenyuk, who was caught with stolen tobacco, simply explained that tobacco was expensive and she and her husband were poor.[59] Georgy Pazdernik, an eighteen-year-old student in a trade school, provided the investigative committee with a detailed description of his activities that day. He had spent Orthodox Christmas day, January 7, on his family farmstead, a few miles outside of Zhytomyr. The next day, he went into town to meet up with some schoolmates and check out the action. He explained that he was drawn toward the gunfire on Bolshaya Berdichevskaya and Kievskaya streets because "I am a generally curious person, and I always go where something is happening."[60] At first, Pazdernik explained, he assumed the gunfire was coming from Jews shooting at the soldiers from their apartments: "there were rumors of this type, and I had heard them as well."[61] When he noticed that it was the soldiers—not the Jews—who were doing the shooting, he felt safe. He knew they were only shooting Jews. "When I saw the scene of the pogrom, it didn't particularly bother me. I had noticed how poorly the Jews treated the Russians, so it didn't strike me as remarkable that the Russians would also treat the Jews poorly," he stated, generalizing the entire non-Jewish urban population as Russian.[62] He claimed that he wandered into a plundered apartment to see what it looked like but insisted that he took nothing. He was just an inquisitive onlooker, not a thief. Several witnesses, including some Christian observers, however, testified that they saw Pazdernik leaving the apartment with a bundle of goods wrapped in gray canvas hidden under his coat.[63] One Jewish witness, Polya Dorfman, claimed that when she asked Pazdernik what he was doing, he laughed and continued looting the house.[64] A witness who identified himself as a family friend expressed disgust with Pazdernik's behavior during the episode, insisting that this was not how Pazdernik was brought up. If Pazdernik's father had known what he was up to during the pogrom, he "would have killed him with his own hands."[65]

Some looters even socialized in the same circles as their victims. Meyer Frenkel and his parents were sitting in their apartment at around five p.m. on January 8 when they heard a knock on the back door. Through the window they could see the top of a *papakha*. "Open up faster," the man yelled. When Meyer opened the door, a uniformed soldier walked in and ordered everybody to raise their hands. When the soldier caught Meyer's eye, though, he excitedly threw his weapon down on the table, exclaiming: "I didn't expect to see you here! I thought you were in Kyiv." Meyer realized that he knew the man from his high school days; since then, they had seen each other at various social events around Zhytomyr. The soldier made himself at home and took the liberty of inviting his companions, who had been waiting in the foyer, into the apartment. The whole squad took their seats at the table, as though they were invited guests. Meyer's terrified father, Lvov, poured the intruders wine while Meyer's mother prepared snacks. The soldier sent one of his men out into the street to pick up some nuts. When the soldier returned, they all chatted about political events in the city and about the pogrom raging outside, seemingly oblivious to the fact that the Frenkels were experiencing this whole episode from a very different perspective. The soldiers bragged about all the loot they had "requisitioned" at various stores, and even displayed some of their plunder for the Frenkels to admire: jewelry, rings, and bracelets. The soldier boasted that his battalion had taken the railway station and killed the station head. "Our Ukrainian forces are seriously hostile toward the Jews, as the soviet and commissariat are made up mostly of Jews," he remarked as he munched on his nuts. Before they left, they all shook hands, except for one of the soldiers who politely apologized that his hand had been shot. He tipped his hat in respect instead. Meyer's classmate approached Meyer's mother, clicked his heels, and kissed her hand as he left through the front door with his entourage.[66]

SOME LOOTERS MOMENTARILY became distracted from their quest for booty and beat up Jews, whipped them, raped them, and even murdered them outright. At about six-thirty in the morning on Wednesday, January 8, Moyshe Feldman left his house to go to synagogue, as was his usual custom. The streets were quiet, and there was no sign of unrest. But by two o'clock in the afternoon he had not returned, and word of the pogrom was already spreading. His wife, Khana, began to panic and ran to the synagogue to see what was going on. Nobody at the synagogue, though, had seen Moyshe that day. It became clear that Moyshe never made it to prayers. It wasn't until Friday afternoon that an employee of the synagogue found Moyshe's body in the courtyard near the seminary building. His head was cut off.[67]

Avrum Makaron was at home with his wife, three daughters, and son-in-law on Wednesday afternoon when soldiers in *papakha*s with red ribbons appeared at his door with revolvers and rifles in hand, demanding money. Makaron gave the bandits what he had—some cash and a watch. It was then that one of the soldiers noticed Makaron's eldest daughter, grabbed the young woman, and led her into another room. Makaron could hear his daughter's cries. But before the soldier could do his worst, she came running back out: the soldier, realizing that she was ill, had let her go. He then ordered her at gunpoint to play something on the piano while he forced Makaron's youngest daughter into the room with him instead. The first sister played the piano in tears in the living room while the other let out ghastly screams from the back of the house. The ordeal only ended when one of the other soldiers got fed up with the racket and ordered the rapist to stop.[68]

When two drunken soldiers entered Moyshe Pressman's apartment, one ordered his mate to guard the door while he grabbed Moyshe's daughter, Zhenya, by the waist, took her aside, and began to "commit nefarious acts on her." When Moyshe and a neighbor tried to intervene, the soldier fired his revolver, killing them both.[69] Witnesses who survived the night in hiding recalled hearing "the constant sound of bottles clinking," punctuated by the occasional sound of gunfire, coming from the building where the soldiers had set up camp.[70]

A pile of bodies was accumulating near the tracks by the railway station. Fyodor Bobr, a station guard, told investigators that he was disturbed by the shootings. At one point that night, he explained, he left his post to get some cigarettes. He noticed two mounted soldiers escorting a young man in an open-collared khaki tunic—a "French jacket," similar to those worn by French and British soldiers, and favored in Russia by Kerensky—toward the station. A crowd of children was following the small procession, hoping to watch the spectacle of the coming execution. The sight disgusted Bobr. He chased off the children and watched as the soldiers took the young man's boots, forced him to stand up against a fence, and cocked their guns. The prisoner turned out to be Aleksandr Stakhovsky, an eighteen-year-old student; he had been arrested in his apartment, where his father had just been shot. Stakhovsky started to cry and beg for his life. Bobr had had enough; he called out and persuaded the soldiers to release the young man. Warning him that he would be captured again if he walked around town in an expensive French jacket, Bobr secured a soldier's overcoat and a military cap for him and sent him on his way.[71]

ON SATURDAY, JANUARY 11—the fourth day of the pogrom—Palienko permitted his men one final day to secure provisions. The soldiers went to exceptional lengths to squeeze out more profit by holding members of high society for ransom or forcing them to withdraw their savings from the banks. They turned their attention particularly to the wealthy Jewish estate holders. At around four in the afternoon, a group of thirty to forty armed men wearing the *papakha*s and red ribbons of Palienko's battalion found their way through a break in the fence into the courtyard of 3 Teatralnaya Street, where thirty-eight wealthy Jewish families had been able to lock the gates and hold off the soldiers for most of the pogrom. Now the soldiers gathered the residents together in one apartment, interrogated them, and conducted a full search of the building on the trumped-up charge that machine-gun fire had come from inside. In the course of the search, a soldier shot and killed one of the residents, Nukhem Epshteyn.[72] Soldiers then detained the rest of the men and led them in a convoy through town to the station. It was already dark, but there were still civilians out on the streets. The prisoners reported that they called to passersby for help, but nobody paid attention.[73]

At the station, the Teatralnaya Street prisoners were handed over to a man in his mid-thirties wearing a black peacoat and a *papakha*. They noticed that they were not the only captives: about three dozen other wealthy members of the Jewish community had been assembled as well, including the secretary of the city government. One soldier ordered everyone to undress down to their undergarments and hand over all their goods. Other soldiers began to beat the group with fists, clubs, shovels, and rifle butts. Nakhman Lyubarsky reported that he passed out from the beating. When he came to, his coat, wallet, and identification papers were gone, and he was left with only his over-coat, covered in blood. He felt a keen pain and realized he had been stabbed.[74]

The soldiers accused the prisoners of being Bolsheviks, despite the obvious fact that they were wealthy elites unlikely to feel sympathy for Bolshevism. Leading them into a railway car, they separated the prisoners into individual compartments and beat them again. "I begged them to shoot me," recalled Lyubarsky.[75] The soldiers then brought the prisoners one by one to an officer, who negotiated a ransom with each one for his release, threatening to kill them if it was not paid.[76] When they agreed upon a price, soldiers would escort the prisoners back to their apartments to secure the money.[77] Shmul Kashuk, a captive who worked at the savings and loan bank, reported that he was escorted to the bank and forced to break into the vault and hand over the cash to secure his freedom.[78]

ON JANUARY 12, Vozny and the city council agreed to a power-sharing agreement that would transfer the city back to civilian control and allow Vozny to resume his position as commandant. The next day, satisfied that the Bolsheviks had been defeated and Directory authority restored, Petliura dispatched the unruly local regiments to the western front and sent in eight hundred Galician sharpshooters to put an end to the pogrom: these former Austrian soldiers were well armed, well disciplined, and willing to take the steps necessary to stop the killing and the robbery. They were the most reliable force under Petliura's command. Palienko's troops abandoned the town center to the Galicians and swept through the outskirts of the city, where the violence tapered off over the next forty-eight hours.[79]

There were still corpses on the streets and in the courtyards of Zhytomyr when local civilian authorities in collaboration with the Jewish community sprang into action, organizing relief efforts, counting the dead, and collecting evidence and testimonies in order to punish the wrongdoers. Fifty-three people were confirmed killed between January 8 and 13, although many estimates put the toll at closer to ninety.[80]

Whatever the actual number, there is widespread agreement that nearly every store in the center of town was ransacked, as were about three-quarters of all stores throughout the city.

Efim Eliasberg, the banker and Jewish community official, responded by organizing a delegation to Kyiv to brief the Directory on what had happened. He demanded a serious governmental investigation into the behavior of Palienko's troops, and financial assistance from state coffers to provide for those devastated by the pogrom. According to Eliasberg, Petliura maintained that the Jews had started the fighting by shooting at Palienko's forces from inside the synagogue, a claim the delegation insisted was false. Opanas Andriivsy, one of Petliura's close associates, looked directly at Eliasberg and asserted that the Jews were the "most active participants in the Bolshevik movement" and were "engaged in speculation."[81]

Despite its initial reluctance, the Directory finally agreed to provide money for relief and to establish a committee of inquiry to investigate the pogrom. Petliura also announced, to the surprise of the delegation, that Palienko had already been arrested in Rivne, where he had fled after leaving Zhytomyr. On January 17, Directory forces had searched his train car and discovered it was full of looted silver and gold.[82] Palienko's story—that he had confiscated the gold and silver from the real robbers with the intention of returning the booty to its rightful owners—failed to convince anyone.[83] Eliasberg, though, came away from the meeting dejected: he interpreted the chilly reception the delegation had received as a message that the government did not care about the fate of the Jews.

In reality, the Directory was in no position to undertake more than a perfunctory investigation, even had they wanted to. On the night of February 2–3, almost exactly one year from their last invasion, Bolshevik soldiers crossed the Dnipro River into Kyiv, forcing the Directory out. Retreating from the city, dispirited Directory soldiers attacked Jewish houses and individual Jews, charging them with spying for the Bolshevik enemy. "Houses burned, and feathers flew from slashed feather beds. Every day there were tales of fresh pogroms, of girls raped and old men with slit bellies," recalled the novelist Ilya Ehrenburg.[84]

Facing the loss of the Ukrainian capital and the surrounding land, Petliura called upon the tsar's wartime allies of Britain and France, both of whom had retained a military presence on the northern coast of the Black Sea, for support against the Bolshevik advance. Vynnychenko, the head of the Directory, along with most of his ministers, resigned in protest, viewing an alliance with "the imperialist Entente" as a reactionary move. Petliura was left alone in charge of the government, and assumed the position of head of state in addition to the military command he already held. Having fled Kyiv, he set up temporary offices in Vinnytsia's Savoy Hotel. Only seven years old at the time, the Savoy was already a relic of a bygone era. With its rounded corner towers, elegant bay windows and balconies, three-story-tall classical pilasters, and intricate decorative cartouches, the lavish Beaux Arts building represented the height of local architect Grigorii Artynov's attempts to turn Vinnytsia's Nikolaevsky Street into the Champs-Élysées. It served as a bitter reminder of Ukraine's gilded age, of a time when the rapid growth of the railroad

Savoy Hotel in Vinnytsia

promised new markets for the sugar beets of Podilia. Petliura's presence there symbolized a newfound embrace of the old regime.

THE OFFICIAL COMMITTEE of inquiry quickly found that without the authority to compel testimony and order arrests, its power was limited. Instead, the aid worker Isaac Giterman, who arrived in Zhytomyr soon after the departure of Palienko, gathered together local jurists to establish a Legal Bureau that would build a case against the perpetrators and demand aid from the government. By February 3, Giterman's team was already collecting its first testimonies and photographs of the dead, the wounded, and the destroyed property.[85]

Over the next month, between February 3 and March 14, Giterman's Legal Bureau collected 358 testimonies and was able to identify many of the local perpetrators—most of whom were still in the area, having gone back to their regular lives.[86] Some witnesses who spoke with Giterman's committee, though, were reluctant to name names for fear of reprisals. Several people confessed that they knew who the culprits were but, recognizing the Directory's tenuous position as the Red Army approached, would give their names only once they were convinced that the government was stable and that they would not be accused of collaboration if a new regime was established.[87]

Critics contended that Vozny egregiously allowed the pogrom perpetrators to remain on the loose. For instance, one victim of the pogrom who gave testimony to Giterman's committee, Moisei Vinokur, was incensed to learn that a police officer was in possession of the record player, nickel samovar, and silver bowl stolen from his house. Despite his appeals to the city government, he was unable to get his property back.[88] Vozny was accused of rejecting repeated requests to provide arms for night watchmen, to establish an effective police force, and to arrest those responsible for the pogrom. He seemed incapable of taking decisive action.

Many witnesses complained that even some of Palienko's collaborators had received positions in Vozny's government, pointing to Anton Bek as one obvious example. Bek, a former chauffeur, had been in and out of prison for years and was most notorious in town for his 1917 attack on a municipal rations stockpile. In the words of the official report that was eventually prepared by the committee of inquiry, he was "an individual well known to the city government as a glaring criminal with a long record."[89] He was a wanted man, missing since a large-scale prison break; to the surprise of the city council, he had suddenly reappeared by Palienko's side in the midst of the pogrom.[90] Now, Bek's newfound employment as an aide to Vozny became a symbol of the commandant's failure to effectively reestablish order and punish those responsible. Testimonies contended that Bek was using his new position to terrorize the Jewish population.[91]

Moyshe Toybenshlak, meanwhile, stated that he saw officers who tormented him and robbed his apartment going to the theater with some of Vozny's men.[92] More disturbingly, Zelman Fayner reported that he overheard one of Palienko's officers who was now serving in Vozny's administration discussing the need to avenge the damage the Jews had provoked.[93]

It was clear that Vozny had little interest in bringing the perpetrators to justice. A common refrain among those Giterman questioned was frustration with the failure of the authorities to unequivocally condemn the violence. Some city officials instead sympathized with the perpetrators of the pogrom and were pleased to see many Jews flee the city in its wake. Witnesses were particularly disappointed that the more respectable members of society, the urban intelligentsia, had neglected to defend the Jewish community. Instead, it protected the culprits and had even profited from the plunder.[94]

Vozny, for his part, placed all blame on Palienko. "With regard to Palienko, I can say that the pogrom in Zhytomyr took place completely with his connivance," he told the committee of inquiry. "Without doubt soldiers of his brigade took part, and he not only didn't stop them, but permitted stolen goods to be taken from the city to the station."[95] The committee concluded that "the announcements and actions of Palienko and his closest collaborators during the first days of the pogrom affirmed that the military command, in whose hands all authority was concentrated at the time, not only failed to oppose the pogrom, but even encouraged it."[96] Yet the Directory shielded Palienko from punishment. Weeks after being detained in Rivne, he was spotted in the Savoy Hotel in Vinnytsia, where he was being protected by powerful figures in Petliura's government. Mykhailo Kovenko, the conqueror of Kyiv, reportedly lauded Palienko's battalion as "the pride of the Ukrainian army."[97]

The committee of inquiry sought to portray the pogrom in Zhytomyr as a replay of the one in Ovruch: both sanctioned by an overzealous military commander acting under the authority of the Directory government, but without approval from his superiors. This narrative—a pair of unruly officers taking advantage of the chaotic situation on the ground to enrich themselves—provided the ruling regime with a convenient way to deflect responsibility. It was in their interest to avoid the type of punitive actions that a full accounting of responsibility would have required, and to pin the blame exclusively on one individual. Many Jewish activists, still trusting the Directory to protect Jewish national autonomy in Ukraine, were also satisfied with these explanations. In both pogroms, though, the Directory authorities were also to blame. By failing to properly equip and feed their army, they required the soldiers to pilfer from the local population. More important, they failed to send a clear message that violence against Jewish civilians would not be tolerated.

Accounts of the pogrom in Zhytomyr differed from the one in Ovruch in at least one important way. The Ovruch pogrom was the tragic product of a warrior gone amok, with easily identifiable villains carrying out their own circumscribed killing by subjecting the population to a reign of terror focused on the Jews. The Zhytomyr pogrom, on the other hand, was a much more complex ethnic riot. It was perpetrated not just by marauding troops but by an array of ordinary citizens: trusted servants, neighboring peasants, students, women, and children, and even, eventually, sophisticated urbanites.

The French psychologist Gustave Le Bon, one of the founders of the study of group psychology, wrote in 1895 about the characteristics of crowds. In a large group, he posited, individuals become part of "a sort of collective mind which makes them feel, think, and act in a manner quite different from that in which each individual of them would feel, think, and act were he in a state of isolation."[98] A generation later, in 1921, Sigmund Freud challenged Le Bon's analysis, expressing doubt that new personalities could suddenly appear ex nihilo. Instead, Freud proposed, the seemingly uncharacteristic ways in which individuals behave as part of a crowd are actually already embedded within the individual but are usually repressed. In a crowd, he wrote, "the individual is brought under conditions which allow him to throw off the repressions of his unconscious instincts."[99] Le Bon may have argued that in Zhytomyr the crowd turned individuals into antisemites, whereas Freud would have said that it just gave them the opportunity to express previously repressed antisemitic feelings.

Decades later, both these arguments were challenged by the American sociologist Mark Granovetter, who questioned the notion that the kind of sudden changes in people's behavior observed in riots resulted either from the emergence of new norms and beliefs or from the stripping away of the veneer of civilization. Instead, Granovetter took as his starting point the idea that the "cost to an individual of joining a riot declines as riot size increases." Each individual, he suggested, has his or her own threshold for joining a riot, a point at which the costs of staying out of the riot exceed the costs of participating. Some are instigators and will be the first to smash windows; others will join only if it seems that everybody else is doing so.[100]

This theory seems to best explain the dynamics of the Zhytomyr pogrom. The pogrom began with local soldiers garrisoned in the city, taking advantage of the revolutionary disorder to take what they believed was their due from the predominantly Jewish urban elites. But as the days went on, the circle of those partaking in the riot widened. Once the soldiers breached military discipline and began to loot Jewish property, local townswomen and children—those least likely to suffer negative consequences—joined in as well. Eventually, otherwise respectable members of Christian society—the *dvornik*s and the milkladies—calculated that the costs of staying out surpassed the costs of participating, and they, too, joined in the looting, risking their jobs and their communal status for fear of losing out on the spoils.

Why was the riot directed specifically against Jews? The main reason seems to be that they were believed to hold the wealth in the city.
Although Palienko's soldiers were officially dispatched to stamp out
the soviet's uprising, and there are several reports of Jews being derided
as Bolsheviks, there is little indication that rioters in this case were
motivated primarily by anti-Bolshevik sentiment. In fact, the worst of
the violence was directed against the wealthy bourgeoisie—the seg-
ment of the population least likely to be sympathetic to Bolshevism.
The pogrom provided an opportunity for hungry peasants and soldiers,
as well as workers and students, to acquire food and money from the
privileged classes. It was an act of leveling, giving the upper classes
their comeuppance. But what could have been an ordinary bread riot
became instead a deadly ethnic riot, because the rioters equated the
Jews with the urban bourgeoisie. The charge of Bolshevism was just a
pretext.

The American political scientist Donald L. Horowitz notes that
deadly ethnic riots frequently arrive as two waves, with the second
one worse than the first. "Often the first such riot looks in retrospect
like an intimation of what is to come, a prelude, a warning to the pru-
dent. After an episode of violence, the atmosphere is likely to be quite
propitious for another episode. The first riot is anticipatory, a tryout
that, if successful, makes massive violence feasible."[101] Although they
did not formulate it in precisely these terms, the Jews of Zhytomyr had
enough experience with ethnic riots over the past decades to recognize
this threat. As Avrom Revutsky put it: "The danger was that Palienko's
'Battalion of Death' would become some type of wandering pogrom-
army, touring from city to city."[102]

The Proskuriv Pogrom

The revolution was not supposed to begin in Proskuriv.[1] It is true that the coming of the railway line in 1870 had turned this once-sleepy backwater into an important transit point in the export of Russian lumber, textiles, and grain. Many of the Jews in the town were involved in this trade either directly or indirectly; by 1881, 90 percent of the commercial permits in Proskuriv were granted to Jews.[2] The four daily trains—two passenger and two cargo—that traveled from Proskuriv to Austria since the 1880s, along with lines added in the early twentieth century to other destinations, brought with them a dramatic increase in population. About half of the newcomers were workers, flocking to the sugar, candle, brick, and tobacco factories, the iron foundry, or the breweries and mineral-water bottling plants. (Solomon Barak's bottled mineral water was all the rage at the turn of the century; he could barely keep up with the demand for his "Korol" (King) brand of seltzer, which he bottled in his barn and delivered to restaurants around the city.)[3] The population of Proskuriv increased sixfold between 1861 and 1913, making it the fastest-growing town in the province of Podilia. By 1913, with a population of forty thousand—eleven thousand of them Jews—it was the third-largest Podilian city, behind only Vinnytsia and

Kamyanets-Podilskyi.[4] But Proskuriv was still a sleepy, regional munic-ipality, the type of place in which a favorite pastime was to spend the afternoon idling away at the station, watching the 13:51 from Vienna come by, and three-quarters of an hour later the 14:35 speed off in the other direction.

Proletarian uprisings were only supposed to happen in industrial powerhouses, places bustling with workers eager to rise up against their factory owners. Proskuriv did not fit the mold.[5]

At least that's what Lev Shenkman thought as he patrolled the streets on a freezing February night. He was the deputy chief of the ward guard, a volunteer neighborhood police force reporting to the city council, and as part of his job he tried to get to know as many people as possible in the town. The city council was comprised of well-respected members of the local intelligentsia, representing an array of predomi-nantly leftist political parties, who had resolved to work together for the benefit of the city. Shenkman recognized that community policing is most effective when the guards and the citizens they are protecting are on familiar terms. Tensions were high throughout Ukraine and had been for years, but on the streets of Proskuriv, on an individual basis, things were fine. Among the ward guards, for instance, Christians and Jews often worked alongside each other, and politics rarely interfered in their joint commitment to keeping the people of Proskuriv safe.

Proskuriv train station

Shenkman had no problem working as deputy to Chief Ostkevich-Rudnytskyi, a Christian. And while some residents didn't like the idea of Jews patrolling the streets with weapons, most people were more tolerant and saw the benefits of a guard force that mirrored the ethnic makeup of the city.

Recently, though, policing had become more complicated. A group of students had formed a youth militia intent on defending the city against the type of anti-Jewish violence that was becoming more common throughout Ukraine. But Yuri Kiverchuk, the military commandant of the city, accused the students of Bolshevism and shut down their enterprise—even though, as one observer noted, "It was clear to everybody that the accusation of Bolshevism was unfounded, as the student militia was made up of wealthy elements. . . . It was no secret that the primary reason for its liquidation was that Jews were predominant among the students."[6] Kiverchuk, who had had a distinguished military career in the Russian imperial army and in various Ukrainian insurgent divisions before becoming commandant of Proskuriv under the Directory, had for several weeks been leading a crackdown on alternative militias in the city, maintaining that security should be a monopoly of the state. Critics, though, accused Kiverchuk's militia of plundering the homes of Jews, and seizing cash and valuables under the pretext of searching for weapons, even though possession of arms was legal.[7]

Kiverchuk's goal was to secure Directory control of the city, an ambitious task at a time when the government itself had just been forced out of Kyiv and was regrouping under Petliura at the Savoy Hotel in Vinnytsia. Recognizing the deteriorating situation, Petliura, too, saw Proskuriv as a crucial bulwark against the encroaching Bolsheviks. On February 5, he sent a paramilitary band that called itself the Third Haidamak Regiment, and a Cossack brigade under the command of the twenty-five-year-old former agronomist Ivan Semosenko, to aid Kiverchuk. Semosenko, a short man with chestnut hair barely concealing his bald spot, watery green eyes, and a pointed face, hardly projected a fearsome image; but his soldiers, with the long locks of hair they wore in emulation of eighteenth-century Cossack fighters, immediately began to make an impression.[8] Kiverchuk and Shenkman both knew of Semosenko's reputation: how he had held up railroad traffic, creating bottlenecks over a Dnipro bridge, in order to solicit huge bribes, and how he had abandoned his wife and his position as chief security officer of the Apostolove railway station in Kherson Province to join Petliura's army.[9] He was known as a law-and-order type and promised to show no mercy to miscreants.[10] With Semosenko's Cossacks in town, Kiverchuk thought that the ward guards were superfluous.

The presence of Semosenko's soldiers, though, only strengthened Shenkman's convictions that the ward guards were essential to calm the situation and prevent any violent flare-ups. He watched as the heavily armed Cossacks paraded around the streets on horseback, displayed their cannons and rifles in a show of force, and shattered the calm restraint that had previously prevailed. They relished their reputation as tough guys who refused to play by the rules and made it clear that they had little patience for Jews and their legalisms. According to Ilya Joffe, who headed the socialist bloc in the city council, as soon as Semosenko arrived a "pogrom atmosphere" pervaded the city. Others recalled that "people stayed locked in their houses and were afraid to show themselves on the street."[11]

ON THURSDAY, FEBRUARY 13, during one of Shenkman's patrols, a Jewish citizen he knew asked him whether it was true that the Bolsheviks were going to stage a coup in the city the next day. Shenkman had certainly heard rumors of an impending uprising, but he imagined, like everyone else, that the revolutionary cells in Proskuriv would stage a local revolt only after a regional insurrection had begun in a larger industrial center or in a transportation hub like Zhmerynka, where the railway workers were often striking. It was unlikely, he thought, that local radicals were planning such an action without him knowing about it. People talked, and he had sources everywhere, particularly within the local leftist groups. And surely the Bolsheviks knew that their success depended upon the support of the ward guards. Nevertheless, he felt uneasy. Was something brewing? He searched out some of the radicals he knew. They confirmed that an uprising was in the works but denied that a precise time or date had been fixed.[12]

The odd thing was that on February 13, everybody seemed to be hearing the same rumors. The municipal police chief cornered Ilya Joffe, the socialist councilor, that same day and accused him of being part of a plot. (The rebels had even selected the members of a Military Revolutionary Committee, the police chief asserted.) Joffe shared Shenkman's skepticism but also his concern. Late that night, he learned that some of the trade unionists were indeed preparing an imminent seizure of power. Joffe was furious: the socialist bloc was strongly opposed to an uprising and had been working productively with the left-leaning Directory government. As a Jew—like many members of the socialist bloc—Joffe was acutely aware of what had happened to the Jews of Zhytomyr after the Bolsheviks tried and failed to seize power. He blamed the plot on a group of young firebrands, uneducated workers, and criminal elements among the Bolsheviks and their Left SR allies, who, he claimed, lived off money sent from Soviet Russia and acted as Russian agents agitating for the overthrow of Ukrainian independence.

Joffe's conspiracy theories were closer to the truth than he may have realized. What neither Joffe nor Shenkman knew at the time was that only a few weeks earlier, the radical terrorist and Left SR Ivan Alekseev, also known by the code name Nebutev, had been assigned by his handlers in Kyiv to stage an insurrection in Zhmerynka. Zhmerynka was an important strategic site for the insurgents; they were convinced that a revolution in the major railway hub would quickly spread to the west. "The path to Galicia went through Zhmerynka," wrote Alekseev.[13] The uprising was planned for February 10. As preparations were underway, though, six echelons from the army of the Ukrainian People's Republic arrived in Zhmerynka—Petliura's counterintelligence had uncovered the plot.[14] The conspirators abandoned the Zhmerynka scheme and instead decided to target neighboring Proskuriv, believing that the two regiments of the army of the Ukrainian People's Republic stationed in the city would be supportive. They were convinced that once they had attained power in Proskuriv, the revolution would quickly spread back to Zhmerynka. As Alekseev put it, "A Proskuriv uprising would inevitably draw several military units from Zhmerynka to restrain it, and we could use the situation of panic it would create to act in Zhmerynka as well."[15] The date was set for Saturday, February 15.[16]

JOFFE RUSHED TO City Hall; it was nearly midnight and the city council was just wrapping up a session. Despite the late hour, he conferred with fellow members of the socialist bloc. Councilman Simkha Vasserman reported that he had heard talk of revenge against the Jews for plotting an insurrection. Councilman Voloshin, a non-Jewish Ukrainian socialist, had overheard an officer of the Ukrainian People's Republic state that "the Jews must be exterminated, the Ukrainians don't need them. Let them all go to Jerusalem."[17] The socialist bloc agreed to call a general meeting for the next morning at nine o'clock.[18]

At the appointed time on the morning of Friday, February 14, as the councilors were gathering, two of Joffe's Bolshevik acquaintances showed up together with a third person Joffe didn't recognize. The unknown visitor introduced himself as a Left SR. It is possible that this was Alekseev himself. The men confirmed they were members of the Military Revolutionary Committee planning an insurrection. Joffe urged them to reconsider, but the revolutionaries refused to be persuaded. They only came to ask whether the socialist bloc would support them. Joffe made it clear that his party was opposed, primarily because it did not believe they would succeed but also, he explained, because such a drastic measure should be taken only with the acquiescence of all the socialist representatives of the city government. The visitors assured Joffe that the insurrection was part of a coordinated action across the province directed from afar. Proskuriv had been selected to be the spark, but the railroad workers of Zhmerynka would immediately follow with a general strike that would bring the province to a halt. Everything had been taken care of; even the soldiers of the local regiments were on board, they assured him. The Military Revolutionary Committee was leaving nothing to chance.[19]

The more experienced city councilors angrily warned the young radicals against taking action but to no avail. So when the revolutionaries left late in the afternoon, the councilors sent councilman Yankl Marants, who was also a member of the ward guard, to warn Shenkman. The councilors also recommended that Joffe get out of town—they had heard about the military's attacks on Jews in Zhytomyr and feared that as a prominent Jewish socialist, he was too easy a target. Joffe headed to the station, planning to take an evening train to nearby Yarmolintsy. When he saw a convoy of soldiers arrive, though, he decided to spend the night at the station instead.[20]

That afternoon, at about five o'clock, as Shenkman was talking with Marants, two young representatives of the Military Revolutionary Committee—probably the same men who had spoken with Joffe—arrived at the guard's headquarters. They asked to speak with Shenkman and his chief, Ostkevich-Rudnytskyi, alone. As Marants waited outside, they explained that they were sent to seek the support of the ward guards for the upcoming revolt. They asked for maps of the city and other information regarding the locations of police and military outposts, which they claimed they needed to avoid unnecessary bloodshed.[21] Shenkman tried to talk them out of it, contending that the plot would inevitably end in a pogrom, as had happened in Zhytomyr. He told them that the ward guards were sworn to neutrality, had the sole goal of protecting the city from violence, and would never support an insurrection. But the visitors were set in their plan. Shenkman had a terrible sense of foreboding when they left. He decided to spend the night at headquarters and ordered all the guards to be on high alert throughout the night.[22]

At around ten, he received a visitor, a Bolshevik who introduced himself as the new commissar and presented him with a document signed by the Military Revolutionary Committee. The commissar appointed Shenkman as liaison between the committee and the guards and invited him to the revolutionary command post. Shenkman went with him but was not impressed: "I found several people there, of whom one, I came to understand, was the obvious instigator. I saw that their work was disorderly and the people were inexperienced."[23]

He pleaded with them to postpone the uprising, but they insisted it was to begin within hours, saying that they had already pushed the start time back from midnight to 5 a.m., when reinforcements were expected to arrive. Shenkman returned to the guard headquarters with the understanding that he was in for a long night.

THE MILITARY REVOLUTIONARY Committee met one last time to coordinate action. "The meeting took place in an atmosphere of nervous tension," Alekseev wrote in his memoirs; "nobody spoke a superfluous word."[24] The conspirators were ready. According to Alekseev, at midnight the committee moved into the Proskuriv train station and arrested the commanding officers, as the artillerists protecting the station fled into the frozen night. Within twenty minutes, his team had secured the station. At the same time, in a coordinated action, about two hundred workers seized the post office and telegraph station and arrested Commandant Kiverchuk. In the early hours of Saturday, February 15, several dozen Bolshevik workers arrived at the local barracks and informed the Eighth Podilian regiment there that the revolution was underway. The soldiers initially protested that the timing was premature, but after they were reassured that reinforcements were soon arriving with fifty machine guns, they overwhelmingly decided to support the revolution, declared their officers under arrest, raided the arsenal, and handed out arms to the workers.

At six-thirty in the morning, Shenkman, who was still on guard at headquarters, reported hearing a volley of shots, confirming intelligence that the revolution was to begin at daybreak. Minutes later, the phone rang. It was a call from Semosenko's staff, assuring Shenkman that Kiverchuk remained in control and that the Bolshevik uprising would fail. Then the line went dead. The revolutionaries had cut the phone wires.

The mutinous soldiers of the Eighth Podilian headed straight from their barracks to the train station, where they expected to easily rout Semosenko's forces and greet the Bolshevik reinforcements arriving from Zhmerynka. Instead, they were confronted with three hundred heavily armed Cossacks and six hundred Haidamak soldiers loyal to the Directory and prepared to fight. The peasant recruits of the Eighth Podilian realized they were outnumbered and evaporated into the countryside, fleeing to their home villages and abandoning the revolution. Meanwhile, the Military Revolutionary Committee waited for the reinforcements, but nobody came, not even the railway workers from Zhmerynka. By eleven o'clock, it had become clear that the uprising had failed spectacularly. With the station firmly under control, Semosenko led his battalion into the city to punish the rebels.

From his window, Simkha Vasserman watched as they moved into town: "I assumed they were heading toward Grechany, where there was a depot and where there had probably been a Bolshevik uprising. But it later turned out that this same detachment of Cossacks scattered around the city and began to slaughter the Jewish population."[25] They set up machine guns around Vasserman's building and in his attic to guard against snipers. Vasserman watched in shock as they shot and killed Abram Marants, a wealthy and prominent merchant, who became one of the first casualties of what was about to be a gruesome day.[26]

As Shenkman later explained, about an hour after he heard from Semosenko, fifteen armed men appeared at his headquarters. Shenkman tried to justify the mission of the ward guards, but the armed men were dismissive, mocking it as a "Jew agency with Jew commissars." They detained Shenkman for the rest of the morning, but by noon, as word spread that the uprising was over, they left. Exhausted from the long night and eventful morning, Shenkman went home to sleep.

THAT SAME SATURDAY morning, city councilor Trofim Verkhola was waiting in a hotel room for his nephew—they had planned on meeting for a morning steam at the *banya*, the traditional Russian sauna. Verkhola was a popular social-democratic politician who had served in a variety of high-level positions around the district and had only recently moved to Proskuriv to assume a seat on the city council. A former schoolteacher, he was well regarded as both a fighter for ordinary people and a defender of the Jews.[27]

Verkhola's nephew arrived in an agitated state, bursting with questions about the Bolshevik uprising. Verkhola had slept through the unrest the night before, despite an uncomfortable encounter he had had with Kiverchuk and Semosenko earlier in the day. In retrospect it was obvious that something was not right. Commandant Kiverchuk had been in an angry mood and had accused Verkhola of harboring Bolshevik sympathies. The night had left Verkhola with feelings of anxiety, but as the saying goes, "*banya parit, banya pravit, banya vse popravit*"—the steam of the *banya* makes everything all right. It was only when he and his nephew returned from the bathhouse at around ten o'clock that the sound of gunfire rekindled his alarm. Verkhola made his way to City Hall as the shelling intensified. There he found several other concerned councilors discussing the situation and awaiting news from Kiverchuk. Nobody had heard from the commandant, Verkhola learned, so a councilman named Stavinsky had gone in search of him. Soon after Verkhola's arrival, Stavinsky returned with the news that the Bolsheviks had arrested Kiverchuk and had seized control of the city.

Verkhola had good relations with many of the radical workers and believed he could negotiate the release of the commandant. But it was a cold February day, and he was wearing his fine fur coat. He was suddenly feeling very self-conscious. Would the fur coat identify him as a member of the bourgeoisie and subject him to arrest? Or, if bandits were roaming the lawless streets, would he become an easy target for robbery and assault? Since he didn't have another coat with him, he wrapped a Red Cross band around his arm, and, together with Stavinsky, headed into the streets.

They had hardly left City Hall when they bumped into Kiverchuk himself, riding a horse. The commandant explained that he had been arrested by the Bolsheviks, "but there were very few of them. The uprising has already failed."[28]

As they spoke, they heard gunfire coming from the vicinity of the station. Kiverchuk headed toward the shooting while Verkhola and Stavinsky returned to City Hall. On the way, they noticed that soldiers were shelling the secondary school on Dvoryanskaya Street, where the

Bolsheviks had installed machine guns. Stavinsky, whose apartment was near the school, along the hills where the wealthier residents lived, left Verkhola to check on his family. He then returned to City Hall, having dropped off his children for their safety at a priest's house on the other side of town. When the guns died down about an hour later, it seemed to the city councilors that peace had been restored. Stavinsky went to retrieve his children and invited Verkhola to join them for lunch at his house.[29]

Since it was Saturday early afternoon, Jewish worshippers were just finishing reciting the morning prayers in the synagogue and sitting down for Kiddush when word spread that there had been unrest in the city that morning. The pious rushed through the blessings, swigged a shot of schnaps, and gulped down a slice of bread and herring before heading out into the street. By the time they were done with Kiddush, the uprising was over and the streets were eerily calm. Moshke Stambulchik recalled that when he was walking home from the synagogue, the streets were completely deserted. The only people who could be seen were Jews, like him, making their way home from services.[30] Yosef Shpigel noted that Bolshevik proclamations had been plastered all over the city. They were already outdated.[31]

VERKHOLA AND STAVINSKY were in the midst of their lunch when a servant interrupted with news that soldiers were slaughtering Jews in the streets. Verkhola put his fur coat back on, Stavinsky put on a soldier's overcoat, and together they ventured to the city center, where most of Proskuriv's Jews lived, often in apartments attached to their stores. They made their way to Sruel Oksman's apothecary, an ornate building commonly known as the House with Dragons, owing to the stucco dragons gazing out of the pediments. There they hoped to check on the city's medical preparedness. Oksman, who was extremely distraught and fumbling with supplies, explained that he was trying to gather all of his bandages to aid the injured. "Go out onto Aptekarskaya Street, and you will see corpses lying around," he told them. They ran into the street and saw the bodies of elderly Jews, women, and children. They stopped next at Ludwig Derevoed's apothecary, the largest pharmacy in the city, which included a full laboratory, a dry cellar, an icebox for cold storage, and a wine cellar, all of which had helped make Derevoed one of the wealthiest citizens of Proskuriv. A field surgeon affiliated with Semosenko's battalion had gotten there ahead of them and was already demanding all of the dressing material in stock to assist injured soldiers—sixty soldiers, he claimed, had been hit by Bolshevik fire. Verkhola and Stavinsky entreated him to leave some dressing material for the injured Jews, and he promised to do so. When they left, they found more bodies on the streets, but the city was generally quiet. The soldiers had returned to the station.[32]

With victory over the attempted Bolshevik uprising at hand, Semosenko gathered his troops at the San Remo restaurant to celebrate with a grand banquet and free-flowing cognac and vodka, "obviously in honor of the coming slaughter of the Jewish people," according to one testimony.[33] In his long-winded, nervous way of talking, Semosenko explained that he did not want a repeat of Zhytomyr, during which the reputation of the Ukrainian army was sullied by looting and theft. Following a common procedure for sending troops into battle (and one often replicated in riots), he filled his men up with vodka and ordered them to take an oath on the flag. In this case, the oath proclaimed that they would kill "from the old to the young" but not steal.[34] The massacre was to begin anew at two in the afternoon.

SHENKMAN, WHO HAD fallen asleep at home, was awakened by his mother a couple of hours later: Kiverchuk wanted to speak with him on the telephone, the line having been restored. Shenkman steeled himself for terrible news, but he couldn't have imagined what would befall him before he could even get to the phone. He had barely risen from his bed when his youngest brother arrived in a panic with word that another brother of theirs had been killed. Shortly afterward, soldiers invaded the home. Shenkman yelled for everybody to run into the bedroom and hide under the beds. From under his bed, he watched in horror as soldiers barged into the room and stuck a bayonet into his grief-stricken mother, killing her on the spot. When his father rose up in rage, the soldiers fired two shots at him. One killed him; the other hit Shenkman's sister, injuring her. When Shenkman's younger brother got up to kiss the body of his mother, the soldiers stabbed him as well. They then turned toward the beds and began prodding the mattresses to make sure nobody was hiding. Shenkman recognized one of the soldiers: "at dawn he had been at the guard headquarters, claiming that Jews were shooting at him."[35]

Lazar Shapiro, who testified before a Soviet investigative committee in 1926, remembered that his father came home from synagogue talking about the terrible rumors he had heard about a coming pogrom. Soon after, their home was surrounded by soldiers. They decided to appease the invaders, and his father immediately offered a large sum. According to Shapiro, "they responded that they didn't need money, just Jewish souls. I remember well the words of one of them: 'we have received an order not to rob, but to kill.'" With those words, the soldiers fatally shot Shapiro's father and severely wounded his mother. They then "literally riddled with bullets" his three brothers, aged eighteen, twenty-five, and twenty-seven, and two sisters, aged twelve and nineteen. Shapiro testified that he was hiding behind the buffet, from where he witnessed everything.[36]

Muka Akselbandt similarly testified to the Soviet committee that she was sitting with her family in the apartment behind the family store when she saw soldiers through the window in the door. She gathered money to save her family, but the soldiers responded that they didn't need money; they were under orders to kill Jews. With those words, they took out their rifles and sabers. They killed Muka's husband, Moyshe; cut off Muka's finger; and seriously injured their daughter, who was still suffering from her wounds when the testimony was taken, eight years after the pogrom.[37]

Semosenko's soldiers specifically targeted Jewish homes, made efforts to ensure that no Christians were harmed, and often verified that the residents were Jewish before massacring them. Shlem Kibrik testified that one soldier broke into his apartment, examined those present, and concluded: "Everybody here is Jewish; there aren't any

Russians here." He then returned with two other soldiers, who opened fire on the room, immediately killing Kibrik's bedridden father. When Kibrik tried to bribe the intruders, one soldier declared that he "does not need money, he only needs our heads; money he can take on his own."[38] They then slaughtered the rest of his family with sabers and bayonets. Kibrik survived by lying motionless on the floor underneath a table. By the time they were done, Kibrik reported, his wife's head resembled "a bloody piece of meat"; two of her fingers had been cut off as she tried to shield herself with her hand. Two of Kibrik's daughters and his brother were also killed in the attack, while his mother was severely injured. The soldiers left, but a few minutes later one of them returned to ensure that everyone was dead. He scanned the bodies scattered around the room and muttered "to hell with all of you" before going on his way.[39]

Sofia Gershgorin testified that two soldiers entered her apartment and asked if there were Jews in the house. When she answered that it was a Jewish home, "they hacked our entire family to pieces with bayonets and sabers." Her fifty-year-old mother; her ten-year-old sister, Sonia; and an eighty-five-year-old relative, Riva, were all killed. Gershgorin was wounded nine times, but survived. "I cannot understand," Gershgorin said in her testimony, "why they killed innocent women who knew nothing more than homemaking."[40]

The soldiers rarely articulated their reasons for targeting Jews, but the statements they made during the killings give some clues. In a few cases, Jews seem to have been targeted for religious reasons. In a house on Sobornaya Street where twenty-one people were massacred, for instance, a survivor reported that "before the murder, the Cossacks demanded that the Jews cross themselves. In the event of a refusal or indecision, they killed with the cry, 'Die, Jew!'"[41] Soldiers also massacred some Jews at prayer. About twenty people were in the synagogue later in the day for a study session when soldiers barged in. Leyb Kozovy, who was present, described how the worshippers insisted that they were simple pious Jews at prayer and had no interest in politics. "The soldier near me smiled," Kozovy recalled, "and drove his bayonet into my neighbor." Kozovy was wounded in the back and survived by pretending to be dead; all the other worshippers were killed in the attack. Kozovy spent the next six months in the hospital.[42]

For the most part, though, religion was beside the point. Jews were targeted primarily because they were associated with Bolshevism. Khaim Dayter testified to the 1926 Soviet investigative committee that the soldiers who burst into his apartment—no less than fifteen of them—shouted, "There are Bolsheviks here."[43] Yakov Zaydman recalled that when he heard knocking at about three o'clock in the afternoon, his children, "unaware of the goings-on," opened the door. A group of soldiers stormed into the house, declared "We are looking for Bolsheviks," and proceeded to slash him and his wife in the head with sabers. Yakov survived, but his wife was mortally wounded.[44]

The soldiers who invaded the home of Gitl Zemelman around the same time made the conflation between Bolsheviks and Jews explicit. "There are Jew-Bolsheviks here. We must kill them all," they yelled before bayoneting her twenty-year-old son, Ilya; her eighteen-year-old son, Shlem; her thirteen-year-old son, Moyshe; and her eleven-year-old daughter, Mariya. Zemelman reported that she was screaming and pleading with the soldiers, insisting that her kids were "little children who don't know anything." How could her eleven-year-old daughter be a Bolshevik? she asked.[45]

Zemelman had a point. Even if the soldiers truly believed that all adult Jews were tainted with Bolshevik sympathies, they could not have believed that children, let alone babies, were influenced by Marxist-Leninist political ideology. Yet children and babies were still targeted, and often killed with exceptional cruelty. This hatred ran deeper than politics. Khaim Baran testified that his four-year-old brother, Boris, was impaled upon the bayonet of a soldier. A neighbor who witnessed the killing told him that the soldier "spun the dead body around on the bayonet for a while."[46] Wolf Brukhis reported that soldiers who burst into his home on Aptekarskaya Street killed his entire family, including his teenage sister, two teenage cousins, and his two-week-old baby nephew, Mendl.[47] Khaim Tenenboym mentioned that among his thirteen family members who were killed was a one-month-old baby, Sonia, who was thrown in the air and stabbed with a bayonet.[48]

There are also numerous reported instances of sexual assault. Soldiers tossed a hand grenade into seventeen-year-old Khayke Balagur's home, smoked her out of her hiding spot in the cellar, and then seized her and tore off her clothing before she managed to break free.[49] A woman was raped at the Einbinder house, where four people were killed.[50] Soldiers from the same unit killed ten people in the Kitsis home, including the entire Kitsis family of two parents and three daughters; first, though, they raped each daughter, including 14-year-old Khana, who survived for two days until she succumbed to her wounds.[51] A dogcatcher who gave testimony to Hirsch Zekcer, an investigative aide to Hillerson, reported that he witnessed a red-haired soldier raping a girl "as she was breathing her last breath." He had never gone after dogs the way these soldiers went after human beings, he added.[52]

Despite Semosenko's orders to kill and not to steal, his Cossack troops could hardly resist looting. Moyshe Plotkin was taking an afternoon nap when he heard terrible screams. He hid in the attic with his family just as soldiers entered his house. "In a short period of time, twenty-two people were killed," he testified. "When the murderers left, different soldiers came and made off with the family's possessions."[53] Zalman Presayzen recalled that the four soldiers who barged into his house, their sabers caked in blood, established that the inhabitants were Jewish and demanded money. Presayzen emptied his pockets and gave what he had. One soldier, noticing that Presayzen was wearing a gold ring, slashed at his finger with a saber until he turned it over. His wife was killed and his six-year-old son was stabbed with a bayonet.[54]

Klimenty Kachurovsky, the archdeacon of the Nativity of the Blessed Virgin Mary Cathedral, stands out as an exception to the general indifference displayed by local officialdom. Witnesses report that Kachurovsky pleaded with the soldiers to have mercy on the Jews. He was holding a child, yelling, "Christians, what are you doing?" when soldiers attacked him with spears, killing him. Dr. Serhy Polozov is also credited with providing medical assistance to Jews during the pogrom and even hiding several families in his house.[55] But such acts of sympathy were rare. Multiple witnesses reported that Kiverchuk's police and even civilian nurses sometimes accompanied the soldiers in their raids on Jewish households; the police stood guard at the door while residents were massacred, and nurses helped expropriate medical supplies.[56]

The entire massacre lasted four hours. In the early evening, the city council telegraphed the army general staff, which ordered Semosenko to end the bloodshed. Semosenko instructed his soldiers to return to the station. As they departed, local townspeople streamed out of their homes and began looting the apartments that had belonged to murdered Jews.

THE PROSKURIV POGROM was an altogether different type of atrocity than previous incidents. For one, it resulted in a dramatic increase in the number of fatalities. Estimates vary on exactly how many

[UNITED STATES HOLOCAUST MEMORIAL MUSEUM]

Victims of the Proskuriv pogrom

people were killed, but a comprehensive report counted more than twelve hundred killed that day and over six hundred wounded, of whom three hundred would soon also succumb to their wounds. An additional six hundred Jews were killed in the neighboring town of Felshtin when some of Semosenko's Cossacks split off and continued the killing spree.[57] Locals estimated that between three and four thousand people altogether were killed or wounded, and numbers in this range were reported to first aid societies. A handwritten list of the dead names 911 victims, which is the most conservative count.[58]

But it is not just the scale of the event that made it novel. Unlike in Ovruch, the perpetrators of violence were not confined to a small circle of militants under the command of a sadistic warlord but rather encompassed hundreds of soldiers from multiple divisions, as well as ordinary citizens. And unlike the Ovruch pogrom, which stretched out across several weeks, or the Zhytomyr pogrom, which built up slowly over the course of three days, the events in Proskuriv were condensed into just a few hours. The pogrom took place within what the Dutch sociologist Abram de Swaan has called a "killing compartment," a narrowly circumscribed period of time in which ordinary norms are suspended for the purpose of mass destruction against a clearly defined set of victims. It had an explicit starting point and an end point.[59]

Yet what really distinguished the crowd that attacked Jews in Proskuriv on February 15 was its eliminationist intent. The pretext of the massacre was the failed coup planned by the Bolsheviks and their Left SR allies, but it was the Jews of the city who suffered the consequences. When Semosenko unleashed his men to wreak havoc in the city, they understood it as a license to attack Jews. The association between Bolsheviks and Jews was already part of the affective disposition of the soldiers, an ingrained part of their worldview. Hence, Jewish children could be bayoneted on the charge of Bolshevism, wealthy Jewish businessmen could be seen as radical leftists, and elderly Jewish men could be blamed for an uprising that took place without their knowledge while they were at prayer in synagogue. The fight against Bolshevism, the perpetrators believed, demanded the elimination of the Jews.

Indeed, the report Hillerson compiled later that year on the pogrom was prophetic in noting that "beginning with Proskuriv the basic purpose of the pogroms in Ukraine appears to be the total destruction of the Jewish people."[60]

AT SEVEN A.M. the day after the pogrom, Sunday, February 16, Verkhola made his way to City Hall through streets littered with corpses. Stavinsky was already there along with a few other councilors. They called a meeting of the council and ordered Semosenko and Kiverchuk to appear before them. "There were only a few councilors present," recalled Verkhola, "and all of them were Christians, except for one Jew."[61] The Jewish councilors were all either tending to the wounded or still too afraid to be out in the streets.

The members of the City Council watched in horror as Semosenko

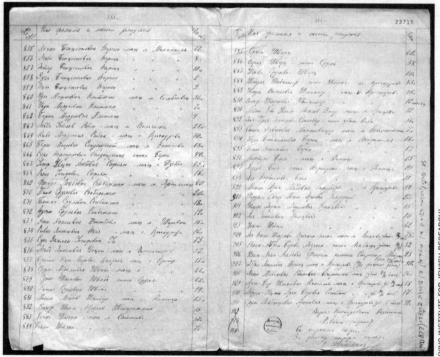

The final page of a list of 911 names of Jews murdered in the Proskuriv pogrom

pulled up in a car soon after the session opened and two members
of his entourage killed a Jewish passerby just as Semosekno entered
the building, adding an exclamation point to the recently concluded
pogrom. The commander shrugged and continued into the hall.[62]
Kiverchuk followed close behind. Verkhola spoke first, addressing
Semosenko directly:

> What are you doing, Otaman? Do you think that you are a
> Ukrainian? . . . You are not a Ukrainian, and you are not a Ukrainian
> Cossack. Our Cossacks have a valorous history. You do not get to
> wear Cossack dress for simple robbery and call yourself an otaman.
> You claim to be fighting the Bolsheviks, but are the elderly, women,
> and children really Bolsheviks? Are there only Jewish Bolsheviks? Do
> you not know that there are also Bolsheviks among other peoples, and
> even among Ukrainians?[63]

Semosenko retorted, "Everybody is saying that my Cossacks slaughtered peaceful residents, women, and children. This is nonsense! According to my orders, they only fought Bolsheviks. I gave a command to root
out Bolsheviks. If Jewish women, children, and the elderly are Bolsheviks,
it is their fault, not mine."[64] The blame for the violence, Semosenko continued, lay with the city council for having failed to stop the Bolshevik
uprising and with the Jews for their Bolshevism.

After the meeting, Verkhola issued a statement: "By order of the
otaman and with the approval of the city council the slaughter of
peaceful citizens has ended. The Cossacks have withdrawn from the
city [. . .] and the city council guarantees complete peace to the residents. Life must return to normal."[65]

Semosenko responded with his own statement: "In the night of
February 14/15, some irresponsible men without honor or conscience
attempted an armed uprising against the authorities of the district
and of the town, men who, according to precise information that has
reached me, belong to the Jewish nation and wanted to seize power,
sow confusion in the government, and plunge our Ukraine, which has
already suffered so much, into anarchy and disorder. I have taken the

most decisive steps to suppress the uprising. It is quite possible that among the victims who fell by the arms of my Cossacks there were innocent persons, but nothing can be accomplished without making mistakes."[66]

On Monday, the city hired peasants to dig a huge trench in the Jewish cemetery. Khaya Greenberg, a nurse who was working for the Ukrainian Red Cross, remembered the scene eight years later: "I shall never forget the reddened snow-sleds filled with the hacked-up bodies going to the cemetery to deposit their sad burden in a common pit. [. . .] The wounded were brought to the hospital, armless and legless men, mutilated babies, and young women whose screams became faint as they succumbed to their wounds."[67] Sruel Finkel recalled seeing wooden sledges filled with corpses heading through the deserted streets toward the cemetery. There, peasants tossed hundreds of corpses into the trench. Thieves were already searching among the bodies, looking for money sewn into the clothing of the dead. "These marauders were very numerous in the cemetery, not just Christians, but also Jews," Finkel recalled with disgust. He spent the day helping mourners identify the corpses of their loved ones.[68]

Verkhola was appointed commandant in place of Kiverchuk and sought to restore order. Semosenko remained in town, holed up at the Palace Hotel. He was suffering from gonorrhea as well as what a doctor attending to him diagnosed as a tumor of the seminal tract and testicles, and a catarrhal condition of the lungs. His room was secured by layers of guards.[69] Both Verkhola and the doctor attending him recalled that in his feverish state, Semosenko was raving to anybody who would listen that the Jews were plotting to seize power.[70]

Though relieved of his duties as commandant of the city, Kiverchuk retained a senior position in the district and was never arrested or tried for his behavior during the pogrom. He soon moved to Kalisz, Poland, where he remained active in Ukrainian diaspora circles.[71]

Semosenko, for his part, was arrested in May and held in Kamyanets-Podilskyi. Aleksander Khomsky, a Jewish member of that city's housing commission who was convicted—in what was widely regarded as a sham trial—of leading armed opposition on behalf of the

Bolsheviks, coincidentally shared the same cell. According to Khomsky, Semosenko claimed he was arrested not for murder (although he boasted exaggeratedly of killing eleven thousand Jews) but rather for having embezzled the money he stole during the pogrom. "I am not guilty," Khomsky recalled Semosenko bellowing. "I was sent to put an end to the Bolshevik uprising and the Proskuriv Jews turned out to all be Bolsheviks." He was released in July.[72]

The Second Zhytomyr Pogrom

The Bolsheviks failed to take Proskuriv in a popular uprising, but after its victory in Kyiv, the Red Army continued to inch westward. Korosten fell to the Bolsheviks on February 20, and on March 1, the Red Army was in Radomyshl, just fifty miles east of Zhytomyr. The authorities in Zhytomyr began preparing for the possible evacuation of the municipal administration. The city, ostensibly under Directory control, was being patrolled by three separate units: Vozny's militia; a civilian joint force composed of police and ward guards; and, until they were recalled toward the end of the month, some highly trained Galician riflemen. Additionally, there were quite a few reservists in the city garrison. Vozny's officers resented the ward guards, accusing them of meddling in the work of law enforcement, and derided them as the "Jewish police."[1] Many Jews, on the other hand, distrusted Vozny's forces, alleging that they had profited from the January pogrom and were sheltering perpetrators.

It was only a matter of time before skirmishes broke out. The first took place late on the morning of March 2, when a group of eighty reservists surrounded the market square and searched the mostly Jewish dressmakers on charges that they were hoarding material needed for military uniforms. The ward guards came to the dressmakers' defense, leading to a melee that threatened to unleash another pogrom and resulted in four injuries among the guards, one of whom—Yosef Shamis—died of his wounds.[2]

The city was on edge. Vozny was receiving reports of a widening Bolshevik front stretching from Ovruch in the north to Korostyshiv, a mere twenty miles to the east. The Bolshevik movement in Korostyshiv, he heard, "has grown and threatens Zhytomyr itself."[3] Vozny's counterintelligence was convinced that many of the Bolshevik agitators responsible for the January uprising had escaped and were strengthening their forces in Ovruch and Korosten, waiting for the next opportunity to strike again. Three agents sent by Vozny on an investigative mission to Ovruch had not returned after a week, and a second expedition to Korostyshiv had ended in disaster: an agent was captured by the Bolsheviks, taken to the cliffs above the Teteriv River on the outskirts of the city, and shot, falling into the frozen waters.[4]

In preparation for another showdown against the Bolsheviks, Vozny sought out new recruits and announced a draft. Morale was low, though, and many potential recruits were sick, suffering from typhus or starvation as conditions in the city and surrounding countryside had deteriorated over the winter. Few showed the enthusiasm they had demonstrated during the December drive, when thousands of peasants had flocked to join the fight for Ukrainian independence.[5] Many of those who did appear at the mobilization points took their rations and uniforms and went home. And those who stayed often didn't last long— the Ukrainian army's preference for garrisoning soldiers close to home made it easy for them to desert as soon as the going got tough. Higher-ranking officers insisted on desk jobs and were "wasted as clerks."[6] The only thing that seemed to motivate prospective recruits was the threat that if they didn't take up arms, they'd become "slaves of the Jews."[7]

In fact, the Bolsheviks were closer than even Vozny's intelligence recognized. On March 7, in an apartment on Volskaya Street, seven revolutionary activists had already formed a new Military Revolutionary Committee with the intention of seizing power in the name of the soviets. Judging by their names, two were from Jewish families, including Abram Gilinsky, who had been one of the leaders of the January uprising.[8]

The next day, on March 8, Red Army units took the towns of Kotelnya and Andrushivka, about twenty-five miles from Zhytomyr. Vozny once again fled the city with his administration. His troops followed four days later. Many Ukrainians who had familial roots in the countryside also returned to their ancestral homes. As a result, the city was once again left with mostly Jews, who had nowhere to run and were forced to bear the brunt of Bolshevik rule. Early on March 13 Bolshevik forces arrived, and the next day the Military Revolutionary Committee declared soviet rule in Zhytomyr. On March 15, the committee dissolved the city council and put a new commissariat in its place; it consisted of five commissars, one of whom had a Jewish name. This time the new government garnered immediate support from key constituencies, including the major trade unions. On March 16, the public education system was put at the disposal of the government, and the next day the official newspaper of the Communist Party, *Izvestiia*, was published on the city printing press. Having established soviet rule in Zhytomyr, the Red Army conquered Vinnytsia on March 18 and Zhmerynka on March 20, forcing the Directory government to flee further west, to Proskuriv.

The new government in Zhytomyr implemented some of the harsh measures for which Bolshevik rule had become notorious: it demanded a contribution of ten million rubles from the bourgeoisie of the city and began requisitioning what little property the elites retained. A local Cheka sprang into action, shooting counterrevolutionaries and suspected bandits in the basement of the prison on Chudnovskaya Street.[9] Official estimates put the number of executions at anywhere between six and twenty-five, but rumors were rampant that the casualties were astronomically higher, that the "Cheka and the Jews" had "executed several thousand Christians, including priests, officers, and students."[10] The figure of seventeen hundred Cheka victims floated around town. Other gossip more preposterously maintained that the Jews "had caused the death of six hundred gentiles by selling them poisoned bread and meat" and that they were planning on bombing the churches.[11]

If the Bolsheviks intended to carry out additional offenses, though, they had little time to do so. Within days, Directory forces camped out in the suburb of Vrangelevka, prepared to retake the city. Recognizing that they were outnumbered, the Bolsheviks withdrew on March 20–21.[12] Hundreds of Jews accompanied them on foot and in carts, abandoning their homes and their property. As Duvid Khasis put it in his testimony to the Legal Bureau of the Central Committee for Relief of Pogrom Victims, "rumors were circulating that all the Jews would pay for the deeds of the Bolsheviks."[13] In a self-fulfilling prophecy, the massive flight of Jews and Bolsheviks fed the narrative that the Jews were in league with the enemy.

Vozny resumed his position and worked with local lay and religious leaders in an attempt to avoid a repeat of January's violence. Both the Orthodox and Catholic bishops issued statements appealing to the military for calm. On Saturday, March 22, a delegation from the city council went out to Vrangelevka to assure the Directory troops that the rumors of massive executions were false and to plead with them to spare their city another bloodbath. On their way, the councilors encountered one of Petliura's lieutenants, who warned them that if there were any Jews among the delegation they would all be in danger. The one Jewish councilor in the group was persuaded to return home. Walking back into town, he came across a body lying on the road: a seventy-year-old man with a tallit in his hand had been shot on his way to synagogue. A trail of blood followed the body for several feet, evidence of the mortally wounded man's futile attempt to get to safety.[14]

The delegation was met in Vrangelevka by an officer who introduced himself as the head of a forward detachment of Petliura's army. A city councilor explained that the Jews were fearful of a pogrom; the officer responded by accusing the councilors of shielding the Jews. The soldiers under his command, he continued, could not be blamed for wanting to seek revenge for the bloody repressions carried out by the Cheka. A pogrom, he warned, was unavoidable.[15]

As CIVILIAN AND religious authorities tried to negotiate a peace, Directory soldiers were already hunting for Jews in the hospital, where hundreds were hiding. They demanded to see a list of admitted patients and searched throughout the hospital, in the shed, in the storage facilities, and in the ice cellar. Most of the Jews were hiding in living quarters of hospital employees, but the soldiers found a group of six men in the basement, led them out into the yard, and shot them. A few hours later the soldiers returned to raid the hospital laundry and pharmacy. They even made off with hay from the shed.[16]

On Saturday evening, Directory soldiers moved into town in force and immediately began tormenting the Jewish population. Mikhail Skokovsky, a liberal attorney and member of the city council, described watching a group of soldiers on horseback in the center of town, on Zhytomyr's biggest thoroughfare, torture two Jews—an elderly man with a long gray beard and a young man of fifteen or sixteen years of age. The right hand of the old man was tied to the left hand of the young one, and both were bound together with rope as a soldier on horseback stabbed them repeatedly with a sharp lance. A military band was playing to the delight of a celebratory crowd that cheered on the spectacle.[17]

That same evening, soldiers and townsfolk spread out from the square, as they had done in January, marched into homes, and demanded money and property. The stores were still largely empty, having been plundered only two months earlier, and many of the wealthier members of the community had fled. The victims this time were those too poor to have left—seamstresses, tailors, bootmakers, leatherworkers, and tinsmiths. Nearly five hundred later gave testimonies to the Legal Bureau. Mikhlya Volkis, a twenty-eight-year-old seamstress, testified that at around seven o'clock in the evening, a gang of eight men dressed in civilian clothes and carrying rifles burst into her apartment, demanded to know if she was hiding any weapons, and proceeded to rummage through her cabinets and trunks. They left the house with money, coats, and other articles of clothing. On their way out they slashed her husband, Avrum-Gdal, with a saber, cutting off three of his fingers. An hour later more men appeared at their house, again demanding money. Persuaded that the house had already been robbed, they left taking only sugar and leftovers.[18]

Whereas in January soldiers used the threat of execution to extort funds from their victims, but rarely carried it out, now they showed no such restraint. For instance, when soldiers discovered about fifteen people hiding in a basement on Sobornaya Street, they first took their money and then ordered eight men outside into the street and executed them.[19] Many of the soldiers who did the killing were locals, new or old recruits from the neighboring villages or even from Zhytomyr itself. Those who had taken up the Directory's calls to service were often the poverty-stricken jobless eager to satisfy their hunger, or criminal elements who seized upon the prospects of operating under the cover of a military uniform.

Armed soldiers came to the apartment of Rivka and Duvid Braverman on Chudnovskaya Street and began to rob the house. "One of them," Rivka Braverman testified, "who I recognized as our neighbor, a young fellow named Mishka, began to beat me with a whip after I expressed astonishment that he was among the thieves. This Mishka took my husband into the courtyard and shot him with a revolver."[20] Blyuma Goldfeld reported that armed men in military uniforms came to her house and demanded money and goods, forcing her father to dig up the yard, where he had hidden some valuables. Once they secured their loot, the bandits shoved the family—Blyuma, her father, and two sisters—into a room and shot them. Everybody was killed instantly except for Blyuma, who fainted, leaving the bandits to assume she, too, was dead. Blyuma believed that her family was shot because they knew the intruders: "They therefore decided to kill us all, so that nobody would turn them in."[21]

As had been the case in January, the marauding soldiers lowered the threshold of participation in the looting, encouraging peasants and townsfolk to join in. Shakhno Shats explained that at around eleven o'clock on Saturday night, eight men wearing civilian greatcoats and armed with rifles burst into his apartment. They seemed to be locals, from the villages nearby. They robbed the house, taking clothing, silver, gold, and money. On their way out, one of the men fired a single shot into the forehead of Shats's wife, Mariam.[22]

Borukh-Pinkhas Tsybulevsky heard the commotion outside and recognized what was happening. He ran toward the Jewish cemetery, where many Jews were hiding, but was stopped at the gate by a mounted man in a military uniform and a young peasant. The peasant stabbed Tsybulevsky with a saber; when he fell to the ground, the soldier shot him in the head. Tsybulevsky's wife, Riva, heard about these events from a neighbor who witnessed them, and went running to the cemetery with her fifteen-year-old son, Avrum. They found Tsybulevsky's body lying on the ground and brought it inside the cemetery to the morgue. When she got home, Riva remembered that her husband had cash hidden inside his boots. She managed to return to the morgue the next day to retrieve the money, but Tsybulevsky's boots were already gone.[23] Shlomo Reibel similarly testified that when he discovered his son's body in his courtyard the day after he had been murdered, "his coat and shoes had been taken."[24]

On Sunday, March 23, Petliura himself passed through the city and commended his soldiers for their victory over the "Muscovite bandits," while noting the anger that Bolshevik rule had roused against "those new Muscovite robbers and Jews."[25] His army was firmly in control of the city, yet soldiers continued their hunt for Jews, searching in cellars, attics, and gardens. They forced those they discovered into the streets, where they executed them in front of indifferent witnesses. Skokovsky counted twenty-three bodies in the main square and the corner of Kievskaya and Sobornaya streets.[26]

Together with others from the city council, Skokovsky implored the military commanders to halt the violence. One officer claimed that he was doing everything he could but that the crowds—including some of his own soldiers—were so riled up that short of firing on them with machine guns there was no way to stop them. "It's Asia here," he declared, "and I will destroy it and set up Europe."[27]

The murder spree continued until Tuesday, March 25, when once again Galician sharpshooters were called in, this time together with troops led by Pavlo Bohatskyi, a former journalist who had become a military commander under Petliura. Bohatskyi's soldiers quelled the violence by publicly executing those they caught stealing and murdering, which quickly put an end to the rampage. The committee of inquiry counted 317 Jewish bodies and noted that the majority, judging by their clothing, were not wealthy people.[28]

The committee's investigation, which was concluded in July, when the city was under Bolshevik rule, laid the blame for the violence squarely on the military authorities of the Directory. "The attitude of the government in both the first and second pogroms," it noted, "was one of inaction and even outright instigation, giving the ignorant elements of the population the impression that participation in the pogrom does not constitute a criminal violation. The pogrom took place completely in the open under the eyes of the authorities and with the participation of many representatives of the commanding structure of the army, including officers."[29]

The authorities' cynical substitution of Jews for Bolsheviks had played a major role in inciting the pogrom. The military had difficulty motivating peasants to fight against an abstract idea like Bolshevism but was easily able to muster recruits when the Jews were presented as the threat. The peasants knew that the Bolsheviks had promised land and bread, yet somehow they had received neither. Many peasants concluded that the promised redistribution of property had been usurped by the Jews, who always seemed to come out ahead anyway. It was a notion that many officials were eager to promote and that Vozny himself was willing to go along with.

On Sunday evening, the sounds of gunfire could be heard from the direction of the road to Berdychiv. Bolshevik forces were approaching. Rumors were widespread that if the Bolsheviks captured Zhytomyr again, "the Jews will slaughter all the Christians."[30] As the Bolsheviks renewed their attack on the city, securing the environs and reestablishing control, another flood of refugees came streaming out. This time it was peasant workers who had moved to the city in search of work who were fleeing back to their home villages, fearful of what they thought would be a Bolshevik-Jewish massacre of the Christian population.

VOZNY, AS WELL, recognized that he was not safe in the city anymore. He fled along with several members of the officer corps to Rivne. There he was appointed to the position of commander of the Fifty-third Novograd-Volynsk Regiment. When the Bolsheviks caught up with him in the spring, he was too ill with typhus to flee again. He was arrested in his hospital bed and brought back to Zhytomyr for questioning.

On June 7, 1919, he was hauled out of his cell in the Zhytomyr head-quarters of the Cheka to explain what he had done during the violence in Zhytomyr three months earlier. His interrogator, Yakov Livshitz, had been one of the investigators with the committee of inquiry. Together with two prosecutors who were also at the hearing, Livshitz listened carefully as Vozny described how he had attempted to de-escalate tensions when he originally arrived in Zhytomyr by permitting the soldiers to form a soviet. Vozny claimed that during the January pogrom his men drove off bands of armed fighters who were terrorizing Jews, and that he himself had shuttled back and forth between the civilian authorities in the municipal government and the Ukrainian military forces occupying the city in an attempt to quell the violence. Other witnesses who testified before the committee had described Vozny as a dedicated civil servant and patriot. Ivan Voronitsyn, a member of the city council, told Livshitz that during the pogrom Vozny "went through the streets with a rifle and dispersed the robbers himself."[31] On the final day of the unrest in January, they said, Vozny had even gone to the train station to secure the release of all the Jewish hostages who were still being held by the occupying forces.[32]

Vozny had barely begun to tell this story when officials from the Cheka abruptly ended the interview. They took Vozny back to his cell and instructed Livshitz and his team to return in two days. Languishing in his cell, Vozny had ample time to contemplate his change of fortune. He must have resented being held a prisoner in the city whose forces he once commanded, let alone being forced to justify his actions before a Jew.

Livshitz arrived at the appointed time on June 9 for the second interview but was unable to complete his questioning. The chair of the Cheka informed him that the case was closed. Vozny had been "killed while trying to escape."[33] Bolshevik rule was still fresh, but Livshitz must have already recognized this phrase as a euphemism for extrajudicial execution, a sentence the Bolsheviks inflicted on many of those who had served counterrevolutionary causes.

PART III

POWER VACUUM

MARCH 1919–AUGUST 1919

The Entente

In November 1918, Béla Kun, a thirty-three-year-old Hungarian Jewish journalist and former soldier in the Austro-Hungarian army, returned to Budapest from Russia, where he had been a prisoner of war and, upon his release, had become active in Bolshevik circles. With stunning speed, aided by Lenin's support, he built up the "Party of Communists" in Hungary, and on March 21, 1919, overthrew the government of Mihály Károlyi and established a Hungarian Soviet Republic. For nearly five months, he ruled Hungary with a committee of largely Jewish commissars, heightening fears of a Europe-wide Jewish-Bolshevik takeover. The Reds were on the verge of building a communist corridor between Soviet Ukraine and Hungary, which would have wiped the Ukrainian People's Republic off the map and created a contiguous Bolshevik state stretching into the heart of Europe.

Petliura controlled only a sliver of territory around Proskuriv at the time and was facing a threat not only from the Bolsheviks but also from the Whites' growing Volunteer Army in the south, an irredentist Poland in the west, and regional warlords challenging his authority throughout Ukraine. He had also lost the support of his erstwhile socialist allies, and a pair of prominent Jews within the government had resigned on account of the pogroms: Revutsky as minister of Jewish affairs and Margolin as deputy minister of foreign affairs. "I found it hard to occupy an official post in a country in which my brothers were being slaughtered," Margolin explained.[1]

Without the socialists in his cabinet to hold him back, the chief otaman lurched rightward. He doubled down on his appeals to the Entente Powers for military aid and official recognition, offering in return a Ukrainian commitment to join a Europe-wide anti-Bolshevik front. But the French and the British saw the Whites as a more reliable bulwark against the Reds: they trusted the Volunteer officers, who were making gains along the Don Basin and northern shores of the Black Sea, to defeat the Bolshevik enemy and restore a united Russia, a goal threatened by an independent Ukrainian state. "No hope can be placed on the Separatist movement under Petliura," concluded one report from the British Political Intelligence Office. "The real danger in the Ukraine is Bolshevism, and Bolshevism in the Ukraine can only be fought by assisting the Russian Volunteer Army."[2] The Allies were also concerned that Petliura was to blame for the recent anti-Jewish violence. Many French military officials shared an antipathy toward the Jews and agreed that Jews were responsible for the spread of Bolshevism, but they objected to the type of frenzied violence plaguing Ukraine. Recognizing that rumors of pogroms perpetrated by Directory troops had sullied his reputation and endangered the Ukrainian cause in the west, Petliura made sure to send two Jews to plead his case and convince the French they were backing the wrong horse: Margolin, who remained committed to the cause of Ukrainian independence even after his resignation, and Pinkhos Krasny, the new minister of Jewish affairs. They took their negotiating skills to Odesa, where the French had established a stronghold on the Black Sea.

Although it was 150 miles from the front, Odesa had been transformed by the Great War. The population had vacillated between 500,000 and 650,000 as refugees poured in from Galicia and Volhynia, prisoners of war were transferred to newly established incarceration facilities, freshly mobilized soldiers and sailors arrived for training and deployment, and Odesans themselves were deployed to the front lines.

GERMANY

LITHUANIAN-BELARUSIAN
SOVIET SOCIALIST REPUBLIC

Orel

RUSSIAN SOVIET-SOCIALIST REPUBLIC

Warsaw
Brest-
Litovsk

POLAND

Polish
advance

Kraków

Kursk   Voronezh

Chernihiv

Ovtuch
STRUK   SOKOLOVSKY

Rivne   ANGEL   UKRAINIAN
SOVIET REPUBLIC

Red Army
Apr. 1919

UKRAINIAN
PEOPLE'S REPUBLIC

Zhytomyr
Kyiv
ZELENYI

Lviv
Berdychiv   Bila   Red Army gains
Tserkva   March 1919

Kharkiv
(capital of Ukrainian
Soviet Republic)

Proskuriv
TIUTIUNIK Cherkasy   Poltava

WEST UKRAINIAN
PEOPLE'S REPUBLIC
Kamyanets- Vinnytsia
Podilskyi
Uman
KAZAKOV
Elizavetgrad   Katerynoslav

HUNGARY

GRIGORIEV
MAKHNO

Mariupol   Advance of the
Army of South Russia
(Whites)
May 1919

ROMANIA   Mykolaiv   Melitopol

Odesa   Kherson

Sea of
Azov

UKRAINE, MARCH–MAY 1919

Area claimed by
Ukrainian People's Republic

Area controlled by
Ukrainian People's Republic

Territories controlled by warlords

Entente control
until April 1919

Crimea

Sevastopol

Black Sea

In the city's industrial sector, armament and aviation factories replaced boarded-up textile plants; off the coast, Russian battleships patrolled the Black Sea, engaging in cat-and-mouse operations against formidable German cruisers. When the Hetmanate's military governor, Vassili Biskupsky, was forced to flee to Germany in December 1918, French naval ships stationed in the Black Sea moved in and, in alliance with the Whites, attempted to establish authority in the city to prevent the port from falling to the Bolsheviks. The former commander of White forces in Siberia, Aleksei Grishin-Almazov, a thirty-two-year-old dandy and ladies' man, was appointed as the new military governor of Odesa. He disbanded existing municipal institutions and tried to rule the city like a dictator, but his ambition and power were tempered by his penchant for boozing and gambling. The real power brokers in the city were the French.[3]

By March 1919, Odesa's grand avenues were being patrolled by some fifty thousand foreign troops. Most were French colonial conscripts from northwest Africa, who had little interest in risking their lives fighting for an imperial power so far from Paris, let alone Senegal. Influenced by the French communist press in wide circulation in the city, some came to harbor more sympathy for the anti-colonialist Bolsheviks than for their own French officers. The population at large, however, treated the French with reverence: they controlled the telegraph lines, introduced the first tanks into Ukraine, and were the only officials who seemed able to secure passage on any railway car. If the French would only dedicate a few battalions to the effort, everybody believed, for better or worse they could decide the fate of Ukraine.

Throughout the winter of 1919, tens of thousands of former landowners, imperial officers, tsarist bureaucrats, and Jewish merchants poured into Odesa from all over the southwestern provinces of the defunct Russian Empire, hoping that the French would protect them from the Bolsheviks. The city's soup kitchens and shelters could hardly keep up with the influx. Under the French tricolor, White officers, Ukrainian nationalists, Greek infantry, Polish cavalry, North African recruits, Zionist poets, anarchist activists, British businessmen, and all types of profiteers, speculators, and spies mingled along the city's famed Deribasovskaya Street—Rue de Ribas, to the French. Art, criminality, and the revolution collided in Odesa, as plots were hatched in cabarets while swindlers and charlatans led revolutionary campaigns. Mishka Yaponchik, the "king of thieves," ruled over the Moldavanka district, where the lavish banquets he threw for the impoverished Jews

[IMAGE COURTESY OF BLAVATNIK ARCHIVE FOUNDATION]

Odesa, early 1900s

turned him into a gangster hero, a role he put to good use by establishing a powerful Jewish self-defense brigade. The prototype of Isaac Babel's Benya Krik, Yaponchik became a symbol of the chaos and decadence of revolutionary Odesa.

Every move of the city's rich and famous was shrouded in intrigue. When the popular silent film starlet Vera Kholodnaya died in February 1919, it was widely rumored that a French official with whom she was having an affair had poisoned her after discovering she was a Bolshevik spy.[4] Kholodnaya in fact died from the Spanish flu, but the rumors were not as far-fetched as they might seem: Odesa under the French was also the stomping grounds of Sidney Reilly, Ian Fleming's reported inspiration for James Bond. Reilly was born Sigmund Rosenblum into a Jewish family near Grodno before moving to Odesa and then to London, where he joined the British secret service as an anti-Bolshevik agent. Sipping Turkish coffee in elegant cafés with his "long, straight nose, dark, penetrating eyes, large mouth, and black hair brushed back from his forehead," he collected intelligence for the British on the situation in what they still called "South Russia."[5] Having gotten his start in the business of counterfeiting Russian rubles in Britain and engaging in foreign arms deals, Reilly's mission to channel money and arms to the Whites was familiar territory for the man known as the "Ace of Spies."[6] At times, though, Reilly's escapades read more like Monty Python than James Bond. In August 1918, he had hatched a plot to detain Trotsky and Lenin and march them through the streets of Moscow "with their nether garments missing," as another British spy put it. Better to ridicule them than to make martyrs of them, Reilly had reasoned. The plot was abandoned only when Fanny Kaplan put two bullets into Lenin before the British de-pantsing scheme could be implemented.[7]

At night, the city came alive. In clubs, cafés, brothels, theaters, and cabarets with names like the Yellow Canary and the Blue Dog, spectators tried to ignore the hunger and scurvy gnawing at them, and forget about the arrests and shootings taking place outside. The former White officer Prince Andrei Lobanov-Rostovsky recalled that one night when he was enjoying a cabaret, the manager interrupted the performance to notify the guests that a curfew had been imposed, prohibiting anybody from going out on the street. "We did as best we could. The artists joined the spectators; everyone got acquainted; we danced and had a merry time until morning."[8] On the first floor of the Variety Theater on Grecheskaya Street, audiences swooned over the Russian-Greek baritone Yuri Morfessi. For those in search of more risqué entertainment, a cabaret satirizing pogroms, the war, and the French played on the second floor. On the third floor, the most trusted guests gambled at cards in a race against the depreciating currency.[9] Inflation was so rampant that one resident quipped that the price of a shave rose by 60 percent as he waited his turn at the barbershop.

Widespread anxieties over the Spanish flu as well as encroaching Bolshevism and the Jews who allegedly supported it, though, cast a cloud over the city. The worldwide flu pandemic ravaged the port, infecting thousands who had not already succumbed to the cholera and typhus epidemics spread by returning troops. In desperation, a group of Odesa merchants even organized a wedding in a cemetery, a Jewish folk custom to ward off disease.[10] At the end of January 1919, White forces backed by the French raided popular leftist hangouts and trade unions, conducting searches and arresting suspected communists.[11] Drunken Volunteers chased Jewish teenagers down Gogolevskaya Street, screaming, "Down with Communism, down with the Jews."[12] Later, as the Bolshevik threat became more pronounced with Red Army victories to the north and west, suspected communists were interrogated and shot. One witness who arrived in the city in early February recalled that "they began these shootings, of course, with communists, but later, when these enthusiasts developed the taste for it, they began to execute and rob simple inhabitants on account of some type of personal allegation or counter-intelligence."[13] Soon, the killings expanded to target Jews everywhere, even those "who had nothing to do with politics."[14]

MARGOLIN SUCCEEDED IN meeting with French officials, who expressed their skepticism about the prospect for success of the Ukrainian People's

Republic, but assured him they would not abandon Odesa to the Bolsheviks. Margolin may have believed the assurances, but he would have been hard-pressed to find anyone else in the city who did. On March 25, the Bolshevik-allied warlord Nikifor Grigoriev began threatening Odesa with hundreds of insurgent fighters. "You have only one choice," he brashly declared: "throw your governor into the sea, raise the red flag, put down your weapons, and come to us, instead of 'God save the tsar' singing 'Arise, ye workers from your slumber.'"[15] "He gives the impression of a man who knows no fear," recalled a Soviet Information Bureau correspondent who met Grigoriev in Odesa.[16] It was widely rumored that Grigoriev threatened to flay Grishin-Almazov and "make a drum out of his skin."[17]

Odesa's terrified citizens were already assembling at the port, eager to climb aboard any seaworthy vessel casting off. Margolin hitched a ride on an Italian ship heading to Romania. Although the pogroms that had accompanied Ukrainian independence had deeply depressed him, he was still convinced that the government of Petliura had done "everything in its power" to fight against them. Krasny was able to secure a seat on a special government train to meet up with the rest of the cabinet in Proskuriv. He also managed to arrange a seat for his predecessor, Revutsky, who subsequently caught a military supply train into Galicia, from where he eventually made it to Palestine.

As word of a potential uprising in support of Grigoriev spread through the streets, the French began a hasty retreat, abandoning the city to the Bolsheviks. Lobanov-Rostovsky, who was staying at Odesa's grand Hotel de Londres at the time, recalled the moment when the venerable guests learned the French were leaving:

In an instant bedlam reigned in the hotel. The lobby was filled with wildly gesticulating people. The elevators were jammed. Two streams of humanity, going up and down the stairs, met on the landings between floors, where free-for-all fights took place. Women caught in the crush were shrieking, and from these landings valises came tumbling down on the heads of those who were below. To add to the confusion, a huge and menacing crowd of ruffians had assembled in the street and with shouts of death were trying to force their way into the hotel.[18]

At the port, tens of thousands of desperate refugees bustled to get on passenger steamers, many of which were grounded as the crews had gone over to the Bolsheviks and were refusing orders to fire up the boilers. Retreating French soldiers were rolling armored trucks off the breakwaters—better the sea get them than the Reds.[19]

The last French troops sailed away on April 6. The French armored cruiser *Waldeck-Rousseau*, with her battery of heavy guns, remained anchored in the Black Sea throughout the spring, its distant silhouette a bitter reminder to those trapped in the city that the prospect of salvation lurked just beyond the horizon.

GRIGORIEV'S INSURRECTIONARY FORCES moved in on April 7, dynamiting bridges and tearing up the railway tracks. As the writer Ivan Bunin, who was in Odesa at the time, put it: "Roughly six hundred of Grigoriev's men blew into town, bowlegged youths led by a pack of convicts and hooligans, who somehow captured an extremely well-to-do city with a million people in it."[20] Odesa had become Red.

Grigoriev introduced himself to the city with a parade down Pushkinskaya Street. A makeshift orchestra of clarinet, violin, trumpet, accordion, and tambourine made its best attempt at the Internationale.[21] The short and stocky warlord, dressed inappropriately for the warm weather in a brown "French jacket" and a large fur hat, greeted well-wishers who ran up to him and kissed his hands.[22] Representatives from the local unions arrived to offer their services in setting up a soviet government. Grigoriev insisted that they first drink to the success of the revolution. The elated union members hustled to produce a bottle. After celebratory toasts, they were ready to get down to business and present the reports they had diligently prepared, detailing the local organizational strength and the procedures they had worked out for a transition of power. But Grigoriev had no patience for the bureaucratic niceties of official reports. All he

Entry of Red Army into Odesa

needed from the unions, he said, was fifteen thousand pairs of shoes. His soldiers would take care of the rest.[23] The dispirited union men left, suddenly realizing that the revolution Grigoriev had in mind was more about pilfering loot for his soldiers than securing equality for the workers.

Grigoriev was born Nechypir Servetnyk in 1885, most likely in a village near Proskuriv.[24] He had served in the tsarist cavalry, fought in Manchuria during the Russo-Japanese War, and was awarded the Saint George's Cross for bravery during the Great War.[25] Over the summer of 1918, he formed his own insurgent army to fight the Germans and the Hetmanate. Starting with a force of two hundred peasants, he attacked a guard outpost and captured four machine guns. He used his new firepower to storm an Austrian armory, where he seized bullets, grenades, rifles, and more guns.[26] When Skoropadskyi was overthrown, Grigoriev fought for the Directory but soon broke with Petliura over the chief otaman's negotiations with the French, which Grigoriev saw as a betrayal of the revolutionary cause.[27] Instead, he made overtures to Antonov-Ovseyenko, commander of the Red Army in Ukraine.[28] An inspector whom Antonov-Ovseyenko sent to Grigoriev's headquarters downplayed reports that Grigoriev had unleashed pogroms and other excesses, and reported back that the warlord "lives like a townsman of modest means" and "has considerable military ability." "It should be quite possible to keep him under control," the report concluded.[29]

In the spring of 1919, Grigoriev began to achieve spectacular successes against the foreign powers occupying the northern shores of the Black Sea. On March 10, he captured Kherson from the French; on March 15—despite Antonov-Ovseyenko's orders to stand down—he took Mykolaiv and its shipyards, following the hasty evacuation of the stranded German garrison that had been left to defend the city.[30] With command of these two ports, Grigoriev controlled the Dnipro Gulf of the Black Sea and two of the major staging grounds of the Entente Powers. He also acquired a treasure trove of abandoned arms—heavy guns, tanks, munitions, and even armored trains. According to the historian Arthur Adams, it was "enough to transform his Cossack and peasant rabble into a well-equipped army, enough perhaps to make him the most powerful man in the Ukraine."[31] Grigoriev's stunning victories drew thousands of fighting men to his command.[32] "Recruits now poured into Grigoriev's camps in small groups, in whole companies, even in roughly formed regiments flying homemade flags and marching to the music of their own bands," Adams writes.[33] By early spring Grigoriev had over ten thousand troops at his disposal.

The Bolsheviks had little choice but to incorporate the warlord and his men into the Red Army's Ukrainian front. It was a mutually beneficial arrangement. Grigoriev was a conqueror, not a ruler; when his men had taken their loot, he was largely willing to deliver the cities he had subdued into the hands of the Bolsheviks. And the Bolsheviks, for their part, were eager to take credit for Grigoriev's victories.

Once in control of Odesa, the Bolsheviks requisitioned property from the bourgeoisie, plundered wealthy houses, and arrested prominent businessmen and professionals. According to one witness, "the arrival of the Bolsheviks caused panic, and the ban they imposed on free trade of bread, as well as their requisitioning of the most essential goods, caused sharp increases in the price of bread and all other foods."[34] A fuel shortage ensued as well. "The entire city is in darkness except for the thieves' dens," wrote Ivan Bunin in his diary.[35] The situation was so desperate that local authorities destroyed a wooden pier for firewood. Since the water pumps depended upon fuel to work, water, too, was in short supply. Factories ground to a halt.

The Cheka, which moved into an office on Catherine Square—opposite the bronze statue of Catherine the Great, which had been installed with great pomp in 1900 only to be unceremoniously dismantled twenty years later when the empress went out of style—sent nearly two thousand people to the firing squad between April and August 1919.[36] The newspapers regularly announced the execution of so-called counterrevolutionaries. "I recently read about the shooting of twenty-six men, but it didn't seem to faze me," Bunin wrote in his diary. "Yes, twenty-six men, and not just any old time, but yesterday, here, right next to me."[37]

On May 13, 1919, the Bolsheviks declared a day of peaceful protest, during which citizens of the city would have free rein to confiscate goods from the propertied classes.[38] Bunin recalled seeing acquaintances wearing two shirts and two pairs of pants, for fear that anything not on their bodies at the moment would be taken.[39] In the end, the protest was called off in the middle of the afternoon as the looting got out of hand and a hailstorm came through.

ON APRIL 8, the day after Grigoriev's capture of Odesa, Proskuriv, where Petliura's government was then based, fell to the Bolsheviks as well. The Directory was forced yet again to move its headquarters farther west, this time to Kamyanets-Podilskyi. Petliura, who had little to show for what his critics characterized as prostrating himself before the imperial powers, found himself embattled politically as well: Borys Martos, the former minister of agriculture and the Treasury, formed a new socialist cabinet committed to peace with Bolshevik Russia and an end to foreign assistance from the Entente. But as head of state, Petliura remained the public face of the Ukrainian national movement and retained control of the remnants of his army. Against the odds, he continued to believe that the Great Powers could be persuaded to

come to his aid, if not with military assistance, then at least with diplomatic recognition.

In order to get their support, he realized he would have to crack
down on excesses within his army and prove that Ukraine could live up
to the promise of tolerance enshrined in the Law on National Autonomy. Thus, on April 9—one day after Proskuriv fell to the Bolsheviks—
Petliura established a committee to investigate the February pogrom
in the city. With the Bolsheviks in control, he could be confident that
access to witnesses would be limited and the inquiry would go nowhere.
But by publicizing his determination to get to the bottom of what happened, he hoped to score political points in the West. On April 12, in
an appeal to the Ukrainian people, Martos followed up with a warning
that "the government will root out bandits and perpetrators of pogroms
and inflict on them the most severe punishments. The government will
not tolerate pogroms against the Jewish population under any circumstances, and will take all measures at its disposal to fight these loathsome
and traitorous evils, which disgrace the Ukrainian people in the eyes of
all civilized nations."[40] Finally, on April 17, an edict concerning Jewish
communal self-government affirmed the continued existence of Jewish
community councils and gave them authority over educational and welfare organizations, community records, and cemeteries, enshrining the
national autonomy that the Central Rada had granted eighteen months
earlier into the law of the Ukrainian People's Republic.[41] Everything was
thus in place for a formal appeal to the Great Powers, who were at that
very moment deciding the fate of Ukraine in Paris. Once again, Petliura
turned to Margolin to make his case.

MARGOLIN ARRIVED IN Paris on April 17 as part of the Ukrainian delegation to the peace talks then underway. There, in the private sitting
rooms and public lounges of the Astoria, the Majestic, and the Cril-
lon hotels (where the British and American delegations were based),
hundreds of statesmen, aides, diplomats, soldiers, regional experts, and
aspirants from states both real and imagined made their cases for a postwar peace to the Supreme Council led by American president Woodrow

Wilson, French prime minister Georges Clemenceau, British prime minister David Lloyd George, and Italian prime minister Vittorio Orlando.[42] On the streets, the atmosphere was constrained. "To my great astonishment," Margolin wrote, "there was lacking any trace of the gaiety and enthusiasm among the population that one might expect in view of the victorious end of the war."[43]

Margolin recognized that following the rise of the Hungarian Soviet Republic and the Bolshevik capture of Odesa, the Allies were increasingly alarmed over the spread of the revolution. Most of Ukraine was in the hands of the Bolsheviks, who ruled the territory from Kharkiv, and the Red Army was rapidly moving toward the Polish borderlands. Margolin blamed the thousands of Russian aristocratic refugees in Paris, who "knew Western European customs and manners of behavior," for convincing the French to support the Whites rather than the Directory. However, he saw an opening for securing Allied support in Eastern Galicia, where local Ukrainians had proclaimed the West Ukrainian People's Republic in November 1918 and were now battling Polish forces for control of the region—the last defense against Bolshevik expansion into the European heartland. The West Ukrainian People's Republic was still allied with Petliura, and with the seat of the Directory now located in Kamyanets-Podilskyi—closer to Lviv than to Kyiv—Eastern Galicia became the focal point of Petliura's ambitions. This made Poland his most pressing adversary.

Margolin and the rest of the Ukrainian delegation in Paris thus presented their republic as a multinational alternative to the ethnonationalist state emerging in Poland. The Ukrainian principle of national autonomy, they contended, offered a unique solution to the "Jewish Question," the problem of how best to accommodate Jewish minorities within the European nation-state. Ukraine alone could be trusted to respect the rights of its minorities if the government just had sufficient strength to curtail the ongoing violence. As the second Zhytomyr pogrom raged on the other side of the continent, Hryhory Sydorenko, the head of the delegation, boasted that Ukraine was the first of the new European states to grant complete liberty and equality to Jewish subjects.[44] "The Ukrainians as a nation, having suffered centuries-long oppression owing to the Russian régime, take very near to heart the claims of another still more oppressed nation—the Jews, who for centuries have been subjected to still greater sufferings and political and social degradation," he wrote. "The Ukrainian nation has always supported the Jews in their fight for full emancipation."[45] The Joint Foreign Committee of British Jews, under the leadership of the philanthropist Claude Montefiore, agreed that the Ukrainian Law on National Autonomy was a model for the newly independent Polish Republic, which, the committee argued, should be required to follow Ukraine in guaranteeing for the Jews "the autonomous management of their religious, educational, charitable, and other cultural institutions."[46]

It may seem inconceivable that many of the leading representatives of world Jewry supported Ukraine after the pogroms of Ovruch, Zhytomyr, and Proskuriv. But throughout most of the year, Ukraine was considered too dangerous for foreigners to access, and only vague rumors were filtering out of the war zone. It was not until the last days of February that reports of the January pogrom in Zhytomyr had begun to reach London, and even then they were unsubstantiated. And although there was some mention of violence in Proskuriv, the Yiddish press would publish details of the pogrom only when cable dispatches reached them in late May and early June.[47] Until then, the Jewish press was still celebrating the Ukrainian People's Republic's grandiose claims of mutual understanding articulated in the Central Rada's four Universals, the Law on National Autonomy, and the liberal reputations of the Directory leaders. Many Jews were inclined to believe the claims of the Ukrainian National Committee in the United States that "there are not and have not been pogroms in Ukraine outside the zone of Bolshevism."[48]

By contrast, news of the November 1918 pogrom in Lviv, which was widely blamed on Polish troops, quickly became an international incident due to the ease with which foreigners were able to travel to and around Poland, and because of the publicity surrounding the Polish Republic during the peace talks. Thus, when the fate of Eastern Galicia emerged as a major point of contention in Paris, much of the organized Jewish community openly favored Ukrainian claims over those of Poland.

JEWISH ACTIVISTS SOUGHT to capitalize on Poland's vulnerable position to secure minority rights for the Jews in Poland akin to those granted by Ukraine and, at the same time, to promote Jewish migration to Palestine in the hopes of establishing a state that would serve as a Jewish haven from persecution.[49] Garnering sympathy for the plight of eastern European Jewry, though, was not easy. The American public was riled up against a Bolshevik and anarchist threat personified to many by Leon Trotsky and Emma Goldman, while demagogues like Henry Ford were arguing that Jewish finance was funding anti-American terrorism. But Louis Marshall, the president of the American Jewish Committee, and Lucien Wolf, the cofounder of the League of British Jews, succeeded in keeping the plight of European Jewry in the headlines—and in the minds of key decision makers and power brokers—by publicizing Polish mistreatment of Jews and highlighting the need for the Polish state to grant Jews national minority rights akin to those they enjoyed by law in Ukraine.[50]

Their task became more urgent when news emerged that on April 5 in Pinsk, Polish troops had broken up an assembly of Jews discussing the distribution of matzo for the coming Passover holidays. Mistaking the meeting for a Bolshevik conspiracy, they had executed thirty-five Jewish men and assaulted and robbed dozens of others.[51] Pinsk, largely isolated by the Prypiat River and marshes surrounding the city, was in disputed territory between Belarus, Ukraine, and Poland. The city had fallen under Bolshevik rule in January, but the Bolsheviks had only been able to hold it for two months before the Polish infantry arrived, taking charge without a fight. In its report on the incident, the Polish military justified the April 5 executions on the grounds that "a predominant proportion of Jews in Pinsk sympathize with the Bolshevik movement and are unfavourably disposed to the Polish Army and the idea of Polish statehood in general." It also blamed the Bolsheviks for having "ensured that the ruling class in the town consisted only of Jews, who

Jews marching to protest Polish pogroms

took over the most important public positions" while the city had been under Bolshevik rule.[52] The report failed to note that the twenty-two thousand Jews in the city made up 85 percent of its population; even under the Bolsheviks, they were in fact statistically underrepresented in positions of power. But it was a novelty to see any Jews in charge at all.

The incident in Pinsk was followed by the murder of seventeen Jews in Lida during the city's occupation by Polish troops, and by fighting in Vilnius that left sixty-five Jews dead on April 20, including the well-known Jewish writer and activist Ayzik Meyer Devenishski (better known by his pseudonym, A. Vayter). Both incidents, widely covered in the foreign press, further mobilized Jewish public opinion against Poland. With anti-Jewish violence in the news, the peacemakers in Paris took up the issue of minority rights again, devoting sessions over the Easter weekend to the subject. "Good Friday we spent about the Jews," wrote James Wycliffe Headlam-Morley, a member of the British delegation. "In the old days I believe the right method of spending

Good Friday was to massacre the Jews; this custom still prevails in Eastern Europe," he quipped.[53]

Polish patriots resented the international Jewish campaign for minority rights, viewing it as an effort to tarnish Polish heroism. Rather than take responsibility for the murder of Jewish civilians, many blamed the Jews for their alleged perfidy and failure to rejoice in the triumphant celebration of Polish statehood.[54] Roman Dmowski, the leader of Poland's far-right Endecja (National Democratic) movement and president of the National Polish Committee, saw the Jewish attempt to secure national rights as an untenable limitation on the sovereignty of the Polish state, and even as a betrayal of the Polish nation. A domineering figure with piercing eyes, Dmowski had spearheaded the 1912–1914 boycott of Jewish businesses in Poland and was widely blamed for placing antisemitism at the forefront of Polish political culture. Dmowski's vision of nationalism pitted nations against each other in an eternal struggle for survival. The Poles, he believed, had to contend not only with foreign adversaries but also with domestic enemies. Chief among these, in his mind, were the Jews, whose nature, according to Dmowski, rendered them unassimilable and parasitic.[55]

These attitudes were shared not only by ethnonationalists but also by cosmopolitan moderates like Ignacy Jan Paderewski, the renowned pianist who in January 1919 became the first prime minister and foreign minister of the Polish Republic and Poland's most potent weapon on the international stage. Paderewski charmed his fans during his many foreign visits; with his fluent French, German, and English, he presented a suave and cultured face of the new Poland. (The Steinway he played on a triumphant US tour is now owned by the Smithsonian.)[56] He cultivated Zinfandel at his California estate and gave charitably in support of music education around the world. His long flame-red shock of hair was instantaneously recognizable and even replicated in a popular children's toy—a windup wooden pianist whose hands would glide across a tiny grand with a turn of the key. Clemenceau, Lloyd George, Wilson, and Orlando all agreed that "no country could wish for a better advocate."[57] Colonel House, Wilson's assistant, commented that in the presence of Paderewski, the American president "did not want to offend the Poles as he thought more of the Poles than he did of the Jews."[58]

Paderewski felt a particular distaste for the more recent Jewish immigrants from Ukraine. These refugees from tsarism and Bolshevism, he argued, "came to us by the thousands and brought with them the very seeds of discord and hatred. The newcomers entered our country like conquerors."[59] He chastised the Jews of Warsaw for favoring Jewish candidates in elections to the Duma, for continuing to speak Yiddish, and for allegedly preferring the Russian language and culture to Polish.[60]

Paderewski was frustrated that his attempt to showcase the new Poland on the international stage as the genteel land of Chopin was

[MCCOOL / ALAMY STOCK PHOTO]

Polish prime minister Ignacy Jan Paderewski walks down the stairs at Trianon Palace after peace talks in Versailles

thwarted by Jewish demonstrations. He claimed to empathize with what he saw as the Jewish attraction to Bolshevism—"It is the penalty Eastern Europe is paying for the mistreatment of Jews in Russia in the past," he suggested—but he faulted the Jews for blaming the misdeeds of the tsars on the Polish state. "New Poland has given the Jew every liberty of the Gentile," he asserted.[61] As a result, he was unwilling to take responsibility for the anti-Jewish violence that had accompanied Polish independence and instead drew upon the familiar theme of Jewish disloyalty. "The present discord," he claimed, "is caused by the attitude adopted by the Jews, who, considering the Polish cause as being a lost one, on many occasions sided with Poland's enemies."[62]

Paderewski opposed the Great Powers' efforts to enshrine minority rights in the Polish constitution on the grounds that such a move singled out Poland for censure. Jews, he granted, could certainly be afforded complete equality of rights as individuals, but should not have the added privilege of separate schools and an autonomous religious organization of the kind set up by the Ukrainan Law on National Autonomy, as many Jews demanded. Poland, he assured the Supreme Council, had joined the West as a force of civilization, and with the West's support could serve as a firewall against the spread of Bolshevism.

THE PEACE TREATIES were already being finalized in Paris on May 1 when President Wilson requested that guarantees to the Jews be included in the terms. "The Jews were somewhat inhospitably regarded in Poland," he observed. In the ensuing discussion, the three world leaders offered their thoughts on the subject. Lloyd George suggested that "the Jews had themselves to blame to a considerable extent," to which Wilson responded that "they were only disloyal in countries where they were not treated properly." Lloyd George and Clemenceau agreed that in England and France the Jews "were very good citizens," and, referring to their penchant for commerce (and what he regarded as their monopolistic hold on certain industries), Clemenceau added that "in Poland, a Pole who wanted to carry out any transaction—for example, to buy a horse—would send for a Jew."[63] In the end, they agreed that when "properly treated" Jews could be productive citizens.

And so, over the weekend of May 2–4, the Great Powers instructed the Committee on New States to draft clauses ensuring the protection of national minorities, for insertion into the Allies' treaties with Poland as well as Romania. The newly created League of Nations was tasked with enforcing the terms. In addition to guaranteeing national minorities equality before the law, the new states would be required to provide them with an equitable share of public funds for the purpose of managing and controlling their own educational, charitable, and religious institutions. An additional clause would specifically prohibit the state from compelling Jews to perform any act that violated their Sabbath.[64]

In order to press their case and force Poland to accede to the Allies' demands, Marshall organized a demonstration in New York on May 21, followed by a mass rally at Madison Square Garden. The *New York Times* estimated that between 150,000 and 200,000 people took to the streets for the event. "Men and women began to put black bands on their sleeves by way of mourning for their fellows murdered in Poland. The demand for black bands soon outran the supply. The excitement ran so high in some quarters that the crowds began tearing umbrellas to pieces in order to tie strips of black on their arms."[65] The philanthropist Nathan Strauss, who had made his fortune as a co-owner of the behemoth department store R. H. Macy & Company, opened the rally. "Nations which permit persecution of the Jews will themselves come to an ignominious end," he predicted. As the campaign went on, Marshall enlisted the support of sympathetic congressmen, including Isaac Siegel and Fiorello La Guardia, who introduced resolutions on the House floor on behalf of the Jews of Poland. Secretary of the Navy Josephus Daniels declared that "America has committed itself to the welfare of the world and stands against autocracy and cruelty no matter in what land. The day will never come when America will not with all the power behind it stand against injustice and inhumanity in any part of the world."[66]

The American ambassador to Poland, Hugh Gibson, though, was having difficulty confirming the rumors of mass anti-Jewish violence.

He found that despite terrible episodes in the major Polish-controlled cities of Warsaw, Vilnius, and Lviv, the violence in Poland was less widespread than the press and Jewish public opinion had intimated; he was beginning to suspect that the accusations were an "attempt of American Jews to hurt Poland in the eyes of the world," or even part of a German-Russian plot being orchestrated by the Jews. He recognized that there were instances of Jews being killed in Poland, but in private letters he downplayed the violence. The reality, he proposed in an argument that hardly bolstered his case, was that the situation of the Jews in Poland was no worse than that of the Black people in the United States. Indeed, in 1919, hundreds of African Americans were murdered in racial riots throughout the United States, the deadliest of which took place in Elaine, Arkansas—an incident that reminded some of the pogroms. American Jews were making a big deal out of nothing, he charged. And Polish Jewry would eventually pay for their troublemaking: "If the people in their resentment do rise up and massacre Jews on a scale never before known, the blood guilt will be on the foreign Jews who with wicked disregard of the facts or the danger to human lives have played with this tremendously delicate situation."[67]

— 10 —

Warlords

As world Jewry continued to press for minority rights in Poland, the status of Jews in Ukraine—where those rights had already been guaranteed—continued to worsen. Petliura's government was virtually homeless, nominally based in Kamyanets-Podilskyi but in practice forced to meander around Podilia in a railway car. "There were moments when the Ukrainian government exercised authority only over the few miles of railroad tracks occupied by the official cars, in which its cabinet, party, officials and 'troops' were temporarily living. Something like a Gypsy camp," wrote Vynnychenko from Vienna, to where he had emigrated after his resignation.[1] "It was impossible at that time to confirm whether the government's orders were being fulfilled in places farther than a few miles from its location," Margolin similarly recalled.[2] By spring of 1919, the chief otaman had largely lost control of the armies he once commanded, as his territorial claim was squeezed further and further between the Bolsheviks in the north and east, the Whites in the south, and the Poles in the west. A typhus epidemic had decimated his army, and his soldiers had no shoes, no clothing, and no medicine. Petliura could rely upon fifteen thousand soldiers at most—the rest of his army, in Margolin's words, had "turned into hungry bands sustaining themselves with pillage and extortion."[3]

In this power vacuum, charismatic peasant leaders emerged to take charge. These ranged from local strongmen, who lorded over a couple of villages with the help of their kinsmen, to regional warlords like Grigoriev, who at one point managed to amass up to ten thousand well-armed men organized into military units that rivaled those of the Red Army. Dozens of mini-otamans ruled fiefdoms, often loosely grouped under the command of more prominent warlords, each with his own territory and his own subservient regional chieftains. Some of these insurgent rebels received direct commands from their superiors; others simply mimicked the actions of fighters they admired, taking inspiration from proclamations that haphazardly reached them on yellowed newsprint.[4]

Most of the warlords had first tested the waters during the summer of 1918 insurgency against Skoropadskyi and the Germans. Many had some military experience in the Russian imperial army, or later in Petliura's army, but deserted as the promise of a redistribution of noble land to the peasants faded. Instead they formed militant bands to raid urban centers and take aristocratic estates by force. Often they allied themselves with one or more of the parties claiming authority over Ukraine— the Directory, the Whites, or the Reds—but ultimately clashed with the intelligentsia, autocratic generals, and urban workers whose interests each of the established militaries represented. None of the organized armies was able to excite the countryside as much as the regional warlords did; they shared the villagers' interests and understood their needs the most. The otamans spoke for the countryside.

Many of the warlords leveraged anti-Jewish sentiments and the promise of Jewish loot to gain popular support. They convinced their rural followers that the only obstacle barring the peasants from their rightful ownership of the land was the Jews. Jewish Bolsheviks, they charged, had co-opted the peasant revolution; Jews were profiting from farm labor by speculating on grain and were destroying the countryside by turning churches into communes. The only way to fulfill the promise of the revolution was for the peasants to take their due by force.

As state power faded, many peasants—particularly young and disillusioned fighters—took matters into their own hands and joined the insurgency headed by these charismatic strongmen. Some did so enthusiastically; others were coerced, sometimes as child warriors. These peasant bands attacked the heavily Jewish urban centers, often targeting Jewish shops and stores and leaving bodies in their wake. To the peasants they were anti-Bolshevik raids; to the Jewish victims, they were pogroms. Between January and March 1919, approximately 150 such incidents took place, but by the summer the number had increased to about 90 each month. One survey counted 148 "pogroms" and "excesses" in the month of May, and 159 in August. Most of these occurred in the province of Kyiv, where the Bolsheviks' hold was tenuous and stable state power wanting.[5]

Although there were numerous local bands of insurgents, each ruling its own circumscribed territory, some of the largest gangs were those of Grigoriev, the Sokolovsky brothers, Ilya Struk, and a commander known as Zelenyi. The pogroms they perpetrated terrorized the Jews of Ukraine throughout much of the summer.

AFTER GRIGORIEV'S CAPTURE of Odesa, Commander Antonov-Ovseyenko and the Bolshevik military leadership realized that he was clearly "going rogue" and had to be tamed. Antonov-Ovseyenko quickly came to understand the true nature of the insurgent he had backed when his assistant, Anatolii Skachko, reported on the conditions at Grigoriev's headquarters: "I found, instead of a staff, a filthy freight car and a swarm of unorganized bandits . . . a cistern of spirits from which everyone drank. Two or three hundred half-drunken soldiers. Five hundred freight cars littered with all kinds of goods—spirits, benzene, sugar, cloth." "My impression," Skachko concluded, "is that it is impossible to trust Grigoriev. It is necessary to liquidate him."[6]

On May 7, Lenin's deputy Lev Kamenev, who happened to be in Ukraine traveling in an armored train with an entourage of Bolshevik officials, made contact with Grigoriev in the hopes of convincing him to coordinate military action with the Red Army. When Grigoriev failed to show at Skachko's headquarters at the agreed-upon time, Kamenev came to the obvious conclusion and cabled Lenin that Grigoriev had mutinied.

The Bolshevik military leadership saw Grigoriev's rebellion as an existential threat: his peasant-based insurgency was undermining Bolshevik influence in the region by competing with the Bolsheviks for recruits and for the loyalty of the rural masses. Antonov-Ovseyenko immediately issued a statement that traitors would be "dealt with like maggots";[7] Trotsky telegrammed the Central Committee of the Communist Party, calling for the "radical, implacable liquidation of the partisan movement";[8] and the Central Committee ordered the mobilization of twenty thousand workers to fight the insurgency. "The fate of the revolution depends on the success of this mobilization,"[9] declared Lenin and Trotsky.

Over the next couple of weeks, Grigoriev advanced toward Katerynoslav, conquering a string of towns south of Kyiv: Horodyshche, Rotmistrivka, Matusiv, Smila, and the city of Elizavetgrad. He plastered every town he occupied with manifestos that drew upon classic antisemitic tropes, characterizing his erstwhile Bolshevik allies as Christ-killers, foreign lackeys, and bloodsuckers. "Instead of land and freedom, they have forcefully imposed upon you a commune, special police, and commissars from the Moscow gluttons and the lands where they crucified Christ," declared one.[10] "Peasants and workers! You are ninety-two percent of Ukraine. And who rules over you? Those who suck the blood of the people," proclaimed another.[11]

Rousing anti-Jewish hatred was Grigoriev's most potent weapon. Along the railway lines, his troops singled out Jewish passengers, robbed and stripped them, and threw them off moving trains. As his men moved through the districts of Cherkasy and Elizavetgrad, they massacred the Jewish populations they encountered; nearly sixty incidents were documented in approximately forty villages and towns. The total death toll in these encounters has been estimated at six thousand.[12]

One of the worst incidents took place in Cherkasy, a shipping hub located on the western bank of the Dnipro, midway between Katerynoslav and Kyiv. When the Bolsheviks took the city in early April, they had arrested approximately fifty people suspected of counter-revolutionary activity and executed at least ten of them, including a few locally prominent Ukrainian intellectuals.[13] Many observers noted that all of the arrested were Christians, including two priests—while, by contrast, the local heads of the communist party and of the Cheka counterintelligence division, as well as the commissar of justice, were all of Jewish heritage. It mattered little that the head of the Cheka itself and the head of the Bolshevik executive committee came from Christian families, or that the Jewish Bolshevik officials had no relationship with the local Jewish community in Cherkasy, or even that one of the officials was out of town when the arrests and executions had taken place; the presence of three Jews in high office within the city's Bolshevik government fostered the narrative that Jews were attacking Christians.[14]

As a result, when Grigoriev's troops surrounded the city and announced that they had come to free Cherkasy of Jews, they received support not only from ordinary townsmen but even from many of the Red Army's worker and peasant recruits garrisoned in the city. These local recruits had recently been dispatched to put down a pogrom in a neighboring town and were "completely demoralized," in the words of one witness, wondering why they were being sent to fight their Christian brethren in defense of the Jews.[15] Now, motivated by Grigoriev's calls for a peasant revolution, the entire Second Soviet regiment and half of the "Spartacus" Communist battalion deserted their barracks and joined the insurgents against their Jewish commanders.

Having lost the support of the garrison, the Bolshevik leadership fled on horseback and in carts.[16] Before departing, they distributed weapons to the trade unions, allowing for the formation of a motley militia of cobblers, needle-makers, and tailors—most of whom were, as was typical of these professions, Jewish. The sight of an army of Jews prepared to defend the city bolstered popular suspicions that the Bolsheviks and the Jews were one and the same. In the words of one member of the trade union, "People started to talk" at the sight of "a worker's detachment made up almost exclusively of Jews."[17] The detachment, though, was poorly armed—"many Jewish soldiers received in total two cartridges. The rifles were also in foul condition."[18]

On the morning of Friday, May 16, on the outskirts of the city near the sugar factory, the trade union militia, fighting "without machine guns, without cartridges, and without any communication with headquarters,"[19] met Grigoriev's forces. In the midst of the melee, Grigoriev's men convinced the handful of Christian workers in the trade union militia that they must not fight a war "between brothers," that there was "no difference between their goals." The Christians on both sides realized that they shared an enemy in the "Jews and Communists," who were duping them into fighting their own brethren.[20] With all the Christian soldiers firmly on one side, Grigoriev's men opened fire. According to the final report on the pogrom prepared by the Red Cross, "they killed not only Red soldiers, but anybody who looked like a Jew. The Jews who were taken in the field were immediately shot."[21]

By the afternoon, Grigoriev's insurgents had entered the center of the city, where local women and children directed them to Jewish homes. The soldiers arrested Jewish men over the age of sixteen, tortured them, and so disfigured them "that only their relatives could recognize them."[22] They claimed to be searching for communists, but at least one soldier made clear the real goal: "We don't need communists; we need Jews."[23]

The next morning, the bloodshed resumed. According to Abram Shenderov, four soldiers entered his house at four a.m. on May 17, shouting about communists and Jews. His son David, who answered the door, managed to pay off the soldiers, and they left. But at noon another gang came knocking. David again answered the door; this time the invaders shot him dead on the spot, then killed eighteen people in the corridor of the building.

Buzia Gurevich similarly testified that when soldiers shot her husband and two sons, Srul and Samuel, early in the morning of May 17, they declared: "You are a communist; you want a commune."[24] A man by the name of Isaac Trotsky reported that he was hiding in a nearby cellar with about two dozen other Jews when a servant came down and told them to go upstairs—the soldiers, he announced, were searching for communists. As Trotsky made his way toward the stairs, near the end of the line, he heard a shot and saw the body of a student who had been hiding with him tumble down the steps. He hid again, and managed to conceal himself when the soldiers searched the cellar. He noted that the soldiers had by then given up the pretense of searching for communists: "There must still be Jews in the cellar," he heard one of them call to his comrades.[25]

The sixty-year-old wood merchant Getzel Rotmistrovsky stated that at six o'clock in the evening of May 18 four military personnel showed up at his cellar, where several neighbors had taken refuge. The intruders demanded valuables, boots, and shoes. A half hour later, the soldiers returned and ordered the men in the cellar to accompany them to the station, reassuring the women that their detained husbands and fathers would be safe so long as they were not communists. On the street, the prisoners joined a convoy of eleven other Jewish

Victims of the pogrom in Cherkasy

[YIVO INSTITUTE FOR JEWISH RESEARCH]

men aged nineteen to sixty heading toward the station. The soldiers insulted them, beat them with clubs, forced them to strip down to their underwear, and made them sing songs for the amusement of passersby.[26] Rotmistrovsky was fortunate: a man who recognized him at the station shoved him into a departing railway car and locked the door. Rotmistrovsky appealed for help to villagers he saw through a window on the train as it rolled through the countryside, but nobody came to his aid during the night. Finally, when the train reached Smila in the morning, a longshoreman he knew spotted him and brought him a sheet to cover his nakedness.

Rotmistrovsky survived, but eighteen of the people who had been with him—including his two sons, thirty-three-year-old Sruel and nineteen-year-old Shmer—were killed at the Cherkasy station.[27] Others reported seeing another twenty-eight bodies on the way to the station, bringing the total number of casualties in the vicinity to forty-six.[28] "Along the road, toward the station, bodies of Jews were lying about," recalled one witness. "Everywhere were traces of blood and brains; papers and passport books lay around."[29]

Throughout the pogrom, as Grigoriev's men arrested and shot Jewish men, they encouraged onlookers—Christian women and children—to raid the apartments of their victims and scavenge for any goods left behind. Nunia Krasnopolsky, who was mistaken for a Christian, described how one soldier handed her a sack and said, "Go and loot." V. Petrov, the former chair of the city council, noted that "the local petty bourgeoisie, women and children, readily took part in the plundering, pointed out Jewish houses to the soldiers, etc."[30] Marusya Ukrainskaia, who was at the station, also recognized locals mingling with the drunken soldiers: "Boys and girls from the Cherkasy high school, officers, and people who had social standing. All this assembly was dancing to the sound of a gramophone. Shouts, tumult, and the most unrestrained merriment."[31] Several witnesses noted in their testimonies that many members of the professional classes who joined the insurgents had parents and relatives who had been arrested by the Cheka.[32] Now was their opportunity to avenge the indignities the Bolsheviks had imposed upon their families.

As the pogrom raged in Cherkasy, a Soviet counteroffensive was advancing from the south against Grigoriev. The Red Army took back Katerynoslav on May 14, Kremenchuk on May 19, and Aleksandriia on May 21–22. On May 21, when a Bolshevik armored steamship shelled Cherkasy from the Dnipro River, the peasant soldiers fighting with Grigoriev melted into the countryside. As Red Army reinforcements moved back into the city, the remnants of the Soviet Second Regiment and the rebellious Spartacus battalion quickly reaffirmed their loyalty. Within weeks the same soldiers and police officers who had participated in the pogrom—now rebranded, once again, as Red soldiers—were patrolling the streets with the same rifles they had used to execute the city's Jews.[33]

By the time Grigoriev left Cherkasy on May 21, the names of 617 murdered Jewish victims had been recorded, likely only a fraction of the total number of casualties.[34] Three thousand houses had been plundered. The Jewish population, which had once dominated the city's trade in wood, iron, sugar, lumber, and salt, had been decimated.

AFTER THE CHERKASY pogrom, the Bolsheviks were determined to be done with Grigoriev entirely. On May 26, Lenin ordered the Red Army to disarm his band by "shooting on the spot, without mercy, every single person concealing even a single rifle."[35] The war with Grigoriev dominated the headlines of the official party paper, *Izvestiia*. The front page of one issue had a banner headline, UKRAINIAN LESSONS, over the transcript of a speech Trotsky had delivered, signaling the importance the Bolshevik leadership attached to the Red Army's war against insurgents in Ukraine. As Trotsky explained, oppressed people without an organized military acting on their behalf naturally gravitate toward charismatic leaders, creating the type of cult of personality he saw in the Ukrainian insurgent movement. But, he said, those leaders soon turn against the interests of the working people. The Red Army was the working people's only true defender. "Guerrilla warfare has outlived itself and become a reactionary force. We must put an end to it at any cost," he concluded, urging the peasants and workers to abandon the insurgency and enlist instead in the Red Army.[36]

The Bolshevik leadership also undertook a campaign against antisemitism. On May 14, *Pravda* published a front-page article warning TO BE AGAINST THE JEWS IS TO BE FOR THE TSAR,[37] which it followed up the next month with another article on the dangers of pogroms.[38] The party paper, *Bolshevik*, was even more active, running weekly articles educating against antisemitism. At the same time, the Commissariat of National Affairs collected and published information on pogroms, documenting 120 pogroms between March and May with an estimated fifteen thousand fatalities. (These reports deliberately understated the involvement of the Red Army in anti-Jewish violence.) The campaign culminated in August with the establishment of a Committee for the Struggle Against Antisemitism within the Commissariat of Enlightenment. The committee was entrusted with the task of teaching workers and soldiers about the dangers of antisemitism by publishing brochures and leaflets, organizing lectures, and addressing military units.[39]

The Bolsheviks had made a strategic decision to crack down on antisemitic violence and language, in part as a means of recruiting the Jewish population to their cause. And their public stance against antisemitism and pogroms did indeed attract many Jews to their ranks, further enhancing the public association between Jews and Bolsheviks. In August, for instance, a group of prominent Jewish political activists within the Bund joined the Communist Party, including Dovid Lipets, the former mayor of Berdychiv.[40] Lipets eventually settled in Moscow, enlisted in the Red Army, and became a high-level Soviet diplomat.[41] His path was typical. Throughout the summer, Jewish youth flocked to join the Red Army, encouraged to do so by a Jewish Military Section tasked with enlisting Jews, and by their own desire for vengeance. As the historian Leonard Schapiro recalled, "In the Klinovka station I was surprised to see a Red Army company composed entirely of Jews and even including some wearing earlocks. These were yeshiva students from Proskuriv who joined the Red Army after Petliura's riots in order to take revenge."[42] Another memoirist wrote of "Jewish youth

[who] leave the *shtetls* and run to Kyiv for one purpose—to get into the Red Army." He doubted the commitment of the new recruits to party ideology, however, saying they were really enlisting because they preferred to become martyrs rather than be murdered hiding in cellars and attics. "They are not Bolsheviks," he wrote; "they go to the Red Army because there one can die with a 'gun in hand.'"[43]

By midsummer, Grigoriev's fortunes were in decline. The desperate warlord sent out feelers to Nestor Makhno, the most powerful and ambitious of the otamans in the Ukrainian southeast. Makhno, who famously rode around in a *tachanka*—a peasant cart outfitted with a machine gun—ruled a vast quasi-state from his base in the southeastern town of Hulyaipole, where he managed largely to maintain his independence from the Bolsheviks, the Whites, and the Directory.[44] He was the archetypal revolutionary peasant warlord, calling upon the countryside to crush the cities; Isaac Babel wrote of his "hay carts lined up in military formation to conquer towns."[45] Makhno's troops had robbed and killed Jews on occasion but were generally more hostile to the German Mennonite colonists in the south of Ukraine.[46] Motivated more by anarchist principles than a desire for loot, Makhno dismissed Grigoriev as an antisemite and a common criminal.

Having discovered that Grigoriev had also been conducting secret negotiations with the Whites, Makhno came to the same conclusion as Antonov-Ovseyenko—that Grigoriev could not be trusted. He concocted a plan to expose Grigoriev by agreeing to meet the warlord for a public debate. On July 27, 1919, the two came together in a village near Aleksandriia in front of an assembly of thousands of peasants, many of whom were part of Makhno's army. All shared an antipathy toward the Bolsheviks, but Grigoriev's willingness to forge an alliance with the Whites—the party of the old landlords—was anathema to the crowd of peasant revolutionaries. When Makhno angrily accused Grigoriev of being an "enemy of the people" in league with counter-revolutionaries, Grigoriev reached for his gun. Shots rang out.

There are conflicting reports about who exactly fired the bullet that felled Grigoriev, but according to one witness, within a split second of

Grigoriev grabbing his weapon, Makhno's assistant, Semen Karetnik, "shot him with a Colt revolver, while Makhno himself shouted 'Death to the Otaman!' and also shot him." The shooting of Grigoriev was witnessed by the entire gathering of peasants.[47] The next day Makhno issued a statement justifying the killing and declaring, "We cherish the hope that now no one will be found who will sanction Jewish pogroms. . . . Down with Jewish pogroms! Long live the revolutionary uprising of Ukraine!"[48]

To the north of Grigoriev's territory, the Sokolovsky brothers lorded over much of the road between Kyiv and Zhytomyr. Growing up in Horbuliv, a village of about six hundred families a few miles from Zhytomyr,[49] Lesyk Sokolovsky and his siblings had been raised on hostility toward the Jews; those who knew Lesyk as a child, for instance, reported that he used to throw rocks and mud at the windows of the thirty Jewish houses in the village.[50] Lesyk, Mitko, and Vassili had all joined the military when their schooling was interrupted by the Great War. After the boys returned from the front, they organized a division of Free Cossacks, leading the local peasants under the popular slogan "land and freedom" and urging them to take up arms against the Germans and seize their landlords' properties.

When the Germans abandoned the market town of Radomyshl in November 1918, sixteen-year-old Lesyk gathered together a group of teens from Horbuliv and the surrounding villages and raided the town. They robbed the Jewish shops, where the tailors, cobblers, glaziers, and coopers worked and sold their wares. Like much of Ukraine, Radomyshl district was starkly divided between town and country: the urban center of about twenty-two thousand people was 63 percent Jewish and Yiddish-speaking, whereas the population of the surrounding countryside, where Horbuliv was located, was 89 percent Christian and overwhelmingly Ukrainian-speaking.[51] Most of the stores selling groceries, dry goods, and hardware were owned by Jews, as were four of the five tanneries, both of the mills, and the foundry, which produced hammers, threshers, and cultivator tools.[52] Radomyshl was particularly known for its coopers, who fashioned barrels for storing everything from honey to herring to water, as well as large casks for transporting drinking water on horseback from the river, and even wooden bathtubs.[53] Virtually the only business in town not owned by Jews was the brewery—it was owned by a Czech and a German.[54] In regions like this, Jews and townsmen were nearly synonymous, so Lesyk's campaigns against the towns could also be interpreted as attacks on the Jews.

In late November, Lesyk assembled his followers and urged them to join in the fight against Bolshevism by liberating nearby Korostyshiv—where half of the ten thousand residents were Jewish—from what he called the "Jewish Council." Upon attacking the town, Lesyk demanded a massive monetary contribution.[55] However, the stoneworkers at the Korostyshiv quarry, many of whom identified with the Bolsheviks and had formed a Military Revolutionary Committee, ambushed Lesyk, killing him and two other leaders of his band. The rest of the young peasants fled, leaving Lesyk lying dead in a field. It took three days for Lesyk's father to find his body.[56]

With Lesyk's death, his older brother, Mitko, took over leadership of the gang. It was early January 1919, and word had reached Horbuliv of the unrest in Zhytomyr. Mitko mobilized his men to assist Petliura's forces in defeating the Bolsheviks. Riding around the neighboring villages, he drummed up troops under the slogans "Beat the Jews—Save the Christian Faith"[57] and "All Yids are Bolsheviks."[58] Hundreds of Christian peasants joined the group. (Despite the rhetoric, a handful of Jews reportedly did as well.) They traveled the thirty miles southwest toward Zhytomyr, helping themselves to abandoned German weapons and supplies along the way. In Zhytomyr, Mitko's gang joined in the pogrom raging in the city and his men enriched themselves with loot.[59]

For the rest of the winter, Mitko controlled the countryside around Radomyshl and Korostyshiv from his base in Horbuliv, and urged more fighters to join his band. He accepted anybody who could ride a horse and fire a rifle but mostly attracted young, disgruntled peasants—traumatized by the violence of the war and inspired by the promises of taking back the land and the churches from the Jewish Bolsheviks.[60]

Relations between the urban Jews and rural Christians were deteriorating quickly. According to one testimony, "In Korostyshiv, Malyn, and Radomyshl, when anybody caught a Horbuliv gentile, the Jews would beat or kill him. The Horbuliv peasants couldn't come into the towns."[61] M. Feshchenko-Chopivsky, who led a mounted regiment under Mitko, recalled that villagers were turned back from the markets and warned: "Tell your thieves that the Bolsheviks will soon come and burn down your villages."[62] The peasants, while continuing to support Mitko's mission, were becoming frustrated that their access to markets was restricted.[63]

On March 10, Mitko and a small detachment of his men rode into Radomyshl, confiscated weapons, rounded up Jews in the street, and took them to the outskirts of town, where they shot them on charges of Bolshevism. Within a day, the group was forced to retreat as the Reds retook the town. But over the next two weeks, Mitko succeeded in securing the backing of over a thousand men—mostly former soldiers—and procuring nearly two dozen machine guns and two cannons abandoned by the Germans. On March 25, he moved into Radomyshl again. Faced with such a force of arms, the town council turned itself over to Mitko, who declared the establishment of the "Radomyshl Insurgent Republic of Sokolovsky"—a republic that ruled over the town for all of six days.[64] Many of the Jews had fled when the Bolsheviks retreated, leaving Mitko and his men with empty houses and shops to loot.[65] But those who stayed suffered intensely. During his brief reign, Mitko, together with local peasants and his military men, robbed Jewish shops and houses, extracted contributions from the city's remaining Jews, and murdered at least thirty-one of them in the process.[66]

In April, the Red Army again took Radomyshl and issued an order for Sokolovsky's arrest.[67] According to Feshchenko-Chopivsky, the Bolsheviks unleashed a "senseless red terror" in the city, setting up a Cheka that executed dozens of citizens without trial. The Cheka, he asserts, was "made up mostly of Jews" who "began to perform dirty work . . . they weren't even ashamed to play the role of executioners." Feshchenko-Chopivsky cites a former newspaper salesman named Renek, in particular, as being especially ruthless. It was Renek, he claims, who was responsible for the murder of Baron Victor von Ungern-Sternberg, a retired nobleman of German origin who had previously served as a communal leader but played no role in politics at the time of his arrest.[68] The killing of the venerable nobleman made a distinct mark on public consciousness in Radomyshl, but it was the rumor that the Bolsheviks were targeting the church that aroused the most passion among the peasantry. Feshchenko-Chopivsky notes that "several times I heard stories from peasants about Bolsheviks persecuting religion, that when they conquered villages, they would turn the churches into stables. The righteous anger of the people against the Jewish-Commissars was especially manifest in this regard."[69]

In the middle of May, around the Jewish festival of Lag Ba-omer, leaflets appeared in the streets of Radomyshl warning that the Bolsheviks were removing icons from the churches and replacing them with pictures of Hasidic rebbes. The priest refuted the accusation, but rumors of an impending Bolshevik attack on the church spread quickly. Mitko, whose supporters may have been responsible for the leaflets in the first place, took advantage of the situation and barged into the town with a large band of peasant fighters, demanding to know where the rebbe lived. At six a.m. on Sunday, May 25, they made a beeline for the home of fifty-seven-year-old Avrom Yehoshua Heschl Twersky, better known as the Malyner Rebbe. Ripping off the window shutters, they smashed the windowpanes with their rifle butts and climbed through the broken glass to attack the Hasidic leader. According to a family member's account of the episode, "The rebbe and his eldest son tried to give them some money and watches and begged them not to disturb anybody in the house. In a minute, a shot rang out and the rebbe fell severely wounded. He did not live long and left this world calling out psalms." As word of the rebbe's death spread through the town, local peasants flooded into the house to gloat over the dead body and the mourning family. During one of these encounters, the rebbe's son, Mordechai, was also fatally shot.[70]

The murder of the rebbe was only one part of a terrible pogrom.

Over that weekend, peasants under Mitko's command reportedly killed three to five hundred Jews in Radomyshl and the surrounding villages, although the names of just forty-four were recorded.[71] As is the case with many of these massacres, we will never know the precise count of victims.

On Monday, May 26, as Red Army forces approached, Mitko called for an end to the violence and ordered the Jews to bury their dead. In an effort to avoid further unrest, he prohibited a large gathering at the burial of the rebbe, limiting the number of people in attendance to a minyan of ten, and barred the rebbe's surviving children from attending.[72] As the funeral procession moved through the streets, gunfire from fighting between Mitko's men and Bolshevik forces moving into the city could be heard; the pallbearers momentarily abandoned the coffin and ran for shelter. When they returned to finish the final journey of the Malyner Rebbe, they did so under a Red guard.

The Bolshevik commissar warned the Jews that he only had a small entourage of soldiers with him and that the Red Army's hold on the town was tenuous. The Jewish population, he advised, had best seek shelter elsewhere. According to one account, "thousands of people with terrified faces, with little children clutching their hands, left town. Among them were the rebbe's orphaned children and grandchildren. And with pitiable faces, they set out on a great restless wandering."[73] Sheyndl Vaynshteyn, a twelve-year-old girl from Radomyshl, shared her story with aid workers in Kyiv: "After the Bolsheviks came in and told us to flee, we spent the night in an inn. From there we went to Korostyshiv and stayed there a month before we returned home. But there was nobody left in Radomyshl, so we came to Kyiv, where we became ill with typhus and my mother and sister died."[74] Another witness reported that "from that day on, Radomyshl was deserted. The city turned into a graveyard. The main streets have become overgrown with grass, empty stores stand with open doors. The doors and windows of homes are boarded up. There are no more than two thousand Jews left in the city; the remaining ten thousand have scattered in all directions."[75]

Defeated in Radomyshl, Mitko and his forces fled to Zhytomyr and then north to Chernyakhiv. On June 20, they captured the town and unleashed a pogrom that killed 18 Jews.[76] The Bolsheviks soon took Chernyakhiv as well, however, and executed several members of Mitko's band. Mitko managed to escape into the forest, where his insurgent brigade regrouped. Throughout the summer, the gang surfaced in the towns and villages of Zhytomyr district, where they conducted "forcible requisitions" to secure provisions for their forest camps. These raids were often accompanied by Jewish fatalities: 20 dead in Borshchahivka, 80 dead in Skvyra, 148 dead in Pryluky.[77] The Red Cross estimated that Sokolovsky's gangs murdered about 3,000 Jews in sixty-two localities.[78]

On August 8, 1919, Mitko was finally captured and executed.[79] A detachment of about one hundred Bolsheviks attacked his funeral procession in Horbuliv and arrested the mourners.[80] By late summer, as Bolshevik rule solidified in the region, local support for the insurgency declined; the powerful metalworkers' union of Radomyshl turned against the Sokolovsky family, blaming them for ruining the village economy and drowning the region in blood.[81] Still, Mitko's brother Vassili, taking over leadership of the band, continued the rampage. In retaliation for a Red Army attack on their base in Horbuliv, Vassili's men executed the remaining fifteen Jews of the village. They forced the butcher Noyekh Zimmerman and his son Yaakov to dig a pit and then shot them, their bodies falling into the open grave. Shlomo and Etel Nogen, the tailor Bunem Krayzman, the storekeeper Aba Muravsky, and others were subsequently shot and dropped into the pit as well.[82]

A detachment of twenty Bolshevik cavalrymen from Radomyshl captured Vassili later that month and executed him.[83] Leadership of the Sokolovsky gang was then taken over by his sister Aleksandra, who fought under the name Marysia and seems to have retained the loyalty of her brothers' followers, at least until she fled Ukraine at some point in 1919 or 1920. There are unconfirmed reports that she later surfaced in Canada.[84]

ILYA STRUK, ANOTHER powerful warlord, controlled the area around Chernobyl, a city set in the Prypiat marshes at the confluence of the

Dnipro, the Prypiat, and the Uzh rivers north of Kyiv. The city was famous for its Hasidic dynasties long before it gained notoriety for its nuclear reactor. The five thousand Jews in the city constituted 60 percent of the total population. During market days, every Monday and Friday, peasants came to town with carts overflowing with grain. Jewish shopkeepers opened their stalls to sell dry goods, fur, hardware, watches, dishes, and hats. The blacksmiths and wheelwrights repaired the peasant carts and greased the axles with wood tar. On the twentieth of every month, the town held a regional fair, attracting peasants from all along the Dnipro between Chernobyl and Kyiv. Visitors stayed at one of the three inns, owned respectively by Lev Bregman, Mordukh Voloshin, and Meyer Gorodetsky. A factory in town produced agricultural and milling machinery and implements.[85] In other words, it was a typical midsize town.

Struk was born in 1896 into a peasant family in Grine, Hornostaipil district. At an early age he rebelled against what he regarded as the monotony of village life. He fell in love with Nat Pinkerton detective stories—an anonymously authored pulp fiction series set in America that was wildly popular in early twentieth-century Russia.[86] According to one report, from his father Struk "inherited a passion for hard drink and a life of adventure and danger."[87] He was clever and a quick learner, well read, and with an easy way about him. He spent two years in a provincial school, where one of his teachers convinced him to abandon his detective novels and instead devote himself to the Ukrainian national cause. He made a living as a private tutor, teaching Russian and Ukrainian grammar to village children, and supplemented his income with work as a clerk, a porter, and as a petty thief. In 1914, at the age of eighteen, still restless and dreaming of adventure, he enlisted in the navy and shipped out with the Baltic Fleet.

Two years later, Struk became a commissioned officer in an infantry brigade.[88] During the 1917 revolution, he deserted his unit and formed his own brigade of Free Cossacks. Under the Hetmanate he transported goods from Hornostaipil and Chernobyl to Kyiv and back, easing his way into the criminal underworld that controlled much of the transport of goods into and out of the region. He traded in counterfeit currency and used it to fleece state warehouses, acquiring a small fortune and an armed entourage. At one point he was briefly arrested after killing two officials during a heist of a post office and telegraph station.

A hero to many peasants, Struk attracted a following of between six and eight hundred insurgents, described by one observer as "former soldiers unable to return to their homelands, and the dregs of society— peasants, former professional thieves, vagrants, and so on."[89] Another recalled: "They were peasants of the neighboring villages, mostly former soldiers, or simply scum with a very bad reputation. Several young peasants with a penchant for the freewheeling life and a lack of acreage from our village also attached themselves to Struk's band."[90] Most noticeably, they were young, traumatized by war, and looking for adventure. Struk himself lived a life of revelry, fueled by theft and murder. His home in Grine, adorned with stolen luxuries, became known as Tsarskoe Selo ("tsar's village") after the town containing the grand palace of the Russian imperial family outside St. Petersburg.[91] He presented himself as a stylish don: he was popular, slim, well spoken, and a virtuoso on the harmonica. Most importantly, he could drink with the best of them.

In a series of photos Struk staged at the height of his power, the young soldiers he gathered around him seek to present themselves as proud Ukrainian Cossacks, armed with bayonets, sabers, and revolvers. But they are betrayed by their ill-fitting clothes and by their makeshift backdrop, a tattered curtain clumsily tacked onto a wooden batten. In one of the photos, a young man in a *papakha* sits on a toy horse—a staple of Ukrainian folk art—holding a revolver in his hand, the holster visible at his hip. One of the horse's legs is broken, forcing the insurgent to hold his foot firmly on the ground to balance himself. The image is comical: the steed resembles My Little Pony more than Bucephalus. Still, it's notable that these teenage warlords and brigands were interested enough in their public image that they saw fit to play dress-up in a photographic studio.[92]

We know a little more about some of Struk's men from the files the Cheka created when the Red Army took over the region and began

One of Struk's men
on a toy horse

punishing them for banditry. Vasily Boreslavsky, for instance, was born
in 1901 in Galicia. He was a drayman by trade and had served in the
military under Kerensky, Skoropadskyi, and Petliura. But he drew the
line at the Bolsheviks. Witnesses testified that during his robberies,
he refused to take Soviet currency, ripping it up and declaring contemptuously that he didn't need Jewish money.[93] Instead, he was after
Nikolaevkis—the gold coins with the portrait of Nicholas II that traded
for a premium during the civil war, when newer paper currencies were
trusted as little as the regimes that issued them.[94] He was branded a
"notorious bandit and robber" and was accused of murdering Jews
in the course of his plunder, claiming that they were hoarding cash for
speculation. In one instance, he was accused of leading "a number of
young Jews to a landfill, where they were later found dead."[95]

Like Grigoriev and Sokolovsky, Struk gained support by promising
to fulfill the original aspirations of the revolution—to distribute land

Struk's men posing in a
photo studio

and bread to the peasants—but with a specifically antisemitic interpretation. A copy of an undated order signed by Struk and addressed to
"Ukrainian and Russian People" states: "We have a common enemy.
The enemy is the Jews who want to take all of our wealth. We need to
wage a relentless war against them and deal with them decisively. . . .
Down with the Jews of Ukraine. Long live our national character."[96]
Another declaration used the proven technique of disparaging the
commander of the Red Army by using his original name: "As long as
a single Bronstein mercenary plunders our land, we will not lay down
our arms. . . . Trotsky-Bronstein destroys our churches, separates our
faithful from their fertile land, turns us into slaves for eternity."[97]

During the Hetmanate, Struk offered his services to the anti-
German fighters in the hopes they would supply him with arms. Oleksandr Udovychenko, who would become Petliura's deputy chief of
staff, responded favorably, noting on August 16, 1918, that together

they could fight "against our common enemy—the Jews."[98] The next week, Udovychenko recommended an alliance with Struk, noting that Struk had already shown his willingness to fight against "Jewish dominance."[99] Having acquired arms from the fleeing Germans, in December 1918 Struk pledged his allegiance to Petliura. According to one of his comrades in arms, "Struk was a great adventurist who often called himself a Ukrainian colonel and claimed to be close to Petliura and so on, but not even his friends believed that."[100] In reality, Petliura had little control over Struk or the other warlords whose bands he desperately enlisted into his dwindling army. Struk's goal was regional authority, and any alliances he sought were solely functional—meant to provide him with arms and respect.

Struk's power came from his control over the river traffic between Kyiv and Chernobyl. In January 1919, he and his men intercepted travelers on the Dnipro River, robbing them and throwing them off their ships, watching as they crashed through the ice into the freezing water. When Struk left in late February, townsmen hacked holes in the ice to retrieve the bodies. Witnesses recount seeing the bloated corpses, along with soggy identification papers and monetary notes, float to the surface when the river thawed.[101]

As Petliura's power faded toward March 1919, Struk switched sides again. His band became the Twentieth Soviet Regiment of the Ukrainian Front, and Struk returned to Chernobyl "in a sailor's uniform, with a red star on his chest and a military service cap, waving a red banner with the words 'Death to the bourgeoisie' and 'Long Live Soviet Power.'"[102] He embraced the slogans of the Bolsheviks, even as he continued to rally his followers against them.

Struk's anti-Jewish rhetoric shifted as well. He now branded Jews as capitalists and speculators, and at times accused them of being both Bolshevik and bourgeoisie, capitalist and communist simultaneously. In Hornostaipil, in April 1919, he issued an appeal to "those villages, towns and cities where Communist-Capitalist Jews and their dishonest servants and employees hold power and authority."[103] The villagers, he argued, needed to unite to protect themselves from "capitalist Jews, rich merchants and speculators." His appeal concluded:

"Let's stand together as friends for our faith, our dear land, and our freedom."[104] His insurgent fighters went on to kill forty-seven Jews in Hornostaipil, violence he justified by claiming that there can be no revolution without victims.[105] On another occasion, his men implied that the Communist Revolution was the Apocalypse foretold by Christ.[106] Struk's followers interpreted the message as it was intended: a call to arms against the Jews.

In April and May, Struk and his men again attacked ships traveling up the Dnipro River. Shifra Shklovskaya was a passenger on the *Baron Ginsburg* when it was attacked on April 7, 1919. The steamer had been chartered by three Jews to transport a cargo of sugar from Kyiv. As was usual for chartered cargo ships, the steamer had also taken on passengers. During the night, Struk's men shot at the ship and forced it to shore, where "five or six brutal bandits, armed with weapons, rushed on board, stamped their feet and gave the order, 'Jews here, Russians there!'" Shklovskaya testified that "the bandits first seized an old woman and threw her into the river" before drowning some forty additional Jewish passengers.[107]

The same day, insurgent fighters affiliated with Struk's gang attacked another ship, the steamer *Kazak*, traveling from Kyiv to Chernobyl. According to the testimony of Ber Borkhov Mogulevich, who was on board, the ship was fired upon by one of Struk's deputies. The captain thought that officials were signaling the ship to come ashore and brought it in. The insurgents then boarded the ship and again separated the twenty-five Jews on board from the twenty Russians. They took the Jews to shore, robbed them of their valuables, and made them wait together with another group of Jewish prisoners, about forty-five people in total. Several hours later, in the middle of the night, the men led the Jews back onto the deck of the ship. The steamer left the dock, and in the middle of the river the men tossed their captives into the water. Mogulevich recalled, "Everything was still. Suddenly I heard a noise as if a tree trunk were falling into the water. Then my second friend was taken away. Two or three minutes later I heard the same noise."[108] When it was his turn, he jumped into the river and managed to swim to shore in the darkness. In total, the Red Cross estimated that Struk was responsible for the deaths of about a thousand Jewish victims, killed in forty-one different localities.[109]

The Bolsheviks by this point wanted little to do with Struk and his gang. Struk made several overtures toward them, seeking a reconciliation, but the Red Army no longer believed he would be a reliable ally. By late April, Struk saw the winds shifting and changed his slogan once again. "We are fighting against the communes, the stranglehold of Moscow and the Jews," he announced in Chernobyl on April 29.[110] By September he was in Kyiv, fighting alongside the Whites.[111] Whether he was claiming allegiance to the Ukrainian People's Republic, the Bolsheviks, or the Whites, his antipathy toward the Jews remained constant. To many of those who followed him, this was really all that mattered.

TRYPILLYA, A PICTURESQUE village set in a valley amid poplar trees that covered the hills overlooking the Dnipro, was a town of about six thousand inhabitants before the Great War. Most of them made their living farming, fishing, or working in the mills and the small metallurgical factory. There were some grocers and farmers, a restaurant, and a market on Wednesdays, Fridays, and Sundays. The town came alive on fair days four times a year, three in the summer and one in December.[112] Jews and Christians lived side by side, worked in unison, and traded with each other in normal times.

In the spring of 1919, rebel lookouts stationed themselves on the highlands above the city, intercepting steamships and redirecting them to the nearby sheltered port of Plyuty. The plan was ambitious: to stockpile hijacked ships and use them to invade Kyiv.[113] The rebels' commander, Zelenyi—born Danylo Terpylo—had learned the arts of terrorism and insurgency at the age of nineteen, while working in the Kyiv Iron Workshops during the 1905 revolution. He joined a tight-knit cell of Socialist Revolutionaries, but was kicked out for demonstrating national chauvinism—"because I made the mistake of handing

out books in the Ukrainian language," he claimed.[114] He was imprisoned by the tsarist authorities and, after being arrested a second time,
was exiled to the White Sea port of Archangelsk. Released in 1913,
probably as part of the general amnesty to commemorate the three
hundredth anniversary of Romanov rule, Terpylo was drafted into
the tsarist military and served in the infantry on the western front.
He used the opportunity to agitate among the soldiers, distributing
pamphlets and lecturing his comrades in arms about the coming peasant revolution. He embraced all aspects of the radical lifestyle with
vigor. Rejecting the institution of marriage, he instead took up with a
married woman, whose jilted husband joined the Bolsheviks and was
later killed by Terpylo's forces.[115] Soon after he returned to Trypillya in
1917, he started an underground cell of Free Cossacks. It was then that
he took the nom de guerre Zelenyi ("Green") because of its romantic
associations with the green forests of Ukraine.

Starting in Trypillya, his band grew from a family affair—three of
his brothers and a handful of villagers—into a massive peasant army
dedicated to the fight against the Hetmanate and the Germans and to
the distribution of land to the peasantry. He made his mark when his
band attacked the local police station, killed two officers, and disposed
of their bodies in the river. Throughout the summer and fall of 1918,
bodies of local guard units, wealthy landowners, and German soldiers
were found floating in the Dnipro and Chervona rivers—victims of
Zelenyi's gang. By November 1918, Zelenyi controlled Trypillya, Plyuty, and several other villages and was fighting for control of larger
towns like Obukhiv and Rzhyshchiv.[116]

Once the Hetmanate was ousted and the Ukrainian People's Republic was reestablished, Zelenyi threw in his lot with the Directory. He
was a powerful orator and was known to turn Red Army soldiers
against their commanders, convincing them to defend the ideals of
true Cossack freedom rather than "Jewish Bolshevism." When enemy
soldiers he captured refused to join his cause, his "people's courts"
took care of them with peasant justice.[117]

Like Sokolovsky and Struk, Zelenyi presented himself as a defender
of the peasantry against the evils of the city. Most of his followers

understood the city as a euphemism for Jews. "I am neither a lover of Israel nor an enemy of Israel," he allegedly declared:

We are fighting for freedom and land. Freedom must be enjoyed by every inhabitant of Ukraine, but the land belongs only to Ukrainians. . . . A Jew does not need land. The Jew doesn't work the land, just like the Jew doesn't want to go to war. The Jew needs freedom and he will get it. He will be able to trade across the land as much as his heart desires, but the commerce must have a decent and upright character. For the freedom that the Jews get, they will have to help us with their money.[118]

In the spring of 1919, Zelenyi led an alliance of warlords against the seat of Bolshevik power in Kyiv, moving toward the city with a force of twelve thousand peasant soldiers. Most of them, however, abandoned the campaign before it reached the gates of Kyiv, preferring instead to pillage the largely Jewish towns along the way, which made for easier targets.

The marauding was interrupted in early July when a Red Army detachment, composed largely of young Jewish recruits, attacked Trypillya. One Jewish fighter described the scene as they entered the village:

It was a hot day and the sun was burning, so the bullets and the bombs quickly ignited one peasant house after another. The bandits understood, of course, that in a short time the entire village would be in flames, and in order to regroup they all left. The village suddenly became strangely quiet. Confident of the military situation, we entered the deserted hamlet. It was not just the bandits who had fled, but almost all of the peaceful peasants. Only the elderly, sick, and children remained, all hiding in cellars and attics. As a result of the provocations spread by the Socialist Revolutionaries and the Petliurites, the peasants were terrified of the Red Army. They had an image of the Red Army as thieves and murderers, led by communists—Yids.[119]

The Red Army detachment set up camp on the hills overlooking the village, half on a hill to the left and half on a hill to the right, where they conducted exercises and reinforced their positions. Suddenly, the encampment on the right side came under cannon attack from Zelenyi's fighters, forcing the Bolshevik soldiers into the village. The insurgents followed them. The entire right flank of the Bolshevik unit was slaughtered in the village, while the second half of the detachment was captured and held overnight in the town square. Zelenyi's men led the prisoners to the edge of the water. There they stripped them, tied their hands behind their backs, bound them together in threes, and threw them into the river, shooting at anyone who surfaced.

On Saturday, August 2, Zelenyi's men rode into Yustingrad, a village of three thousand people—80 percent of them Jewish—about 120 miles south of Kyiv. Many of its residents were craftsmen.[120] The tanneries, situated along the river, where the waste could flow into the water, supplied leather for the harness makers and saddlers whose shops dotted the unpaved main road. On the other side of the town, closer to the fields, were the wheelwrights and blacksmiths, who catered to the coachmen and to peasants bringing their produce into town for the Monday market. Rope makers twined hemp fiber by stretching ropes along the streets as children played with the stalks.[121] The Jewish community had a small self-defense brigade, which, with the help of Christians from a nearby town, had protected Yustingrad from much of the violence that had engulfed the region during the preceding months. Now, according to the town's memorial book, the community had become complacent. "It was a beautiful day and the people were relaxing."[122]

At dusk, a couple of mounted men entered the home of the local rabbi, Pinkhos Rabinovich, and shot him dead. The memorial book explains: "People think that the bandit leader had heard from the local gentiles that the presence of this righteous leader protected the town. For that reason, the murderers were sent to eliminate the rabbi before they attacked the town."[123] With the rabbi out of the way, Zelenyi's fighters began plundering the village. The next morning, they rounded up 143 young Jewish men, locked them inside the synagogue, and demanded the sum of one million rubles to release them. Terrified representatives of the Jewish community went door-to-door to collect money. When they were unable to come up with the funds after two hours, the insurgents took ten men out of the synagogue and shot them, promising to repeat the action every hour. By late afternoon, when it became clear that the ransom was not forthcoming, Zelenyi's men took the hostages to a bridge on the outskirts of town, shot them all with machine guns, and tossed their bodies into the river.

THE CONDITIONS THAT gave rise to warlords like Grigoriev, the Sokolovsky brothers, Struk, and Zelenyi prevailed throughout much of Ukraine. The complete breakdown of state order and economic stability following the retreat of the Directory and the Bolshevik onslaught provided an opening for dispirited and disgruntled former army men to secure local bases of power. When their military units were disbanded, they found themselves unable to reintegrate into a peacetime routine; the village economies were in shambles, and their familial homes were threatened by the surrounding lawlessness. Instead, they continued with the type of military lifestyle they had come to know while serving in the Russian imperial army or while fighting as independent Free Cossacks. The charismatic leaders found easy recruits among their starving fellow soldiers, as well as among the village youth, who had known only war and whose fathers had long ago traded their plowshares for swords. After five years of war, violence had become normalized, and the distinction between military and civilian authority had disintegrated.

With the countryside destroyed by marauding armies, peasants took up arms for survival—to secure food, clothing, and shelter—or to settle scores with ethnic rivals. The question of which political movement's flag they were fighting under was secondary. They turned to Petliura and his proclamations of freedom; then, after his retreat, they put their faith in the Bolsheviks' promise of land redistribution, only to be disappointed once again. In the absence of any political ideology to believe in, many became susceptible to the conspiracy theory that the Jews were to blame for all their problems. After all, some mused, the Jews had aided the Germans in the occupation; had speculated in produce and currency, leading to the economic collapse; had betrayed the Ukrainian cause by siding with the Russians; and now, in the guise of Bolsheviks, had co-opted the peasant revolution. Many believed the Jews had stolen the land, threatened the churches, and were on the verge of securing control of the entire country. How could the downtrodden peasants of Ukraine not fight back?

Months and Days

Before he moved to Kyiv and became a prominent writer of Yiddish fiction and children's books, Itsik Kipnis lived among the furriers and tanners in the town of Slovechno, about twenty miles west of Ovruch. His house was on the outskirts of town; the courtyard, which his family shared with his aunt and uncle, adjoined a tannery his parents had acquired as part of his mother's dowry. Kipnis's father worked in the tannery, just as his grandfather had. There were two wells in the courtyard, one for the tannery and one for drinking water. The Kipnises also owned a shed and a small room they would occasionally rent out.

On the other side of the Kipnises' garden lived the Lukhtan brothers. It was not unusual in Slovechno for Jewish craftsmen like the Kipnis family and Christian peasants like the Lukhtan family to be living side by side, their fruit trees reaching over each other's fences. In his autobiographical *Months and Days: A Chronicle* (1926), Kipnis recalls that the Lukhtans were good neighbors.[1] Timukh, the middle of the three brothers, was a good-natured former soldier. He rode a horse around town and had an impressive way about him; he was as "tall as a pine." Marko, the oldest, a teller of tall tales, a married man with two children, never seemed to mind when Jews' geese grazed in his yard or when the Jewish children in the neighborhood filched cherries from his tree. Maxim, the youngest, whom Kipnis characterized as having a "face of pure evil," would sometimes try to make an incident out of the trespassing geese or missing cherries, but Marko would just smoke his pipe and laugh in a friendly way. "So what do you care about the little Jews? So they want to grab a cherry." Marko had served in the military and fought the Germans, and when he came back with epaulets on his shoulders he also brought candies for the neighborhood children. And he liked Jews. That's why it was so surprising when on Wednesday, July 16, 1919, Marko helped unleash a massacre of his Jewish neighbors.[2]

Like so many local toughs, Marko Lukhtan had been wrenched from rural life and thrown into combat at a young age. His wartime experience had hardened him, and the collapse of the tsarist military in which he fought—not on the battlefield, but due to revolutionary action at home—had convinced him that the army had been betrayed, stabbed in the back. He was drawn home by the Bolshevik promise of land, only to have the fields occupied by the Germans instead. Somehow it seemed that the Jews were behind it all: Trotsky had made the deal with the Germans, and the Jewish sugar barons and grain merchants were profiting from the rising prices of basic goods. Even in Slovechno, the Jews, who made up about half of the town's two thousand residents, suddenly seemed to be in charge.

Before the war, the Jews of Slovechno were mostly petty traders, leatherworkers, or small shop owners. They dominated the market square—all twenty-two stores listed in a 1913 directory of the town were owned by Jews—but they traded peacefully with their Christian customers.[3] The peasants would bring their grain in sacks to Engel-brekht's mill, where the miller would weigh it, grind it into flour, pack it with a wooden pestle, and help load it onto the peasants' sleds. In the two sawmills, Jews worked alongside their Christian neighbors, cutting timber for railroad crossties, light poles, and even boards for export. The peaceable nature of the town was confirmed by a student, Isaac Goldberg, in testimony he gave to the Russian Red Cross: "Relations of the peasants toward the Jews were entirely neighborly—until the last days."[4] When violence came to Slovechno, it was intimate:

perpetrators knew their victims by name and had generations of history with each other. Unlike in many previous pogroms, where the violence was instigated by outside soldiers or regional warlords, in Slovechno the perpetrators and victims were neighbors. The dynamics were entirely local, informed by personal relations and generational differences, and interpreted through the lens of the ordinary religious symbols that shaped daily village life.

While Slovechno had the feel of an isolated town, it was not politically insular. "There was no newspaper in Slovechno," writes Kipnis. "But still everyone knew everything that happened; every happening spread just like a drumbeat."[5] As refugees flocked to town after the Ovruch pogrom in January 1919, they brought news of events in the area. Stories of the savagery in Ovruch stoked fear in the Jewish population, while giving license to impressionable youth of the region to regard Jews as objects of scorn and disgrace.

That winter, the revolution made its way to Slovechno as the peasants established a soviet in order to represent rural interests. The Jewish townspeople, they complained, had profited from the German occupation at the expense of the villagers. It was said that the Jews wanted to overthrow the peasant council and institute a new Bolshevik one in its place to represent the urban workers. In July, new rumors began circulating: the Bolsheviks were planning to shutter the churches and exile the priest. According to Jacob Melamed, a twenty-four-year-old teacher from Slovechno, the rumors stemmed from the news that the Bolsheviks were preparing to transfer ownership of the metrical books—the official registrar of births, deaths, and marriages—from the priest to the soviet executive committee, as they had done in other towns they had conquered. Such a move represented the encroachment of the state upon the sacraments that had long marked the life cycles of the common people. It also represented a major diminution of church authority. It was often the Bolsheviks' attacks on the church that most antagonized the masses, and that contributed to the popular association between Jews and Bolsheviks: many pious Christians could not imagine one of their own profaning the church. The assaults must be the work of the Jews, they reasoned. In many small towns like

Slovechno, rumors of a Bolshevik crusade against the pious sparked widespread anti-Jewish violence, blending modern economic, political, and social anxieties into long-standing religious resentment.[6]

L. Kaplan, who also gave testimony to the Red Cross, attributed the rumors to a nineteen-year-old peasant with a long face and green eyes named Kosenko, who liked to refer to himself as the "Commissar of the Insurgents." Kosenko charged the Jews rather than the Bolsheviks with the affront to the church: "The leitmotif of his speeches was 'the Jews are stealing our churches and turning them into synagogues, and will force us to register our births, marriages and divorces with the rabbis.'"[7] Kosenko, who was fourteen when the Great War began, had received a basic education and had served in the ration office and as a low-level governmental clerk. Kipnis described him as "short like his father, cunning, a little monstrous, learned: he finished both classes of our school, a chap of twenty years, and a bit of a local writer."[8] Like many of the powerful warlords he emulated, at his young age he had already lived through the disintegration of several states and experienced traumatic violence. Under the Hetmanate, he had briefly joined one of the paramilitary divisions that popped up in the region, but when it was disbanded he found himself at loose ends. In the spring of 1919, when a new police chief came to town—a corrupt Pole whom many witnesses characterized as an antisemite—Kosenko enrolled in the force together with Marko and Timukh Lukhtan. Marko and Kosenko quickly became best of friends.

Jacob Melamed explained that on Saturday, July 12, when the rumors were rampant, he and the town pharmacist (who was also Jewish) appealed to the local priest to use his sermon to calm the peasants. "The priest replied that there was no reason to be afraid of his parishioners and that he would explain all this to them on Sunday," Melamed said. "This reassured us a little."[9] But several months later, as a refugee in Warsaw, Melamed gave a different story to the Joint Distribution Committee, transforming the priest from the neutral arbiter he had been in his initial testimony to an active participant in the strife. Perhaps contact with other refugees had influenced his narrative, or perhaps he had learned new details in the interim. To the

Joint Committee, Melamed testified that when he and the pharmacist approached the priest, the priest retorted: "'The Jews took part in severing the church from the state; they are communists and this is why the peasants are angry at them.' . . . The priest promised, however, that he would try and pacify the peasants. Later it appeared that this priest was one of the instigators of the pogrom."[10]

All the testimonies agree that by the morning of Tuesday, July 15, talk of an impending pogrom filled the air. According to Melamed, at daybreak, "when the Jewish women drove the cattle into the field, the peasant women told them 'today the worst will befall you.'"[11] In the evening, a group of prominent Jews went to the police chief to request permission to form a self-defense brigade for the night. The chief assured them that he and his forces had the situation under control. Although the Jewish petitioners were not permitted to patrol the town with weapons, they decided nevertheless to spend the night on guard, roaming the town unarmed just to keep an eye on the tense situation. They were relieved when toward midnight they saw the chief arrive with several men, including Marko Lukhtan and Kosenko, each armed with five rifles slung over their backs. But instead of providing security and distributing the weapons to the Jewish guards, the two men fired off a pair of volleys. At that signal, the town was surrounded by peasants coming out of the darkness. "The police distributed the rifles to the swine and the Jewish guards fled," writes Kipnis. The police chief, he says, had planned the whole affair in advance together with Marko Lukhtan and Kosenko.[12]

Hannah Gozman, a forty-five-year-old mother, had disregarded the rumors and was sound asleep when the shooting awakened her in the middle of the night. She told the Red Cross that about ten minutes later, thirty to forty men descended on the town square from the surrounding villages, armed with rifles, pitchforks, and crowbars.[13]

Roza Zaks was just seven years old when the pogrom began. Many decades later, in 1996, sitting in her West Hollywood home, with a gold Star of David on her necklace, she told the Shoah Foundation that she remembers her mother waking her and her siblings in the middle of the night to hide in the loft of their neighbor's pigsty. From their hiding spot, they saw an elderly Jew come running to seek cover, only to be shot by an armed peasant. They managed to stifle their screams and avoid detection. At the next opportunity, her mother moved Roza and her siblings to the house of Ukrainian acquaintances in a neighboring village: "They were very good people," Zaks remembered.[14]

The peasant insurgents were shouting the slogan of the tsarist-era Black Hundreds paramilitary forces: "Hurrah! Beat the Yids!" They smashed windows and pillaged homes the entire night. They had even brought along sacks to carry the looted goods. Melamed managed to find shelter in the cellar of the local post office. Hannah Gozman, whose husband was away on business, took her children and hid in her cellar for the night. When she emerged, all her windows had been broken.

Kipnis described the scene the next morning: "The streets looked like they did after a fair, or before Passover"—when Jews thoroughly clean their houses—"but in a nasty way. Dust and garbage in front of every door. Papers thrown about with broken glass."[15] As Ayzik, Kipnis's autobiographical narrator, wanders through the street, he sees Serhy, "a well-built goy, an old man from a nearby village, old but without a single grey hair on his head," and Timofeiko, "a neighbor about my age." Both of them are looting the houses, including Ayzik's own home—carrying away their teacups, their bedding, everything from their cupboards, even their salt supplies.[16] Surveying the damage in his bedroom, Ayzik expresses his sense of personal violation: "Now our room is no longer our room. It's more like a public bath. Sure, it's still our room, but we no longer have anything to do with it."[17]

On Wednesday, the Jews of Slovechno buried the dead as their neighbors continued looting. There were seventeen bodies—four locals and thirteen Jews from the surrounding villages.[18] Some survivors managed to get back into their homes and hide any valuables that had not yet been stolen. As night fell, many Jews fled to the countryside to sleep out in the open, in the hemp and rye fields that surrounded the town. Others sought shelter in non-Jewish neighbors' cellars or among acquaintances in nearby villages. Many of those who fled to other villages did not survive: Melamed told the Red Cross that eight Jews were killed in Begun, a few miles away, and two in Verpa. Gozman reports that she approached several peasants she knew for protection, but only one was willing to allow her and her children to hide with him.

Ovsey Freink, a fifty-three-year-old tailor, told the Red Cross that when the violence began, he fled with his family to his hometown of Begun. With the help of a peasant acquaintance, he found shelter there inside a barn. Peering through the slats, Freink saw several peasant insurgents with revolvers approach, among whom he identified Kosenko. The men found Ovsey and his family in the barn—possibly tipped off by the peasant who had aided him—and robbed them at gunpoint. They shot Ovsey's son Dovid in the leg, and then, when Ovsey's wife protested, shot her as well. Kosenko and his men next shot Ovsey's other son, eighteen-year-old Khayim-Leyb, killing him instantly as Khayim-Leyb's wife, who was holding their baby, stood watching. Dovid and his mother suffered for two hours before they both succumbed to their wounds. As Ovsey describes the scene, when the men left, he was drenched with the blood of his family. Aside from him, only his daughter-in-law and the baby survived. The three of them remained hidden in terror until the next day. When they emerged from hiding, they found no help in the village. Ovsey reports that the peasants and Christian townspeople looked at him and his traumatized daughter-in-law with the baby in her arms and simply laughed.[19]

In Kipnis's chronicle, Ayzik recalls learning of Dovid Freink's murder the next morning. As he wanders through town, he hears a woman singing in the middle of the marketplace. Only once he approaches does he realize that the singer is Dovid's delirious widow and "she is not singing. She is preaching like a priest. No, she is declaiming with a hoarse, bedraggled voice, as though she were in the theater. And, yes, she does sing a little too, in a moderate voice as though she were talking to someone. And she walks with a slow gait, with dangling hands, as though she were in no rush."[20]

ON THURSDAY AFTERNOON, the Slovechno town rabbi, Ber Borukh Zion, called for a conference with the insurgents and asked the priest to serve as a mediator. When they met that afternoon in the town square, the rabbi made entreaties for peace, but, according to Melamed, was quickly shouted down. The priest followed the rabbi, condemning bloodshed in general terms but adding that the Jews deserved whatever was coming to them. The meeting concluded with the Jewish community agreeing to pay a large sum of money, ostensibly to reimburse the peasants for the destruction of the previous days. The Jewish community then held a meeting of its own in the synagogue and collected forty thousand rubles, which it turned over to Kosenko and his men in exchange for a commitment to stop the violence.[21]

In his chronicle, Kipnis describes the gathering in the town square in language that echoes the testimonies. "It was a strange assembly today! A day that was neither holiday nor workday. In the middle of the marketplace there was a bit of a fair, yet without any trade,

[YIVO INSTITUTE FOR JEWISH RESEARCH]

Four wounded survivors of the Slovechno pogrom: Y. Zilberband, M. Lender, Motl Feldman, and Kh. Y. Zilberband

with the rabbi and the priest standing in the middle of the circle."[22] In Kipnis's rendition, the priest explains that both the Jews and the peasants will have to restrain themselves, making Ayzik wonder how the Jews could act any differently to halt the carnage of which they are the victims. One of the perpetrators, Stodot Popak, then speaks: "The Jews are foreigners. The Jews are harmful. Jewish cattle eat the entire pastures. The Jews cut down all the forests to make brooms. Jewish geese spoil the wheat fields." Stodot continues his accusations, claiming that the Jews aided the Germans during the war and are now communists. Marko Lukhtan then steps in and demands that the Jews give up their money in order to put an end to the bloodshed. It is clear to Kipnis that Marko is in charge: "He counts the money; he issues the commands."[23]

On Thursday night, many Jews, including the rabbi, resolved to spend the night together in Motl Ratner's house. Ratner was a prominent Jewish figure, and he owned one of the only two-story houses in town. In Kipnis's words, "Motl's place was like a railroad station, not like a home. People were always coming and going, both Jews and peasants. . . . They won't let anybody kill Motl."[24] But as it turned out, Ratner's house was not a safe place to hide. At three o'clock in the morning, Kosenko led a group of peasants armed with axes and rifles into Ratner's house, where they immediately slaughtered five people and seriously wounded the rabbi. On the street outside, the peasants unleashed another wave of fire, killing and wounding many more until the shooting died down at daybreak. A total of twenty-five people were reportedly killed around Ratner's house, including Ratner's daughter-in-law Yokheved.

Once the city quieted, the surviving Jews came out of hiding to assist the wounded. But the peasant insurgents returned and began yet another round of violence. They sought out the wounded in particular, finishing them off with their bayonets. The gravely injured rabbi was stabbed to death when a group of Jews carrying him to the infirmary was attacked.

On Friday morning, Jacob Melamed, who had been hiding in the postmaster's basement, decided to leave town. Peasants, he had heard, were going door-to-door hunting Jews. "I came out of the cellar and saw the entire road flooded with Jews—women, children and old people dragging along for miles without stopping. It looked like the Exodus."[25] Melamed headed to Ovruch with a crowd of refugees, but villagers tried to stop them all along the route; they survived by dispensing bribes to any peasant with a scythe. He also reports that seventeen Jews were shot, including three small children: "They lay on the road until Saturday evening when they were taken to the town."[26]

Hannah Gozman, too, decided that it was time to leave. Together with her children, she gathered her belongings in a cart to flee to Ovruch. On their way out of town, though, Gozman was warned that Slovechno was surrounded and there was no way out. She returned and hid her valuables in a garden. The tailor, Avrum-Ber Vaysband, invited her and her children to hide in his house, where many Jews were already taking advantage of the iron door and reinforced window frames. The transcript of her testimony continues: "It is difficult for me to convey our time in that earthly hell [fainting] yes, yes, yes, all the rooms were packed with the Jews of Slovechno—elderly, women, children, many had hidden under beds, tables, couches, etc."[27]

Srul Ber Berger, who was also hiding in the house, described the scene in his testimony: "Some of us were shut in a bedroom, the rest stayed in the front room."[28] Soon after, Kosenko burst into the tailor's house, leading a band of peasant insurgents. According to Berger, "a company of peasants began to break windows and shoot into the rooms. We lay on the floor, one on top of another, ten or fifteen people in a heap. A number of peasants entered the house with Kosenko at their head. Kosenko announced that he was going to kill all of us. The bandits took our money, and then struck us with axes and sabers."[29] Berger pretended to be dead and lay in a pile of corpses as the peasants rummaged through the bodies searching for valuables. "It was not until I heard Yiddish words that I raised my head: it was Jews who had come to take away the bodies. Blood everywhere, and all around the groans of the wounded. I went out to help lay the corpses in the cart. I laid the body of my sister in the cart. As I did so, I saw with horror a dress I knew all too well. I looked closer: it was my wife."[30]

Avrom Leyb Melamed, a fifty-three-year-old worker, also fled to Vaysband's, bringing his wife and three children. He, too, recalled Kosenko's attack on the house: "The bandits began to shoot at us and to chop at the skulls and bodies of my wife and children. I saw how Kosenko hacked my wife in the head and how she breathed her last breath. He fell upon me as well. I was injured in the head and in my right hand, which I can no longer use." Kosenko then took his coat and shoes and left.[31] A fifteen-year-old student named Motl Kaplan also reported that he was at Vaysband's with his mother, who was struck by a bullet in the heart as they ran out of the house.[32]

Gozman testified that Kosenko ordered all the Jews out of the room and beat them as they left. Kipnis also recounted this episode in his chronicle: at Vaysband's, he writes, "Kosenko opened a window and told the Jews they should flee to save themselves, but he stood there and chopped off every head that stuck out the window."[33] Roza Zaks, who had returned from hiding under the mistaken impression that the massacre was over, and had joined the others at Vaysband's, was beaten and left for dead. Only when the corpses were being thrown into mass graves later in the day did someone hear a grunt from one of the bodies near the top of the pile. Roza's face was disfigured but she was alive.

As Hannah Gozman fled Vaysband's, she saw corpses and wounded Jews on the roads. "I will never forget it: among the slain lay the wounded wife of the synagogue caretaker, and some peasant was kicking her in the head." She recalls that Maxim Lukhtan stood nearby with a gun. Gozman managed to escape with her children toward the neighboring village of Petrushki.[34] But the flight did not end her ordeal: on the way to Petrushki, she was stopped by "a peasant boy, twelve or thirteen years old, armed with a little pistol, who demanded that we hand over whatever we had left." She reports that other peasants ridiculed them for their bloody clothing and taunted them as Bolsheviks and communists. Only when they reached the house of a peasant near Petrushki did they find safety. He fed them, let them spend the night, and, on Saturday, took them into the woods where other Jews were hiding. Gozman traveled with this group until morning, when Motl

Ratner picked them up with his cart and took them to the town of Valednik. Eventually, they made it to Ovruch, where her children got medical attention.

Describing these events in her testimony, Gozman suddenly remembered a crucial detail: "Excuse me, I forgot to say that as we were passing the house of Kosenko, his mother washed my daughter's wounds with water, saying, 'Get out fast or it will be bad for you.'"[35] It was not uncommon for parents to stand apart from the violence of their children. "In my opinion," writes the student Isaac Goldberg, "the most active participants in the pogrom were young peasants." Most of the perpetrators had grown up in a time of total war and chaos and had few memories of a country at peace. Instead of spending their youth harvesting the fields alongside their fathers, young boys in Slovechno imagined their fathers shooting Germans with revolvers at the front and heard whispered stories and rumors of death and destruction.

Indeed, the parents of perpetrators are often portrayed as sympathetic to the Jews, seeking to put a stop to the brutal behavior of their children. Roza Zaks, for instance, tells of one Ukrainian woman whose son wanted to join the insurgents "ransacking Jewish homes." But she "cried and implored him not to do it: God would punish him, the stolen things would not do him good. Her son obeyed and went home to sleep."[36] The insurgency was, in other words, also a rebellion of youth, of young people who saw no future for themselves in the turmoil of the civil war and who had no recollections of the delicate peace that had once been the norm.

Several testimonies refer to episodes in which Jewish victims were threatened with forced conversion or taunted with religious symbols. Moyshe Feldman, for instance, a nineteen-year-old forester, reported that on his way to the cemetery to help bury the dead he was accosted by peasants who said: "After you bury all the slain, we will kill you and bury you ourselves; you've caused us enough trouble. . . . But if you want to live, then go to the priest and ask him to baptize all your sins out of you."[37] Kipnis, as well, writes that before Kosenko ordered the surviving Jews to bury the dead, the peasants blocked their path out of town and assembled the Jews in the town square, by the church, where they ordered them to kiss the cross. Whether portrayed as a mediator or an instigator, the local priest also appears prominently in many of the testimonies. The root causes of the conflict may have been more about economic rivalries and political strife, but these details are reminders of the continued role that time-tested religious resentments played in motivating violence.

On Saturday morning, a detachment of Red Army soldiers—"salvation," in Kipnis's words—arrived from Ovruch and surrounded the town. Goldberg, who had managed to escape Slovechno on Thursday, returned with the detachment as a new recruit; the pogrom was enough to convince him to enlist. He recalled the scene as he entered town on Saturday evening: "It was difficult to believe that this was reality and not a nightmare. There was not a soul on the streets, just a herd of cows that the peasants had released when they heard about the approach of the Bolsheviks (the livestock belonged to the Jews). Corpses and destroyed property were scattered about; trails of blood were everywhere. There were signs of destruction on the outside of the houses—broken windows, doors, and gates. In the courtyards everything was dug up. Corpses were lying in the houses we managed to look into, corpses of children."[38] Feldman also remembered that day: "Until evening we were busy at the cemetery. We didn't bury everyone. Many corpses remained in the homes and on the streets. There was a stench of putrefaction in the summer heat and pools of human blood everywhere."[39] Another Red Army soldier, Arya Tereshko, recalled his first impressions of the city: "The bodies were piled one on top of the other. There were bodies of women and children. In one house, I saw a decapitated corpse with the head lying nearby."[40]

The Red Army troops engaged in a skirmish with Kosenko and his men. Four of the insurgents were killed; two soldiers also fell in battle, one of whom was of Jewish background. By nightfall, four days after it began, the pogrom was over.[41] Once they established control, the Bolsheviks called a meeting of the peasants and urged them to redeem themselves by joining the Red Army and fighting for the revolution. They also urged the Jews to join the battle, to repay their debt to their communist saviors. Victims and perpetrators would serve under the red flag together.[42]

The main ringleaders of the pogrom escaped and faded into the countryside, but the Bolsheviks captured a dozen insurgents. As Kipnis tells it, the Red Army detachment "sat twelve peasants in a great wagon of hay; their hands were bound to the rails. And all twelve were big, strong and angry. Nine were local. . . . Only the chiefs were missing. There was no Kosenko, no Marko, and no police chief."[43] Justice was swift: four of the peasants "were stood up next to the jail with blindfolded eyes and shot."[44] According to one report, the detachment killed twenty peasant insurgents on the spot and arrested another ten whom they took with them to Ovruch.[45]

THE SLOVECHNO POGROM shattered a balance between town and country that had existed for generations. Christian villagers who had lived in close proximity to the town, regularly coming in for market days and church services, often knew the Jewish merchants and tradesmen whom they now accused of speculation and Bolshevism; the Jewish townspeople, in turn, could identify by name those who wielded a sword against their kin and carried off their dining sets. This familiarity made it difficult to forgive when power shifted once again, leading to a cycle of violence.

Fourteen months later, in September 1920, a revolutionary tribunal acting on evidence provided by nineteen witnesses arrested and indicted three individuals—Dmytri Dubnitsky, Oleksandr Khilevich, and Ivan Kuprash—on charges of actively participating in the pogrom. Kuprash managed to escape, but further investigations were conducted regarding the remaining two defendants.[46] The twenty-six-year-old Dubnitsky and eighteen-year-old Khilevich denied any involvement in the pogrom, claiming that the Jews had accused them "out of spite." The indictment contains extensive witness statements given by a group of Jews who attested that they personally saw both Dubnitsky and Khilevich among the insurgents armed with rifles, shouting "Beat the Jews, beat the communists, kill them all." The tribunal concluded that both defendants were motivated by "national hatred toward the Jewish population" and indicted them for murder. The two were handed over to the Volhynian Revolutionary Tribunal.[47]

On March 31, 1921, the Volhynian Revolutionary Tribunal, chaired by a Comrade Feldman, heard the case. The secretary of the tribunal was named Ratner, possibly of the same prominent Ratner family that had been targeted during the pogrom. The tribunal concluded that the two took part in a premeditated agreement to carry out a pogrom that killed seventy-two people and injured one hundred. The tribunal declared that the two were "the most wicked enemies of the working people" and sentenced them to "the highest measurement of punishment, that is, execution by shooting."[48] Many Jews watched the proceedings unfold with reverence and awe at the willingness of the new regime to crack down finally on anti-Jewish violence. On the other hand, many locals likely viewed the Revolutionary Tribunal, with Feldman and Ratner at its head, as little more than Jewish vengeance, a Jewish court eager to carry out reprisals against the Christian youth of the village.

The two convicts appealed to the Supreme Appellate Tribunal, and on May 28 the appellate tribunal ruled in their favor. The chief judge, with the Slavic name of Yanskii, and assisted by officials with the Slavic names of Semenova and Rudenko, found that the Revolutionary Tribunal had failed to take into account a November 7, 1920, decree issued by the Communist Party on the occasion of the third anniversary of the revolution, which provided an amnesty for "individuals accused of banditry who belong to the proletarian elements or are unmarried villagers and became involved in criminal activity as a result of ignorance or thoughtlessness."[49] Such amnesties were regularly issued in order to retain mass support, alleviate prison overpopulation, and ease ethnic and class tension. Amnesties also helped project an image of the new Soviet government as benevolent and merciful. However, they had the corollary effect of alienating populations seeking justice.[50] Where the tribunal of Jews had sentenced the perpetrators to death, the tribunal of Slavs had spared them. It was a lesson that was likely to be remembered in town for a long time: it seemed to confirm suspicions that the Jews were a harsh people, incapable of exhibiting Christian mercy.

Marko Lukhtan, for his part, somehow managed to escape the tribunals. He was less successful in escaping vigilante justice, however. Kipnis tells us that eventually, "in the middle of the day, three shots could be heard behind the town.... Marko killed the Jews and the Jews killed Marko."[51]

— 12 —

Poland and Ukraine on the World Stage

On Saturday, June 28, 1919—five years to the day since Gavrilo Princip's fateful assassination of Archduke Franz Ferdinand—lancers in blue uniforms and tin hats lined the square in front of the Château de Versailles as motorcars ferried Clemenceau, Wilson, Lloyd George, and their aides into the palace. Escorted by the French Republican Guard, Clemenceau, the host, led the stately convoy up the Grand Staircase, through the staterooms, and into the Galerie des Glaces, the same place where Bismarck had declared the establishment of the German Empire back in 1871. Now, the leaders of the Great Powers sat on a slightly elevated dais in the middle of the magnificent room, surrounded by gilded bronze capitals, red marble "Rouge de Rance" pilasters, and hundreds of mirrors. A throng of distinguished guests—sixty people for each of the Great Powers—looked on. There were no elaborate speeches; the mood was subdued. It was a sharp contrast with the grandiose setting, so rich with historical symbolism.

At three in the afternoon, the German delegates were escorted into the crowded room. "They looked like prisoners being brought in for sentence," remarked British statesman James Wycliffe Headlam-Morley.[1] The audience strained to see the Germans signing the papers in which they accepted responsibility for "all the loss and damage" of a war caused "by the aggression of Germany and her allies." In the agreement, Germany lost 13 percent of its territory and 10 percent of its population, and agreed to military restrictions and reparations. It was a humiliating way to end the war. The signing itself was so quick and methodical that when a cannon was fired, few of the guests peering over each other's shoulders could discern if the ceremony had ended or just begun. Elsewhere, though, celebrations filled the streets. In Paris, "impromptu orchestras appeared on every corner. Young and old danced, and everyone kissed everyone else," reported the *New York Times*.[2]

The peacemakers declined to recognize an independent Ukraine and spurned all Bolshevik claims on former tsarist territory. Instead, they encouraged "at opportune times, the reunion with Russia" of Ukraine within "a federalized or genuinely democratic Russia," and committed their support to the Whites in furtherance of this goal.[3] But their attitude toward Poland was more favorable. At a side table during the ceremony in the Galerie des Glaces, Dmowski and Paderewski put their signatures on the Polish Minority Treaty, in which the Great Powers agreed to recognize the Polish Republic as a sovereign state in return for its commitment "to protect the interests" of its ethnic, religious, and linguistic minorities. Specifically, the Poles granted the Jews the right to observe their Sabbath and educate their children in schools funded from the state treasury. The League of Nations would enforce the provisions. Many Poles still regarded the Minorities Treaty as an intolerable restriction on their sovereignty, as a stain on what was otherwise a triumph of the Polish national spirit, and resented the Jews for intervening with the Allies to curb Polish autonomy.[4] "There exists a Jewish propaganda campaign against the Polish state," declared one Polish parliamentarian the week the treaty was signed. His allegation was greeted with shouts from the backbenches: "True!" "Absolutely!"[5]

UNABLE TO INFLUENCE events in Ukraine but buoyed by their Polish successes in Paris, the Jewish emissaries Louis Marshall and Lucien Wolf

The signing of the Treaty of Versailles in the Galerie des Glaces

[ARCHIVIO GBB / ALAMY STOCK PHOTO]

continued to campaign on behalf of eastern European Jews, now advocating for the establishment of an American-led investigation into the pogroms that had taken place in Poland. When Paderewski announced that he would welcome such a commission, the matter was settled. US secretary of state Robert Lansing charged the commission with investigating "the various massacres, pogroms, and other excesses alleged to have taken place," for the purpose of "seeking to discover the reason lying behind such excesses and discriminations with a view to finding a possible remedy."[6] As chair of the commission, Wilson appointed Henry Morgenthau, the German-born Jewish former ambassador to the Ottoman Empire who had raised awareness of Turkish atrocities against the Armenians in 1915. But as a staunch assimilationist and an outspoken opponent of Zionism, Morgenthau had few friends among Jewish activists. He was one of the signers of a declaration sent to President Wilson that contended that Zionism "not only misinterprets the trend of the history of the Jews, who ceased to be a nation two thousand years ago, but involves the limitation and possible annulment of the larger claims of Jews for full citizenship and human rights in all lands in which those rights are not yet secure."[7] Years later, in his memoirs, Morgenthau disparaged Zionism as "the most stupendous fallacy in Jewish history" and characterized the movement as "wrong in principle and impossible of realization."[8] He even blamed the pogroms on the influence of Zionism: "It was quite evident that one of the deep and obscure causes of the Jewish trouble in Poland was this Nationalist-Zionist leadership that exploited the Old Testament prophecies to capture converts to the Nationalist scheme."[9] His appointment to lead the commission was a great disappointment to Marshall and the other Jewish advocates, who felt Morgenthau was more interested in coddling the Poles than defending the Jews.

On the day the Treaty of Versailles was signed, Morgenthau dined with Paderewski, Dmowski, and Lansing at the Ritz. In the midst of the dinner, Lansing and Paderewski left to bid farewell to President Wilson, who was boarding the train to Le Havre for his return to America. Morgenthau was left alone at the table with Dmowski. Expressions of antisemitism were still acceptable in polite society, so it was not shocking when Morgenthau turned to Dmowski and said, "I understand that you are an Anti-Semite, and I want to know how you feel toward our commission." Far from denying the characterization, Dmowski replied, "My Anti-Semitism isn't religious: it is political." He assured Morgenthau that he had no quarrel with Jews, so long as they were not in Poland. "He wanted Poland for the Poles alone—and made no secret of this desire," recalled Morgenthau. "There never was a pogrom in Poland," Dmowski insisted, taking the position that the violence in Lviv, Pinsk, and elsewhere were brawls rather than massacres. Before the ink on the Polish Minorities Treaty was even dry, Dmowski gave Morgenthau a dire warning: "Unless the Jews would abandon their exclusiveness, they had better leave the country."[10]

Morgenthau's commission arrived in Warsaw on July 13, moving into the rococo seventeenth-century Raczynski Palace, where they received guests and collected statements from Polish dignitaries and representatives of the Jewish community. "Day after day, we sat there, listening, questioning, taking voluminous notes, making bulky records," recalled Morgenthau.[11] In his memoirs, he wrote of the oppression he witnessed and the faith that the Jewish representatives he interviewed placed in his commission. Rabbi Rubenstein from Vilnius, for instance, "displayed a pathetic faith that here at last was a tribunal anxious to dispense justice. Imagine a face like that of some medieval artist's 'Christ,' lined with the horror of his recent experiences; eyes wide with the grief that they had suffered in witnessing the massacre of the flower of his flock."[12]

Like everyone else, Morgenthau was enthralled by Paderewski. But he was less impressed with the Polish head of state, Józef Piłsudski. Like Dmowski, Piłsudski dismissed foreign reports of pogroms as exaggerations and accused the commission of having come "to stir the whole thing up again" and "still further hurt our credit abroad." Morgenthau laid out his strategy to Piłsudski: "Though we would have to rap Poland's knuckles and blame some of the Poles severely for certain excesses and economic persecutions, which I strongly condemned, we would present our conclusions with fairness to both sides."[13] According to Morgenthau, Piłsudski replied by reciting the long history of friendship between Poles and Jews but lamented that "it was unfortunate that, in the recent war, some Jews had informed against the Poles in Galicia and thereby created prejudice against them," repeating the canard of Jewish disloyalty.[14]

Ultimately Morgenthau's mission found that about 280 individual Jews had been killed and thousands had been assaulted and robbed in eight specific incidents in what they considered to be Polish territory: two in November 1918 (Kielce and Lviv), three in April 1919 (Pinsk, Lida, and Vilnius), two in May 1919 (Kolbuszowa and Częstochowa), and one in August 1919 (Minsk). The "excesses," as the report termed them, were "the result of a widespread anti-Semitic prejudice aggravated by the belief that the Jewish inhabitants were politically hostile to the Polish State."[15] The report placed ultimate responsibility on "the undisciplined and ill-equipped Polish recruits, who, uncontrolled by their inexperienced and ofttimes timid officers, sought to profit at the expense of that portion of the population which they regarded as alien and hostile to Polish nationality and aspirations."[16] The committee was confident that "when the boundaries of Poland are once fixed, and the internal organization of the country is perfected, the Polish Government will be increasingly able to protect all classes of Polish citizenry"[17] and "the relations between the Jews and non-Jews will undoubtedly improve in a strong democratic Poland."[18] In his memoirs, Morgenthau reflected: "There was no question whatever but that the Jews had suffered; there had been shocking outrages of at least a sporadic character resulting in many deaths, and still more woundings and robberies, and there was a general disposition, not to say plot, of long standing, the purpose of which was to make the Jews uncomfortable in many ways: there was a deliberate conspiracy to boycott them economically and socially. Yet there was also no question but that some of the Jewish leaders had exaggerated these evils."[19]

The Morgenthau report disappointed many in the Jewish community, who felt that it whitewashed anti-Jewish atrocities. Some felt that by narrowly interpreting his instructions to include only territories firmly controlled by the Polish military, Morgenthau had neglected the far more severe pogroms in the contested regions to the east. Confusion over what exactly was meant by "Poland" was understandable, as many in Poland continued to lay claim to the historic lands of the Polish-Lithuanian Commonwealth, including much of Ukraine. At a time when borders were constantly shifting and the status of the entire region was being disputed, few understood the fine distinctions that Morgenthau—and Hugh Gibson, the American ambassador to Poland, before him—were making when they spoke of "pogroms in Poland." As a result, the American investigation inadvertently gave the false impression that the Jewish situation throughout the entire region was less dire than previously imagined.

PETLIURA, FOR HIS part, tried to take advantage of the anti-Polish sentiment among Jewish activists in order to rally support for the Ukrainian People's Republic in its conflict with Poland over Eastern

Galicia. In May 1919, while the fate of Poland was being decided in Paris, Petliura issued a series of statements unequivocally condemning pogroms. Calling for the prosecution of perpetrators, he established an Extraordinary Commission for the Investigation of Anti-Jewish Pogroms, with the power to determine the guilt of individuals and summon them before a military court for sentencing.[20] On July 9, days before Morgenthau's commission arrived in Warsaw, he issued a proclamation reminding his army that the Jews were fighting alongside Ukrainians in the battle for independence.[21] These sentiments were reaffirmed in a cabinet decree of August 18, which blamed pogroms on "the common enemies" of the Ukrainian and Jewish people: the Polish ruling classes, the White "reactionary clique," and the Bolsheviks. The decree affirmed that the leaders of the Ukrainian People's Republic "have set themselves the most urgent task of doing away with all possibilities of provocations, pogroms, or other excesses, and of calling to account all persons hostile to the Ukrainian state, who are executing treacherous and provocative pogroms in Ukraine."[22] Finally, on August 26, as Petliura's troops approached Kyiv in a new offensive, he issued Army Order No. 131: "It is time for you to understand that the peaceful Jewish population, the women and children, have been oppressed and deprived of national freedom just as we have. They cannot be separated from us, they have always been with us, and they have shared with us their joys and sorrow."[23]

Order 131 was addressed to Petliura's officers and soldiers, but it was also directed at international audiences—particularly the peacemakers in Paris, whose representatives continued to debate the status of Eastern Galicia, which was not resolved by the major treaties signed at Versailles. As the order stated:

The whole world admires our victorious fight for liberation. Do not stain those deeds—even accidentally—by disgraceful actions, and do not shame our country before the whole world. Our many enemies, external as well as internal, are already taking advantage of the terrible pogroms: they are pointing their fingers at us and inciting against us saying that we are not worthy of an independent

national existence and must again be harnessed to the yoke of slavery. I, your Chief Otaman, tell you that the question of whether or
not we will have an independent existence is being decided right
now in the international court.[24]

Petliura had been unwilling to issue such unambiguous declarations when he actually held power, during the period when his troops
were actively committing atrocities against the Jewish populations of
Ovruch, Berdychiv, Zhytomyr, and Proskuriv. As many critics pointed
out, it was only once his army had disintegrated and he was soliciting
Allied support that he was willing to return to the founding principles
of the Directory government and embrace a multiethnic Ukraine.

And the declarations came too late to make a difference, particularly in Petliura's bid for international acceptance of Ukraine's claim
to Eastern Galicia. Britain and France recognized that the Jews of
Eastern Galicia "have given an incontestable proof of their unwilling-
ness to be subjects of the Polish State on account of pogroms perpetrated on them" and "have manifested their desire to be included in
the Ukrainian State," still believing in the promise of national autonomy under the Directory—but with the Bolsheviks occupying Kyiv
and with talk of an alliance between Bolshevik Ukraine and Béla Kun's
Hungary, the Great Powers concluded that it was too risky to rely
upon Petliura.[25] They anticipated that the Ukrainian Republic, such as
it was, would soon fall to either the Whites, the Poles, or the Bolsheviks; their primary interest was ensuring that it was not the Bolsheviks.
So, turning a blind eye to Polish offenses against the Jews, the Supreme
Council led by Wilson, Clemenceau, and Lloyd George supported Polish claims to Eastern Galicia and authorized the Polish military to
occupy the region as a temporary measure to hold back the advance
of Bolshevism.[26]

In June 1919, Polish legionnaires secured Lviv and drove out the
Ukrainians, effectively destroying the Western Ukrainian People's
Republic. Many Galician Ukrainian nationalists went into exile, to
Munich, Berlin, Paris, London, and western Canada, where they would
continue to advocate for an independent Ukraine from afar. Others

joined Petliura's army as a last-ditch effort to fight for an independent Ukraine without Eastern Galicia. Although the Allies claimed they did not intend the Polish occupation to prejudice the final disposition of the region, the League of Nations subsequently granted Poland a temporary mandate over Eastern Galicia, and then, in 1923, acquiesced to permanent Polish sovereignty over it. That sovereignty would last until the German and Soviet invasions of September 1939.[27]

WITH THE STATUS of Poland settled for the time being, world attention finally turned to the slaughter taking place in Ukraine. By late August, evidence of terrible violence in the region was overwhelming.[28] On September 2, the Yiddish-language *Der morgen zhurnal* ("The Morning Journal") opened with a banner headline reporting on half a million pogrom victims in Ukraine.[29] A few days later, the Federation of Ukrainian Jews in America warned of six million Jews in peril and asserted that 127,000 had already been killed in Ukraine,[30] while the *New York Times* published detailed accounts of pogroms.[31] In October, the Jewish aid workers Meir Grossman and Abram Koralnik arrived in London from Kyiv and delivered firsthand reports of atrocities. The French writer Anatole France, who had been a prominent critic of the French military during the 1898 Dreyfus affair, once again came to the defense of the Jews as the lead signatory of an October 1919 letter calling for the Great Powers to defend the Jews of eastern Europe: "In the very midst of civilized Europe, at the dawn of the new era for which the world awaits its charter of liberty and justice, the existence of a whole population is threatened. Such crimes dishonour not only the people that commit them, but outrage human reason and conscience."[32]

Letters continued to reach London and Paris almost daily from Ukrainian Jews telling of the violence, leading the American Jewish Committee and the Joint Distribution Committee to organize a mass demonstration. The "Day of Sorrow," as it was called, took place on November 24, with twenty-five thousand New Yorkers marching to Carnegie Hall accompanied by bands playing funeral dirges. PEACE ON EARTH AND MASSACRES IN THE UKRAINE. WHAT ARE THE WORLD'S

DIPLOMATS THINKING ABOUT? asked one banner, referring to the recently concluded peace talks in Paris.[33] The Canadian Jewish Congress also held a rally, demanding that the government "terminate these frightful conditions which prevail in Ukrainia and which are a blot on the name of civilization."[34]

But, still believing in the principle of national autonomy, many Jewish activists remained sympathetic to the Ukrainian People's Republic. For instance, Israel Zangwill, president of the Jewish Territorial Organization (and author of the influential 1908 play *The Melting Pot*, which featured a pogrom survivor as its protagonist), commended Petliura in an open letter: "The national rights you have given to the Jews are a manifestation of true statesmanship and in shining contrast with the Jewish policy of Poland, and I can only hope that your Republic will be preserved to give the rest of the world an example of the strength and the exalted patriotism that comes from the cordial co-operation and mutual respect of all the varied racial and religious elements that make up a modern state."[35] Margolin, continuing his defense of the Ukrainian government, argued that Petliura could not be held responsible for violence in areas where his meager forces had no control and placed the blame on the great powers for failing to intervene: "American mammoth freighters were belching smoke in every seaport of Romania. If only some power could find the will to enforce order, even just in the Odesa and Kherson areas, then the markets would be flooded with desperately needed nails, caps, boots, clothing, not to mention agricultural machinery. That by itself would root out the anarchy and Bolshevism . . . nails and boots could do more than guns."[36] Leo Motzkin, chair of the Committee of Jewish Delegations, and the Zionist activist Nahum Sokolow agreed. "It is our opinion," they wrote, "that, if at any moment during the course of this criminal butchery . . . the public opinion of the civilized world and the Governments had expressed strongly [their] firm determination to put a stop to this state of things, the massacres would, in spite of all, have ceased."[37]

Official spokespeople of the Ukrainian People's Republic also fostered the narrative that its government lacked only the means to combat pogroms, not the will. Ukrainian representative to the United States Julian Batchinsky acknowledged the role of Petliura's forces in the Proskuriv pogrom but claimed that the soldiers had acted without Petliura's knowledge and "against his strictest orders and against the purpose of the Ukrainian People's Republic." The perpetrators, he said, were "adventurers and brigands," "the same as lynching mobs in America." Despite "proclamation after proclamation against pogroms and order after order against evildoers," the Directory had been unable to put a stop to the violence. The solution, Batchinsky concluded, was not to attack the Ukrainian government but rather to strengthen it, so that it could better control its territory. As Margolin put it in an interview with the *London Jewish Chronicle*: "There is no antisemitic tendency in the Ukraine Government, which differs in this respect, very notably, from that prevailing in Poland. It is to the progress of democratic ideals in the Ukraine that we must look for the elimination of the evil pogrom element."[38]

PART IV

THE TRIUMPH OF BOLSHEVISM

AUGUST 1919–MARCH 1921

The Volunteer Army

In the spring of 1919, while the Bolsheviks were preoccupied with putting down Grigoriev's rebellion and Petliura was retreating toward Galicia, the Volunteer Army of South Russia began its march from the Don river basin toward Kyiv. Within four months, the Whites would conquer a vast territory in the south and east of Ukraine, before being beaten back by a new Bolshevik advance in December. Having inherited the Russian imperial army's distrust of the Jews, the former tsarist officers who comprised the leadership of the Whites saw the Jews as the progenitors of Bolshevism and as an internal enemy whose perfidy had led to Russia's defeat in the Great War.

The propaganda tools the Whites had at their disposal allowed them to foster this narrative, broadcasting it across the region and eventually around the globe. In addition to their own intelligence services and information agency, the Whites could rely upon a network of sympathetic Russian-language newspapers and an array of like-minded civic organizations to spread their antisemitic conspiracy theories. During the three months of their advance, for instance, the Whites were able to print one and a half million leaflets and over four million posters, whose messages they supplemented with agitational

lectures, brochures, and films they screened in the mobile movie theaters that accompanied their troops.[1]

In his 1923 study of the Whites' pogroms, Nokhem Shtif observed
that the pogroms perpetrated by the Volunteer Army were distinguished by their military character, by the mass rape of women, by
the humiliations and tortures to which the victims were subjected, and
by the goal the Volunteers set for themselves to eradicate entire Jewish communities, often burning them to the ground. "No other group
before the Volunteers had done this on such a massive scale, so systematically and thoroughly," Shtif wrote.[2] The aid worker Nokhem
Gergel charged the Whites with responsibility for 213 pogroms and
"excesses," resulting in the confirmed murder of 5,235 Jews—a figure
that does not include those whose deaths were not registered because
they were killed outside of city limits, as well as those who subsequently perished from their injuries or from disease and starvation
attributed to the pogroms. The total death toll from the anti-Jewish
actions of the White army was not less than 8,000 and possibly double
that.[3] These numbers are particularly striking given that the pogroms
perpetrated by the Army of South Russia were concentrated during the
brief period of their advance from July to September 1919, and then
again during their retreat in December.

In contrast to the pogroms carried out by the armies of Petliura
or the various warlords, which were perpetrated by peasant soldiers, alienated troops from city garrisons, or local toughs, the White
pogroms were instigated by uniformed Russian officers of the former
tsarist army sworn to uphold law and order, people of "refined manners" and "good upbringing" who read philosophy and played classical music but were also inculcated with the antisemitism of the old
tsarist elites. As the folklorist Shmuel Rubinshteyn put it, "The Jews
had already lived through pogroms, but pogrom-mongers with university diplomas in their hands, with noble titles, with French words on
their tongues—this was new to them."[4]

Since April 1918, the Volunteer Army had been led by Anton Denikin, whose shaved head, prominent black eyebrows, silver goatee, and
handlebar mustache projected the image of the distinguished tsarist

officer he was. His father, who was born a serf, had found his sense of dignity and self-worth as an officer in the tsarist army and passed down his gratitude toward the military to his son. The younger Denikin saw action in Manchuria during the Russo-Japanese War, was promoted to colonel, and by July 1914 had reached the rank of major general. He was a strict believer in discipline and order who felt at home with the camaraderie of the officer corps. "At that time," he wrote, "we seemed to understand one another and were not strangers . . . a common life, common sufferings and common fame brought us still closer together, and created a mutual faith and a touching proximity."[5] As commander of the Russian Eighth Corps, he gained the respect of his soldiers and a reputation for being a capable leader with a modest demeanor. But he never felt quite at ease with the rest of the officer corps, who looked down upon his peasant origins.

Denikin was a true Russian patriot, who saw the church, the tsar, and the army as the three institutions that held the nation together. The dissolution of the tsarist empire and the potential loss of what he called "South Russia," the regions claimed by the Ukrainian People's Republic, were to him the greatest travesties. He was dedicated, above all, to restoring a united Russia. He had an easy way with his French and British allies and closely collaborated with them on the blockade of Odesa in early 1919. He also respected the stately German officers and disciplined soldiers he had fought against during the Great War as worthy rivals. The real enemy he loathed was internal: the "Pharisees—the leaders of the Russian Revolutionary Democracy." He regarded them as defeatists and traitors who had brought down the empire.[6]

Denikin's use of the word "Pharisee"—the ancient Judaic sect imagined in Christian theology as self-righteous opponents of Jesus—was no accident. For centuries, Jews had been blamed for manipulating governments into doing their evil bidding. Now it was the Bolsheviks who were accused of being stooges in the global Jewish plot to destroy Russia. The most ambitious Jewish conspiracy, Denikin believed, was the Russian Revolution itself. Those who brought down the tsar, he wrote in his postwar memoirs, were characterized by an "exceptional preponderance of the alien element, foreign to the Russian national idea."[7] According to John Ernest Hodgson, a British war correspondent embedded in Denikin's army, the general and his officer corps had it all figured out: "The officers and men of the army laid practically all the blame for their country's troubles on the Hebrew. They held that the whole cataclysm had been engineered by some great and mysterious secret society of international Jews, who, in the pay and at the orders of Germany, had seized the psychological moment and snatched the reins of government."[8] Hodgson, who was himself sympathetic to this viewpoint, was nevertheless shocked by the "terrible bitterness and insistency" with which Denikin's men maintained their conviction of a vast Jewish conspiracy. Copies of *The Protocols of the Elders of Zion* circulated widely among the troops and updated variations of the infamous hoax proliferated. One poster distributed by the Army of South Russia, for instance, was titled WHO GAVE THE PEOPLE SOCIALISM AND BOLSHEVIKS? It answered: "The Yids." The poster emphasized the alleged Jewish backgrounds of many prominent revolutionary leaders by referring to them by their birth names, with their new identities in parentheses:

> Bronstein (Trotsky), Nakhamkes (Steklov), Tsederbaum (Martov), Rosenfeld (Kamenev), Kats (Kamkov), Apfelbaum (Zinoviev), Zilberstein (Bogdanov), Goldman (Gorev), Kibrin (Kerensky), Goldenberg (Meshkovsky), Goldstein (Solitsev), Liberman (Chernov), Goldfarb (Parvus), and Fayshteyn (Zvezdich) have no need of Russia and do not care for the welfare of the Russian people. They dream of and strive for the destruction of Russia and the weakening of the Russian people.[9]

The document repeated the fallacy that Kerensky was Jewish, but otherwise got the names mostly (though not entirely) right. Another petition circulating at the time warned: "Awake, Russian people! Not long ago the sun was shining and Kyiv was visited by the Russian tsar, but now Jews are everywhere. We will shake off this yoke; we cannot endure it any longer. They will lead our country to destruction. Down with the Jews! Unite, Russian people! Give us a tsar!"[10]

It was Trotsky, though, who emerged as the most visible symbol of the revolution and purported Jewish power. A White propaganda poster, for instance, showed Christ being led to Golgotha by Red Army soldiers as Trotsky looks on in approval, invoking the perennial association between Jews and Christ-killers, and portraying Trotsky as a modern Caiaphas. The soldiers mock Christ, who glares at Trotsky. Another White postcard was labeled THE COAT OF ARMS OF LEON TROTSKY and showed a two-headed man with his legs grotesquely spread, in scandalous mockery of the imperial eagle. One of the faces wears Trotsky's distinctive round spectacles; both of them feature large hooked noses, full lips, enormous ears, goat's beards, and skullcaps. Four hands protrude from the figure: two of them grasp a garlic clove and a fish, representing stereotypical Jewish foods, and the other two hold aloft a prayer shawl in place of the eagle's wings. A hammer and sickle hover above the figure, and a crest with a Star of David and the word "Talmud" appears in the middle. Another poster urging Ukrainian peasants to mobilize into the Volunteer Army attacked "the little Jew, Leyb Bronstein" who "sits in Moscow in place of the tsar."[11] In order to emphasize Trotsky's Jewish roots, Denikin and White propaganda regularly referred to him by his birth name, "Bronstein," or at the very least "Trotsky Bronstein." The calculated effort to frame the

[HOOVER INSTITUTION LIBRARY AND ARCHIVES]

Christ being led to Golgotha by Red Army soldiers, with Trotsky in the foreground

Bolshevik revolution as a Jewish conspiracy proved to be an effective means of galvanizing support for the White movement.

Denikin's most significant base of support came from the Don, Kuban, and Terek Cossack bands in the south of Russia and the Northern Caucasus. As one observer noted, "It was well known that the overwhelming majority of the population of these territories was anti-Soviet."[12] The Cossack leadership was deeply committed to the frontier culture of independence they had retained under the tsars and, after an intense struggle, managed to negotiate autonomous status under Denikin's supreme command. Their military regiments had been the most hardened units in the imperial Russian army, known for their fearsome cavalry that would swarm the enemy in open fields, encircling them with rattling sabers and intimidating battle cries. Owing to their mobility and versatility, they were also typically tasked with reconnaissance and requisition missions in urban areas, terrorizing the Jews who often lived there. The Cossacks' militaristic culture and tribal loyalties presented a stark contrast with the marauding bands of peasant soldiers that constituted the other armies in the vicinity. The Cossacks of the Northern Caucasus were also free of the local

"The Coat of Arms of Leon Trotsky"

commitments that bound Petliura's peasant soldiers.[13] They were seen as an invading force of "foreigners." "They advanced as if across a strange country, seeing enemies everywhere," wrote the novelist Ilya Ehrenburg.[14] But like all the other fighters in the region, they were persuaded to continue the battle only in exchange for the right to avail themselves of the spoils of war. The constant flow of looted furnishings, jewelry, and food back to the Don Basin and Northern Caucasus helped compensate for the sacrifices the Cossack warriors were making in leaving their homelands to embark upon what many considered to be a foreign campaign.[15]

The White offensive toward Kyiv was so overwhelming that at some points they were not even able to find the Bolshevik front: it had evaporated like mist as the Volunteers approached. The Cossack cavalry rode through the empty steppe and Denikin's armored trains had complete control of the rails. The Volunteers entered the Soviet stronghold of Kharkiv on June 24 in a triumphant procession, led by priests bearing banners, lanterns, and icons as the church bells rang. General Vladimir May-Mayevsky—whom a fellow general described as looking like "a comedian from a little provincial theater," "round as a barrel" with a "chubby face and bulbous nose"[16]—followed the priests, seated in a litter. Behind him marched a military band and White troops, outfitted in British uniforms and looking every bit the Englishmen with their clipped mustaches. Ladies in silk and gentlemen in dress coats threw flowers and shouted "hurrah" as the general passed by.[17] Many in the city had tired of Bolshevik requisitions and Red Army recruitment drives, and greeted the Whites with enthusiasm.[18]

After the fall of Kharkiv, Denikin's army swept through the coal and iron districts of Katerynoslav, capturing the city itself on June 30. Farther to the east, with the assistance of British tanks and Sopwith Camel biplanes, they defeated the Bolsheviks in a massive battle at Tsaritsyn—the industrial city that a generation later would become the site of one of the most decisive battles of another war under its new name, Stalingrad. The Volunteers then captured the railway hub and grain distribution centers of Kremenchuk, where they acquired three fully equipped armored trains.[19] White forces overran Poltava on July 29, Kherson and Mykolaiv on August 18, and finally retook Odesa from the Bolsheviks on August 23.[20] As the victorious Whites swept through Ukraine, their counterrevolutionary allies in Hungary overthrew Béla Kun's Soviet government and unleashed a reign of terror against the Bolsheviks and against Hungarian Jews.[21] The Red tsunami that threatened to overwhelm Europe seemed to have been stopped.

The Volunteer Army supplemented its military victories with a propaganda campaign intended to solidify their base against perceived enemies. The military's first order after conquering Cherkasy, for instance, celebrated the unification of the city "with a single indivisible Russia" and called for the removal of all "Bolsheviks and Jews" from the city government.[22] Denikin's operational reports warned his soldiers to be on the lookout for Jewish enemies and "Zionist regiments," particularly as the Whites moved into cities like Kherson and Odesa, with their large Jewish populations and a history of Zionist activism. His propagandistic Special Commission for the Investigation of Bolshevik Crimes publicized real and exaggerated stories of the Red Terror, using tales of Cheka torture chambers to stir people against the Bolsheviks—and against the Jews.[23] The commission reported on gruesome methods of torture purportedly performed by the Cheka, including the "glove trick," in which a victim's hands were scorched in boiling water until the skin could be pulled off like a glove, and the "ice statue," in which victims were drenched with cold water and exposed to the winter cold until they turned into human ice statues.[24] John Hodgson, the British journalist embedded in Denikin's army, said that he had personally examined exhumed bodies of White soldiers the Bolsheviks had captured, and described unimaginable tortures—"live coals had been pressed into their stomachs, and a number appeared to have been scalped."[25] He wrote of mass graves inside public parks, which the Whites disinterred to show the public what the Bolsheviks had done. "All these things have left behind them a bitter and implacable determination . . . to exact vengeance the moment that circumstances, as they indubitably will, lead to the overthrow of the Soviet dominance," he warned.[26] And since the Volunteers "held all Red Commissars to be

Jews," he continued, "crimes of revenge against the Jews will be constant throughout the country for many years to come."[27]

Indeed, many noticed the prominence of Jews in the Cheka. Isaak Shvartz, the first head of the Ukraine Cheka, was a longtime Bolshevik party activist. The head of the Kyiv Cheka, Yosif Sorin, was of Jewish descent; so was his deputy, Yakov Lifshitz, who would go on to become the head of the Cheka in Chernihiv and a high-level Chekist in Zhytomyr. Some three-quarters of the staff of the Kyiv Cheka in the early months of its existence were Jews. (Latvians—another largely urban ethnic group with high levels of education—were also prominent.)[28] The deputy head of the Cheka in Odesa, Boris Severnyi, had been born with the Jewish surname Józefowicz and patronymic Samoilovich and had come from a family of dentists, well recognized as a Jewish occupation.[29] As the historian Leonard Schapiro wrote in 1961, "Anyone who had the misfortune to fall into the hands of the Cheka stood a very good chance of finding himself confronted with and possibly shot by a Jewish investigator."[30]

Despite the rhetoric of White propaganda, many Jewish property owners, shopkeepers, mill owners, and factory owners still regarded Denikin's Volunteers as the most viable defenders of private property and classical liberal values, and supported them as the best chance for defeating the Bolshevik dictatorship and restoring calm. "They believed, or at least they wanted to believe, that Denikin was some type of righteous messianic figure whose disciplined army would bring law and order to the Jews of Ukraine," recalled Shmuel Rubinshteyn.[31] Jewish officers and soldiers had joined the White ranks in the early days of the movement, and Jewish philanthropists had helped fund some of its first efforts, believing Denikin was committed to continuing the reforms that the tsar had promised in the last years of his reign.[32] Jewish overtures, though, were not always welcomed. By the summer of 1919, the Whites stopped accepting Jews into their ranks altogether because, as Denikin explained, "no one wanted to live in the same building as them or share a kitchen with them."[33]

Jews who had suffered under the Bolsheviks and yearned for White liberation were quickly disappointed when the Cossacks arrived in their cities. British parliamentarian Cecil L'Estrange Malone, who was on a mission to Ukraine at the time, described how the Volunteer Army treated Jews upon their entry into Kharkiv: "Jewish Red Troops were separated into a special group and handed over to the Volunteers, who shot them all with machine guns on the spot."[34] More than 200 mostly Jewish workingmen were hanged from four gallows in the town square and from lampposts around town. In the next three weeks, White armies perpetrated a string of atrocities, killing 130 Jews in Kremenchuk, 129 in Cherkasy, and 30 in Smila, to name but a few examples.[35] Many liberals who had previously supported the Whites were deeply concerned by what they saw. The Alliance for the Regeneration of Russia, for instance, warned in September that rather than bringing law and order to Ukraine and uniting the people of the former Russian Empire, Denikin was instead inciting chaos and divisiveness: "While the continuous outrages are terrorizing *one* part of the population, they are simultaneously corrupting the *others*, sustaining the growing conviction that it is necessary to kill, massacre and rob Jewish citizens."[36]

THE WHITE ADVANCE forced the Bolsheviks to retreat, giving Petliura a new opening. He was joined now by more disciplined Galician soldiers from the defunct Western Ukrainian People's Republic, who came under his command following the Polish occupation of Eastern Galicia. As Petliura's forces fought their way back from Kamyanets-Podilskyi, heading toward Uman, the Whites advanced through Elizavetgrad, a hundred miles to the east. Both armies were converging on Bolshevik-held Kyiv. Petliura had sent signals to the Whites suggesting an alliance, a position favored by the British and French, who saw a joint Ukrainian-Russian advance against the Bolsheviks as the best chance for defeating the Red Army. But Denikin was not interested in cooperating with Petliura, whose Ukrainian Republic infringed upon his dream of a united Russia. Nevertheless, Petliura ordered his soldiers to avoid conflict with Denikin's forces and the two reached a temporary understanding that they would use the Dnipro River as a dividing line

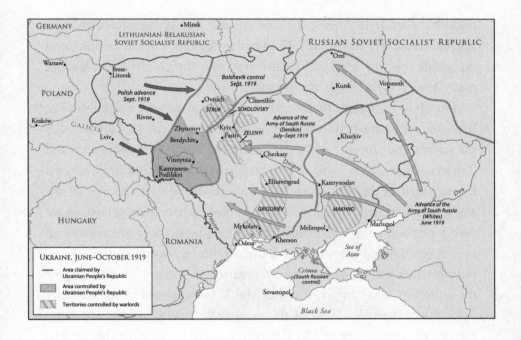

GERMANY   •Minsk
            LITHUANIAN-BELARUSIAN
            SOVIET SOCIALIST REPUBLIC   RUSSIAN SOVIET SOCIALIST REPUBLIC

Warsaw•   Brest-   •Orel
                 Litovsk   Bolshevik control
POLAND   Polish advance   Sept. 1919   •Kursk   Voronezh•
                        Sept. 1919   •Ovruch •Chernihiv
Kraków•   Rivne•   STRUK SOKOLOVSKY
            GALICIA   Advance of the
            Lviv•   Zhytomyr Kyiv•   Army of South Russia
                         Berdychiv• Fastiv ZELENYI (Denikin)   •Kharkiv
                                                   July–Sept 1919
                                        •Cherkasy
                  Vinnytsia•   Dnipro
                  Kamyanets-
                  Podilskyi•
                                  •Elizavetgrad   •Katerynoslav
HUNGARY   GRIGORIEV   Advance of
                                            MAKHNO   Army of South Russia
                                                        (Whites)
            ROMANIA   June 1919
                         Dnister •Mykolaiv   Melitopol• •Mariupol
┌─────────────────────────────────┐ •Odesa •Kherson
│ UKRAINE, JUNE–OCTOBER 1919   │   Sea of
│ ---- Area claimed by   │   Azov
│   Ukrainian People's Republic│   Crimea
│   Area controlled by   │   (South Russian
│   Ukrainian People's Republic│   control)
│ //// Territories controlled by │ Sevastopol•
│   warlords   │
└─────────────────────────────────┘   Black Sea

between their operations in Kyiv. On August 22, a Galician unit led by the Austrian general Anton Kraus moved into Bila Tserkva, fifty miles southwest of Kyiv.

Next in line was Fastiv, a town of twenty-two thousand located between Bila Tserkva and Kyiv. When the Red Army had taken the town on February 19, the Jews, who constituted about 40 percent of the population, were relieved. They remembered the bodies that had been found near the railway lines under the Directory and the harassment Jews had faced from Petliura's soldiers. The Red Army, though, did little to endear itself to them. Many of the members of the local party organization were ill-disposed toward Jews, viewing them as bourgeois speculators.[37] Soon after their conquest of the city, Red soldiers removed two Jewish passengers from a train and executed them for pickpocketing.[38] The whole town suffered from the Bolshevik requisitions, but the Jewish craftsmen, petty traders, and workers bore the brunt of the hardship. The Bolsheviks nationalized the leather factories, butter production facilities, hulling mills, and iron storage facilities, most of which were owned by Jews—instantly turning wealthy notables into virtual paupers. But despite the economic turmoil, a Jew could survive in the city. The Bolsheviks kept out the bandits and insurgent soldiers who had been terrorizing the countryside, leading many Jews to grudgingly accept soviet rule.

Jewish women and children from nearby towns—from Radomyshl, Brusyliv, and Tarashcha—had been flooding into the city all through the spring and summer of 1919, fleeing the bands of Sokolovsky and Zelenyi.[39] The pious came in the belief that they would be protected by the spirit of Avrom ha-Malach (Avrom the Angel), the son of the eighteenth-century Hasidic leader Dov-Ber of Mezritsh, whose grave was a popular pilgrimage site. The more pragmatic were convinced that the Red Army would never abandon this important railroad junction. Neither the pious nor the pragmatic got it right. By late August the question was simply whether the Whites would reach the city before the Galicians. Most of the local Jews, having previously experienced the turbulence of Ukrainian rule, were rooting for the Whites, who, at least, held out the promise of restoring law and order.

In the end, it was Kraus's Galicians who arrived first. After only two hours of fighting, the well-trained former Austrian soldiers

Привѣтъ изъ Фастова

Postcard: "Greetings from Fastiv"

defeated the ragtag Red Army troops, many of whom had been forcibly recruited and had little interest in fighting. On their way out of
town, the Red soldiers managed one final round of requisitions, taking
watches, shoes, and any other valuables they could collect.[40] Kraus's
soldiers were accompanied by a motley crew of brigands and bandits,
who raided Jewish stores in the center of town, killing at least four
Jews and injuring many others.[41] Acting decisively, Kraus quickly put
an end to the violence by executing two of the ringleaders. The worst
seemed to be over. A few days later, Kraus departed for Kyiv, leaving a
small contingent of troops in Fastiv. The town quickly reverted to its
state of anarchy as insurgent bands took over.

But then, on Saturday, September 6, 1919, the *Vityaz*, an armored
train belonging to the Volunteer Army and carrying the Second Terek
Cossack Brigade, pulled into the Fastiv station.[42] Its 75-millimeter

[TsDKFFA]

Petliura's reception in Fastiv after the expulsion
of the Red Army in August 1919

cannon surveyed the station and its surroundings, rotating like a peri-scope on the top of the tank that had been installed on the open flatbed. Although armored trains had been used as early as the Boer War, they became a major part of the constellation of forces during the civil war. The Reds were the first among the combatants to reinforce old passen-ger trains and flatbeds with armored walls and outfit them with Maxim guns and naval cannons. Riflers fired through embrasures and from turrets built on top of the trains. The Whites soon followed suit, build-ing their own armored trains or, more often, capturing Bolshevik trains, which they rebaptized and used to quickly shuttle troops to the front lines. Most had been hastily assembled: steel coal hoppers lined with pressed straw and mounted steel plates. The *Vityaz*, named after the warrior hero of medieval Slavic legends, was not one of the military's best-equipped war machines, but it sufficed to threaten the garrisons of medium-sized towns like Fastiv.

An elated crowd greeted the train. "So many children, women and old folks came out into the street—what joy could be seen in their faces. Everybody thought that their saviors had arrived," one witness reported.[43] Jews came out to the station holding Torah scrolls and dancing in celebration. One Jewish community leader wrote to a friend in Kyiv: "You, of course, understand how eagerly we awaited them [the Volunteer Army], as it seemed to a great majority of the Jewish population that, now, finally, a capable government would be installed that would put an end to the horrors and torments."[44] Isaac Berliand, a teacher in Fastiv who volunteered for the Red Cross, wrote that most of the Jews in town "were anticipating with great impatience the arrival of Denikin's troops, being persuaded that they are the bearers of the principles of private property, of free trade, of freedom of speech, and in general of all that characterizes a middle-class republic."[45]

In two neighboring villages, both with largely Jewish popula-tions, retreating peasant gangs and insurgents attacked the civil-ian population, killing twenty-three Jews and, in the words of one report, "violating almost every woman, from 12-year-old girls to 55-year-olds."[46] But in Fastiv itself, optimism reigned. Jewish and Christian communal leaders were convinced that the Whites were about to restore the liberal civic institutions created by Kerensky's provisional government, and immediately set to work reinstating the previous municipal government. Kiosks and stalls reopened and the streets were filled with craftsmen, traders, and peasants buying and selling their wares. "The population," wrote one witness, "having endured so much under the authority of Petliura, Zelenyi, Sokolovsky, and other bands, awaited the arrival of the new soldiers with excitement, hoping for the onset, finally, of a little calm and perhaps even a respite from the constant requisitions by the Bolsheviks and the outright plunder by all kinds of otamans."[47]

Townsfolk were genuinely surprised when at ten o'clock in the evening of September 6, they heard shooting and commotion. A few rogue Terek Cossacks had begun to rob Jewish homes. They were soon joined by others. Screams and shots pierced the night as plunder and assault ravaged the city.[48] "During the day it was usually quiet, but the night was a terrible nightmare," recalled one witness.[49] According to one anonymous report sent to the Central Committee for Relief of Pogrom Victims: "The Jews lived through a torturous night. They hid in forests, gardens, ravines, attics, basements, cellars, and pits. Sometimes whole families managed to remain together, but often they were separated from each other, husbands from their wives and children, each of whom found their own hiding place. They spent the night in deathly fear for their lives and their families."[50] As the Jews stayed out of sight, soldiers looted the town, stealing from individuals on the streets and burglarizing homes. Seven or eight women were reportedly raped that night.[51] At several points around the city, Christians auctioned off stolen Jewish goods: "They were selling expensive fur coats, clothing, sewing machines, mirrors, pictures, and household goods at bargain prices."[52]

Many witnesses insisted that the plunder was authorized from above: "A significant part of the officers actively participated," wrote one.[53] The commander of the brigade himself, Colonel Vladimir Belogortsev, personally summoned Rabbi Raphael Moyshe-Meyerovich Kligman and demanded an exorbitant monetary contribution by the next day. Kligman succeeded in raising most of the sum, but when he presented it to the colonel, Belogortsev scolded him for trying to pass off worthless Soviet currency. He ordered the rabbi to come back with Nikolaevkis—tsarist gold coins. Kligman made the rounds again and delivered the money the next day.[54] Three officers searched Kligman's own apartment and walked away with cigarettes, cash, and clothes.[55] "From everywhere could be heard inhuman cries of Jews who were being slaughtered, violated, and robbed," the rabbi reported. "When we brought this to the attention of Colonel Belogortsev, he said that he had already taken measures against it and they would soon be implemented."[56] Within a few days an uneasy calm set in, as the city accustomed itself to White rule.

THE WEEKS-LONG RESPITE in Fastiv was shattered early in the evening on Sunday, September 21, when cannons and gunfire again rattled the windows.[57] Residents who took shelter in their basements or in one of the few brick buildings in town recall hearing the sounds of machine-gun fire and shouts of "hurrah" coming from the vicinity of the train station, where six to seven hundred Red Army troops had just arrived. Christian townsfolk grumbled that the Jews were celebrating the return of the Bolsheviks. Jews who gave testimony, though, insisted that the cheers were most likely coming from the soldiers themselves, as virtually every Jew in the city had gone into hiding as soon as the gunfire began; certainly none were anywhere near the station.[58]

The next morning, Red Army soldiers were patrolling the town square, looking on edge, as though they, too, were shocked to be in control and were fearful of what was to come. In their haste to retreat, the Whites had left behind trainloads of foodstuff and clothing that fell into Bolshevik hands. A few women ventured outside to buy sugar and leather from soldiers eager to make money off the captured trophies, but most people stayed in their homes and observed the scene from their windows.[59] It was clear to everyone, including the Bolsheviks themselves, that their hold on the town was tenuous: the new government didn't even bother to issue orders. The Bolsheviks just

seemed to be waiting, counting down time until the inevitable counterattack.

Sure enough, at around four o'clock in the afternoon on Monday,
the windows started to rattle again and the thunder of cannons shattered the eerie calm. Within two hours, the Second Terek Cossack
Brigade moved back in, now with an additional artillery division,
forcing the Bolsheviks back toward the Unava River, where they
remained encamped at the edge of town, near the station.

As evening turned to night, smoke rose from the Bolshevik encampment as it sustained White bombardments. Under the cover of darkness, Cossack soldiers plundered Jewish homes, aided by local youth
and peasants, who showed them the way. Some Cossacks justified
their raids as a search for weapons or for the field telephones that Jews
were allegedly using to communicate with the enemy. According to the
journalist Ivan Derevensky, who interviewed witnesses the following
week, the Cossacks "broke into every storage space. They smashed furniture, walls, stoves, floors, and cupboards, and dug through firewood
in sheds, all in the pursuit of money."[60] Officers could even be seen
loading pianos onto peasant carts, awkwardly balancing the instru-
ments and strapping them down with rope as they wheeled them off.[61]
Derevensky described gardens that had been dug up in search of buried
treasures. Survivors were deprived of even their beetroots and turnips.

The violence spread from storefronts and houses into the open.
Derevensky writes that "groups of Cossacks openly went around the
city stopping Jews on the street. Sometimes they would simply ask 'Are
you a Jew?' and shoot them in the forehead. But much more often they
would first search them, even strip them naked, and then shoot them
in that state right there on the street."[62] Others tell of Cossacks torturing Jews until they revealed their hidden valuables or weapons. Those
who had neither were hanged on the spot. The story of one Jewish
family who beat back marauding Cossacks in their home was inflated
into the absurd allegation that Jewish craftsmen were attacking the
Army of South Russia.

Isaac Berliand recorded numerous instances of rape: "How many times did I see those scoundrels drag young girls, children even, into the destroyed and empty apartments."[63] Another witness testified that over two hundred women and girls were raped: "This was a new method of war surpassing every abomination. In the presence of mothers, fathers, and dozens of strangers, the victims were pushed to the ground and raped, even right on the street by fifteen to twenty people each. . . . The cries lasted for hours but nobody paid attention."[64] Cossack regiments fighting for the Whites were accused of sexual atrocities in neighboring Smila as well, where doctors treated ninety-five women and girls for injuries. "The Cossacks were especially energetic in their pursuit of Jewish girls and women, who were violated right on the street, in view of everyone," wrote I. Galperin. Galperin further reported that two of his brothers-in-law, hiding in a cellar, witnessed "a group of around twenty drunken Cossacks committing a vicious act of violence against a Jewish girl. The rape was accompanied by awful torments. Each of the abusers had come up with ways to torment the victim. I was later told that after these events this unfortunate girl took her own life."[65] In some cases, men killed themselves after witnessing the violation of their daughters.[66] Most of those who received medical attention for rape were adolescents, some as young as ten, but that may have been because older victims were less likely to seek medical attention. There are reports of women as old as seventy being subjected to sexual assaults.[67]

Many Christian residents painted crosses on their doors to signal to the Cossacks to spare them, thereby acquiescing in the violence. But others resisted by taking Jews into their homes. One officer, most likely of the former tsarist army, sheltered some three hundred injured and sick Jews at the school. The Jewish community rewarded him with a handsome sum for his troubles.[68] A peasant named Timofei Sadnikov wrote to the Central Committee for Relief of Pogrom Victims to let them know that his sister hid two young Jewish women in the nearby village of Potievke during the pogrom. Sadnikov wanted to be sure that the committee knew "our people, the peasants of Potievke, did not take part in either the pogrom or the looting. There are rumors that our people took part in the looting and stole goods from Fastiv and gave them to the village elder. But this was rare. For the most part, the goods were stolen by the Cossacks."[69]

THE FIRES BEGAN on Monday evening. The first victim was Aba Markman: Cossacks filled his house with gunpowder, doused it with kerosene, and set it alight. Soon, the homes of Perets Feldman, Yakov Zabolotsky, Motel Shlak, Dovid Neishtat, Aron Mestechkin, Eliezer-Dovid Feldman, Yosef Kogan, and many others were also set on fire with incendiary bombs. The fire easily devoured the houses, with their thatched roofs and walls made of clay and straw over wooden frames. By daybreak, the entire Jewish quarter, where merchants lived behind their storefronts, was in flames. The systematic torching of houses represented an escalation in the violence and the level of hostility: the conflagration rendered the damage irrevocable, transforming the physical landscape of the town center into ash and embers, a warning to the inhabitants never to return.[70] Fedor Zalevsky, a Christian who owned a bakery near the market, could not believe his eyes. He threw his hands up to the heavens and shouted, "How do you not heed Jewish blood and cries?"[71]

A Christian field nurse by the name of A. O. Nikolaidi who lived in a nearby village reported that she looked out across the open wheat fields and saw the sky glowing red in the distance. She gathered her medical supplies and headed toward the flames. In her testimony, she recalled seeing victims with gunshot wounds, with appendages cut off by sabers, and several women who had been raped and sexually assaulted.[72]

Throughout the week, the fires continued. Isaac Berliand wrote that the Cossacks compelled residents to set fire to their own homes and then forced them back into the burning houses.[73] In one house alone, twelve charred corpses were discovered. Derevensky reported that a total of two hundred buildings burned, half of which were residential. The entire market square was destroyed and nearly all the buildings on the main commercial streets were torched.[74] Even Yisroel Berlin's mill was consumed. There would be no grain for the survivors.

According to a press report: "At the end of the fifth day, when the fire began to threaten Christian homes as well, the local Catholic priest and several other citizens appealed to the commandant to cease the pogrom, and particularly, to control the fire, which would not discriminate by nationality."[75] And so, on a frigid Thursday night, five days after the violence began, the Cossacks ordered the surviving Jewish population to gather near the synagogue and hand over their outer garments. Wearing only their underclothes, the assembled crowd was driven into the synagogue. The Cossacks locked the doors and threatened to burn the building down in a final inferno unless the terrified Jews could raise a ransom.[76] The Jewish quarter was in ashes and there was little left that could be handed over. But they promised to give whatever they possessed. When the hostages were released, the Cossacks took the Torah scrolls out of the ark and tore them apart but spared the synagogue. The pogrom was over. The bodies of the dead were still smoldering inside the locked houses.

ON FRIDAY MORNING, hundreds of Jews, many disguised in peasant clothing, headed to the station, hoping to stow away on any passing freight car to escape the shattered town. The rail line to Kyiv, which had been a battlefront during the pogrom, had just been cleared. But even so, the fleeing Jews were not safe. Cossacks stopped the trains on their way out of town and hunted for Jews aboard; those they found were forced to disembark before the train was allowed to continue on its route. When the train started to move again, passengers reported hearing gunshots from nearby in the forest.[77]

As the Jews fled the city en masse, long chains of peasants pushing carts or carrying empty bags could be seen heading in the opposite direction, into Fastiv from neighboring villages. By evening, nothing of value was left inside the burned-out homes.

According to Nikolaidi, "The bodies of murdered Jews lay all over the place. There were around a hundred corpses (exclusively men) in two squares in the city—one near the Catholic Church and the other between the market and the hospital. Despite the constant flow of elderly Jewish men carrying the dead on stretchers along the streets in the direction of the synagogue, many victims of the pogrom remained uncollected. Near the Catholic Church I saw with my own eyes a pig gnawing the body of one of the murdered Jews. Some bloody rags were hanging out the window of one basement. I went over and looked through: there on the floor of the empty room lay a bloody corpse of a Jew with a bullet through the head."[78] Derevensky painted a similar scene: "The smell of corpses lingered near a few of the burned-out homes. Often the bones of unidentified victims could be found at locations where arson had occurred. Many people's relatives had not been accounted for. Pigs and dogs fed on some of the bodies in the ravine behind the prayer house."[79] The Joint Distribution Committee reported, as well, that "a great many Jews have been found hanged in the neighboring forest." The number of dead recorded came to a staggering 1,036; in the cemetery alone, 540 victims were counted.[80] Many more were severely injured or burned, and many corpses were too badly charred to be identified. Later estimates by the Jewish Public Committee set the death toll even higher, at 1,800.[81]

On the Monday after the pogrom, as Nikolaidi boarded a train to return to her home village, she witnessed a few barefoot Jewish men clearing garbage off the tracks under the watch of some Cossacks. "The communists dirtied the place up, let them clean it up," one of the guards snarled.

Weeks later, a thousand sick and starving victims were still being held in two locations: a single-story building and the synagogue. As Berliand reported: "Dead bodies had been lying in hospitals, dormitories, and private homes for ten to twelve days; disease spread from the dead and dying to the living."[82] By November, the Red Cross worker G. I. Rabinovich estimated that another thousand Jews had died of typhus, hunger, and exposure; hardly a Jewish home remained standing, and those that remained had broken windows and doors, making it impossible to keep out the bitter cold.[83] "The situation is very serious for the sick and injured; every day the epidemic spreads, especially because some one hundred and fifty people are living in incredibly difficult and unsanitary conditions," the Red Cross reported.[84] The most

seriously injured were evacuated to Kyiv, where, according to Rabinovich, many victims perished soon after arrival. He estimated the
death toll, including those who fell victim to disease in the aftermath
of the pogrom, to be over eight thousand.

WITH FASTIV UNDER White control, the road to Kyiv was clear. On
August 30, Kraus's unit was the first to reach the city, secure the
bridges over the Dnipro, and hoist the blue and yellow Ukrainian flag
over City Hall. But by evening the next day, the Don Cossack cavalry attached to Denikin's army under the command of Major General
Nikolai Bredov arrived from the east and brazenly rode into the center
of the city. After two days of heavy fighting, the forces of Bredov and
Kraus defeated the Bolshevik armored trains, heavy artillery, observation balloons, and gunboats and occupied Kyiv. With the departure
of Red Army troops, Bredov turned on the Galicians, giving them an
ultimatum to either lay down their weapons or leave the city. Kraus
ordered his men to comply, thereby handing the capital over to Denikin. With Kyiv in their possession, the Whites looked to discredit the
Ukrainians and restore the ancient capital to a united Russia.

Large segments of the city population—Jews and non-Jews alike—
celebrated the Whites' victory, anticipating that Kyiv would become
Russian again and that normalcy would be restored. It was the ninth
time the city had changed hands since 1917 and the economy was
in shambles. With a population that was largely Russian-speaking,
many in the city had been wary of Ukrainian statehood. The Bolsheviks, who had controlled the government since February, were equally
disliked. It had been a time of tribulation and extremes as the Bolsheviks experimented with social engineering in the city. "In every
institution," recalled Ehrenburg, "it seemed, grey-haired eccentrics
and young enthusiasts were drafting projects for a heavenly life on
earth."[85] But the discrepancy between their discussions and reality
was staggering: "Gangs prowled about the city; every day there were
new stories of pogroms and killings."[86] During the winter, the Bolsheviks had levied substantial contributions, taken over private shops,

requisitioned residential houses, nationalized banks, rationed bread, and imposed a ten p.m. curfew.[87] It was enough to turn even their erstwhile supporters against them. Jews, who were overrepresented among the private shop owners, suffered in particular. "All Jewish life, both on an individual and a societal basis, was under the yoke of a terrible physical and moral terror," declared representatives of the official Jewish community after the Bolsheviks had been forced out.[88] "For the last three months, I slept half dressed, waiting to be searched or arrested," complained one student in September.[89] At the same time, Jews were blamed for the excesses of the Bolsheviks. As Ehrenburg put it, the Russian majority in the city "quarreled among themselves. All, however, cursed the Bolsheviks, the Ukrainian nationalists, and the Jews."[90]

As usual, what had most terrified the population was the implementation of Red Terror under the Cheka, which the Whites exploited for the purpose of propaganda. As a London *Times* correspondent who arrived in the city on September 17 wrote, "Kyiv today is a city of horrors. I do not know whether in any other town in which they have ruled the Bolshevists have left such ghastly traces of their fiendish work as they have here." He estimated that two thousand people had been murdered by the Cheka but noted that popular rumors put the figure at thirty to forty thousand victims. In the holding cells used by the Cheka, he continued, "the walls are pitted with revolver bullets and splashed with red stains; the floor is still glutinous; the smell makes one turn away sickened after a very short inspection." He wrote of hundreds of bodies left to rot in makeshift prison cells. The entire city, he complained, reeked of "a terrible odor, which chloride only partially stifles."[91]

The *Times* correspondent identified the main culprit within the Cheka as a "Jewess" named Rosa Schwartz: "I say this," he wrote, "because the figure of a Jewess as a prominent member of the [Cheka] is becoming legendary."[92] In an extended version of the article, he blamed the entire Terror on the Jews, repeating the canard that both Christian Rakovsky, who headed the Soviet government in Ukraine, and Martyn Latsis, who headed the Cheka in Kyiv, were Jewish. In fact, neither was—Rakovsky was of Bulgarian and Romanian descent and Latsis was Latvian.[93] But many were convinced that it was the Jews who were responsible for the horrors the city had endured. According to one witness, when the Don Cossacks arrived with the Volunteer Army,

> various types of merchants with various types of products approached them. These merchants strongly agitated among the Cossacks against the Jews, blaming them for all the deeds of the Cheka. The first day, however, was completely quiet: the Cossacks didn't touch any of the Jews. But on the next day, the Cossacks sent a delegation of four people to inspect the Cheka [building]. When the delegation returned the attitude of the Cossacks immediately changed; all were in a terribly agitated mood and threatened to slaughter all the Yids. In reality, from this moment they began to beat every Jew who passed by on the street.[94]

The inspection of the Cheka facilities turned prejudices into retribution. The Whites arrested anybody suspected of aiding the Bolsheviks, sending hundreds of Jews to overcrowded prisons in the city. Mobs roamed the streets, enraged by stories of Red Terror, randomly attacking anybody who looked Jewish. At the railway stations leading into the city, Cossack soldiers attacked and murdered dozens of Jewish travelers on the charge of Bolshevism.[95] Denikin, however, fearing that the disturbances would get out of control, distributed flyers calling for an end to the violence against Jews, calming the situation and allowing for a tense peace to prevail for nearly six weeks.[96]

On October 16, 1919, however, two days after the Bolsheviks launched an offensive to retake Kyiv, the Volunteers responded with a new counterattack of their own.[97] "The cannons roared furiously and shells fell throughout the city, carrying out their destructive mission," recalled Charles Jacobovitz, the secretary of the Belgian consulate in Kyiv. "The sky was low and covered with clouds. A cold wind roared, as though wailing. The streets were deserted apart from a few soldiers and passers-by." By midmorning, he continued, the Whites had reestablished control but used their reentry as a pretext to attack the Jews: "Organized bands of soldiers and officers from the Volunteer Army arrived by car, on horseback, and on foot with the deliberate intention of attacking and looting defenseless Jewish homes."[98] There were rampant rumors, fueled by the right-wing press, that the majority of the Jewish population had sided with the Bolsheviks during the interlude, and that Jews were shooting at the Whites and pouring boiling water onto the troops from their windows and balconies. The Volunteers' own military intelligence warned its officers to be on the lookout for a Jewish communist fighting organization that had allegedly acquired machine guns, rifles, and grenades.

Claiming to be scouring the city for collaborators, White officers and Cossack forces responded by systematically raiding the wealthy Jewish mansions along the tree-lined boulevards of the downtown core, emptying stores of supplies stockpiled for winter, ransacking private homes, and occasionally leaving estates in flames. Their underlings were permitted to scavenge the poorer outer suburbs.[99] The warlord Ilya Struk, now fighting alongside Denikin, took over the heavily Jewish Podil district of the city.[100]

In one of three hundred testimonies given to the Central Committee for Relief of Pogrom Victims, Shmuil Gankin said that a colonel, three officers, and some soldiers arrested him on the false charge that he had been looking out his window with binoculars. He testified that he handed over his documents, which provided no evidence that he had anything to do with communism. "But the colonel said that the Jews are always fabricating papers and that even if I am not a communist I must answer for other Jews." The colonel searched his apartment, took all his clothing, leaving him only his waistcoat and cap, and ordered the soldiers to escort him outside, where they beat him and forced him to chant the contradictory slogans, "Long live the Volunteer Army" and "Long live Lenin and Trotsky."[101]

A. Teitelbaum reported that an officer and soldiers who came to his home accused him of shooting from his window. The officer pointed to one of his soldiers who had a bandaged arm and promised to get even; Teitelbaum insisted he didn't even have a gun.[102] Samuil Meltser was on his way to his apartment in the middle of the day when two

Cossack officers accosted him and demanded his watch, his coat, and his money. As he was talking with them on the street, a neighbor appeared on a second-floor balcony: "one of the officers shot him with his rifle, killing him outright."[103] At least five people recovering from wounds sustained during the Fastiv pogrom were murdered in the hospital by soldiers who barged into the surgical ward demanding to know which patients had come from Fastiv.[104] Semen Burakovsky, a thirty-nine-year-old merchant, was mortally wounded in his apartment by soldiers who, according to his widow, shouted, "All Yids must die; they are all communists."[105]

The looting and murders continued for four days, becoming more brazen each night. Many witnesses hinted at sexual violence. "As long as I live, I will not forget the screams that echo relentlessly in my ears," wrote Jacobovitz, the Belgian consulate secretary, of the sounds he heard coming from a neighbor's house. "The cries continued for around an hour and then ceased. The lone voice of a woman that resembled the bark of a dog could then be heard." In another apartment he was able to enter, "a whole family—father, mother and a little girl—were lying in a pool of blood, their bodies terribly mutilated, their hands torn off, separated from the body by saber blows."[106]

"This was not Petliura's band of riffraff," noted Shmuel Rubinshteyn: "These were people with manicured hands, with noble faces of princes, accompanied by their fiery, dark, and beautiful friends from the Caucasus, who learned the way of the pogrom from the old Petersburg military elite."[107] "In Kyiv," he continued, "the true face of the 'benevolent army' with its high aristocracy was uncovered."[108] "They killed plenty of Jews," Ehrenburg mused, "but they did not save their old Russia for all that."[109]

The Whites accompanied their physical attacks on the Jewish residents of Kyiv with an antisemitic propaganda campaign. Papers, brochures, and posters blaming the Jews for the crimes of the Bolsheviks were distributed along the railways, among military companies, and widely within the city. They accused the Jews of communist sympathies or of fighting for the enemy. They alleged that "Jews shot at our valiant defenders from their attics, balconies, and windows," warned that

"Trotsky-Bronstein will close the Orthodox churches and divide up our rich land among his co-religionists," and urged a boycott of Jewish businesses.[110] The Whites worked in conjunction with a sympathetic and widely circulated press that incited further violence, laying the blame for all the unrest the city had experienced on the Jews, who were accused of having brought on the turmoil by murdering the tsar and supporting the Bolshevik government that took his place. One Jewish student expressed amazement that his own maid, who had personally witnessed how the Bolsheviks had harassed him, came to believe that he was connected to the Bolsheviks. "The propaganda," he noted, "had done its job."[111]

The Bolsheviks, wrote the Russian-language newspaper *Kievlianin* on October 19, "were assisted by the local Jewish population, which shot indiscriminately" at the Volunteers and formed "Jewish party fighting organizations, which they called self defense brigades."[112] Two days later, the paper questioned the loyalty of the city's Jews and urged them to denounce their coreligionists: "Will the Jews learn anything from these terrible nights . . . will they learn what they need to do?

[TsDKFFA]

Jewish delegation greets Petliura after his return from Galicia

Will those Jews whose hands are all over this catastrophe be publicly cursed in the synagogues? Will the majority of the Jewish population that attacked the old regime also renounce the new [Bolshevik] government with the same passion?"[113] The antisemitic publicity campaign reminded many of Kiev's Jewish residents of the darkest days of tsarism and was regarded by some as a greater affront than the physical violence they endured.

The Jews were not entirely abandoned by the city's largely Russian inhabitants: the powerful union of metallurgists issued a statement condemning the pogrom, as did the workers' trade union council.[114] Many members of the liberal intelligentsia spoke out against it, and there are reports of at least one Orthodox priest coming to the defense of his Jewish neighbors.[115] But it was not enough. By November 1, 294 Jewish bodies had been buried at the cemetery. And as one observer writing on that day noted, there were still bodies in the streets, and many people, unable to get to the cemetery, had buried their neighbors in yards and green spaces throughout the city.[116] Representatives of the Central Committee for Relief of Pogrom Victims went door-to-door to distribute hundreds of questionnaires asking for details of the pogrom.[117] Final estimates of the dead ranged from four to six hundred.[118] Assessing the impact of the pogrom on the political loyalties of the Jewish population, one memoirist noted: "If these people were indifferent before, now they will become Bolsheviks."[119]

The Tetiiv Pogrom

The Red Army launched another major counteroffensive against both Petliura and Denikin in December. Petliura's army once again evaporated into the countryside and, on December 5, 1919, the chief otaman himself fled to Warsaw to seek new alliances within Poland. The Whites were forced into a retreat, leaving the Ukrainian heartland as quickly as they came. The Bolsheviks entered Kyiv on Thursday, December 11. "The city wasn't bombed," recalled one resident, "but we could hear the crackling of the machine guns and the cannonade from the armored trains." The Whites and their supporters surrendered or fled without a fight. "Refugees were waiting until Tuesday at the station, sitting in passenger cars with no locomotives and no train conductors."[1]

After their retreat from Kyiv, Denikin's Volunteer Army crumbled along with its dream of a united Russia. Typhus ravaged the ranks, officers squabbled over tactics, the British ended their support, and the Cossacks abandoned the effort. Completely demoralized, the retreating soldiers sought revenge against the Jewish residents of the towns they passed by.

They reached Tetiiv, a small town in the Dnipro Uplands on the

Ros River, on December 25. The four thousand residents, almost half of whom were Jewish, remembered the Whites from their advance through the town earlier in the fall. Before then, the town had been led by a local Bolshevik named Volf Lederman, whom the peasants contemptuously called "the Yid Tsar."[2] Under Bolshevik rule, the five mills, soap factory, and seltzer water plant had largely ground to a halt, and many of the groceries, dry goods stores, and hardware stores had closed up shop.[3] In September, weakened by economic collapse and disease, residents had eagerly welcomed the Volunteer soldiers, who spoke in elegant Russian and promised a restoration of law and order. But instead, about thirty Cossack horsemen together with a dozen members of Denikin's counterintelligence forces had burst into homes in search of valuables, even swiping blankets off bedridden patients.[4]

As a result of this experience, when the Volunteer Army returned during its December retreat, residents were already on edge. Aron Sery testified that he was in bed, sick with typhus but "fully aware," on the evening of December 25. Neighbors were hiding in his house, sitting in the darkness, when at around eight o'clock "somebody started banging at our window, cursing at us to open the door." About ten Cossacks and one Chechen soldier fighting under Denikin barged into the room demanding to know who the homeowners were. When Sery's parents stepped up, the Cossacks hit his mother in the chest with a revolver and struck her a second time in the head, drawing blood. The soldiers turned to Sery's father and beat him, yelling all the while: "Jews, money!" Sery's father offered some money, but the Cossacks were not satisfied, and they struck him in the face. Sery himself handed over a silver watch and all the money he had on him. The soldiers ordered Sery and his father to place their heads on the table and raised their sabers in mock execution. Then they left, taking with them clothing and other valuables. They also grabbed three geese from the yard and slaughtered them right there, taking the birds for their meal. Throughout the night, Sery reported hearing screaming, the sound of glass breaking, and the rumbling of rolling carts, as soldiers looted his neighbors.[5] "The most noble men just like the simplest soldiers took part in the wildest robberies and atrocities—many people were injured, many people were tortured and humiliated; they even violated women, young and old alike (from the oldest, a 60-year-old, to the youngest 14- and 15-year-old girls)," remembered one witness.[6]

On Friday afternoon, December 26, as the Volunteers prepared to move on, they began gathering hay and straw, setting it alight, and throwing the torches into Jewish shops and houses. Many of the stores in the market square burned to the ground, as did ten houses, including those that belonged to Shloyme Gorodetsky, Moyshe Peker, and Moyshe Rabinovich.[7] Sery counted fifteen people killed; other reports put the number of dead at twenty to thirty. All witnesses documented numerous additional incidents of rape and assault.[8] The Whites' brief occupation had aggravated ethnic relations, raised the town's tolerance for violence, and foreshadowed the crimes to come.

Similar episodes occurred along the route of the Volunteer Army's retreat. In Kryve Ozero, for instance, a town of fifteen thousand near Odesa, White soldiers plundered Jewish homes, attacked the Jewish population with swords, knives, axes, and bayonets, and forcibly confined several young Jewish girls to a house that the soldiers used as a brothel. According to witnesses, "On Christmas night, under the sound of the church bells, a wild killing began."[9] The Whites celebrated the season with "a ball, with music, dancing and card games in the very center of the town, on streets that were streaming with blood," where they toasted their victory over the "Communist-Yids."[10] On January 10, the Volunteer soldiers, hearing news of a Bolshevik approach from the north, began torching the town. By the time the Red Army secured control two weeks later, the Jewish community had been completely ravaged. One witness, a Christian schoolteacher, described "corpses lying around the street like garbage." He assisted the surviving Jews in transporting over four hundred bodies to the cemetery and digging a massive pit in the frozen earth. "One didn't hear any noise and one didn't see any tears. Everybody was silent and looking at me, the only Christian among them," he recalled.[11]

By March, the Whites were pushed back to Crimea. In the face of defeat, Denikin resigned and fled to Constantinople along with many of his former comrades in arms. He later settled in Paris. The Bolsheviks had achieved a major victory, permanently ending the Whites' military presence in Ukraine. But White propaganda proved in the end to be more resilient than their power. The last pockets of peasant resistance had internalized the conspiratorial worldview that linked all Jews to Bolshevism, and the counterrevolutionary movement began to adopt the scorched-earth tactics of the Volunteer Army. When the Red Army finally crushed the opposition, the Jews were widely blamed. As a famous quip put it: "The Trotskys made the revolution, but the Bronsteins paid the price."

AFTER THE DEPARTURE of the Whites from Tetiiv, local Bolsheviks under the leadership of Grigorii Vynnychenko (no relation to the Central Rada leader Volodymyr Vynnychenko) immediately declared themselves in charge of the smoldering city and ruled for the next three months.[12] According to one report, Vynnychenko "was a staunch defender of the Jews and often took revenge against the peasants; it was enough to point out that a peasant was a bandit and he would immediately have him killed."[13] For the first time since the Great War began, the Jews of Tetiiv felt safe; now it was the peasants of the region who were terrorized. Stories of Vynnychenko's brutality circulated around the countryside. It was said that when his men captured one band of thieves in the forest, they led the prisoners into the center of the village, forced them to line up, and chopped their heads off one by one. Children would take turns playing "Vynnychenko," mimicking acts of cruelty they had heard about from the adults.[14] Sadistic types of all stripes gravitated toward the Bolshevik leader, pleased at the opportunity to exercise sanctioned violence. Twelve-year-old Sonia Lev reported that her family's maid had a brother, Simon Doginsky, who was a real troublemaker and used to spend time at their house while his sister worked: "He was a bad person, simply a bad person."[15] When Vynnychenko came to power, Doginsky was one of the first to sign up as a Bolshevik.

Vynnychenko's men were motivated more by power and sadism than ideology, a fact that Vynnychenko was only too aware of. "I can guarantee that I am a Bolshevik myself, but I cannot say the same of my soldiers," he is reported to have confessed.[16] Indeed, his own police chief, Ilya Chaykovsky, a former officer in Petliura's army, was a double agent, sharing Bolshevik intelligence and passwords with anti-Bolshevik insurgents.

In March 1920, a group of peasants rose up against Vynnychenko and the Bolsheviks. Their leader, Overko Kuravskyi, joined with Chaykovsky to form an insurgent band. Most of those who flocked to the cause were local toughs, the type of men who had been in and out of Petliura's army, joining when the tides favored him and wandering back to their villages when the going got hard. Kuravskyi was a highly successful recruiter: according to one report, "every day gangs of twenty-five to thirty people arrived from the villages, all armed."[17] He managed to bring aboard some one thousand heavily armed men, including sixty cavalry, in addition to many more who were "ready to take up a pitchfork any minute, as they consider themselves to be always mobilized . . . spades work for those without gunpowder weapons."[18]

But Kuravskyi's biggest strength was the backing he received from Vassili Perevalov, the powerful head of the district bank of Tetiiv. Only thirty-five years old, he had the professional profile of a mid-level district bureaucrat rather than an insurgent warlord. Like most bankers, Perevalov despised the Bolsheviks, who sought to nationalize the banks. He also resented his Jewish competitors who directed many of the banks in the region. He ran an anti-communist ring out of his bank and used his position to agitate against the communists and the Jews. As one report bluntly put it, his bank was "a nest of antisemites."[19] Thanks to the support of Perevalov and his money, Kuravskyi was able to purchase an arsenal consisting of five Maxim guns, numerous Lewis guns, and a generous supply of magazines.[20] He even had some Chauchats, the light machine guns favored by the French during the war.

Kuravskyi's insurgents attacked passing Red Army detachments and gained a reputation for ruthlessness. Not only did they shoot the prisoners they captured, they even executed nurses and surgeons, particularly when the medical personnel were Jewish. They also regularly attacked Jewish merchants traveling through their territory, reportedly killing two brothers, for instance, who were on their way to sell soap in a nearby village.[21]

ON THE NIGHT of Wednesday, March 17, 1920, a small group of Kuravskyi's insurgents conducted a raid on Tetiiv itself to restock their supplies. They looted the shops in the center of town and left five Jews dead. Vynnychenko was enraged. As Efraim Joffe, a sixty-year-old resident of Tetiiv who fled to Berdychiv, recalled, "After this incident, Vynnychenko went after the bandits with even more passion."[22] He sent out an expedition that slaughtered as many as twenty peasant men.[23] The locals, Joffe continued, "took out all their anger at Vynnychenko on the Jews."[24]

On March 20, Vynnychenko left town to travel through the region, as was his usual Saturday routine. But this time he failed to return the next day as expected. The Jewish residents of Tetiiv became alarmed, concerned that he had been captured or killed. Those with the means to do so gathered their things and prepared to flee to nearby Bila Tserkva. Chaya Goldenberg rented a cart, packed her stuff, and hired a peasant driver with the intention of leaving early on Wednesday morning.

When Vynnychenko finally returned on Monday night, March 22, he called a group of Jewish leaders together and warned them of the obvious: the insurgents were preparing to attack and a pogrom would likely ensue. He promised that the Bolsheviks were on their side and he would try to protect the Jews but indicated that he would need them to reconstitute their self-defense brigade. The Jewish leaders demurred. In the past, when they had taken up arms against peasant insurgents, they had been overwhelmed and the episodes had resulted in horrifying violence. This time, the Jewish leadership instead resolved to buy off the attackers.[25]

Many Jews were hiding in cellars and garrets when, as everyone expected, the insurgents arrived in town during the night between Tuesday and Wednesday, March 23–24. Most of the twenty to thirty men came from the nearby village of Telizhyntsi; only a few were local Tetiivers. [26] The first thing the insurgents did was shut off the electricity, leaving the town in complete darkness. Witnesses remembered the sounds of explosions and gunfire tearing through the night. Thanks to Chaykovsky's insider information, Kuravskyi and his men were able to quickly get past the guards at Vynnychenko's headquarters, where they opened fire. One insurgent, who some witnesses identified as Oleksandr Sahatyuk, threw a grenade toward the building; unfortunately for Sahatyuk, it rebounded off the window frame and blinded him in the blast. Vynnychenko's men easily captured him. When residents awoke on Wednesday morning, Sahatyuk's limp body was hanging from a noose slung over Vynnychenko's balcony; evidence of the tortures he had endured was displayed for all to see. [27]

Undeterred, Kuravskyi attacked. Many Jews, upon hearing renewed gunfire, sought refuge in the synagogue's attic, which could only be reached from a second-floor window and through a curtain. From there they were able to witness up close the atrocities that were about to occur. By four o'clock in the afternoon, as it became clear that Vynnychenko could not hold the town, he left together with his last supporters, promising he would soon return with a Red Army detachment. By the time he reached the next town along the road, he had only one man by his side: the rest had declared their loyalty to the insurgents or simply abandoned him.

In the hours after Vynnychenko's departure, about two hundred peasants flooded into town, several on horseback, and all armed with the implements of the countryside: axes, knives, and pitchforks. One child witness interviewed in an orphanage in Bila Tserkva recounted, "The town was full of peasants, and all of them with axes." Only a few carried rifles and sabers. [28] The insurgents were accompanied by a massive crowd of villagers, young and old. This mixed multitude demanded that the Jews accept responsibility for the crimes perpetrated by the "Jewish Commissar." It seemed futile to point out that Vynnychenko was not even Jewish. [29] Leading the rebel crowd was Chaykovsky, Vynnychenko's turncoat police chief; he brought with him about twenty former Bolshevik policemen who had gone over to the insurgents' side. Among them was Simon Doginsky, the brother of Sonia Lev's maid, who had acquired a revolver and sword to go with the rifle he always carried.

According to one witness, the insurgents, once in control of the city, "convened a meeting and in a fiery speech called for the extermination of all the Jews from two-day-old children to ninety-year-old men. Only then would peace come to the town."[30] Holding up two fingers in the traditional form of a soldier taking a military oath, one of their leaders ordered everyone assembled to swear they would show no mercy and not be distracted by the temptation to loot.[31]

The insurgents then set the Jewish section of town on fire. Local peasants helped. Teme Novofastovskaya, who was interviewed in a homeless shelter in Bila Tserkva, had been at home when she heard shooting. At around three o'clock in the morning, she noticed neighboring houses in flames. She recalled watching as locals gathered sheaves of straw, lit them, and threw them into houses and stores. She saw her neighbors, distinguished members of the community, pointing out which houses to burn, and witnessed her brother's home going up in flames. Eventually, she ran outside and spent the rest of the night hiding in a garden. Later she found protection from a Pole, who sheltered her and gave her food.[32]

As peasants set the Jewish quarter alight, armed insurgents rounded up Jewish men, women, and children and forced them into the synagogue. Witnesses estimate that there were over a thousand Jews trapped in the building when the mob outside began to hurl burning logs through the windows.[33] The insurgents loaded their rifles and fired into the synagogue, the ejected cartridges showering the courtyard. A few men tossed grenades into the sanctuary.

Chaya Goldenberg, who had been watching the fires from the synagogue attic, recalled: "We saw everything. But when we realized that the synagogue was burning, we decided to get out."[34] The entrance to the women's section was already burned and the whole synagogue was full of smoke. The main door was engulfed in flames.

Men and women were shoving each other on the stairs to the attic, where the windows promised the prospect of escape. But the smoke and flames were heading in that direction as well. Bundles of burning straw continued to fly into the synagogue through the windows, adding fuel to the fire. The wooden bimah and the ark containing the Torah scrolls went up in flames together with hundreds of men, women, and children. "The sanctity of the Torah scrolls did not protect them," Joffe mused.[35] Among the victims was the local rabbi, Shimen Rabinovich.

Goldenberg managed to throw herself out an attic window and landed on the ground, dazed and injured. She lay in pain and shock for a few minutes, drifting in and out of consciousness, listening to the screams, the roar of the fire, and the thumps of other bodies landing nearby. After some time, she came to. There were others lying near her, some injured, some dead. She tried to get up, stumbled a few times, and managed to make her way to safety.[36]

The insurgents shot at the Jews as they hurled themselves out the upper windows of the burning synagogue. Peasants chased those who survived the fall, beating them and stabbing them with swords, knives, and pitchforks. The grocer Hinde Feldman reported that she escaped through the attic window with her mother. Her mother survived the fall but was attacked as soon as she landed. Hinde ran to the body: there was no life left in it. Hinde herself was stabbed in the hand and head.[37]

Moyshe Peker, a town elder well respected among the local peasants, managed to escape the synagogue but was quickly captured by Kuravskyi's men. Local peasants, recognizing him, tried to save him. According to one witness, Kuravskyi himself came over and declared, "Even if he is a good man, he is still a Jew and needs to be exterminated." According to the witness, "Peker was chopped into little pieces."[38]

Nokhem Bikov, a forty-five-year-old fishmonger, managed to flee the burning synagogue and jump into the river. Two peasant acquaintances on the riverbank saw him and called out, offering shelter. When he managed to reach them, they shot him.[39]

Moyshe Lev and his uncle, Berl Baltok, were hiding in a neighbor's cellar when they smelled smoke. Lev and Baltok ran to the Russian cemetery and spent the night hiding in a grave. Early the next morning, on their way to a nearby village, they bumped into a peasant named Mykytyn; Lev had occasionally hired him to pick up supplies from Uman. This time Mykytyn was in no mood to serve. He knew that Lev had money at home and ordered the Jew to lead him to his house. Located on a mixed Jewish and Christian street, the house had been spared from the fires. Mykytyn rummaged through the family's belongings and came across tsarist rubles hidden in a trunk. Taking the cash, he led Lev out into the courtyard and shot him with a single bullet.[40]

On Friday, there was a lull in the violence. Joffe recalls hearing "wild and heart-wrenching screams" as the first survivors came out of hiding and discovered the charred bodies lying around town. "We saw a corpse with a pig at its side nibbling on him," he remembered.[41] More survivors emerged from their cellars early Saturday morning and immediately headed toward the synagogue, "but there was no synagogue, only burned walls and unrecognizable scorched corpses. Hands, feet and other limbs were lying here and there."[42]

Joffe returned to his smoldering house to see what he could salvage. As he got to work dousing the embers with water, an insurgent approached his yard and ordered him to "go tell the Jews to bury their dead." The man then walked into the house, stabbed Joffe's wife, Shifre, with a stake, and proceeded to take their last possessions from the charred cupboards. After he left, Joffe took his wounded wife to a neighboring cellar, where he hoped he could hide her from further harm. As he opened the cellar door, he saw twelve dead bodies. He laid his wounded wife among them.[43]

It was Saturday and Joffe realized he was hungry—he had barely eaten since the pogrom began four days earlier. He sought charity from his non-Jewish neighbors but "the local Christians didn't acknowledge me—they gave me nothing." Wandering through the town in search of food, he came to realize the scope of the massacre. "Corpses were lying around like garbage. Dogs and pigs were pouring in from everywhere. From some of the corpses, only a half remained. . . . Many corpses were not covered. The majority of houses had been burned down. Here and there you could find a few that had, by some accident, remained whole. You heard frightful stories. Many people were burned and could not be saved."[44]

THE NEXT DAY was Palm Sunday, March 28. A Red Army detachment of eighty soldiers arrived, engaged the insurgents, and killed fifteen of them. The commissar gathered the surviving Jews: the Bolsheviks would not be able to hold the town, he advised; they should seek shelter in neighboring Pohrebyshche, where the Red Army was in firm control.[45] There were no carts available, so over one thousand men, women, and children set out to make the trip by foot: "Many old men and children did not have the strength to continue and were left on the road where the bandits later killed them . . . many children were trampled under the feet of the panicked refugees," according to one report signed by five witnesses.[46] Villagers cocked their rifles and shot at the passing convoy, killing the survivors for sport.[47] The refugees arrived in Pohrebyshche on Tuesday. Local Jews provided them with food but insisted that they move on; the Jewish community of Pohrebyshche was itself too poor and devastated to provide for them. The Tetiiv refugees eventually arrived in Kozyatyn. Using the biblical phrase that would later be adopted to refer to the survivors of the Holocaust, one man wrote, "From Kozyatyn, the *sh'erit ha-plitah*, the surviving remnant, dispersed in various directions—to Berdychiv, Kyiv, Odesa, and so on."[48]

Eighteen-year-old Velvl Tsap, who fled with a small group of five, was captured in a nearby village. Recognizing them as Jews, his captors accused the group of being Bolsheviks, led them to a clearing on the edge of the village, ordered them to lie facedown in the dirt, and slashed them with their sabers. Tsap lost consciousness. Some time later—he estimates it was a few hours—he became aware that peasants were lowering the bodies of his companions into a freshly dug grave. When a peasant came to him, Tsap opened his eyes. The peasant jumped back in fright.

"You are still alive?"

"Yes," he replied.

"But we have to bury you."

One of the peasants piped up: "Let's leave him and tomorrow we will see. If he is dead we will bury him then." Tsap managed to get himself up and walked three days through the fields toward Pohre-byshche.[49]

On April 2, the night of the Passover seder, about ten insurgents arrived in Tetiiv. Mykytyn, the peasant who used to bring Lev supplies from Uman, was among them, riding on a horse. The insurgents gathered all the wounded Jews together, took the men behind the hospital, and shot them. They ordered the women and children to leave town.[50]

Estimates of the number of Jews killed during the ten-day pogrom range from 3,000 to 5,000, although those figures may be exaggerated. One list of victims includes 631 names; another, compiled among refugees in Odesa, counts 704 names.[51] Other reports cite 1,127 people burned to death in the synagogue fire and up to 2,000 more killed during the rest of the pogrom.[52]

One witness recalled the horrifying aftermath: "After two months, I returned to the town of Tetiiv in order to fulfill my last obligations to my parents. I didn't recognize the town. Not a single building had survived. There were open spaces everywhere, charred stumps and debris everywhere, everywhere the remains of people's paltry possessions and piles of bones. It was impossible to recognize anyone. There were no complete corpses, only skeletons and bones. Everywhere lay human hands, feet, torsos."[53] She went searching for her family but could hardly even recognize her own home among the ruins; all that remained was her cellar. She ventured down and, amid the shelves for compote and dried fruits, discovered human bones and skulls. Among these, she assumed, were her mother, Freyda Krasnaia, and her two sisters, seventeen-year-old Evie and twelve-year-old Toybe.[54]

———

ON JUNE 27, 1920, three months after the pogrom, while traveling with some companions by cart, Vassili Perevalov, the banker, was stopped on the road from Bila Tserkva to Kyiv by Bolshevik special agents, who had been tipped off that Perevalov was responsible for the Tetiiv pogrom. Perevalov insisted that he was just a poor peasant bringing farm products to starving relatives in Kyiv; in these times of scarcity, countryfolk needed to help out their city kin. The story was plausible, but the special agents had good reason to doubt it. Their informant was Volf Lederman, the former Bolshevik leader of Tetiiv. The special agents searched through Perevalov's freight and found about 150 pounds of millet, 15 pounds of sugar, and 10 pounds of lard—nothing unusual for peasants bringing their goods to market. But then they discovered a pouch containing 200,000 rubles. They confiscated the money and brought the group to Bila Tserkva for further questioning.

Perevalov defended himself: he was not a pogrom instigator, he insisted; on the contrary, he had sheltered Jews in his home. He could even name them: Leyzer Shvarts, Moyshe Peker and two of his sons, Shleym Grosman and his two daughters, and others as well. But when asked if they were still alive, Perevalov was at a loss. He had heard that Leyzer Shvarts was living in Kyiv, but he didn't know the fate of the others. A medic who served as a witness in the case suggested the answer: "He apparently turned them over to the bandits, who carried out the bloody massacre."[55] At least one witness was able to confirm that Peker had been killed.[56] Further investigation revealed that after the pogrom Perevalov suddenly seemed to be doing very well for himself; he had even purchased a house, leading many to suspect that he had profited from the massacre of Jews and the theft of their property.[57] With this evidence in hand, on August 12, 1920, the Commission for the Struggle Against Banditry concluded that Perevalov was guilty. The Kyiv regional Cheka subsequently sentenced him, together with several of his traveling companions, to be shot.[58] As in Slovechno and other locales, Bolshevik justice was firm and quick.

The Polish-Soviet War

In April 1920, Polish and Ukrainian forces advanced toward Kyiv from the north, beginning what came to be known as the Polish-Soviet War. Their goal was to challenge Bolshevik ascendency in the region and reclaim the historic lands of the Polish-Lithuanian Commonwealth. Petliura, who was then in exile in Warsaw, had agreed to an alliance with Piłsudski in which Poland would support Ukrainian independence in the provinces of the former Russian Empire in exchange for Petliura's renunciation of Ukrainian claims to Eastern Galicia.[1] Polish forces had already made gains in Belarusian territory, conquering Mazyr and Kalinkavichy in March.

The Red Army was completely unprepared for the assault. Polish soldiers were amazed at the bedraggled appearance of the Bolsheviks. "Some were barefoot, some had shabby soft shoes, others had rubber galoshes," wrote Franciszek Krzystyniak, "while on their heads they wore a variety of headgear—some even had women's hats—and winter caps or kerchiefs, and some were even bareheaded, their hair flying in the wind. They looked like ghouls. Their rifles were either suspended on string, or without any straps—but they did have plenty of ammunition in their pockets and their aim was good."[2] The Bolsheviks' tenuous hold over Ukraine seemed to be evaporating just as it had in the face of the Whites eight months earlier.

The Polish Third Army, comprised largely of recruits from German-speaking Posnania in western Poland as well as volunteer legionnaires from America who had returned to Poland to join the fight for independence, easily took Zhytomyr on the morning of April 26. Polish officer Mieczysław Lepecki recalled that "the people of Zhytomyr, fed on falsehoods about Poland and the Polish Army put about by Soviet sources, thought that our units were some sort of marauding bands, dressed in tatters and living off requisitions. Instead, they saw something quite different."[3] Ivan Voronitsyn, the former chair of the city council, agreed that at first the Polish soldiers comported themselves like "gentlemen": "They wanted to present themselves as European."[4] The city councilors, he claimed, greeted the Poles respectfully and carried out all the assignments the incoming soldiers gave them. As Lepecki put it, "People were literally snatching Polish officers from each other, offering them quarters in their own homes."[5] They hoped that cooperation would guarantee them safety. Many were also pleased to see the Bolsheviks go.

But after only a few days, the Poles began harassing elderly Jews, cutting or even tearing off their beards. Voronitsyn claimed that even the liberal attorney Mikhail Skokovsky, whom the Poles appointed as their representative on the city council, began to adopt the antisemitism of the new regime: "He expressed quite openly a Judeophobia that we had never suspected of him."[6] After the Poles were briefly forced out of the city by Soviet cavalry, they returned on May 9, and according to Voronitsyn, "the pogrom began immediately." That very day "the city council received information about several murdered Jews, even though there were relatively few Poles in the city."[7]

Krzystyniak, the Polish soldier, described his comrades' behavior in the conquered territories: "Our soldiers knew how to make the most of every opportunity, with no holds barred," he wrote. "When we captured a village there followed a free-for-all—in the houses of the most affluent villagers, they looked for money hidden behind the pictures on the wall. . . . There were plenty of Jews in every village and they had all sorts of shops, which were well-stocked . . . our soldier-boys immediately opened up all the shops and looted what they could."[8]

THE POLES WERE stunned by the rapidity of their own advance. On May 6, the Red Army, which had held Kyiv since December, abandoned the city and the first Polish unit marched in. The Polish Third Army, together with allied forces of the Ukrainian People's Republic, occupied the city the next day. On May 9, the Poles held a victory parade down the city's main thoroughfare with flowers in the muzzles of their guns. "This was so unexpected, we could hardly believe our ears," recalled Zofia Krauze, a Polish resident of the city. "There had been no firing, no sounds of battle, we did not even know that the Polish Army was advancing on Kyiv."[9] It was the thirteenth time Kyiv had switched hands in three years, but the first time the Poles had conquered it.

The Polish soldiers immediately turned on the city's Jews, publicly humiliating them in a show of dominance. In the Demiivka district on the outskirts of Kyiv, Polish soldiers invaded the synagogue,

[PICTORIAL PRESS LTD / ALAMY STOCK PHOTO]

Polish soldiers in Kyiv

where they set the holy books on fire, tore apart the Torah scrolls, and ripped up tefillin. They roamed the side streets, harassing any Jews they could find. According to one report, "they often cut off the men's beards with sabers, sometimes with knives—in the process they cruelly mocked the Jews: forced them to dance, to sing, to twirl around, to get on their knees, while groups of soldiers and Christian members of the public amused themselves at the scene."[10] Borukh Shvartsman gave a statement to the Kyiv Jewish Community testifying that "on May 27 at noon, as I was walking past 184 Bolshaya Vasilkovskaya Street, where a detachment of Polish soldiers was quartered, one of the soldiers jumped me and cut off half my beard."[11] Borukh Ostrovsky explained that he was walking past the same house when "two soldiers standing at the gate threatened me with a revolver and forced me to go in. There, in the presence of four additional soldiers who threatened to beat me with whips, they cut my beard."[12] Nuty Kigsman testified that soldiers beat him with ramrods, ordered him to shout Ukrainian slogans, and to "lie under the table and howl like a dog."[13] Polish soldiers gathered about two hundred elderly and infirm Jews on the pretext of taking them to "work," but in reality made them dance and sing, or marched them to the station along the gutters, forcing them to pick up the waste with their bare hands.[14] Others testified that Polish soldiers broke into their homes and stole money and valuables, or beat them on the charge of speculating in currency. On one occasion, on June 10, a Polish patrol barged into the Merchants' Synagogue on Malaya Vasilkovskaya Street in the middle of evening prayers and began firing at the worshippers, injuring nearly twenty men, at least one of whom, Fayvl Zeltsman, perished from his injuries.[15] In contrast to the earlier White pogrom in Kyiv, which had targeted Jews as Bolsheviks, these attacks by Polish soldiers drew from more archaic forms of religious hatred: they were directed primarily toward Jews as a faith group, focused on marks of Jewish religious difference. They were also designed more to demean the Jews than to murder them.

A representative of Piłsudski's who met with a Jewish delegation

[TsDKFFA]

Polish soldiers punishing a civilian

soon after the Polish conquest of the city agreed that, unfortunately, Polish troops had committed some excesses. However, he said, "these obscene acts were perpetrated not by our Poles and not by the Posnanians, but by legionnaires from America. You probably know that in America," he explained, "there is a particular aversion toward beards."[16] As for the other incidents, he explained, "you must not forget that we are living during a time of war."[17]

Thousands of terrified Jews fled Kyiv into Bolshevik territory to the east. The Yiddish novelist Israel Joshua Singer described the scene in the railway hub of Bakhmach, Chernihiv Province, as refugees from Polish-occupied Kyiv streamed into a former bank that had been converted into a refugee center:

> At the barred cashiers' windows, where people used to withdraw money, sat badly dressed clerks and unshaven, unkempt young men or short-haired young women. The rows of people in front of the

[YIVO INSTITUTE FOR JEWISH RESEARCH]

Men trying to salvage Torah scrolls in Demiivka after the Kyiv pogrom, 1920 windows were long, weaving, full of men and women evacuated from Kyiv, the city near the Dnipro that had been occupied by the Polish military. They were abandoned, sleep deprived, weary, broken, lost people in a strange place, and they besieged the officials' windows, asking for bread, clothing, a corner in which to lay their heads. Others were searching for their things, which they had lost while fleeing, or their relatives, from whom they had been separated in the chaos of leaving their homes. Men were looking for their wives, women for husbands, parents for children. The clerks, unsure of what to do with these people, sent them from one department to another, demanding documents or asking them to come later, tomorrow, next week. Any time except now.[18]

The Bolsheviks had lost much of the Ukrainian territory they had held, including Kyiv, but they had one final weapon in their arsenal: the famed Red Cavalry led by the charismatic commander Semyon Budyonny, whose handlebar mustache, renowned bravery, and intimacy with the Cossack way of life (although he was himself a Russian) would become legendary in Soviet lore.[19] Kicking up dust as they swept through the plains on their stallions, the Red Cavalry with their *tachanka* mounted machine guns proved to be an effective shock force that disrupted the enemy lines and swung the war in favor of the Bolsheviks. Composed mostly of Cossacks who had defected from the Whites, the Red Cavalry also welcomed any riffraff who could ride a horse. "To the horse, Proletarians," Trotsky had famously declared in September 1919 in an effort to counter the White Cossack horsemen who were threatening the Bolsheviks from the south. Singer wrote of them:

Riding on small Siberian horses, they were traveling in endless rows, sunburned, dusty, curious and wild, unshaven, with forelocks and one sidelock. Even though the sun was blazing, they wore fur hats and coats. They carried rifles and spears, daggers, and silver swords and knives. Accompanying the men were their equally sunburned, dusty, curious and combative wives. Loudly, they all sang their long, savage songs about the Ural River, about fighting and carousing.[20]

On May 27, 1920, the Red Cavalry advanced from their staging ground in Uman; they broke through the Polish lines and arrived in Zhytomyr during the first week of June. On the morning of June 9, though, they abandoned the city as quickly as they came to continue their drive toward Kyiv. With the Bolsheviks gone, three open trucks full of Polish soldiers with their rifles aimed at rooftops and windows returned to retake the city, turning Zhytomyr into a killing ground once again. The Poles had no doubt that the Jews were responsible for the Red Cavalry's success: the Jews, they claimed, had attacked the Poles as they retreated the week before, firing from machine guns installed on top of the city hospital. On this pretext, Polish troops patrolled the main streets, raided Jewish homes, and opened fire on Jewish passersby. One of the first victims was a sixteen-year-old boy, Samuil Ogyshevsky, who was shot in the head while walking through a schoolyard on his way to work at a barbershop. An eight-year-old boy, Borukh Belogolovsky, was killed in his home, struck by a bullet fired through the window from outside. On Thursday, June 10, Polish soldiers assembled dozens of Jews in the square and shot them, killing about thirty. On Saturday morning, as word spread that the Reds had taken back Kyiv, Polish soldiers panicked and set fire to several Jewish homes, killing eight more people. In total, between forty-two and sixty-four Jews were killed by the Poles in the city over four days. Voronitsyn is particularly adamant that during the course of the pogrom, "not a single Pole raised a voice of protest. Neither the priest nor a representative of the Polish women's charity approached us in the city council."[21]

Having retaken Kyiv from the Poles, the Red Army continued a westward advance in the hopes of spreading the revolution through all of Europe. By July 10, the Poles were forced back to Rivne, from where they had begun their Ukrainian adventure. But the Bolsheviks pushed onward: "Soldiers of the Red Army! The time has come to settle scores," declared Mikhail Tukhachevsky, commander of the western front. "Turn your eyes to the west," he continued. "The fate of world revolution will be set in the west. The road to worldwide conflagration leads over the dead body of a White Poland. Our bayonets will bring joy and peace to the working masses. Onwards and

Westwards!"[22] By mid-August, Budyonny's cavalry had control of the Galician oil fields and was on the verge of taking Lviv. Meanwhile, regular Red Army units had made it to the outskirts of Warsaw. The Red soldiers, though, were exhausted and had little incentive to be fighting so far from home. According to the British diplomat Edgar Vincent, who was stationed in Warsaw at the time, the Bolshevik fighters were "apathetic about the joys of victory" and displayed an "entire lack of enthusiasm or conviction regarding the Soviet government." They hated taking orders from Jewish commanders and fought only for fear of the Cheka if they refused. "The general impression conveyed was that the Jews and Jewish Commissars were universally detested and the latter particularly feared," continued Vincent.[23] The soldiers were perfectly content to be taken prisoner, where "they realized they were more or less safe, that they would have adequate, if not abundant, food, that there would be no Jewish Commissars to shoot them if they ran away."[24]

Thus, in what the Poles would remember as "the Miracle on the Vistula," Piłsudski's forces held back the Reds from taking Warsaw, forcing a Bolshevik retreat. "There is not the slightest doubt that if we had been victorious on the Vistula the revolution would have set the whole continent of Europe on fire," lamented Tukhachevsky.[25] He was certainly right. It was the farthest Bolshevik advance of the war, but the soldiers had faltered with Warsaw in sight. The Red Army would not reach that far west again until the summer of 1944, when Soviet tank crews watched from the eastern banks of the Vistula as the Polish Home Army's Warsaw Uprising failed amid German bombing.

THE POGROMS WERE not yet over, though, as the Red Army was by no means immune to the appeal of plunder and murder during its adventure in Poland.[26] "Our men are going around indifferently, looting where they can, ripping the clothes off the butchered people . . . it's pure nonsense that our army is any different," wrote Isaac Babel, who was embedded as a journalist with Budyonny's troops.[27] Babel told of how the Red Cavalry victimized Jews in particular, despite the Jews' eagerness to welcome the Reds as liberators: "They looked to the Soviet regime as saviors, then suddenly yells, whips, Yids."[28] Red Army soldiers billeted themselves in private homes, often belonging to Jews, where the terrified homeowners were forced to feed the hungry soldiers from their meager provisions. The soldiers slaughtered their hosts' geese for food and requisitioned their carts, their horses, their harnesses, their clothing, and their boots. "As soon as the Bolsheviks had entered the town they immediately gave orders that the inhabitants of the three main streets should leave, taking with them only what they could carry in their hands," one Polish newspaper reported regarding the Bolshevik conquest of the Galician city of Ternopil. "Then there followed an orgy of looting in these streets, while in the next days the remainder of the town was subjected to unceremonious pillaging."[29] In the Galician town of Sokal, Babel recorded: "The Jews ask me to use my influence so they won't be ruined, they're being robbed of everything. . . . The little stores, all of them open, whiting and resin, soldiers ransacking, swearing at the Yids, drifting around aimlessly, entering homes, crawling under counters, greedy eyes, trembling hands, a strange army indeed."[30]

[TsDKFFA]

Semyon Budyonny's Red Cavalry

Battle-weary soldiers living in the cramped quarters of Jewish dwellings eyed the young women in the house and frequently demanded sexual satisfaction. Babel, for instance, described his traveling companion, a young Cossack named Prishchepa, who, "in the grip of lust," assaulted a Jewish woman as he requisitioned her family's cart.[31]

In his Red Cavalry story cycle, Babel provided more background on Prishchepa, telling his readers that during the civil war, the "rough-neck" Cossack had run away from the Whites: "As a reprisal, they took his parents hostage and killed them at the interrogation. The neighbors ransacked everything they had." When Prishchepa returned home, he "went through the village picking up his gramophone, kvas jugs, and the napkins that his mother had embroidered . . . the bloody prints of his boots trailing behind him. In huts where he found his mother's things or his father's pipe, he left hacked-up old women, dogs hung over wells, icons soiled with dung."[32] Having been a victim of unimaginable violence in his own childhood, Prishchepa would grow up to become the murderer and rapist described by Babel. Violence begat violence.

Seventeen-year-old Manya Shvarts reported that some of Budyon-ny's cavalrymen entered her apartment and tried to force themselves upon her. When her grandmother started to scream, the soldiers turned on the elderly woman with their swords. Manya used the distraction to flee. When she returned her grandmother was lying dead in a pool of blood.[33] Babel wrote that outside a house in which he was billeted "a couple of Cossacks were getting ready to shoot an old silver-bearded Jew for espionage. The old man was screeching, and tried to break free. Kudrya from the machine gun detachment grabbed his head and held it wedged under his arm. . . . Kudrya pulled out his dagger with his right hand and carefully slit the old man's throat without spatter-ing himself."[34]

Babel also portrayed the brutality of Polish soldiers in one of the early pieces he wrote for the newspaper *Krasny Kavalerist* ("The Red Cavalryman"). He tells of one "modest, hardworking pharmacist" who lived in Volhynia near the Polish border and "had no connec-tion to politics at all, and quite possibly thought that Bolsheviks were monsters with ears above their eyes." But he was Jewish, and "for the Poles that was enough." They beat him and tortured him on the trumped-up charge that he killed a Polish officer. "If I had not seen that lacerated face and that shattered body with my own eyes, I would never have believed that such shocking evil could exist in our era."[35] When Babel's own division arrived in the Polish town of Komarów on August 28, he wrote:

We found the town's Jewish population robbed of everything it had, wounded and hacked to pieces. Our soldiers, who have seen a thing or two in their time and have been known to chop off quite a few heads, staggered in horror at what they saw. In the pitiful huts that had been razed to the ground, seventy-year-old men with crushed skulls lay naked in pools of blood, infants, often still alive, with fingers hacked off, and old women, raped, their stomachs slashed open, crouched in corners, with faces on which wild, unbearable desperation had congealed. The living were crawling among the dead, bumping into mangled corpses, their hands and faces covered with sticky, foul-smelling blood, terrified of leaving their houses, fearing that all was not yet over.[36]

WITH THE BOLSHEVIK retreat from Warsaw, the active front moved to the north, to Belarus, where Polish-allied armies under the command of Stanisław Bułak-Bałachowicz pushed back against the Bolsheviks and sought to create a Belarusian People's Republic. Bułak-Bałachowicz was a veteran of the tsarist army who had commanded a cavalry division on behalf first of the Reds and then the Whites, and had gained notoriety for his penchant for hanging suspected communists from lampposts. "I don't fight for the tsar, I don't fight for the Russian manors; but for the land, bread and for all people," he had declared in one manifesto.[37] In February 1920, he had sworn a new allegiance to Piłsudski and gathered an army comprised of what one hostile report termed "drunks and adventurists" to fight against the Bolsheviks.[38] One Polish officer who spent an evening with him characterized him as "a man with no ideology, a brigand and a murderer."[39]

The Belarusian front was particularly chaotic during the fall of 1920. "The behavior of our troops in the territories which we have captured leaves a great deal to be desired," the Polish ministry for military affairs admitted in an internal communiqué. "There are frequent complaints that, in their dealings with the local people, who have been robbed of everything by the Bolsheviks, the soldiers often resort to indiscriminate commandeering, and even theft, and this applies both to individual soldiers and to entire units."[40]

On November 14, 1920, Bułak-Bałachowicz announced that he had freed the Christian people from the Soviet-Jewish yoke and encouraged them to wreak revenge, "to murder the Jews, to take their property, and to erase them from the face of the earth."[41] Over the next week, in the village of Chojniki, locals together with Bułak-Bałachowicz's men stole "dresses, underwear, dishes, livestock, foodstuff, books, talliths, and furniture," killed more than sixty Jews, and raped at least thirty women. The violence only stopped thanks to the intervention of two priests and several important townsmen, demonstrating the principle that when authority figures spoke out, the violence often ended.[42] In March 1921, after the Bolsheviks secured control of the region, a Revolutionary Tribunal indicted fifty-one locals for participating in the pogrom.[43]

Bułak-Bałachowicz's men also destroyed many of the smaller Jewish communities in the Mazyr region. Mazyr itself, a town in which the nearly ten thousand Jewish residents constituted a solid majority, was completely devastated after its occupation by Bułak-Bałachowicz's troops on November 9, 1920. The soldiers plundered and terrorized the Jewish population, blaming them for the excesses of the Bolsheviks, who had conducted mass arrests of those suspected of "counter-revolutionary" activity. Bułak-Bałachowicz's soldiers murdered all eleven Jews who lived in the town of Koshevichi and drowned all eight Jews who lived in a village nearby.[44] In other towns, they simply chased the Jewish population out, leaving their empty houses for the Christian residents to take over.

Several child witnesses reported on the situation in Pietrykaŭ when Bułak-Bałachowicz's men arrived. All recalled the feelings of dread as rumors of atrocities in neighboring villages filtered into the town in early November. Thirteen-year-old Hirsh Shapiro heard in the marketplace that Bułak-Bałachowicz's men had already entered neighboring Smidin and ran to tell his father. His father, still skeptical, went out to the street to investigate for himself. He came back yelling that there was shooting outside and that two Jewish neighbors had been killed. The boy recalled seeing the soldiers carrying a white flag on which the slogan BEAT THE JEWS, SAVE RUSSIA was written. He watched as about twenty soldiers came into town and in front of the church ordered the rabbi to collect valuables for them by the next morning. From an upstairs window of a neighbor's house, he could see Christian residents wandering into Jewish homes, helping themselves to whatever they could find.[45] One anonymous report describes the scene: "A father threw himself on the warm corpse of his murdered son, and a Bałachowicz hero killed him on the spot. Another father wanted to tear the corpse of his son from between the teeth of a pig, and he met the same fate."[46] The plunder continued for the next few days. On their way out of the village, the soldiers set fire to the marketplace. When the Bolsheviks returned two weeks later, Makhlya Gokhman recalled, "the Jews were very happy, but the Christians said that a Jewish regime had arrived."[47]

One study submitted to the Jewish Public Committee in January 1921 on the basis of material gathered by the Society for the Protection of the Health of the Jewish Population blamed Bułak-Bałachowicz for the murder of 435 Jews in seventeen locations between October and November 1920.[48] The society also counted a total of 617 incidents of sexual assault in seven towns, including the repeated rape of a twelve-year-old child by three officers.[49] The report held locals responsible for having actively participated in the pogroms, or at least having done nothing to stop them. In the village of Horodyshche, near Mazyr, for instance, the Committee accused the local population of having slaughtered 72 of the 84 Jewish residents in town as soon as Bułak-Bałachowicz's soldiers arrived.[50]

Reports commended a few local Christians for rescuing Jews: Dr.

Kovsky in Pietrykaŭ hid a group of Jews in the hospital and provided medicine and first aid to the injured. In Zhytkavichy, the local priest, with the support of the rest of the villagers, reportedly saved the entire Jewish population—forty-eight families—from a decree ordering them shot.[51] Jewish sources credit the Polish Catholic priest of Yuravichy with hiding the rabbi and leading a delegation of Christian residents who demanded that Bułak-Bałachowicz's soldiers release the Jewish hostages they were holding. One member of the delegation is even said to have removed her own gold earrings to present to the soldiers as a bribe to release the Jews.[52] When a larger group of Polish soldiers arrived in Yuravichy the next day, the soldiers handed out rifles to twenty Jewish men and pleaded with the Jews to testify on their behalf before the inevitable revolutionary tribunal. It was a worthwhile gambit—a few days later, when the Red Army arrived, the Jewish community intervened to save the Polish commander from execution.[53]

By LATE 1920, the Polish counteroffensive was stalling, Bułak-Bałachowicz's army had retreated and been disarmed, and the Bolsheviks had lost much of their advantage. The war seemed to be coming to an end, and the sides came together to talk. The Bolshevik government in Moscow, which had renamed itself the Russian Soviet Federative Socialist Republic, formally united with the Bolsheviks in Kharkiv, who now controlled almost the entire territory once claimed by the Ukrainian People's Republic and had renamed it the Ukrainian Soviet Socialist Republic. Together with the Belarusian Soviet Socialist Republic, they were working on establishing a Soviet Union. But first, they needed to end the war with Poland.

In August 1920, Adolph Joffe, who had led the first round of talks at Brest-Litovsk for the Bolsheviks, once again sat down at a negotiating table, this time across from his Polish adversaries. The Poles, who had promised Petliura not to make a separate peace, broke their agreement, decisively putting an end to Ukrainian dreams of independence. Petliura left Poland dejected and spent the next several years in Budapest, Vienna, and Geneva, before settling in Paris in 1924, where he helped establish a Ukrainian-language newspaper, *Tryzub* (Trident), which catered to the growing Ukrainian diaspora in the capitals of Europe.

The Bolsheviks, for their part, were convinced that an imminent worker revolution in Poland would render any agreement irrelevant, and so regarded all territorial concessions as provisional. Negotiations began in Minsk and continued in Riga, where on March 18, 1921, the Bolsheviks formally renounced their claims to Eastern Galicia and permitted Poland to retain its hold over Vilnius. The border between Poland and Ukraine was set along the Zbrucz River. Proskuriv and Kamyanets-Podilskyi were incorporated into Soviet Ukraine, Minsk into Soviet Belarus, and Rivne and Pinsk into the Polish Republic. The treaty also stipulated that individuals living in territories granted to the Soviet states who could claim historic ties to Poland might opt for Polish citizenship and be repatriated. By the fall of 1921, over three hundred thousand people—POWs, hostages, civilian prisoners, and refugees—had left Soviet territories for Poland. The war was over, but a global refugee crisis was just beginning.[54]

PART V

AFTERMATH

1921–1941

Refugees

The Peace of Riga ended major military conflicts, but the impact of the violence continued with massive population displacement. New tensions emerged as hundreds of thousands of Jewish refugees arrived in European capitals, claiming to be fleeing "Ukrainian Cossacks," while at the same time similar numbers of Ukrainians showed up claiming to be fleeing "Jewish Bolsheviks." The westward migration of poverty-stricken eastern European Jewish refugees had begun even before the Great War, but the civil war increased the flow and stigmatized the newcomers as dangerous Bolsheviks intent on spreading revolution. At the same time, the pogroms alienated Jews from the Ukrainian cause to which many had once contributed and led them instead to turn to the new Soviet bureaucracy for justice and protection. The association between Jews and Bolsheviks became a self-fulfilling prophecy.

In the fall of 1921, as the Bolsheviks consolidated their control over the lands once claimed by the Ukrainian People's Republic, the newly renamed Ukrainian Soviet Socialist Republic was suffering from famine, disease, and political turmoil. Poor crop yields were exacerbated by Bolshevik requisitions, which transferred food reserves and grain from the previous year's harvest to the Russian interior and had discouraged farmers from planting surplus seed. The resulting malnutrition contributed to the spread of typhus and scarlet fever and led to the deaths of an estimated 250,000 to 500,000 people.[1] The impact of the famine was devastating for all residents of Soviet Ukraine, but the Jewish population, still recovering from the pogroms and having to care for some 600,000 orphans, widows, and internal refugees, was particularly hard hit. As Jews abandoned the towns and villages they had called home for generations and sought shelter instead in larger cities, the needy could no longer rely on the local networks of support that had sustained them through difficult times in the past. Tetiiv, for instance, which had once hosted a small but thriving Jewish community, was completely ethnically cleansed, while some 20,000 Jewish refugees, 6,500 of them children, were living in makeshift dormitories in the basements of synagogues in Uman. Similarly, 50,000 Jewish refugees had fled to Odesa.[2] By 1926, when the first Soviet census was conducted, a staggering 42 percent of the 1.5 million Jews counted in Ukraine were no longer living in the locale in which they were born. In urban areas, 60 percent of Jews had been born outside the city environs; the largest number had moved between the years 1917 and 1920.[3] In the new Ukrainian Soviet Socialist Republic capital of Kharkiv, 80 percent of the 84,000 Jews in the city were newcomers.[4] In Kyiv, where Jewish residence had been restricted before the revolution, 62 percent of the 154,000 Jews in the city had arrived from elsewhere—old-time residents "were heavily outnumbered by the multitude of refugees," wrote Ilya Ehrenburg. Kyiv, he continued, "was the first halt of the Russian emigration: before the Odesa quays, before the Turkish islands, before the Berlin boardinghouses, and Paris attics."[5] The fortunate in the city found work in sugar beet factories or leatherworks, where they were paid in kind, selling molasses and finished hides for profit. Others took up their former occupations, working in cottage industries as artisans. Many remained destitute.

Foreign aid was essential for support of those who stayed in Ukraine, but Jewish relief organizations were haunted by a July 1920 episode in which two Jewish aid workers—Israel Friedlaender, a Polish-born professor of biblical literature at the Jewish Theological Seminary in New

York, and Bernard Cantor, a young Reform rabbi at the New York Free Synagogue—had been mistaken for Polish officers and murdered in a Bolshevik ambush near Proskuriv.[6] Recognizing the risks of going in alone, the Joint Distribution Committee concluded that the only means of offering aid within Ukraine was "with the co-operation of the Soviet government."[7] There was, however, only one organization with which they could work: in the preceding months, as they solidified their hold over the region, the Bolsheviks had centralized all voluntary associations, effectively closing down prerevolutionary organizations and rebranding them as Soviet institutions under strict governmental control. Thus, in June 1920, the Central Committee for Relief of Pogrom Victims and the charity divisions of the major Jewish political parties were all merged into a government-controlled Jewish Public Committee.[8] The Joint indicated its willingness to work with the Bolshevik committee and agreed in principle to provide food, clothing, drugs, soap, shoes, and money to Jews suffering from the war and pogroms. However, in order to deal with the Soviet government, which was still not recognized by the United States, American aid organizations needed permission from the US State Department: even the American Relief Administration, the congressional aid mission led by Secretary of Commerce Herbert Hoover, was not permitted to work in Bolshevik territory until 1921.[9]

Since the fall of 1919, the Joint and the American Jewish Congress had been petitioning the State Department to send a high-level delegation to Ukraine and managed to receive a formal hearing before Secretary of State Robert Lansing on December 10, 1919. If the pogroms in Ukraine "are not brought to a stop there is a possibility that the entire Jewish population in the Ukraine may be exterminated," the congress had warned, "for this is not a thing that is occurring in one isolated instance, but it is an organized massacre to exterminate the Jews in the Ukraine."[10] Lansing had responded: "Until there is a change in the political situation in the Ukraine, we are almost helpless. We have no one to whom we can send a protest; there is no one with whom we can reason."[11] Now that Ukraine had been firmly incorporated into the Soviet orbit, Louis Marshall recognized that it would look bad for American Jews to be perceived as providing aid to the Bolsheviks,

but he saw no other option to stave off the suffering of his coreligionists. On August 11, 1920, Marshall sent a letter to Lansing asking the
United States government to support the Soviet Jewish Public Committee. The State Department responded in October that "while it cannot in any way help" and "it will not encourage American citizens to
enter territory controlled by the Soviet authorities . . . it will not inter-
pose any objection to the Joint Distribution Committee commencing
relief work under the terms of the Agreement."[12] It was a remarkable
concession by the United States government, achieved through years
of extensive lobbying and public campaigns organized by the American Jewish community.

The lead role in the distribution of American Jewish aid was played
by Boris Bogen. After being naturalized as an American citizen in
1904, the Moscow-born educator had given up his job as principal of
a trade school in New Jersey to work on behalf of refugee relief, eventually becoming director of the Joint and moving to Warsaw as general
director of the committee's relief operations in Europe. No stranger to
human suffering, he was still taken aback when he arrived in Ukraine
in 1922 as part of the American Relief Administration. In an orphanage in Proskuriv, he observed "boys and girls crowded together in a
heap of tatters on the floor without any clothing wherewith to cover
their bodies. They could not step beyond the threshold, for they had
nothing to put on. They could not move, for there was no free space.
All looked extremely emaciated, some of them like skeletons. That was
a terrible sight." Scarlet fever and typhus ran rampant as the sick lay
on the ground covered in filthy rags, infecting their healthier neighbors; there was insufficient clothing, underwear, mattresses, and blankets.[13] "But," Bogen continued, "the most unforgettable impression
was made upon us by the extraordinary timidity of the children, which
was betrayed by every move they made. Fear was in their eyes and they
lay motionless."[14]

As Bogen noted, the dislocation, suffering, and trauma were having
a deep psychological impact likely to outlast any physical wounds.
It was a threat recognized by other aid workers as well. The Federation of Ukrainian Jews, a London-based relief committee, predicted as

early as 1919 that the violence the refugees had witnessed as children
would shape future generations: "Starving children are always the
potential parents of discontented and anti-social men and women. But
the demoralized urchins from the Ukraine, with their childish memory
of seeing a father shot or a mother violated by savage soldiery, present
a problem beyond the reach of ordinary methods of relief. Such children seem bound to grow up with a grievance against society, unless
a remedy is found for their moral as well as their physical wants."[15]

Outside of the orphanages, though, Bogen noticed a radical shift
in power structures since the revolution: "The Jews who had been
the oppressed were now the rulers of the town, holding the principal
offices, and they loitered in and about the town hall with an air of
familiar possession, though in former times they entered its portals
only by suffrance. Where the portrait of the tsar once hung they had
placed an image of Trotsky."[16] Bogen's characterization was a realization of the most incendiary peasant fear: traumatized Jews with a
"grievance against society" in control of the levers of power, preparing to mete out justice to their former tormentors. Indeed, in Uman,

[TsDKFFA]

Jewish refugees from Uman

Zhytomyr, Mykolaiv, Cherkasy, Berdychiv, and countless other cities and towns throughout Ukraine, it was undeniable that for the first time in the long history of Jewish life in the region many top positions were now held by Jews. The pogroms of the preceding years, which had been justified on the specious grounds that Jews were responsible for Bolshevism, were having the paradoxical effect of driving Jews toward Soviet power, where Jewish ethnicity posed few barriers to advancement.

But while a select few were able to capitalize on the new opportunities offered by the Soviet state, the vast majority of the Jewish population—the artisans, shopkeepers, merchants, and members of the bourgeois class—suffered terribly from the Bolshevik ban on private enterprise, state control of foreign trade, and the nationalization of industry. The economic niche that Jews traditionally filled was, in fact, the sector most targeted by the new regime. As a result, the number of impoverished Jews increased dramatically.

Faced with these conditions, hundreds of thousands of Jews left the region entirely. Between 1917 and 1923, the Jewish population in what became Soviet Ukraine decreased by about 35 percent, from 2.3 million to 1.5 million. Many Jews relocated to the Russian interior, where the Jewish population swelled by more than 75 percent between the census of 1897 (the last before the civil war) and 1923. The number of Jews in Petrograd nearly tripled from 20,000 to 54,000, and the Jewish population of Moscow skyrocketed by a factor of eleven, from 8,000 to 88,000.[17] In these cities, many Jews found work as shopkeepers, artisans, and merchants, much as they had in Ukraine, or came to populate the entrepreneurial class—the so-called NEP-men, who benefited from the New Economic Policy (NEP), the state's strategic retreat from the stricter economic policies of "war communism." Jews also gravitated to government employment: in 1923, 44 percent of all Jews in Moscow worked for the state bureaucracy. Jews were playing a visible and disproportionate role in the nascent Soviet government.[18]

But the same dynamic that characterized Jewish life in Soviet Ukraine was replicated in Moscow and Petrograd: while a small number of Jews began to appear in the most privileged state offices, the majority of the Jewish population continued to suffer from the economic turmoil and social breakdown. The most needy were the dislocated children who had lost their parents during the pogroms. The artist Marc Chagall, who was working as an art teacher in a Jewish orphanage in Malakhovka, outside of Moscow, remembered the refugee children he taught as "the most unhappy of orphans."

> All of them had been thrown out on the street, beaten by thugs, terrified by the flash of the dagger that cut their parents' throats. Deafened by the whistling of bullets and the crash of broken windowpanes, they still heard, ringing in their ears, the dying prayers of their fathers and mothers. They had seen their fathers' beards savagely torn out, their sisters raped, disemboweled. Ragged, shivering with cold and hunger they roamed the cities, clung on to the bumpers of trains until, at last—a few thousand among so many, many others—they were taken into shelters for children.

It was a sight that would continue to haunt Chagall, who returned to the theme of pogroms several times in his work, most famously in his 1938 *White Crucifixion*, which depicts Jesus, wrapped in a prayer shawl, on the cross in front of a burning synagogue as Jewish refugees flee a pogrom.

JEWS NOT ONLY fled into the Soviet interior, they also sought to move entirely beyond the reach of the Bolsheviks. An estimated six hundred thousand Jews joined nearly two million White soldiers and activists, members of the Russian aristocracy and bourgeoisie, tsarist government officials, and other opponents of the new regime who fled Bolshevik rule into Poland, Romania, Germany, Austria, France, and across the Black Sea to Constantinople. Although Jews constituted only about a quarter of the total number of refugees from the former Russian Empire, their visibility within the group and popular associations between Jews and Bolsheviks ignited anti-Jewish and

[AMERICAN JEWISH JOINT DISTRIBUTION COMMITTEE ARCHIVES]

Liebe Messer, who was orphaned by
a pogrom in Ukraine

anti-immigrant sentiment, spurring governmental action and the rise
of right-wing movements across Europe.[19]

Throughout the continent, the Joint assisted refugees by renting dormitories and building orphanages. It provided clothing, blankets, towels, soap, and food packages of flour, canned milk, rice, oil, beans, and
cocoa, as well as monetary loans, sewing machines and other trade tools,
legal assistance, and English, Spanish, and Hebrew lessons. It amounted
to the most extensive Jewish relief project to date. The Joint also kept
receipts and records, documenting the flow of humanity as it passed
before the aid workers.

The most common route of escape for Jewish refugees, as had been
the case before the war, was to cross the Zbrucz River into Galicia, now
firmly part of Poland. Between 1919 and 1923, about two hundred
thousand Jews took this path. Many of them were returning home
after having been deported during the war.[20] "It seems that whole cities
are moving," wrote aid worker J. M. Kowalsky, "and in some instances

orphanages and other communal institutions are moved along with the entire community."[21]

The crossing was not always easy. The spread of typhus in Ukraine during the fall of 1921 prompted Poland to set up disinfecting stations and quarantines at the border, but the flood of immigrants quickly overwhelmed their capacity.[22] Refugees and repatriates were directed into overcrowded and lice-infested quarantine stations, set up in former army barracks; nearly fifteen hundred people died at one station, waiting under difficult conditions to enter Poland.[23] By January 1922, five thousand Jews had arrived in the border town of Brest-Litovsk, where over half the buildings in the city had been destroyed by the war. One observer wrote to the Joint that "every family in Brest is housing some returned refugees, and likewise every family has an active or convalescent case of typhus under its roof."[24] The Joint even funded the construction of a model refugee camp in Brest—the Felix Warburg Colony—to house ninety-six families.[25]

Repatriates returning to Galicia often found that their former homes had been destroyed or occupied by Christian neighbors, forcing them to find shelter in synagogue basements, school buildings, cellars, and even caves. The nationalist Polish government unleashed a steady stream of laws intended to restrict the movement of refugees and prevent them from settling permanently in Poland; new migrants were required to register with the police and were barred from settling in frontier regions and county seats.[26] As a result, by 1923 only about eleven thousand Jewish refugees remained in Poland, while at the same time tens of thousands of Polish Jews were themselves fleeing the Polish Republic.[27]

The disputed territory of Bessarabia, which had been occupied by Romania since March 1918, became the next most common destination for Jews fleeing Ukraine. Estimates of the number of Jewish refugees in Bessarabia in February 1921 range from twenty-two thousand to forty thousand, and refugees continued to arrive by the thousands throughout the year.[28] Romanian gendarmes guarded the bridges over the Dnister to prevent more Jews from crossing. Desperate refugees flung themselves into the water attempting to beat the current, and untold numbers drowned when the river froze and they tried to cross the thin ice.[29] Many hired smugglers and contrabandists to get them across, only to be robbed of their possessions on the other side. "The worst is that a great deal of this shameful robbery is perpetrated by Jews against Jews," bemoaned one Joint report.[30] The region was under martial law, so once they arrived, refugees were at the mercy of soldiers who swindled and abused them.[31] The flood of humanity quickly overwhelmed small border towns that were themselves recovering from war and disorder. Thousands died of disease, exposure, and violence in the makeshift camps established near the banks of the river.

As the number of refugees in Bessarabia reached seventy-five thousand in May, 1921, Romanian authorities began evicting the newcomers from the border towns where they were settling.[32] Military convoys shepherded those who had managed to ford the river back across the Dnister.[33] Others fled into the regional capital of Kishinev—the site of the infamous 1903 pogrom. There they were kept under guard and forced to live huddled together in synagogue basements; fifteen

hundred refugees were sleeping on synagogue floors in June 1921 and
another six thousand were living in various group lodgings throughout
the city.[34] By November, the number of refugees in Kishinev peaked at
eighteen thousand.[35]

Bessarabia was, for many, merely a stopping point on the way to
the Old Kingdom of Romania, the territories included in the prewar
Romanian state, where living conditions were better. There many settled in the city of Iași, attracted by its university and its large Jewish
population. However, the university was also a hotbed of Romanian
nationalism and political antisemitism. The influx of Jews seeking
admission led to anti-Jewish student demonstrations, organized by
radical nationalists who accused the Jews of importing Bolshevism
and corrupting the student body. In December 1922, a nationwide
general strike demanded a quota on Jewish admission to the university, and throughout the year the right-wing press stoked xenophobia
and warned of the racial corruption of Romania. In the midst of this
climate of hyper-nationalism, Romania reluctantly adopted a constitution that granted citizenship for Jews, in accordance with the minority
treaties signed in Paris. But an administrative rule required that appli-
cants for naturalization demonstrate continued residence in Romania
since before the Great War, an impossibility for the eighty thousand
Jewish refugees then living in the country.[36]

Some former Russian subjects who had fled Ukraine through Romania made their way to Hungary, where they joined twenty to forty thousand mostly Galician Jewish refugees. There, in the midst of the White
Terror reaction against Béla Kun's failed Soviet Republic, they were
accused of being hostile invaders and Bolshevik agents. According to
the Warsaw-born American Yiddish writer Isaac Unterman, "There was
an order to detain and strictly inspect all Jews from the former Russian
territories, as they were all, God help us, caught up in Bolshevism."[37] On
September 20, 1920, the Hungarian minister of the interior ordered the
expulsion of all Jews who had arrived in Hungary after January 1914,
setting off months of police raids as local authorities engaged in Jew
hunts. The law was used to expel even Galician Jews who had been living in Hungary for thirty years or more. Many were interned in refugee

camps, like the ones in Piliscsaba and Zalaegerszeg, where they awaited documents that would allow them to leave for Czechoslovakia.[38]

Czechoslovakia, for its part, was also overwhelmed with about fifteen thousand Jewish refugees from Hungary, Galicia, and Ukraine. "The congestion in the larger Czechoslovakian cities was so great that no proper accommodations of any kind could be found for thousands of refugees," the Joint reported, noting that eight hundred Jewish families were living in abandoned railway cars.[39] In response, on March 5, 1921, the generally liberal Czechoslovakian government ordered all refugees to leave the country by the end of the month. The Joint was able to intervene and arrange for them to be held at Czech barrack camps, where some four thousand were detained until homes could be found for them in other countries. By the spring of 1921, the Joint was still receiving an average of forty applications for assistance per day from refugees in Prague and even more in Bratislava.[40]

By 1923, Poland and Romania, the two nations on Ukraine's western border, were becoming impatient with those migrants who had neither settled permanently and become self-sufficient—a task made difficult by a dizzying array of legal restrictions—nor moved on to another country. Poland ordered the expulsion of all remaining refugees dependent upon public assistance by the end of March 1923, and the Romanian government ordered its police to do the same by October 1 of that year.[41] The pipeline out of Ukraine was largely frozen. Tens of thousands of Jewish refugees without citizenship papers were stranded in Poland and Romania.[42] But an even bigger problem lay elsewhere, as those migrants who did manage to get through Poland and Romania sought more permanent homes in Germany, France, the United States, or Palestine.

ATTRACTED BY THE cheap currency that made for easy living, about seventy-five thousand Jewish refugees from the former Russian Empire arrived in Germany between 1919 and 1923, joining about two hundred thousand recent Jewish immigrants, mostly from Galicia.[43] Already in June 1919, a report by the Committee for the Assistance of

Poor Russians in Berlin noted that "monthly, a fresh lot of Polish Jews, whose circumstances arouse the deepest commiseration, joins the thousands [already here]. Owing to the bloody proceedings in Poland and Galicia thousands of people fly across the frontiers in disorder . . . at least 3–400 of those wretched outcasts pass the German frontiers weekly."[44] Many of these migrants had originally come from lands now claimed by Ukraine. "They come from Ukraine, from Galicia, from Hungary," wrote the novelist Joseph Roth. "Back home they fell victim, in the hundreds of thousands, to pogroms. The survivors make their way to Berlin. From here they head west, to Holland and America, or south, to Palestine."[45] The Yiddish writer Israel Joshua Singer characterized the refugees similarly: "They had come here from Galicia . . . from Poland, Romania, Russia—from wherever the war and the carnage had driven them. . . . They all somehow eked out a living, crowded the small kosher restaurants and every inch of the neighborhood's living space. The police made frequent raids, seeking persons without proper credentials, and the old quarter throbbed with hustle, bustle, and strife. Brokers arranged deals, peddlers bickered, beggars clamored for donations, policemen blew whistles, moneychangers bartered foreign currencies, and pious Jews prayed with fervor."[46]

All came to Germany with the firm belief that, as Margolin claimed German foreign minister Walther Rathenau assured him, "those terrible pogroms that occurred in Russia never could or would occur in Germany."[47] Margolin himself, who arrived in Germany in 1921 after having already seen his political hopes crushed in Ukraine, was less sanguine: in response to its total defeat in the Great War, he wrote, Germany "could become the seat of incalculable calamities in Europe and the entire world."[48] But most Jews were convinced they would be safe in Germany. Nevertheless, about half of the migrants moved on to other destinations by the end of the year, mostly for economic reasons, with the bulk heading to the United States, Canada, Argentina, Palestine, or various European locations.

Among those who stayed in Germany, the largest number gravitated to Berlin. "The whole world passes before you there," remarked Abe Cahan, editor of the *Jewish Daily Forward* upon his return to

[YIVO INSTITUTE FOR JEWISH RESEARCH]

Jewish orphans in Berlin on their way to Paris

New York in 1921.[49] The city was in flux: "The Germans were living as though they were at a railway station, no one knowing what would happen the next day," wrote Ilya Ehrenburg, who arrived in 1921. "Herds of foreigners wandered along the Kurfürstendamm: they were buying up the remnants of former luxury for a song. In the poorer quarters several bakeries were looted. It seemed as though everything was bound to collapse, but factory chimneys went on smoking, bank clerks neatly wrote out astronomical figures, prostitutes painstakingly made up their faces, journalists wrote about the famine in Russia."[50]

"There people did not trade in dollars or mourn the Kaiser," continued Ehrenburg, "There people went hungry, worked, and waited for the revolution to break out."[51] Jewish writers and poets congregated in the smoke-filled rooms of the city's coffeehouses, arguing about the form the revolution would take. "Never in my life have I met so many miraculous Hasidic rabbis as in inflationary Berlin, nor such crowds of constructivist artists as at the Romanisches Café," wrote Marc Chagall when he arrived in 1922.[52] Other Jewish writers who found themselves in the German capital included the Hebrew poet Hayyim Nahman Bialik, whose poem "In the City of Slaughter" about the Kishinev pogrom had become a rallying cry for Jewish self-defense organizations; Shmuel Yosef Agnon, whose evocative Hebrew-language literary portraits of his hometown in Eastern Galicia would win him the 1966 Nobel Prize for Literature; and Ehrenburg, who would describe the horrors of war for tens of millions of Russian readers during the Second World War. The Yiddish writers Dovid Bergelson, Moyshe Kulbak, and Der Nister also made Berlin their home during this period, as did the Hebrew writers Shaul Tchernichovsky and Uri Zvi Greenberg. The leaders of the Central Committee for Relief of Pogrom Victims—Elye Tsherikover, Nokhem Shtif, Jacob Lestschinsky, and Nokhem Gergel—arrived in the city in 1921–1922 and established the Eastern Jewish Historical Archive to hold the tens of thousands of papers they had brought with them documenting the recent pogroms in Ukraine. The Russian Jewish historian Simon Dubnow, one of the chief theoreticians of Jewish national autonomy, arrived in the city in 1922. Avrom Revutsky, the former minister of Jewish affairs in the Directory government, was also in Berlin, editing the Zionist Marxist journal *Der Kampf.*[53]

About twenty thousand Jewish refugees lived in the seedy Scheunenviertel district near Alexanderplatz among a quarter-million Russian-speaking immigrants. Internationalist Marxists, Zionist Jews, Russian monarchists, and Ukrainian nationalists all shared the same streets and boardinghouses.[54] Dovid Bergelson portrayed the friction in the city in his short story "Among Refugees," in which he imagined a Ukrainian Jew whose hometown was decimated by a pogrom living in the same Berlin boardinghouse as a Ukrainian warlord who had perpetrated the violence: the Jew in room three, the Ukrainian in room five. "Why, in Palestine, if an Arab kills a Jew, then a couple of hours later you'll find a dead Arab," the alienated and distressed Jewish boarder muses as he tries to acquire a gun. "And here, among so many Jews, all these pogromists are running around scot-free, and there's not a single Jew around to get rid of even one pogromist."[55] Although the story was fiction, it reflected genuine animosities that percolated among Jewish and Ukrainian refugees from neighboring towns and villages, living in close proximity to one another in slums across Europe.

After escaping Kyiv, for instance, Pavlo Skoropadskyi—the leader of the Ukrainian state in 1918—settled in the Berlin suburb of Wannsee, where he and his followers cultivated conservative circles that supported a restoration of the Hetmanate.[56] Vassili Biskupsky, who had been the military governor of Odesa, became vice president of the right-wing Aufbau (Reconstruction) movement in Munich and conspired with the German war hero Erich Ludendorff to invade Bolshevik Russia with a joint Ukrainian-German army in the hopes of reestablishing the Hohenzollern and Romanov monarchies. Biskupsky aimed to put Grand Duke Kiril Romanov, a cousin of the deposed tsar Nicholas II, on the Russian throne and funneled Romanov wealth to Adolf Hitler in support of this goal. Ivan Poltavets-Ostrianytsia, who had engineered Skoropadskyi's coup, also worked with the Hitler movement in 1923, looking to establish a national-socialist Ukraine through his Ukrainian National Cossack Society and its newspaper, *Ukrains'kyi kozak* (the *Ukrainian Cossack*).[57] Likewise, Yevhen Konovalets, a former officer in the army of the Ukrainian People's Republic revered for his defense of Kyiv in 1918, moved to Vienna and then Berlin, and in 1929 established the Organization of Ukrainian Nationalists, which sought to create an independent Ukrainian state with German aid.[58] In 1938, he was assassinated in Rotterdam by Soviet secret agents who treated him to a box of exploding chocolates.[59] The conflicts that had destroyed the Russian Empire continued to resonate across Europe, carried through the continent by new diaspora communities.

Although eastern European Jews never constituted an actual majority of refugees in Germany—Christian émigrés from Russia far outnumbered them—the Ostjuden (Eastern Jews), coming "across the border, often with false passports, at night and in fog, wearing caftans,"[60] were often invoked as stand-ins for refugees in general. A long-standing German aversion toward eastern European Jews, shared by German Christians and Jews alike, intensified with the sudden arrival of tens of thousands of poor, typhus-infected, and politically suspect refugees, rendering the so-called Ostjudenfrage (Eastern Jewish question) one of the most pressing issues of the day. Already in 1919, one Joint Distribution Committee report noted, "It is feared incessantly that the fury of the poor and needy part of the German people will turn against the refugees."[61] Another March 1920 cable from Joint representatives in Europe warned that the influx of eastern European Jews into Germany was responsible for the "ever growing severity of antisemitism."[62] Over the summer of 1920, the threat had hardly subsided: "Gentiles hostile to the Eastern Jews say, not altogether without justice, that the latter are consuming the country's scanty provisions, without paying for them with the labor of their hands," warned one Frankfurt rabbi in an August 1920 letter to the Joint.[63]

Eastern European Jewish refugees were portrayed as rowdy and raucous and generally uncivilized, as having poor hygiene and being carriers of disease. They were alleged to be prone to criminality and were accused of running whorehouses and behaving sexually inappropriately.[64] The conservative *Alldeutsche Blätter* referred to the eastern European Jews as "alien, inferior, and therefore highly undesirable."[65] The *Völkischer Beobachter*, which had been purchased by the recently formed Nazi Party, devoted the front page of its March 6, 1920, edition to an open letter to Bavarian minister of the interior Fritz Endres under the headline AGAINST THE OSTJUDEN.[66] A few days later, in an article entitled CLEAN OUT THE JEWS, ONCE AND FOR ALL, the paper urged that "the Ostjuden must be taken out immediately, and ruthless measures must be promptly enacted against all other Jews."[67] In 1922, the nationalist monthly *Deutschlands Erneuerung* was even more blunt: "The Slavic-Jewish-German mongrel is the most hideous human being that has ever populated the earth."[68]

The German press and government debated various solutions to the flood of eastern European Jews, ranging from expulsion to internment in concentration camps.[69] German society was starkly divided in its attitude toward the Jewish refugees. Socialists, many of whom were of Jewish background themselves, believed it was incumbent upon Germany to provide asylum, whereas nationalists feared that the arrival of Jewish refugees would pollute the racial purity of the German nation and import Bolshevism into the region. Albert Einstein, already a

celebrated physicist and a particularly astute observer of the scene in
Berlin, wrote in 1921: "Eastern European Jews are made the scape-
goats for certain defects in present-day German economic life, things
that in reality are painful aftereffects of the war. The confrontational
attitude toward these unfortunate refugees, who have escaped the hell
that Eastern Europe is today, has become an efficient and politically
successful weapon used by demagogues."[70]

The most nefarious accusation against Jewish refugees to Germany
was the allegation that the Jews as a collective bore responsibility for
the crimes of the Bolsheviks and that the Jews were importing Bolshevism into Europe.[71] It was a charge bolstered by the prominence of
Jews among official Soviet representatives to the West: Adolph Joffe,
who had led the Bolshevik delegations at Brest-Litovsk and Riga, had
since become the first Soviet representative in Berlin; Maxim Litvinov
was the Soviet representative in London and became Soviet commissar
of foreign affairs in 1930; Grigory Zinoviev led the Communist International; Leonid Krasin led Soviet trade negotiations in Europe; and,
of course, Trotsky was the face of the revolution to the world. Karl
Radek, Joffe's successor as Soviet representative in Germany, became a
particularly potent symbol of eastern European Jewish involvement in
the revolutionary movement after he was arrested in February 1919 for
his involvement in the radical Spartacist uprising. And few had forgotten the role that prominent revolutionaries with Jewish backgrounds,
like Rosa Luxemburg and Kurt Eisner, had played in the uprisings of
1918–1919. Those who feared the spread of Jewish Bolshevism from
Moscow were hardly placated by Trotsky's appeals "to the Comrades
of the Spartacus League"[72] or by Zinoviev's prophecy that "the time
is not far off when the whole of Germany will be a soviet republic."[73]

One of the most fervent voices equating Jews and Bolshevism in
Germany was the Baltic German refugee Alfred Rosenberg, whose first
published piece, in the February 21, 1919, edition of the ultraconserva-
tive journal *Auf gut Deutsch* ("In Plain German"), a "Weekly for Law
and Order," was entitled "The Russian-Jewish Revolution." The article
blamed the "Jewish spirit" for the "tolerance of open borders" that
Rosenberg argued was destroying Germany. In Russia, he continued,

the government was "almost purely Jewish," and if the borders remained open those same Jews would soon bring about the destruction of Germany as well.[74] In another article published on April 4, 1919, Rosenberg railed against Germany's tolerance of foreigners, who he claimed were threatening to blanket the country with "shameless Jewish lying propaganda."[75] He subsequently warned that "Jewish Gold from Moscow" was creating anarchy in Germany[76] and cautioned that the "unrestricted power" of "unscrupulous Jewish demagoguery" in Russia could already be seen in the streets of Munich.[77] Rosenberg and other migrants from the former tsarist empire helped define and popularize the narrative that Bolshevik Jewish refugees were destroying Germany, and Rosenberg himself was to become one of the leading ideologues of the Nazi movement and editor of the *Völkischer Beobachter*.

This anti-Jewish and xenophobic rhetoric soon seeped into the Reichstag and the German bureaucracy. Bavarian deputy Georg Heim, for instance, explained on May 19, 1919, that "in Bavaria as in Hungary and as in Russia the eastern Jews prepared the revolution. The eastern Jews, persecuted for centuries, have the spirits of rebels. And they caused all the trouble with us."[78] Munich chief of police Ernst Pöhner shared these sentiments, blaming eastern European Jews for importing Bolshevism into Germany and accusing them of being "a harmful foreign body in the German nation."[79] These ideas were amplified by right-wing papers and pamphleteers and were quickly accepted as conventional wisdom throughout Germany.

The most influential agitator against Jewish migrants and what came to be known as "Judeo-Bolshevism" was, of course, Adolf Hitler. Hitler disparaged the Soviet Union as "satanic" and a "Jewish dictatorship of blood" and obsessively linked the fear of Bolshevik expansionism to the flood of Jewish refugees into Germany. In 1922, he warned "that we too shall sink into the blood-swamp of Bolshevism, and may prove a thousand times that the ultimate cause of all this misery, the ultimate germ of this disease of the race, is the Jew."[80] Later, in *Mein Kampf*, he would write that "in the organized mass of Marxism," the Jew "has found the weapon which lets him dispense with democracy and in its stead allows him to subjugate and govern the peoples with a dictatorial and brutal fist."[81] Hitler deemed that "the Jew today is the great agitator for the complete destruction of Germany."[82] Claiming to be convinced that the Jews had destroyed Russia with Bolshevism, Hitler and his followers were willing to go to extraordinary lengths to ensure that they would not be permitted to do the same to Germany.

As hyperinflation reached new heights in the fall of 1923, the far right's argument that Jewish refugees were to blame for Germany's ills intensified. On November 5, 1923, anti-Jewish rioting began in the Scheunenviertel in what many called a pogrom. That same month the Bavarian government issued an order expelling Jews with Polish citizenship from Bavaria.[83] On November 8, Hitler, with the support of Ludendorff, Rosenberg, and six hundred Nazi storm troopers, marched into the Bürgerbräukeller beer hall in Munich, where Bavarian state commissioner Gustav von Kahr was speaking. Hitler fired his revolver in the air, stood on a chair, and declared revolution. The Beer Hall Putsch may have failed, but Hitler had catapulted himself to the pinnacle of the German right. While serving his sentence in Landsberg Prison, he had the opportunity to articulate a potent narrative of his movement in *Mein Kampf*. Fourteen years later, the führer would speak before tens of thousands of cheering youth in the closing ceremonies of the 1937 Nuremberg Rally and warn that "Jewish Bolshevism is an absolute alien body in this community of European culture-nations."[84]

THE UNITED STATES and Palestine, the two regions viewed as the most likely recipients of Jewish migrants in the early 1920s, were not immune from the Judeo-Bolshevism scare.

Although most migrants preferred America, the world Zionist community saw the prospect of Jewish sovereignty in Palestine as a permanent solution to the Jewish problem. The bloodshed in eastern Europe encouraged wide-scale Jewish migration to Palestine, which was in the process of coming under British control as a mandate territory. The British appointed Herbert Samuel, a Jewish former British home secretary who had become a supporter of the Zionist movement, as high commissioner, lending encouragement to about forty thousand Jewish refugees from Ukraine who sailed across the Black Sea and through the Turkish Straits between 1921 and 1923 to get to Palestine. Large segments of the Arab population responded to the migration movement and the British Mandate with suspicion and anger that occasionally erupted into riots and violence. Although it was more of a reaction to Zionist ambitions than fears of racial or political contamination, many Jewish leaders and migrants interpreted Arab hostility as another version of what they had experienced in Europe. In March 1920 skirmishes between Jewish paramilitaries and Arab militias in the disputed region of the Upper Galilee led to the death of Joseph Trumpeldor, a veteran of the Russo-Japanese War who had inspired Jewish self-defense movements in Ukraine. His death at the settlement of Tel Hai initiated a virtual cult within the Zionist movement and amplified his call for Jewish self-defense. Even a Ukrainian nationalist like Margolin could agree: "Of course, it is better to die by an Arab's knife in one's ancestral land than to become a victim of a pogrom in Ukraine or Poland," he wrote from Germany.[85]

The most notorious clashes during this period erupted during the 1921 May Day parade in Jaffa, in response to the distribution of leaflets by the Jewish Communist Party calling for the establishment of a Soviet state in Palestine. The riots began when a group of Jewish workers, many of whom were new immigrants from Russia and Ukraine, unfurled red flags with Bolshevik slogans in a largely Jewish market on the edge of an Arab neighborhood. The flag-bearers were initially hounded by anti-communist Jewish counter-protestors, but as the demonstration spilled into the Arab residential area, the clashes escalated into an ethnic riot; fierce fighting resulted in the deaths of forty-seven Jews and forty-eight Arabs.[86] Once again, a narrative emerged of Jews being attacked on the charge of spreading Bolshevism. As a British Commission of Inquiry concluded, "The Bolshevik demonstration was the spark that set alight the explosive discontent of the Arabs, and precipitated an outbreak which developed into an Arab-Jewish feud."[87] Many Jewish refugees in Palestine viewed the new violence they were encountering in Jaffa through the lens of the pogroms they had fled in eastern Europe, and the Yiddish press immediately took to calling it

the "Jaffa pogrom."[88] "The pogrom against Israel in Eretz-Israel is still
continuing," proclaimed the Hebrew writer Berl Katznelson.[89] It was
a sentiment shared by future Israeli prime minister David Ben-Gurion
and other Jewish activists in Palestine. Despite the numerous differences between the riot in Palestine and the pogroms of Ukraine—not
the least of which was the high Arab death toll, which signaled a lethal
brawl more than a pogrom—the notion that the violence in the Holy
Land was just another pogrom established a myth that came to define
the right wing of the Zionist movement.

Despite Zionist entreaties, the vast majority of Jewish refugees
expressed the desire to eventually settle in the United States.[90] American
lawmakers, though, were also becoming increasingly suspicious of Jewish immigrants, who they feared were importing Bolshevism into the
country. From September 1918 to June 1919, North Carolina senator
Lee Overman led a congressional committee to investigate the impact
of Bolshevism in the United States. The Reverend George Simons, a
pastor who had worked as superintendent of a church in Petrograd for
ten years before the revolution, testified incorrectly that "out of 388
members" of the Soviet government in Petrograd, "only 16 happened
to be real Russians, and all the rest [are] Jews."[91] He further testified
that *The Protocols of the Elders of Zion* "reflects a real organization," a
"secret Jewish society," seeking "to make a conquest of the world, and
to make the Christian forces as ineffective as possible, and finally to
have the whole world, if you please, in their grip."[92] The committee did
not accept Simons's more inflammatory accusations, but concluded that
"radical revolutionary elements" in the United States had made "common cause" with the Bolsheviks in Russia to "incite revolution" and
"inaugurate a reign of terror." Without mentioning Jews or the Yiddish
language by name, the committee concluded that "foreign-language
newspapers are a danger to the country" and warned that "the forces
of anarchy and violence are utilizing the financial resources plundered
by them from the European people they have succeeded in exploiting,
to import into this country money, literature, and hired agents for the
purpose of promulgating the doctrine of force, violence, assassination,
confiscation, and revolution."[93] Most who read the report would have

recognized the accusations of "exploitation," importing anarchy, and "utilizing financial resources" as references to Jews.

The hearings sparked widespread fear of Bolshevism throughout the country. On April 30, 1919, Senator H. J. Walters, president pro tempore of the New York State Senate, warned, "there is no doubt that there is a thoroughly organized plan worked out by the Russian Bolsheviki to seize the reins of government in this country."[94] American military intelligence agents spread the falsehood that the Bolshevik revolution was part of a worldwide Jewish plot financed by Jewish bankers with the goal of securing world domination. The State Department's Russian Division speculated about the "power and aims of International Jewry" in a report linking Jews and Bolshevism.[95] The Overman committee's report gave credence to the fantasies espoused by fringe pamphleteers. As Henry Ford's *Dearborn Independent* put it, "The Bolshevik revolution was a carefully groomed investment on the part of International Jewish Finance" and "the same forces would like to introduce it to the United States."[96] These same "hysterical American Jews," the paper contended, were using the violence in Ukraine and Poland as an excuse to advance their own nefarious political goals.[97] The *Dearborn Independent* bemoaned in 1920 that "an endless stream of the most undesirable immigrants pours daily into the United States, tens of thousands of the same people whose presence has been the problem and menace of the governments of Europe."[98] Similarly Madison Grant's influential *The Passing of the Great Race* warned that the true American, "the man of the old stock," was being "literally driven off the streets of New York City by the swarms of Polish Jews."[99]

In 1921, 119,000 Jewish refugees arrived in the United States, the vast majority of them coming from the former Russian Empire.[100] These newcomers added to the 1,486,000 Jews who had arrived in the country between 1899 and 1914. Congress responded to growing fears of Jewish immigration by passing the Emergency Quota Act of 1921, which sought to preserve the existing ethnic makeup of the United States by limiting the number of immigrants from each country to 3 percent of their total population according to the 1910 census. Yet Congress was alarmed that in both 1921 and 1922 a plurality of immigrants were still "Hebrews," representing 15 percent of total immigration into the United States during those years.[101] As a result, the Johnson-Reed Act of 1924 reduced the quota from 3 percent to 2 percent and used the 1890 census instead of the 1910 census as the benchmark, thereby further restricting Jewish immigration. Gedalia Bublick, editor of the *Jewish Daily News*, pointed out during the congressional hearings on the act that the Jews fleeing Russia were actually anti-Bolshevik—that's why they were fleeing Bolshevism in the first place.[102] But Congress, responding to constituents riled up by fears of encroaching Bolshevism, passed the law nevertheless. "America must remain American," declared President Calvin Coolidge as he signed the act.

The bill ensured that the United States would be closed to the vast majority of eastern European Jews. The 1925 quota for immigrants from Eastern Galicia (which remained a separate legal category for US immigration despite its incorporation into Poland), Russia (including Ukraine), Bessarabia, and Romania, for instance, was set at 3,758—one-tenth of the 1924 quota of 37,610.[103] The unspoken understanding in the congressional debates was that reducing the number of immigrants from these four regions would effectively ban almost all Jews from entering the country. It also ensured that America would be closed to the tens of thousands of European Jews desperate to flee the rise of fascism.

The Schwarzbard Trial

Throughout the spring of 1926, Yiddish poet and watchmaker Sholem Schwarzbard wandered through the streets of Paris's Latin Quarter with a pistol in his pocket. In his hands he carried two photos of Petliura, one cut out from the *Larousse Encyclopedia*, and another he had found in a recent newspaper from which he learned that the former chief otaman was living in the French capital. Schwarzbard was obsessed. The forty-year-old, who courtroom reporters would later comment looked "more like a clerk than a murderer," short, blond, and "undistinguished in appearance," drew no attention to himself as he sought out Petliura from among the crowds, comparing the features of likely candidates to the photo in his hands.[1] The deposed leader often dined at the cafés and bistros that catered to Sorbonne students. Schwarzbard had found his target on several occasions, but each time Petliura was accompanied by his wife and daughter, Olga and Lessia, with whom he shared two small rented rooms on the rue Thénard.

Finally, on May 25, Schwarzbard encountered Petliura browsing alone through the new releases at Joseph Gibert's booksellers, on the corner of the rue Racine and boulevard St. Michel. When Schwarzbard told a Paris courtroom of this encounter, one reporter noted that his

face came "alive and transparent with boyish exultation."[2] Still unsure
if the man he saw matched the photo, Schwarzbard asked, "Are you
Petliura?" The chief otaman didn't answer. The poet took a chance
and shot the former head of state five times. When police arrived at
the scene, Schwarzbard was waiting for them: "I have killed a great
assassin," he declared.

Born in 1886 in Bessarabia, Schwarzbard was raised in the Podilian
town of Balta. Three of his siblings and his mother died when he was a
child; the young Schwarzbard was apprenticed to a watchmaker soon
after his bar mitzvah. As a youth, he became involved in anarchist
circles, agitating for the overthrow of the tsar. Once, in 1906, when he
was distributing literature inside a synagogue, the pious Jews trying
to pray got fed up with him and denounced him to the authorities.
He was detained but managed to flee across the Austro-Hungarian
border and continued his anarchist activities. He was arrested again in
Vienna on the charge of robbing a small wine bar. The barkeep found
him on the premises at opening time: the would-be thief had carelessly
locked himself inside at closing the night before. The till was short
and Schwarzbard was carrying a tool kit and cash. Undeterred by the
hopelessness of his defense, the brash poet claimed it was a case of
misidentification. After serving four months for the crime, he moved
to Budapest, where he again found himself in custody, this time for
distributing radical literature. He relocated to Paris in 1910, where
during the Great War he served in the Foreign Legion and later in
a regular French infantry brigade. He was injured and awarded the
Croix de Guerre.

The revolutionary cause remained dear to his heart. Upon hearing
news of the overthrow of the tsar in Russia, Schwarzbard returned to
Ukraine in the summer of 1917, just in time to witness the chaos of the
civil war. He floated through several revolutionary fighting brigades,
eventually finding his way to French-occupied Odesa. Soon after Grigoriev's conquest of the city, Schwarzbard joined the Bolsheviks and
traveled with a brigade to the pogrom-devastated regions around
Cherkasy. Disillusioned and traumatized, he returned to Paris, where,
under the pen name of Bal-Khaloymes ("The Dreamer"), he published

vignettes about the pogroms and a series of poems about the war. For his day job, he got work fixing clocks in a small shop and resigned himself to a quiet life. At least until he found the photo of Petliura in the *Larousse*.

SCHWARZBARD'S VIGILANTE ACT of vengeance threw him into headlines around the world and brought renewed global attention to the pogroms and the question of Petliura's responsibility for the violence. Much of the Jewish community saw Schwarzbard's deed as defensible and even admirable. "If murder can be justified after the fact, it should be justified completely for Schwarzbard, because he avenged our blood. He himself is pure," declared the American Hebrew-language paper *Ha-Doar*.[3] In *Davar*, the labor Zionist Hebrew daily, Yehoshua Heshel Yeivin took an even more militant stance, praising Schwarzbard for his bold act while

Sholem Schwarzbard at trial

criticizing the world Jewish community for meticulously documenting the pogroms but failing to act resolutely to stop them: "Material about the pogroms in so many volumes—that was how we responded to the violence in Ukraine. It is a response worthy of the people of the book, of sheep for slaughter."[4] The Yiddish writer Sholem Asch, already known for his controversial hagiographies of Jesus of Nazareth and his salacious portrait of lesbian love in his play *Got fun nekome* ("The God of Vengeance"), wrote that Schwarzbard's sin was "a redemption for us all."[5]

The Ukrainian diaspora community, on the other hand, united around Petliura, collecting some four hundred statements to present at trial defending their leader's honor. Since most of the Ukrainian territories Petliura had once ruled were now under Soviet control, with free speech restricted and nationalist sentiment shunned, the Ukrainian diaspora in Paris, Vienna, Berlin, and Prague became the chief voice of the Ukrainian independence movement. Petliura, who had previously been a controversial figure among Ukrainian nationalists, many of whom blamed him for the ultimate failure of the movement and particularly for his surrender of Eastern Galicia to Poland, was celebrated in death as a national hero. At a memorial service for the slain leader, his former political rivals interpreted his murder as an attack "not on Petliura the person" but on "the cause he served."[6] It was an affront, they argued, to the entire Ukrainian people and the idea of Ukrainian independence. Schwarzbard's deed and the Jewish response even provoked a genuine fear among Ukrainian communal activists that there was "a danger of Jewish terror against Ukrainian leaders."[7]

Many in the Ukrainian diaspora were also quick to dismiss the notion that Schwarzbard had acted alone, insisting that he was a Bolshevik agent. "Ukrainian democratic circles have regarded the killing of Chief Otaman Petliura by a certain Schwarzbard as the doing not of the Jews but of the Bolsheviks, directed against Ukrainian democracy and the person of its leader, who had been leading an armed struggle for the independence of Ukraine," reported Petliura's own *Tryzub*.[8] "This bandit-like crime is the work of the Bolshevik mafia," Mykyta Shapoval, who edited a Ukrainian socialist paper in Prague, confided to his brother, Mykola, a onetime general under Petliura.[9] One popular theory was that the Bolsheviks had purposely hired a Jew for the task in order to drive a wedge between Jews and Ukrainians.[10] In fact, while Schwarzbard had certainly identified with Bolshevism upon his return to Ukraine, there is no evidence that the assassination of Petliura was orchestrated by the Soviet secret police.

Both sides mobilized their bases. Leo Motzkin, who during the Paris Peace Conference had been reluctant to blame Petliura entirely for the pogroms, now took the lead in establishing a Schwarzbard Defense Committee to raise funds for the assassin's legal bills. "It is not about the act itself," he wrote, "but rather about Ukrainian Jewry and the danger they are in."[11] The committee consisted of Léon Blum, the future prime minister of France, and the Russian Jewish legal veterans Henry Sliosberg and Maksim Vinaver. The Ukrainian side followed suit, establishing its own committee in Paris headed by Oleksandr Shulhyn, who had been a cabinet member in the Central Rada and Petliura's representative to the Paris Peace Conference. The Eastern Jewish Historical Archive in Berlin assigned its top historians—Dubnow, Tsherikover, and Gergel—to collect evidence of Petliura's ultimate responsibility for the pogroms to send to Paris.[12] In Lviv, a Symon Petliura League was established to collect evidence of the chief otaman's innocence. It was as though Petliura and not Schwarzbard was the one on trial.[13]

Arnold Margolin, who had settled in the United States in 1922, was one of the few Jewish spokespeople who expressed caution. He saw Schwarzbard's act as a threat to the peaceful coexistence he still believed was possible in the region. "The trial of Schwarzbard may become an arena for an open and bitter fight between the Jews and Ukrainians. This pending danger is very serious and full of perilous possibilities in the future," he warned.[14] Margolin believed that as two of the largest stateless minorities in Europe, Ukrainians and Jews should be cooperating to advocate for the enshrinement of minority rights. It was an idea that had been taken up by the right-wing Zionist activist Vladimir Jabotinsky, who had even sought to collaborate with Petliura in 1921–1922 to reconquer Ukraine with a Jewish gendarmerie attached to a Ukrainian army.[15] Margolin feared the assassination would tear Jewish-Ukrainian relations asunder, further damaging any efforts toward reconciliation, and planting the seeds of future conflicts. Jabotinsky, for his part, worried that the whole affair was further tainting the world image of Jews with the stain of communism.[16] Louis Marshall also refused to allow the American Jewish Committee to endorse vigilante violence: "Although we can understand how a man who continually dreams of wrongs and crimes against humanity and whose relatives were victims of pogroms is compelled to commit such a desperate act," he wrote, "there is no excuse to make of him a national hero and to justify the murder which was committed as a private punishment for the alleged wrongs. Nor should the Jewish people assume responsibility for his action."[17]

PRETRIAL HEARINGS, WHICH began over the summer of 1926 and continued throughout the year, previewed the drama of the trial. Both the prosecution and defense assembled hundreds of witnesses from around the world, each of whom advanced their own narrative to account for what had happened in Ukraine just a few years earlier. The trial preparations provided the opportunity for a communal reckoning. One of the most insightful assessments was provided by former prime minister Volodymyr Vynnychenko, who sent in a testimony blaming the "enemies of an independent Ukraine" for promoting the idea that "the people of Ukraine are only a people of barbarians, bandits, and pogrom perpetrators." These propagandists, he continued, were depriving Ukrainians "not only of an independent existence as a free state but also of elementary respect."[18] Antisemitism existed in Ukraine, Vynnychenko continued, for the same reasons it existed everywhere: "racial differences, religious prejudices, the lack of culture among the masses, social inequality, economic competition of certain classes, etc."[19] It was just that in Ukraine, four years of total war and extreme violence had led "certain elements of the Ukrainian people" to feel an "indifference toward their own life and toward the life of others."[20] The government of Petliura, he concluded, was simply powerless to quash the violence perpetrated by rogue bandits and disgruntled soldiers.

Others pointed to popular hostility toward Jewish Bolsheviks as the key factor in precipitating pogroms. Borys Martos, who had also served as prime minister under the Directory, agreed that Petliura did not have the power to control his army. He, too, noted the psychological impact of war on Ukrainian soldiers but emphasized that "many of these men had been forcibly mobilized by the Red Army, where they had been compelled to serve under Jewish commanders, who marched them against their own people." Martos blamed the revolutionary tribunals for being overzealous in executing Ukrainian peasants for alleged counterrevolutionary activity and claimed that two-thirds of the members of those tribunals were Jews. "Is there any force that could satiate the desire for revenge?" he asked, excusing the pogroms as an understandable reaction to Jewish oppression.[21] If the masses had not been held back by Petliura's military intervention, he continued, "there would have been a complete destruction of the entire Jewish population, without exception."[22] The Directory government should be commended for limiting the bloodshed to what it was, he argued. Yet another member of the Central Rada agreed that the violence was simply retaliation for Jewish Bolshevik repression: "It is important to note that the majority of Bolshevik commissars who agitated against the Ukrainian authorities and military, who raised rebellions and who carried out the arrests, were Jews." It was only natural, therefore, "for the Ukrainian army to take out their frustrations on the people they saw as responsible: the Jews of Ukraine."[23] M. Feshchenko-Chopivsky, who served in an insurgent band, also pointed to the "senseless red terror" that prevailed in Radomyshl, where he was based, as Bolsheviks executed dozens of citizens without trial. The Cheka, he alleged, "was made up mostly of Jews" who "forgot that they were also part of the Ukrainian population, which was fighting for its independence." He justified "the righteous anger of the people against the Jewish commissars" on the grounds that the Bolsheviks would "turn churches into stables" and "some members of the Jewish people" would torture Ukrainians and "play the role of executioners."[24]

By contrast, Jewish members of the Schwarzbard defense committee, completely ignoring how they had once celebrated the Ukrainian
People's Republic's Law on National Autonomy, sought to portray the
pogroms as a deliberate policy of Petliura's government, motivated
by long-standing Jew-hatred. They sent in testimonies challenging the
allegations that the violence against Jews was simply part of the general unrest of the period or that it was a natural reaction to Jewish
involvement in Bolshevik cruelty. As Elye Tsherikover put it, "there
are almost no instances in which pogrom perpetrators attacked the
peaceful Christian population."[25] Petliura held ultimate responsibility for the pogroms, he continued, because "power was in the hands
of Petliura. And he who holds power, holds responsibility."[26] Petliura, Tsherikover charged, deliberately spread antisemitism within the
ranks of his military, "tolerated pogroms, and did not want to punish
those responsible."[27]

Nowhere was the enmity more poignantly displayed than in a
courtroom confrontation between the wives of the two central characters in the drama: Anna Schwarzbard and Olga Petliura. At the conclusion of the second pretrial hearing, on July 21, 1926, according to
news reports, Olga Petliura "rushed up to Mrs. Anna Schwarzbard
and started to beat her with a stick she held in her hand. The police
had to intervene and removed Madam Petliura from the courtroom."[28]

Schwarzbard used his eighteen-month pretrial detention in La
Santé Prison as an opportunity to defend his actions before the world.
In the pages of the New York anarchist Yiddish paper, *Di fraye arbay-
ter shtimme* ("The Free Worker's Voice"), he mused: "I have become
convinced that before being able to emancipate all of mankind, one
must first liberate oneself, liberate the Jewish people from all persecutions and calumnies which never cease to strike this people who have
been abandoned by everyone and are oppressed everywhere."[29] To his
comrades in Ukraine he wrote: "We are the people who gave the world
a god, the bible, morality, we carry with us the grand mission of liberty, and of universal emancipation. [We are] a people of holy martyrs,
a people in search of the emancipation of the world from slavery, from

Petliura's widow, Olga, with her brother at Schwarzbard's trial

crime, and from decadence."[30] He clearly saw himself as a historic, even messianic, figure, a primal defender of the Jews.

THE TRIAL, WHICH opened at Paris's Palais de Justice on October 18, 1927, was held in front of a *cour d'assises*, the criminal court in which France's most serious crimes were tried. Schwarzbard's fate was put in the hands of three judges and twelve jurors, whose verdict could not be appealed. Even though he did not deny that he had shot Petliura, Schwarzbard and his lawyers knew that their odds were good. In a spate of trials over the preceding years, juries had surprised courts by excusing crimes of passion and vigilante acts. Not only were battered wives forgiven for murdering their husbands, but political assassins were not convicted for carrying out hit jobs. Most famously, in 1919 the court had refused to render a guilty verdict in the trial of Raoul Villain, who had fatally shot the socialist politician Jean Jaurès at the outbreak of the war. In 1924, in a case that mirrored Schwarzbard's, the Armenian student Soghomon Tehlirian was acquitted in a Berlin trial of assassinating Talaat Pasha, the former grand vizier of the Ottoman Empire, even though police found Tehlirian at the scene holding a pistol over the dead body. The jury sympathized with Tehlirian's story that he was acting in retaliation for Pasha's role in the Armenian genocide a decade earlier.

Henri Torrès, the prominent Jewish lawyer and communist leader who headed Schwarzbard's legal team, knew that he had to turn the jury's attention away from his client and render the trial instead a prosecution of Petliura. "It is no longer Schwarzbard who is at issue here. It is the pogroms," he pronounced in his booming voice.[31] As the clerk read the indictment, surveying the long history of the Ukrainian revolution before finally addressing Schwarzbard's role in the assassination, the audience of four hundred people packed into the courtroom repeatedly shouted their disagreement and approval, garnering several warnings from the presiding judge, Georges Flory. In keeping with the tradition of the French Revolution that had created the *cour d'assises*, Flory believed the jury's job was not only to determine the facts of the case but also to apply "true justice." Testimony that would explain the extenuating circumstances of the murder was therefore regarded as relevant to the case.

Schwarzbard, for his part, acknowledged that he had carried out the assassination but, relying upon the jury to vote its conscience, pleaded not guilty. When he first took the stand, he provided sensational details of the horrors of the pogroms, directed both at the jury and at the global audience following the news dispatches. One reporter described the scene: "Rocking and swaying in the manner of Jews at prayer, he closed his eyes, tautened his lips and grimly . . . told of streets where corpses were piled upon corpses as on a battlefield."[32] Petliura, Schwarzbard asserted, was not just an isolated individual, but rather the culmination of centuries of Ukrainian antisemitism, dating back to the insurgency of 1648: "It was three centuries ago that the massacres commenced in these valleys of blood and tears. Petliura was the grandson of a great murderer who is named Khmelnytskyi."[33]

Schwarzbard confidently declared that the pogroms were ordered by Petliura and that his assassination was a true rendering of justice.[34]

Over the next week, a parade of witnesses for both sides debated Petliura's culpability in the pogroms, focusing predominantly on the events of February 15, 1919, in Proskuriv. In accordance with French legal procedures of the time, witnesses included not only those with first-hand knowledge of the events but also a range of experts and character witnesses, who spoke both to Schwarzbard's motives and to Petliura's. Oleksandr Dotsenko, for instance, who had worked as an adjutant for Petliura in Ukraine before becoming a stonemason in Paris, testified that his boss had been deeply concerned over the fate of the Jews and turned pale upon hearing of the atrocities committed against them in Proskuriv. On the other hand, Henryk Przanowski, who had been in Proskuriv as a worker with the Danish Red Cross, asserted that Petliura's officers acted only under his direct orders. Albert Baudry, a French chemical engineer whose only connection to the case was that he had lived in Ukraine, solicited sympathy from the jury by affirming that Petliura had always sought the support of the French and the Entente. Elye Tsherikover, who took the stand on Tuesday, October 25, provided detailed testimony on the pogroms he had painstakingly documented over the preceding seven years. Khaya Greenberg, the Red Cross nurse who had been in Proskuriv during the pogrom, gave some of the most harrowing testimony about the aftermath of the massacre.

The most tense moment of the trial came on Friday, October 21, when Oleksandr Shulhyn, the Central Rada cabinet member, testified. Schwarzbard, Shulhyn asserted as he began his testimony, "is not the avenger of the Jews but an agent of the Cheka."[35] According to the news reports, Shulhyn turned "toward Schwarzbard, and shaking his finger so vigorously that his whole body quivered," shouted, "I accuse that man of being the agent of Moscow. I swear it a thousand times." Petliura, continued Shulhyn, was not in the least bit antisemitic. Upon hearing this claim, Schwarzbard "leaped to his feet, flailing the air with his right arm and shouting," as his "body quivered in spasmodic jerks." When Schwarzbard finally managed to get words out, he shouted, "You hate me because I am a Jew." Shulhyn, "who had turned his back to the speaker, whipped around and screamed in a high falsetto: 'No, because you are a Bolshevik.'" Outside the courtroom, supporters of both sides began throwing punches, resulting in "black eyes and split lips."[36]

When the trial resumed, the lawyers went at each other again. They "renewed their verbal battle of yesterday with such ferocity that at times the trial degenerated into something much resembling a street brawl," the *New York Times* reported. "At the height of their unusual and seemingly extralegal battle half the jury was laughing, the other half was perceptibly annoyed and the Chief Justice could not make himself heard above the din."[37]

THE TRIAL ENDED on October 26 with the jury acquitting Schwarzbard of all charges after only thirty-two minutes of deliberation. "The jury, intensely moved by the heart-breaking details of these tragedies as told at first hand by those who had been through them, followed the dictates of its heart rather than of its head in rendering its verdict," the press reported.[38] Upon hearing the ruling and the roar of approval from the packed Palais de Justice, Schwarzbard "had the excited expression of a child on Christmas morning."[39]

In the months following Schwarzbard's acquittal, many of the Jewish activists who had been his staunchest defenders came to reflect upon the impact the trial was likely to have on the Jews who remained in Ukraine and their non-Jewish neighbors. The ordeal had dredged up animosities between the two communities that would be difficult to heal. Whereas Petliura had been a controversial figure for both Ukrainian and Jewish observers before his death, his assassination had opened an unbridgeable chasm between the two sides. Petliura had become a hero to all Ukrainians and an archetypal villain to the Jews—a precursor to Hitler, as some would later put it. Schwarzbard, by contrast, had become a hero to the Jews and a villain to Ukrainians. "This trial is a catastrophe, a catastrophe for Jewish-Ukrainian relations," wrote Shulhyn to Margolin when it was all over.[40]

The Interwar in Ukraine

The murder of Petliura provided an ideal opportunity for the Soviet government to advance its own narrative of the pogroms as a relic of the imperial age that communism had since overcome.[1] During the early 1920s, the Bolsheviks had been touting their successful suppression of pogroms and whitewashing their own complicity in the anti-Jewish violence of the revolutionary era. The government even sponsored a 1923 exhibition on pogroms, which was later reproduced as a book, reminding readers of the ways in which the Red Army had saved the Jews from destruction.[2] Indeed, during its early years, the leadership of the Soviet Union fought against antisemitism, portraying it as a counterrevolutionary weapon of reactionary elites, and sought to appeal to Jews through Yiddish-language schools, theaters, literature, and film. The flourishing of Yiddish culture even prompted some of the Ukrainian Jewish intellectuals who had constituted the heart of the Berlin diaspora to return, as the city of Kyiv emerged as a major center of Yiddish life. In the economic sphere, many Jewish artisans whose cottage industries were frowned upon by the state found employment instead in the growing factories, where they worked on production lines alongside Christian laborers, or in the Soviet bureaucracy. The migration of Jews into larger cities also shattered the tight-knit communities that had kept Jews to themselves in small towns and villages. Jewish integration was a cornerstone of Soviet policy in Ukraine.[3]

At the same time, Moscow continued to view the ill-fated Ukrainian People's Republic as a bourgeois escapade and any expression of Ukrainian nationalism as a dangerous centrifugal force capable of tearing asunder the fragile Soviet Union. Even if it was not directly ordered by the Kremlin, the murder of the chief otaman was welcomed in the Soviet capital. Petliura, *Pravda* claimed in its coverage of the trial, was a "marauder, a murderer, and a pogrom monger," an "agent of foreign intervention" who had led a movement of the Ukrainian elites "against the proletarian revolution" and "was the chief culprit of the terrible Jewish pogroms and mass murder in Ukraine."[4] The wide-scale publicity around the trial made it possible to blame the persecution of the Jews on the personality of Petliura (as well as Denikin) and to deflect responsibility from those who had been Bolshevik sympathizers. Now the government could simultaneously discredit the Ukrainian independence movement and garner the support of the Jewish population at home and abroad.

One of the most significant ways in which the Soviet government earned the trust of large segments of the Jewish population was through its efforts to punish pogrom perpetrators in what was officially termed the "struggle against banditry." In May 1921, in the midst of the famine and faced with growing opposition from the peasantry, the Bolsheviks had launched a major operation against "bandits," a catchall term that included perpetrators of an assortment of crimes. Political commissars were given wide latitude to shoot peasants on the spot if they were suspected of harboring a bandit or concealing weapons. Throughout Ukraine, regional divisions of the Cheka hunted for bandits, uncovered "Petliurite plots," and arrested or shot peasant leaders who had engaged in "counterrevolutionary" activity during the civil war. Villagers were coerced into identifying bandits and were instructed to "voluntarily" expel them from town, after which the accused would be sent to concentration camps or to forced labor in the mines of the Donbas. Newspapers regularly celebrated the growing victory over banditry, announcing the names of convicted bandits and lauding towns and villages for surrendering them. Jewish victims of pogroms quickly learned to call the perpetrators "bandits" in order to provoke a government response.[5]

Recognizing the opportunity to exact revenge for the pogroms and reclaim stolen property, growing numbers of Jews were attracted to and recruited into the Cheka and its successor organizations—the All-Union State Political Administration (OGPU), which replaced the Cheka in 1923, and the People's Commissariat of Internal Affairs (NKVD), which took over secret police functions in 1934. In October 1921 about 10 percent of the nearly fifty thousand employees of the Cheka across Soviet territories had Jewish backgrounds, even though Jews made up less than 2 percent of the overall population.[6] By 1923, Jews constituted 15.7 percent of the leadership of the OGPU, and in 1924, 8.7 percent of the Central Apparatus of the organization. Only Russians and Latvians were more heavily represented within the leadership of the secret police.[7] In Ukraine, where Jews made up 6.5 percent of the overall population, they accounted for approximately 38 percent of leading positions within the state security apparatus in 1929–1931, and an estimated 67 percent in 1932–1933.[8] Nikolai Ezhov, who would purge many Jewish personnel when he became head of the NKVD and commissar for internal affairs in September 1936, is said to have quipped, "When I went to Ukraine, they told me that many Jews worked there. But they deceived me—only Jews worked there."[9] Although exaggerated, Ezhov's joke pointed to a common misconception that the secret police was a Jewish police and that their crimes could be blamed on the Jews. (By 1939, though, Jews would be purged from the organization and would constitute only 4 percent of the NKVD in Ukraine.)[10]

Although many Jews had initially joined to combat pogroms and prosecute perpetrators, they often remained in the secret police once new campaigns were initiated. In the summer and fall of 1927, when the state was arresting "anti-Soviet elements" and forcibly requisitioning grain in Ukraine, many peasants noted the presence of Jews among the activists. Far fewer noticed the number of Jews being arrested as speculators, private traders, and Zionists. The following year, Stalin declared his first five-year plan and began a drive to collectivize agriculture by seizing land from private homesteads and turning it over to state institutions. Twenty-five thousand urban workers and intelligentsia specifically recruited for the project fell upon the countryside to convince peasants to give up their land and join collectives. The Thousanders, as they were known, did not shy away from the use of force in persuading the peasants to comply. Some, like Gershon Shapiro, came from Jewish backgrounds and had first tested their fighting chops defending the towns and villages of Ukraine as Red Army recruits during the civil war. Others, like Lev Kopelev, who joined a brigade in 1932, had been victims of the pogroms themselves.[11] The peasants whose land, livestock, and grain were expropriated often recalled with bemused suspicion the "foreignness" of the Thousanders, many of whom couldn't even tell the difference between a colt and a calf. Miron Dolot, a peasant who recorded his experiences during the campaign, remembered them as "people who had always lived in cities—professors, teachers, and factory workers . . . their personal appearance amused us. Their pale faces and their clothes were totally out of place in our village."[12] The collectivization drive in Dolot's village was led by Comrade Zeitlin, of whom he writes, "He spoke some Ukrainian, but he was certainly not a native."[13] Surely, Dolot and the rest of the village recognized the name and the man as Jewish.

In 1929 alone ten to fifteen thousand peasant families were arrested and shipped in freight cars thousands of miles away, to Siberia or Central Asia, where they were left to fend for themselves in "special settlements," often no more than tents set up outside a railway station. The peasants responded as they had to the Red Terror in 1919—with thousands of mass protests and disturbances. The Soviet secret police fought back with the language of the civil war, accusing the peasants of banditry and Petliurism as though their resistance was premised on a nationalist agenda as opposed to simple survival.[14] At the highest level, Genrikh Yagoda, deputy chair of the OGPU, was widely blamed for the excesses of collectivization. Lazar Kaganovich, who had been the head of the Ukrainian Communist Party between 1925 and 1928, was also held responsible, despite having been transferred back to Moscow before the campaign even began. Both had Jewish backgrounds: Yagoda was the son of a jeweler from central Russia, while Kaganovich came from an artisanal family in a village near Radomyshl.

The forced requisitions resulted in alarming food shortages in the countryside. Local officials warned Moscow of the threat of starvation, but Stalin, who had consolidated his control of the party, was unrelenting in his demand for the fulfillment of procurement goals. Starving peasants watched as brigades entered their villages and farms and forcibly confiscated their grain, their livestock, and their vegetables. "In some cases they would be merciful and leave some potatoes, peas, corn for feeding the family. But the stricter ones would make a clean sweep," recalled Kopelev, who was a member of a brigade near Poltava.[15] The produce was sent to Odesa, where longshoremen loaded it onto ships for export in exchange for the hard currency Stalin needed to fuel his military and industrialization drive. By spring 1932, the situation had turned into a full-blown famine. Fearing increased peasant resistance, Stalin sent Kaganovich back to Ukraine at harvesttime to ensure that future procurements would be carried out as planned, regardless of the astronomical human cost. One of the first to warn the West of what was happening was none other than Arnold Margolin, who visited Germany and Czechoslovakia in the summer of 1932 and reported on what he learned to his friend James Grafton Rogers, an assistant secretary of state under President Hoover. "Since the beginning of wholesale collectivization of the farmers," he wrote, "a great number of hungry peasants are brought from time to time to the hospitals; most of them have swollen arms and legs as the result of starvation."[16] By the fall of 1933, some 3.5 to 4 million Ukrainians had starved to death.[17]

The famine was worst in the countryside. In the cities, where most of the Jews lived, workers continued to receive rations, albeit just above starvation level, and special stores remained open for those with access to foreign currency. Jews suffered terribly during the famine, and thousands if not tens of thousands perished. But the Ukrainian peasants bore the brunt of it. In subsequent years, some would recall the generosity of their Jewish neighbors who shared what little food they had. Others would remember only that when Ukrainian peasants were starving to death, the urban Jews seemed to somehow have food. Many imagined that it had something to do with the presence of Jews in the upper echelons of government, or they blamed Jews for speculating in stolen grain.[18]

ANOTHER POINT OF contention between Jews and Ukrainians was the plan, developed in the early 1920s, to reserve the Ukrainian south and Crimea for potential Jewish settlement and later to designate Crimea as a Jewish republic. The idea was promoted by the American agronomist and communal activist Joseph A. Rosen. Born in Moscow and having emigrated to the United States in 1903, Rosen had already achieved renown for his introduction to the American midwest of "Rosen rye," a Russian variety of winter rye with four rows of long plump kernels on every head, which doubled the yield of the seed then in use in the United States.[19] Rosen subsequently gained the trust of the Soviet authorities through his aid work with the Joint Distribution Committee on behalf of victims of the 1921 famine in the Volga region. In conjunction with the Joint and its subsidiary, the American Jewish Joint Agricultural Corporation (known as Agro-Joint), Rosen helped raise money in the United States to fund the settlement of three thousand Jewish families per year in the Ukrainian south and Crimea. He even gained financial support from Julius Rosenwald, Felix Warburg, and John D. Rockefeller Jr. Rosen sold the plan not just as a solution to the Jewish refugee problem but as a panacea for the predicament of world Jewry. Like the Zionists who were establishing agricultural settlements in Palestine, Rosen believed that by training Jews to become agricultural workers, he could forever remove the stigma of Jews as petty traders, peddlers, and moneylenders. Herbert Hoover agreed, characterizing the endeavor as "one of the outstanding pieces of human engineering in the world today."[20]

The Soviet government supported the plan and in 1925 established the Society for the Resettlement of Jews on the Land and the Committee for the Resettlement of Jews on the Land, both of which raised funds and advertised at home and abroad in support of the project. In

1927, Warburg traveled to the region to inspect the progress; the Joint filmed his trip and released the footage to advertise its achievements. Between 1924 and 1938, dozens of Jewish agricultural settlements were established with optimistic names drawn from Jewish and Slavic languages like Fraylebn (Yiddish: Free Life); Fraydorf (Yiddish: Free Village), Yidndorf (Yiddish: Jewish Village), Ahdut (Hebrew: Unity); Herut (Hebrew: Freedom), and Pobeda (Russian: Victory). In the end, the program attracted some forty thousand Jews to southern Ukraine and Crimea, who joined the seventy-five thousand already resident in the region.[21]

Presciently, Margolin warned that the project could become another point of conflict between Ukrainians and Jews.[22] Indeed, in the eyes of many in the Ukrainian diaspora, these settlements were usurping land that properly belonged to them. Petliura's Paris-based *Tryzub* dubbed the Jewish settlements "Muscovite colonialism" and accused "Muscovite occupiers" of stealing Ukrainian land for the benefit of the Jews.[23]

[AMERICAN JEWISH JOINT DISTRIBUTION COMMITTEE ARCHIVES]

Three young Jewish men in a wheat field at an agricultural settlement in Dzhankoi, Ukraine

Yiddish-speaking militias, claimed one editorial, were aiding in the confiscation of land "where the most Ukrainian blood has been spilt." The blame, the editorial continued, rested not only with Moscow, but also with the global Jewish community for providing financial support. The Jews, the article concluded, should focus their settlement efforts on Palestine and leave Ukraine alone.[24] Another article echoed these sentiments: "When the multinational Americans are proclaiming that America is for Americans, when the Muscovite Bolsheviks are embracing the cry of China for the Chinese, then let us too declare 'Ukraine for the Ukrainians.'"[25] The real reason the Jews were being settled in the region, the article asserted, was to spread Bolshevism in Ukraine.

Within Soviet Ukraine, where public expression of oppositional ideas was silenced by the state, there is evidence that locals also looked upon the new Jewish farmers with mistrust and resentment. "Why did these alien people come?" they asked themselves.[26] In late 1928, a dispatch reached Warsaw that peasants had attacked and killed several Jews in farm colonies in southeastern Ukraine. "Discontent has long been brewing among the peasants of the Soviet Ukraine against the establishment of Jewish agricultural settlements," the news cable declared, "and it turned into open violence when the peasants in broad daylight attacked the colonies."[27] To many Ukrainians, the plan to settle Jews in southern Ukraine seemed to be the fulfillment of the prophecies of Struk, Grigoriev, Sokolovsky, and the other warlords, all of whom had warned in the spring of 1919 that the Bolsheviks would steal Ukrainian land and turn it over to the Jews. Agro-Joint's support for the colonies furthered resentment. The new farmers were trained in the most modern agricultural techniques and experimented with innovative crops. The Joint even sent John Deere tractors and soil specialists to help ensure the success of the Jewish colonists. Very quickly, thanks to American financial support and imported technology, the Jewish colonies were outperforming their struggling Ukrainian neighbors, breeding further animosity.

Soviet agitators accompanied their campaigns with attacks on religion. As Bolshevik city folk with their pince-nez glasses and goatees raided churches and monasteries for the benefit of industrial and military production, many peasants and townspeople were reminded of the proclamations and leaflets they had read a decade earlier warning that with a Bolshevik victory, the Jews would steal their land and close their churches.

In Eastern Galicia, now firmly incorporated into the Polish Republic, both Jews and Ukrainians also faced a turbulent decade. Despite the rights promised to ethnic minorities in the treaties signed in Paris, the various conservative coalitions that vied for power in Poland after 1922 failed to provide state funding for Jewish schools or to protect observance of the Jewish Sabbath. The government also closed down Ukrainian cultural institutions and persecuted the Ukrainian minority. Instead, it promoted a Polish identity based on the Roman Catholic Church with little tolerance for ethnic or religious minorities. Electoral gerrymandering ensured that Eastern Galicia, where Poland's largest minorities of Jews and Ukrainians were concentrated, was allocated fewer seats than its population warranted. Only in May 1926 did Piłsudski's coup d'état bring to power a more tolerant and inclusive government, allowing for a flourishing of cultural, political, and religious life for both minorities. But ethnic and religious tensions continued to run deep and further deteriorated with Piłsudski's death in 1935 and the

[AMERICAN JEWISH JOINT DISTRIBUTION COMMITTEE ARCHIVES]

Jewish family in Ukraine poses in front of John Deere tractor, 1920 rise of right-wing nationalists. As Hitler came to power in Germany and fascism swept through Europe, xenophobic policies aimed at excluding Jews from public life were promoted in Poland too, including segregated seating in university lecture halls and boycotts of Jewish businesses. Many Jews responded by leaving Poland altogether: nearly 10 percent of the Jewish population—four hundred thousand people—left between 1921 and 1937. Others turned to the radical political ideologies of communism and Zionism, further distancing them from the Polish mainstream. At the same time, politically alienated Ukrainian students coalesced around the Organization of Ukrainian Nationalists, whose hyper-nationalist agenda was inspired in part by Hitler's Germany.[28]

SOVIET TROOPS OCCUPIED eastern Poland, including Eastern Galicia, western Volhynia and western Belarus, in September 1939, two weeks after the German invasion of Poland and the start of the Second World War. A month earlier, Nazi Germany had concluded a nonaggression pact with the Soviet Union that stipulated the division of Poland between the two powers. The Soviet conquest was experienced as a disaster for the Polish majority, but Ukrainians and Jews saw it differently. Most Jews were relieved to be conquered by the Reds rather than by the Nazis. Some were also pleasantly surprised to meet Jews among the Red Army soldiers. "A couple of them were Jewish," recalled Simon Feldman in a 1997 interview he recorded with the Shoah Foundation. "They got off and were talking to my grandmother and my aunts. They were dressed neat, the Russian soldiers. And they were Jews. I mean, that was really unique."[29]

Many Ukrainians initially celebrated, too—not out of any love for the communists but because they saw the collapse of the Polish Republic and the union of Eastern Galicia with Soviet Ukraine as a first step toward liberating Ukrainian lands from foreign rule and establishing a united Ukrainian state. But both Ukrainians and Jews soon found themselves victims of the new Soviet regime. Throughout the conquered territory, the Bolsheviks authorized violence against those they identified as counterrevolutionaries, inflaming ethnic tensions and providing opportunities for revenge killings and settling of old scores.

In the twenty-one months that the Soviets ruled the territory, they implemented the same policies that had marked their reign over the rest of Ukraine, but in a vastly accelerated manner. Tens of thousands of city councilors, judges, priests, and government officials were kicked out of office, arrested, and replaced with ill-prepared workers and party hacks; three hundred thousand people—businessmen, wealthy peasants, former elites, refugees from German-occupied Poland, and others accused of being anti-Soviet—were arrested, forcibly resettled in the Russian interior, or executed (and sometimes all three); land-holders' property was requisitioned; villages were collectivized; and churches were looted. The new Soviet prisons that proliferated in the area, crowded with intellectuals and elites, became a potent symbol of Red Terror.[30]

Jewish artisans and shopkeepers lost their stores, businesses, and workshops. Zionist activists and rabbis were arrested, Hebrew was repressed, and Jews were resettled at significantly higher rates than Ukrainians. On the other hand, quotas on Jewish admission to universi-ties that had been imposed by the Polish authorities were lifted, discrim-inatory practices against Jewish access to the civil service ceased, and the number of Yiddish-language schools increased dramatically.[31] In Simon Feldman's hometown of Boremel, a Jewish carpenter was put in charge of the local soviet: "which means he was the main person of the town. And it was kind of unusual to have a Jew that would be involved in that." The Soviet regime removed all the restrictions the Polish govern-ment had placed on the Jews. Edward Spicer, a former resident of Lviv who was interviewed by the Shoah Foundation in 1996, recalled: "In the polytechnical schools, we had a quota, only so many Jews could get into the school. But when the Russians came to town, all of a sudden the doors opened wide and before you know, about half the students were Jews."[32] Forty thousand Jewish refugees from the German occu-pation zone of Poland flooded into the Soviet zone, raising the Jewish population in Eastern Galicia to around 570,000, about 10 percent of the overall population. By the spring of 1941, there were about 150,000 Jews living in Lviv alone, rendering Jews almost as numerous as Poles in the city for the first time.[33]

Throughout the newly occupied territories, many middle-class urban Jews who lost their businesses and professions took white-collar jobs in the new Soviet administrative structure. As a result, whereas the persecuted elites tended to be ethnic Poles, the bureaucrats who replaced them were disproportionately Jewish. Once again, it seemed like the Jews were taking over. As one Ukrainian quoted in a Polish report put it, "I thought this was Ukraine, but really it's Palestine."[34]

These allegations were propagated by right-wing political groups, like the Organization of Ukrainian Nationalists. In Kraków, a faction of the Ukrainian Nationalists led by the Galician agronomist and political activist Stepan Bandera accused the Jews of being "the most faithful support of the ruling Bolshevik regime and the vanguard of Muscovite imperialism in the Ukraine,"[35] and warned in its official documents that "Marxism is a Jewish invention" and "Stalinist and Jewish commissars are the arch-enemies of the people."[36] It was an ominous harbinger of what was to come.

The Onset of the Holocaust

The mass murder of Jews resumed in the days and weeks after the German invasion of the Soviet Union on June 22, 1941, this time with yet a new set of perpetrators—the Nazis and their collaborators. In Ukraine, which was still reeling from the bloodshed of the pogroms and the retaliatory violence that followed it, over five hundred thousand Jews were killed in the first six months of war. By the fall of 1943, the death toll approached 1.4 million, about a quarter of the total number of Jewish victims of the Holocaust. The vast majority were murdered with bullets, at close range, near their homes, while their neighbors watched, assisted, and sometimes pulled the trigger before plundering their property and even moving into their homes. In the territories that first fell under German occupation, these shootings were preceded by anti-Jewish riots instigated by the Germans and carried out with the participation of locals. Survivors called both types of massacres "pogroms"; they were lethal, participatory, and familiar. In contrast to the systematized and unprecedented killing operation the Germans would perfect in the death camps they later established in occupied Poland, these first mass killings of the Holocaust were vast escalations of a known phenomenon. By 1941, the population had come to recognize the singling out and slaughter of Jews as an ordinary part of warfare. The legacy of pogroms was by no means the only factor in accelerating the killing, but combined with Nazi racial ideology, fascist violence, colonial expansion, economic competition, political antagonisms, and the myth of "Judeo-Bolshevism," the normalization of mass murder during the previous conflict emboldened the Germans in their genocidal ambitions.

The Germans knew that Ukraine had been a site of rabid anti-Jewish violence a generation earlier and believed that they could unleash it once again. In the weeks leading up to the invasion, Alfred Rosenberg, the Nazi ideologue whom Hitler placed in charge of the occupied territories in the east, had proposed giving locals a "free hand" to deal with the "Jewish Question," and Reinhard Heydrich, head of the Reich Security Main Office, instructed his commanders "not to hinder the attempts of local anti-communist and anti-Jewish circles in the newly-occupied territories to engage in cleansing activities. On the contrary, they should be carried out and intensified, if necessary, and channeled in the right direction, but without leaving a trace."[1] Stepan Bandera's faction of the Organization of Ukrainian Nationalists was eager to help and allied itself with the Nazis, expecting that Ukrainian aspirations for statehood would finally be met and their grievances against the Soviets would be avenged.[2]

Just as it had in 1918, the new wave of bloodshed in Ukraine began in Eastern Galicia. It took only one week for the German First Mounted Division to arrive in Lviv. It entered the city on June 30 together with volunteer expeditionary units composed of ethnic Ukrainians from the diaspora, whose formation Bandera had encouraged, imagining they would comprise the nucleus of a Ukrainian national army. Over the following days, these militiamen together with local supporters and ordinary citizens would carry out a massive pogrom against the Jewish population, leaving between two to five thousand Jews dead.

Shaken by twenty-one months of Soviet rule, the Ukrainian population of Eastern Galicia largely greeted the German occupation of Lviv with enthusiasm. According to one witness, "the Ukrainians welcomed the Germans with flowers, laughter, joy, full of hope and illusions, as rescuers and liberators."[3] Many believed the occupying army would permit the reestablishment of an independent Ukraine. In this expectation, on the day the Germans arrived, Yaroslav Stetsko, a twenty-nine-year-old son of a Greek Catholic priest from Ternopil who had become a close affiliate of Bandera, declared the establishment of a Ukrainian state, just as his forerunners had done in November 1918, this time under the slogan "Ukraine for the Ukrainians." In the courtyard of Saint George's Cathedral, he registered a company of recruits, mostly men from the expeditionary units, into his Ukrainian militia. "Russia and Bolshevism," he had declared in 1938, were "the main present-day instrument of the Jewish danger."[4] Weeks later, under arrest in Germany, he would write: "I support the destruction of the Jews and the expedience of bringing German methods of exterminating Jewry to Ukraine."[5]

Hours after the declaration of Ukrainian statehood, the new Ukrainian militia under Stetsko's command liberated the Soviet prisons, two of which were located near the Jewish quarter. There, they discovered the bodies of some three thousand Ukrainians, Poles, and Jews whom the retreating Soviet secret police had executed. In retaliation, Stetsko's militiamen, assisted by Ukrainian civilians, rounded up hundreds of Jews from the streets and from their apartments. "Young Ukrainian men wearing stickers in the colors blue and gold on their marine blue epaulettes entered the houses and took Jewish lawyers, doctors, merchants and others" to the prison "from whence they never returned," remembered Anastasja Klymkova.[6] Blaming them for the Bolshevik massacre of prisoners, the militiamen forced the Jews to place the decomposing corpses on public display for identification.[7]

As the bodies were being recovered, relatives of the murdered prisoners arrived to identify the dead. Other ordinary townspeople and peasants also gravitated toward the macabre site, and, as though reenacting familiar roles from twenty years earlier, took out their anger on the Jews, beating them, mocking them, sexually assaulting them, and forcing them to sing communist songs as a symbol of alleged Jewish complicity in the Soviet regime. Witnesses described the perpetrators as "sinister Ukrainians, Petliura supporters, and old pogromists."[8] At least in the minds of the victims, in other words, the violence they experienced in 1941 was directly connected to the bloodshed they had experienced in 1918.

After the war, US forces discovered film footage that German soldiers, who were also present during the violence, had recorded for propagandistic purposes. The grainy silent film begins with scenes of dying men on the pavement. Then, a woman—stark naked—is marched past the camera through a crowded and chaotic street under the direction of a uniformed man. Another man in a bowler hat swings his arm back, and with full force brings a rod or cane down upon the exposed buttocks of the woman. She starts to walk faster as her hand clutches her bruised behind. Another naked man runs past. Crowds are watching; some seem to be enjoying the scene. Others are milling about. In the next scene, a man is dragging a woman through the streets by her hair. Later in the film, lines of people under guard are being marched through the street as crowds look on from the sidewalks.[9] "I saw thousands of mutilated Jews beaten in the most brutal fashion, women stripped until they were completely naked and children covered in blood," recalled Jakub Dentel of that day.[10]

Edward Spicer described how several days later, in a separate incident, he was "caught by Ukrainians, they were all over the city, they were beating up Jews, killing Jews, beating them to death on the street. It didn't matter whether it was a man, woman or a child." He was taken to a place near the railroad station and then to a former hockey rink, where German guards forced hundreds of Jewish prisoners "to lie there with our hands stretched out until the morning." Those who moved were beaten to death with rifle butts. Over the next two days, German guards selected groups of about forty people at a time and took them away on trucks, where they were shot by members of a German Einsatzkommando—a special mobile killing squad subordinated to the Nazi Reich Security Main Office.[11] In total, an additional twenty-five hundred to three thousand Jews were killed in the operation.[12]

On July 26, German Einsatzkommandos with the collaboration of Ukrainian auxiliary police and militia killed another one thousand or more Jews in Lviv. According to the memoirist and witness David

Bystanders watch as Jews are rounded up and attacked in Lviv

Kahane, "Ukrainian policemen swooped down on Jewish houses, removed young Jewish men and women, and marched them to Lecki Street. The operation was repeated throughout that day and the next until the prison was packed with people. Even the prison courtyard swarmed with Jews; only a handful succeeded in getting away. Hair-raising scenes unfolded. No food was brought in. From time to time gangs of Ukrainian policemen burst into the place, dealt blows with rifle butts, and screamed: 'This is for our hetman Symon Petliura.'"[13]

The Germans referred to the whole episode as "Petliura Days," signifying an opportunity for Ukrainians to get back at the Jews for the crimes of the Bolsheviks, for what they portrayed as the Jewish betrayal of the Ukrainian nation, and for Schwarzbard's assassination of the Ukrainian leader.[14] Several weeks later, the Germans imposed a levy upon the Jewish population, forcing Jews to sell their property at heavily discounted rates. "The news of the sale spread quickly among the peasants of the district. They began arriving in the city in droves. For the price of a cartload of vegetables, they dressed themselves like lords and took home expensive furniture," Kahane wrote.[15] The principal beneficiaries, he continued, were the Ukrainian policemen, who "would burst into Jewish homes at night, extorting large sums of money from the residents."[16] Kahane described it as "a brutal pogrom, plain and simple."[17] Other survivors referred to the perpetrators as "Haidamaks," explicitly linking the event to the pogroms of the past.[18]

The pogrom in Lviv was just one of many instances of mass violence that occurred throughout the Baltics, western Belarus, and western Ukraine in the weeks after the German invasion. One of the earliest incidents took place during the night of June 24 to 25 in Kaunas, Lithuania, where an advance command of Einsatzkommandos along with German security police succeeded, "under great difficulty," according to a German report, to "launch a pogrom," which took the lives of some three thousand Jews over the next three days. In this area, though, which had been spared the worst of the civil war pogroms, the local Lithuanian population was, at least initially, reluctant to fully embrace German actions against the Jews. "To our surprise," noted the German officer in command of the operation, "it was not easy at first to set in motion an extensive pogrom against the Jews."[19] Jewish witnesses blamed "organized groups of Lithuanian partisans" for carrying out some of the violence, but even these militias were either formed by the German security police from former Soviet political prisoners or were affiliated with the Lithuanian Activist Front, which was established in Berlin out of Lithuanian émigrés in the city. Lithuanian civilians on the ground are blamed for failing to intervene, but rarely are they accused of active participation. As had been the case in Lviv, after unleashing the initial pogrom, a German Einsatzkommando carried out far more extensive shootings outside of Kaunas the following week.[20]

There was more active local civilian participation in the Białystok and Łomża regions of western Belarus and northeastern Poland. In the most well-documented pogrom of the period, on July 10, a group of Polish men in Jedwabne forced about forty Jews to demolish a statue of Lenin and carry it through town while singing Soviet songs, before killing them and burying them in an open grave inside a barn. Several hundred more Jewish women, men, and children were subsequently locked in the barn, while local Poles doused it with kerosene and set it alight, burning at least three hundred people to death.[21] But Jedwabne, where political polarization along ethnic lines predated the war, was the exception rather than the rule; most of the dozens of anti-Jewish actions in the region took place under the direction of German security police or Wehrmacht units. There were few outbursts of the type of localized anti-Jewish violence common in the Ukrainian territories that first fell to the Germans.[22]

The largest number of pogroms, about 150, took place in the newly occupied territories of Eastern Galicia and western Volhynia, areas heavily impacted by the anti-Jewish violence of 1918–1921. Between 12,000 and 35,000 Jews were killed in these pogroms, many of which were perpetrated by locals, and some without even a German presence.[23] In the village of Peremyshlyany, for instance, locals set fire to the synagogue and threw Jews into the burning building: "The flames were rising up high, parched window frames and benches on which our grandfathers, fathers and brothers used to sit now crackled. Fire turned into an awesome element. A throng of peasants gathered around the fire with their sacks ready to plunder," remembered one witness. "An enthused mob of shrieking peasants, just like locusts, pounced on everything that belonged to the Jews."[24] In Buczacz, Ukrainian militiamen carried out "reprisal" killings against Jews and communists, plundered Jewish homes, forced Jews to perform humiliating tasks, and violated Jewish women.[25] In Złoczów, Ukrainian militiamen posted announcements demanding that Jews appear in the marketplace the next morning, and then led the assembled mass to the Soviet prison, where, as in Lviv, locals beat the Jews and forced them to remove the bodies of executed prisoners. "They brought in Ukrainians from the villages and gave them weapons," remembered one witness. "Some of the peasants didn't even know how to shoot."[26] In Rivne, which was occupied by the German army on June 28, Einsatzkommandos with the assistance of Ukrainian auxiliary police arrested 130 Jews and shot them on the outskirts of the city. In Borysław, where 400 Jews were murdered between July 1 and July 3, witnesses reported that crowds of ordinary Ukrainians killed "with metal rods and sticks with nails" and "with sticks and stones, not guns."[27]

The Operational Situation Reports the Germans sent back to Berlin expressed approval of the enthusiasm that locals in Galicia and western

Volhynia displayed in attacking Jews on their own initiative. A July 5 report boasted of "the gratitude of the Ukrainian people for their liberation by the Germans"[28] and a July 16 report included a section on the attitude of the Ukrainian population: "In the first hours after the Bolshevik withdrawal, the Ukrainian population displayed commendable activity against the Jews: they set the Dobromil synagogue on fire, and an enraged crowd in Sambor slaughtered fifty Jews. In Lemberg [Lviv] the population rounded up, mistreated, and delivered one thousand Jews to the prison."[29] It is possible that such reports expressed wishful thinking or attempted to deflect culpability from German crimes onto the local population, but that seems unlikely: in other instances, the reports presented candid evaluations of the situation on the ground or even boasted of direct German responsibility.

In general, the Germans did most of the shooting, but several witnesses also place blame on the Ukrainian police. "The ones that did the shooting, and the ones that did the arresting, and the ones that carried out these atrocities were not Germans; this was the local Ukrainian police," recalled Simon Feldman of the shooting of ten people, including his father, during the first weeks of the German occupation of Boremel. "They made them dig their graves, they made them undress, and they shot them right on the spot, and then they covered it up with dirt."[30] The pogroms that took place in the initial weeks of the German invasion were encouraged by, and often incited by, the Germans. But, at least in Ukraine, they were also perpetrated by a local population that, thanks in part to a legacy of pogroms, had become inured to bloodshed and primed to target Jews in ethnic violence.[31]

WITHIN A WEEK of Stetsko's declaration of Ukrainian statehood in Lviv, the Germans showed that they had little tolerance for the Ukrainian nationalist movement, quickly disappointing Bandera and his supporters. On July 5, they arrested Bandera in Kraków and, a few days later, detained Stetsko as well, transporting both to Berlin. Keeping the territory under their own control, the Germans established auxiliary police drawn from the local population, at first by seeking out volunteers, later through compulsion. They gave preference to ethnic Germans but sought out anyone with previous military or combat experience.[32] Usually that meant recruiting Red Army POWs or former Soviet police officers eager to prove their allegiance to the new regime; but sometimes, it entailed enlisting those who had fought the Bolsheviks in the civil war. Sergei Sukov, for instance, had served as a warrant officer in Denikin's army before fleeing to Zabolottya, north of Lviv, where he still lived in June 1941. He recalled that when the Germans occupied the town, the whole population "gathered at the station out of curiosity." It was then that "the German officer addressed the people and said that we need to appoint an elder, a person to maintain order. Someone shouted—'Here's a White emigrant. He served in Denikin's army. Let's make him commandant.' At the time, I was a little drunk and I stepped forward. The officer called me and said that 'temporarily you will be the commandant and will help us.'"[33]

Similarly, Fedir Lyashchenko, born in Bila Tserkva in 1899, had been drafted into the tsarist army in September 1916 and had served at various times under both Denikin and Petliura.[34] In August 1941, Lyashchenko was working as a tiler at the First of May Factory when the Germans appointed him chief of police in Bila Tserkva. "Tall, blond, with a military bearing, golden eyes, a straight nose," he looked every bit the part.[35] Other members of the local auxiliary police had connections with the Ukrainian warlords of the civil war era. Andriy Terpylo, who served the Germans in Kyiv, was the son of Saveliy Terpylo, who had been part of Zelenyi's gang (and likely Zelenyi's kin). In addition, Andriy's stepfather, Hryhoriy Kolesnik, had been arrested in 1929 for participating in Zelenyi's gang. Andriy thus had a personal vendetta to fulfill.[36]

Still others who collaborated with the Germans had been part of Petliura's forces. Stepan Grabar, for instance, a native of Khonkivtsi, one hundred miles southwest of Vinnytsia, joined the army of the Ukrainian People's Republic after he was demobilized from the tsarist army. In 1932 he was arrested for failing to meet his bread production quota. His previous service in Petliura's army was an aggravating factor that led to his sentence of eight years in exile. By 1941, he had ample reason to despise the Bolsheviks, and tried to rile up prospective recruits by portraying the current war as a continuation of the civil war: "We need to volunteer for the German army, to fight the Soviets as I fought for Petliura in 1918," Grabar said, according to a witness (Grabar himself disputed this statement in questioning). In December 1941, Grabar joined the regional police of Khonkivtsi and served in that capacity until the arrival of the Red Army in March 1944.[37]

Many of those who served in the local police claimed in postwar testimonies to have been forced to serve or having done so out of fear. Others, though, were candid about their reasons, explaining that they volunteered to secure privileged access to looted goods, to avenge injustices committed by the Soviets against their relatives—or simply, in the words of Stepan Redesha, who also served in Zabolottya, because "I had many enemies in my village" and "I personally harbored a grudge against the Jews."[38] Throughout the period of German occupation, these local police forces would play critical supporting roles in the continuing genocide of the Jews.

WITHIN WEEKS OF the invasion, the Germans moved across the 1939 border between Poland and Soviet Ukraine into the former provinces of Podilia, Kyiv, and eastern Volhynia, where most of the pogroms had taken place in 1919–1920. About half the Jewish population had managed to flee eastward in advance of the German occupation, but some 750,000 Jews remained, the vast majority of whom would be murdered over the next year. When German forces occupied Proskuriv on July 8, Ukrainian militias attacked Jews, pillaged their property, tortured them in the streets, and committed occasional murders. Liusia Blekhman told the Shoah Foundation in a 1998 interview that on the morning the Germans arrived her neighbors plundered her house, which was under renovation and being used to store furniture: "They had been our very good friends, but suddenly they started to say that the Jews are bad, that the Jews are wealthy."[39] David Bershtin, who recorded an interview with the Shoah Foundation in 1996, remembered how in neighboring Felshtin, the Germans first humiliated the

Jews in public displays and then began to shoot young Jewish men. The massacre was organized by the Germans, he maintained, but local Ukrainian "bandits" voluntarily assisted.[40]

The German First Panzer Division took Zhytomyr on July 9, 1941, by which time only some 7,000 Jews remained in the city; over two-thirds of the 30,000 who lived there before the war had already fled. The Germans expressed approval of the support the local population was willing to provide. In one Operational Situation Report, they wrote back to Berlin that "as a result of the behavior of the Jewish population under the Bolshevik regime, the population, with only a few exceptions, is consciously antisemitic."[41] The reason for local support, they explained in another report, was that under the Bolsheviks, "leading positions were almost entirely held by Jews," "the Jews were the sole beneficiaries of the system," and the Jews "exercised absolute rule and had extensive economic freedom."[42] The people were eager for revenge, the Germans maintained. Justifying their actions as retaliation for "robberies and engaging in communist activities," Sonderkommando 4a, a division of the Einsatzgruppen under the command of Paul Blobel, in collaboration with Ukrainian auxiliary police, murdered 363 people, mostly Jewish men, within the first three weeks of the occupation, and an additional 1,281 over the rest of the summer.[43] On July 12, 1941, Blobel's men moved on to nearby Korostyshiv, where they shot 40 Jews on the charge of espionage and sabotage.[44] Boris Kazak, who had fled from Zhytomyr to Korostyshiv where his mother's family was living, told the Shoah Foundation that his uncle, Idel-Gersh Kozak, was killed in his apartment and the rest of the family was shot in a pit located in a pine clearing outside of town. The Germans killed them, but they were helped by locals "who knew where the Jews lived and pointed them out."[45] By July 22, Blobel's men had reached Fastiv, where they shot 261 Jews.[46] Similar incidents took place in dozens of other locales in the month after the German invasion. Each of these episodes, witnessed with little or no resistance by the larger civilian population, further emboldened the Germans and their collaborators, stimulating a rapid escalation of killing.

In total, German forces with the assistance of local collaborators killed about forty thousand Jews in Ukraine within the first six weeks of the invasion. During this crucial period, the Germans typically incited the population by equating the Jews with Bolsheviks, drawing upon the same language with which Ukrainian peasants and Cossack militias had massacred Jews some twenty years earlier. At times, the linkages were made explicit, as auxiliary police volunteered in order to defend the honor of Petliura or seek retribution for the Jewish role in the campaign against banditry. As though reenacting familiar roles from the civil war, ordinary townsfolk, motivated by anti-Bolshevik and anti-Jewish fury as well as the prospect of plunder and loot, participated in the killing operations by assaulting Jews, by pointing out the homes of Jews, by volunteering for auxiliary roles in the massacres, and by otherwise acquiescing in the bloodshed.[47] At least in the initial weeks of the German invasion, during the first round of violence, many Ukrainians believed the Jews were getting their comeuppance.

IN LATE JULY and early August 1941, SS Reichsführer Heinrich Himmler toured the newly conquered territories and summoned commanders to meet directly with him. After these visits, the Germans began to quash local initiatives and establish more complete control. The killings also increased dramatically. Although there are no records of a written order—the Nazis rarely put such orders in writing—some have come to see this as a key turning point in the Holocaust. Himmler may have endorsed or even ordered the murder of entire Jewish communities— men, women, and children—escalating the previous policy of singling out mostly men.[48] The German high command began to see that the physical extermination of the Jewish population need not remain a utopian fantasy but could actually be realized. As if to confirm that a new era had dawned, on August 19, Reich Minister of Propaganda Joseph Goebbels recorded in his diary a conversation with Hitler: "We also spoke about the Jewish problem. The Führer is of the conviction that his earlier prophesy in the Reichstag, that if the Jews succeeded in provoking a world war once again, it would end with the extermination of the Jews—was coming true."[49] This was the first time that the Germans tested the potency of the myth of Judeo-Bolshevism. In Ukraine, the accusation landed on fertile soil.

Himmler made Zhytomyr his Ukrainian headquarters and used the city as a backdrop for grandiose spectacles of violence. On August 7, 1941, on the pretext of punishing the Jews for their role in the Bolshevik secret police, the Germans hanged the Soviet judge Wolf Kieper and his aide, Mosche Kogan, on gallows erected in the market square. German officials held up signs in German and Ukrainian identifying the victims as "Cheka Jews" and claimed the judge was responsible for the Bolsheviks' execution of over one thousand people in the early years of the Soviet regime. About four hundred Zhytomyr Jews were forcibly assembled in the square and ordered to keep their hands over their heads so as not to cover their eyes. Many were elderly survivors of the civil war pogroms. An open truck carrying the two victims drove up to the gallows, as a crowd of locals cheered and scrambled to get a better view. Nooses were put around the victims' necks and then the truck drove off, leaving them to hang.[50] Afterward, Paul

[UNITED STATES HOLOCAUST MEMORIAL MUSEUM, COURTESY OF EVA BETTER-HEITNER SAK]

Execution of Mosche Kogan and Wolf Kieper in the Zhytomyr market square, August 7, 1941. The sign reads: "The assistant of the Cheka Jews, the hangman Mosche Kogan."

Blobel ordered the four hundred assembled Jewish witnesses to be shot. Waffen SS, members of the Wehrmacht, and Ukrainian auxiliary police helped transport the Jews in trucks to the edge of a pit. According to SS Obersturmführer August Häfner, "A group of Jews was lined up by the edge of the grave. There were about ten to twelve of them. They were standing facing the marksmen. There was one marksman for each Jew. Then the platoon-leader of the Waffen-SS platoon gave the order to fire. The victims fell backwards into the grave."[51] In Radomyshl, as well, Blobel's Sonderkommando 4a arrested and shot 276 people over two days in early August, on the trumped-up charges of being "Jewish communist functionaries, saboteurs, Komsomol members, and communist agitators."[52] Dozens of similar episodes followed Himmler's tour.

It wasn't until the second and third weeks of August that the Germans occupied the towns of Korosten, Ovruch, and Slovechno in the north, by which time most of the Jewish population had fled. Yet a detachment of Sonderkommando 4a carried out at least three massacres in the region, murdering 451 people, mostly Jewish men, before turning authority over to Ukrainian auxiliary forces, who later subjected the surviving Jews to mockery, robberies, and additional killings and forced them to complete humiliating and hard labor.[53] "I saw how Jews were gathered near the school," recalled one witness in a 2013 interview with the organization Yahad in Unum about a massacre in Slovechno. "After midday they were driven to be shot." They were forced to walk in a column, guarded by dogs. She remembered the Jews were carrying shovels. They would be digging their own graves.[54]

On August 19, the German military commandant of Bila Tserkva, speaking on the radio, ordered the Jews to come to a rallying point in town with their valuables. There, Ukrainian police marched them in a column to a building on the western outskirts of town. Taking groups of nine or ten people at a time, the police led them to large pits, where the soldiers of Sonderkommando 4a ordered the assembled Jews to kneel, and shot them in the back.[55] Once the adults had been killed, the children were led to a house set back from a side road, where they were guarded by Ukrainian militiamen. Neighbors complained, however, about the crying and whimpering they heard through the night, so the next day, a Catholic military chaplain, Dr. Josef Maria Reuss, investigated: "The children lay or sat on the floor, which was covered in their feces. There were flies on the legs and abdomens of most of the children, some of whom were only half dressed. Some of the bigger children (two, three, four years old) were scratching the mortar from the wall and eating it."[56] The children had not been fed or provided with water for twenty-four hours and were suffering from the August heat. According to Häfner's testimony, he refused orders to shoot the children and assigned the task instead to Ukrainian auxiliaries. On August 22, 1941, he continued, "The children were taken off the tractor. They were lined up along the top of the grave and shot so that they fell into it. The Ukrainians did not aim at one particular part of the body [. . . .] Many children were shot four or five times before they died."[57] According to Ivan Yatsenko, who testified in 1945, Fedir Lyashchenko, the police chief who had served with Denikin and Petliura, "took the most active role in the extermination of the Jewish population" in Bila Tserkva.[58] Another witness confirmed that "Lyashchenko ordered the police to escort Soviet citizens to the shooting site. He often sent Jews who had been detained throughout the city and region to jail. Later those Jews were shot."[59] The mass murder of children, of which this was one of the earliest instances, marked a key moment in the evolution of violence into genocide.

Altogether in the month of August, the Germans and their collaborators shot about sixty-two thousand Jews in Ukraine, including thirty-one thousand in the district around Proskuriv and ten thousand in the district of Zhytomyr.[60] Similar escalations of killing took place in the Baltics and western Belarus. Locals helped by pointing out Jewish dwellings to the incoming Germans, guarding the vicinity during roundups, escorting victims to the killing sites, digging pits for mass graves, and stripping victims of their clothing and property. On their own initiative, locals also beat up and humiliated Jews on the streets, plundered their homes, and watched the massacres—sometimes with binoculars, sometimes just standing a safe distance from the shooting. All these actions lent legitimacy and a sense of normalcy to the mass murders. For many observers, the intensity of killing was new, but the phenomenon of rounding up, torturing, and shooting Jews was not.

AFTER THE INITIAL onslaught, the German military established administrative control, and issued a series of decrees requiring the surviving remnants of the Jewish community to register with the authorities, to move into about 250 designated ghettos, and to wear distinctive markings—usually an armband with a Star of David painted on it. In late August and September, Ukrainian police went door-to-door to enforce the regulations and to select Jews for forced labor. Unenlisted locals, often Ukrainian teenagers or even children, were provided with rolls of barbed wire and gloves to fence in the ghettos. In Proskuriv, for instance, Liusia Blekhman recalled that "the Germans ordered all the Jews in town to assemble together in one place, a ghetto." Local Ukrainian police oversaw the roundup and "whoever didn't move into the ghetto would be shot on the street." The ghetto was surrounded by barbed wire and was guarded by at most "maybe one or maybe two Germans; the rest were Ukrainian gendarmes or police." She recalled that all the Jews were ordered to wear a yellow star and were used as forced labor to harvest the fields and clean the streets.[61] In Zhytomyr, nearly five thousand Jews were held behind barbed wire in an area that included the Jewish synagogue, which was used to house residents. Similarly, the Germans set off a few streets in Korostyshiv, Radomyshl, Fastiv, Chernobyl, and dozens of other cities, towns, and villages. On August 26, about fifteen thousand Jews were confined to a ghetto in Berdychiv, the largest in the region. The Germans relied upon locals to help enforce their rules by disclosing Jews in hiding and reporting on suspicious individuals. Some heroically resisted, saving and hiding their neighbors; many others did not.

The liquidation of the ghettos in Ukraine began in many cases only weeks after their hasty construction; they had never been intended to hold their internees for the long term. On September 6, 1941, Sonderkommando 4a, with the assistance of Ukrainian policemen, liquidated the ghetto of Radomyshl, gathered the Jews together, loaded them onto trucks, and transported them to a clearing outside of town. There, the Germans executed 1,107 adults, and Ukrainian police shot 561 children.[62] In Zhytomyr, the ghetto began to be emptied in mid-September on the pretext that the Jews were dangerous agents of Bolshevism. According to a German Operational Situation Report, "It was ascertained that the Jewish living quarter was the source for the dissemination of [communist] propaganda among the Ukrainians, which asserted that the Red Army would soon return to recover its lost territory. The local police were shot at from concealed positions both at night and in broad daylight." In retaliation, the report continued, "On the evening of September 18, 1941, the Jewish quarter was encircled by 60 Ukrainian policemen. At 4:00 a.m., on September 19, 1941, it was cleared. . . . Once the transport was completed and the necessary preparations had been completed with the assistance of 150 prisoners, 3,145 Jews were registered and executed." The report also noted, "About 25–30 tons of linen, clothing, shoes, dishes, etc. that had been confiscated in the course of the action were handed over . . . for distribution."[63] The Germans revived the accusations that had fueled the pogroms two decades earlier—that Jews were spreading Bolshevism and shooting at soldiers from secret hideouts—and encouraged locals once again to benefit from the massacres and plunder the property of their Jewish neighbors.

Soon afterward, Einsatzkommando 4a liquidated the ghetto of Korostyshiv and shot a reported 700 Jews in a meadow south of town. Others were shot in their own homes.[64] Many of the remaining Jews of the northern Zhytomyr region (Korosten, Ovruch, and Slovechno), about 1,000 people, were murdered in September and October 1941, during an operation that began when Ukrainian police set fire to a school in which they had imprisoned 160 Jews. All were either killed in the fire or were subsequently shot by Germans outside of the city. One woman recalled the humiliations to which Jews were subjected before their murder in the southern Zhytomyr district: "I saw the police brutally mock the Jewish population. They forced them to bring all their valuables, then they forced them to dance and to laugh, and so on. They beat to death those who refused."[65] In Proskuriv, an

A German propaganda pamphlet reads: "This is the Jewish Bolshevism with which Churchill and the British plutocratic clique are fighting a war against Germany! The German people thank the Führer for protecting them from the deadly threat of Bolshevism."

estimated 5,300 Jews were killed on November 4. "They killed the children and the elderly," recalled Blekhman. The shooting started in the morning and "continued without stop for the entire night."[66]

The most deadly massacre took place in Kyiv. On Friday, September 26, 1941, less than one week after the city's occupation, the Germans posted announcements in Russian, Ukrainian, and German around the city ordering all Jews to assemble Monday morning at eight o'clock near the site of a Jewish cemetery. Many were still relative newcomers, refugees who had fled into the city in the aftermath of the pogroms twenty years earlier. Most were women, children, or elderly people; the able-bodied men had been mobilized into the Red Army over the preceding three months. From the assembly point, the multitude was marched under guard through a barbed-wire enclosure, where members of Sonderkommando 4a together with German police and Ukrainian auxiliary police—about three hundred of whom had been recruited from thousands of volunteers at a prisoner of war camp near Zhytomyr—robbed them of their belongings, money, and documents. They were then led into an open meadow, part of the Babyn Yar system of ravines, where estuaries that once fed into a tributary of the Dnipro River had left steep troughs amid the lowland fields. Genia Batashova remembered: "On the opposite side of the meadow, surrounded on all sides by Germans, there was a mound of earth. Behind it machine guns clattered away relentlessly. Passageways in the mound were dug out at an acute angle, so that no one could see what was going on past that point. Here on the green square, people's clothing and underwear were torn off and, beaten with clubs, they were driven toward the passageways."[67] Ukrainian police took away the clothing and loaded it onto trucks. At that point, according to postwar trial records, the victims "were made to lie facedown on the bloodied corpses of victims who had already been shot. If they did not do this willingly, they were beaten and knocked down. Then the gunners climbed over the wobbly mounds toward the victims and shot them in the back of the neck."[68] In an Operational Situation Report, the Germans boasted of shooting 33,771 Jews over thirty-six hours.[69]

THE WAVE OF pogroms that began with the German invasion developed into genocide as the inconceivable became conceivable. The local militias and crowds of Ukrainian civilians who had participated in the early anti-Jewish riots and displays of violence were quickly sidelined by the heavily armed German Einsatzgruppen, German police, and Ukrainian auxiliaries. By late 1941, buoyed by their success in the Ukrainian operations, the Germans began experimenting with gas vans in Kharkiv and Poltava, utilizing technologies developed earlier as part of the Nazi euthanasia program. By December 1941, close to five hundred thousand Jews had been murdered in the newly occupied regions of Ukraine, about a third of the prewar Jewish population. Most of those still alive by the end of the year would perish in ghettos, labor brigades, and camps over the winter, or be murdered in another round of mass shootings when the remaining ghettos were liquidated in the spring of 1942, just as most of the Nazi death camps began functioning to the west. The largest death tolls in Ukraine were recorded in the regions that had once been the Russian provinces of Kyiv, Podilia, and Volhynia, followed by the former Austrian province of Galicia, the very same places that suffered most during the pogroms of the civil war. Twenty-four years after it began, the genocide of the Jews of Ukraine was completed.

When Jewish activists and humanitarian observers warned in September 1919 that six million souls in Ukraine and Poland were in peril of being "completely exterminated," they could not have imagined the systematic, bureaucratic, state-sponsored murder to come, nor would they have suspected that Germans would be the primary perpetrators. The Holocaust, like all history, was unpredictable. But its broad outlines were anticipated. There were many individuals who tried to take action and prepare for what they feared would be a cataclysmic massacre of the Jewish population in Poland and Ukraine. They foresaw it because they recognized that the pogroms of 1918 to 1921 had established a precedent that could be built upon in the future. Many of the historical circumstances that had led to bloodshed in the past remained unresolved: the libel of Judeo-Bolshevism continued to stir those who had suffered from Soviet rule, income inequality between town and country had worsened, the trauma of ongoing barbarity had further inured the population, plundered property had not been restored, and justice had been arbitrarily served—many of the most egregious perpetrators had gone unpunished, whereas lesser accomplices had been sentenced to death by tribunals or vigilantes. Most important, the value of Jewish life had been debased. The repercussions of the 1918–1921 pogroms continued to linger and ripple through the community and across Europe.

Life went on in the twenty years between 1921 and 1941: children grew up, married, and celebrated the births of their own children; adults passed on their traditions to the next generation and struggled to eke out a living in a changing world; friends and families ate together, drank together, and worshipped together; and enmity, grudges, and personal slights played themselves out with the restraint that society

demands. From the fields of Ukraine to the halls of the world's parliaments, decent people reached out to their Jewish neighbors, heeded the
warnings of Jewish activists, and worked to make the world a better,
more civilized place. The tragedy is that it wasn't enough.

When the next war came, when the Germans invaded on June 22,
1941, they deliberately and strategically exploited preexisting anti-
Jewish sentiments and drew upon homegrown patterns to launch a
new wave of killing, to reenact a script written a generation before. The
pogroms of 1918–1921 had already established violence against Jews as
an acceptable response to the excesses of Bolshevism. Those in their thirties and forties had witnessed and sometimes participated in the same
type of action when they were adolescents, the age of many of the men
who had fought in insurgent armies during the civil war. When locals
went out into the forest on German instructions to dig pits, they could
have been wearing the same boots they had stolen from murdered Jews
twenty years earlier. When they returned home, they may have made
tea in samovars stolen from their Jewish neighbors. Those in their late
twenties and early thirties had been among the children running after
convoys of Jewish prisoners in the festive atmosphere of the pogroms.
Older men and women scavenged Jewish property in 1941 just as they
had in their youth.

In Eastern Galicia and western Volhynia, the discriminatory policies of the Polish Republic had radicalized the political environment
and pitted Ukrainian and Jewish minorities against each other. Xenophobic rhetoric emanating from civil and religious leaders further
inflamed antisemitism and bolstered ethnic stereotypes, so that when
a new Soviet regime arrived in 1939 many viewed it as a front for
Jewish power and blamed the Jews for its crimes. In Soviet Ukraine,
on the other hand, the hammer and sickle had dampened ethnic tensions, but the arrival of a new group of soldiers in town soon triggered
responses learned during traumatic childhoods and reignited the cycle
of violence, which the Germans eagerly radicalized and quickly took
over. As children, many locals had seen Bolshevik investigators, a disproportionate number of whom were Jewish, arrest and execute their
heroes—the brash adventurists and "noble bandits" who rose up in

defense of a peasant republic and fought for the redistribution of land to the people who worked it. Some had even seen their parents charged with banditry and counterrevolutionary activity. Many believed it was time to avenge themselves for the excesses of the revolutionary tribunals, the Soviet secret police, the theft of their land and their grain, the closure of their churches, and the murder of their youth. German propaganda, reviving themes that had been rampant during the civil war, convinced many that the Jews were to blame. Those who had lived through the pogroms had seen what was possible in an era of total war. Even in the midst of civilized Europe.

NOTES

ABBREVIATIONS

AHEYM Archives of Historical and Ethnographic Yiddish Memories

CAHJP Central Archives for the History of the Jewish People

DA, CBU Haluzevyi derzhavnyi arkhiv, Sluzhba bezpeky Ukrainy (State Archive, Ukrainian Security Service), accessed at USHMM RG-31.018M

DAKO Derzhavnyi arkhiv Kyivs'koi oblasti (State Archives of Kyiv Oblast), accessed at USHMM RF-31.058M and at Hatcher Library, University of Michigan

DAZhO Derzhavnyi arkhiv Zhytomyrs'koi oblasti (State Archive of Zhytomyr Oblast), accessed at USHMM RG-31–060M

GARF Gosudarstvennyi arkhiv Rossiiskoi Federatsii (State Archive of the Russian Federation), accessed at USHMM RG-22.002M

JDC Joint Distribution Committee

TsDAVO Tsentral'nyi derzhavnyi arkhiv vyshchykh orhaniv vlady ta upravlinnia Ukrainy (Central State Archives of Supreme Bodies of Power and Government of Ukraine), accessed at USHMM RG-31.076

TsDKFFA Tsentral'nyi derzhavnyi kinofotofonoarkhiv Ukrainy imeni G. S. Pshenychnogo (Central State CinePhotoPhono Archives of Ukraine, named after H. Pshenychnyi)

USHMM United States Holocaust Memorial Museum

YIVO Yidisher visnshaftlekher institut (Institute for Jewish Research)

INTRODUCTION: "WILL A SLAUGHTER OF JEWS BE NEXT EUROPEAN HORROR?"

1. *Khurbn Proskurov: Tsum ondenken fun di heylige neshomes, vos zaynen umgekumen in der shreklikher shkhite* (New York: Levant Press, 1923 or 1924). For more on the book's creation see Susan Milamed, "Proskurover Landsmanshaftn: A Case Study in Jewish Communal Development," *American Jewish History* 76, no. 1 (1986): 40–55.
2. H. G. Wells, *The War That Will End War* (London: Frank & Cecil Palmer, 1914); and Margaret MacMillan, *Paris 1919: Six Months That Changed the World* (New York: Random House, 2001).
3. The exact number of incidents is impossible to determine. The Eastern Jewish Historical Archive at YIVO includes information on 1,154 pogroms: YIVO 80/271–276. I have compiled a list of 469 distinct locations in which fatalities were registered. For recent work on these pogroms see Irina Astashkevich, *Gendered Violence: Jewish Women in the Pogroms of 1917 to 1921* (Boston: Academic Studies Press, 2018); Elissa Bemporad, *Legacy of Blood: Jews, Pogroms, and Ritual Murder in the Lands of the Soviets* (New York: Oxford University Press, 2019); Elissa Bemporad and Thomas Chopard, eds., "The Pogroms of the Russian Civil War at 100: New Trends, New Sources," *Quest. Issues in Contemporary Jewish History*, no. 15 (August 2019); O. V. Budnitskii, *Rossiiskie evrei mezhdu krasnymi i belymi (1917–1920)* (Moscow: Rosspen, 2006), translated by Timothy J. Portice as *Russian Jews Between the Reds and the Whites, 1917–1920* (Philadelphia: University of Pennsylvania Press, 2012); Thomas Chopard, *Le martyre de Kiev: 1919: L'Ukraine en révolution entre terreur soviétique, nationalisme et antisémitisme* (Paris: Vendémiaire, 2015); Lars Fischer, "The *Pogromshchina* and the Directory: A New Historiographical Synthesis?," *Revolutionary Russia* 16, no. 2 (December 2003): 47–93; Alexander Gendler, *Khurbm 1914–1922. The Beginning: Expulsions, Hostages, Pogroms* (Skokie, IL: Varda Books, 2019); Victoria Khiterer, *Jewish Pogroms in Kiev During the Russian Civil War, 1918–1920* (Lewiston, NY: Edwin Mellen Press, 2015); Kamil Kijek, Artur Markowski, and Konrad Zieliński, eds., *Pogromy Żydów na ziemiach polskich w XIX i XX wieku. Tom 2: Studia przypadków (do 1939 roku)* (Warsaw: Instytut Historii PAN, 2018); Kamil Kijek, Artur Markowski, and Konrad Zieliński, eds., *Pogromy Żydów na ziemiach polskich w XIX i XX wieku. Tom 3: Historiografia, polityka, recepcja społeczna (do 1939 roku)* (Warsaw: Instytut Historii PAN, 2018); Brendan McGeever, *Antisemitism and the Russian Revolution* (Cambridge: Cambridge University Press, 2019); Lidia B. Miliakova, ed., *Kniga pogromov: Pogromy na Ukraine, v Belorussii i evropeiskoi chasti Rossii v period grazhdanskoi voiny, 1918–1922 gg. Sbornik dokumentov* (Moscow: Rosspen, 2007); Volodymyr Serhiichuk, ed., *Pohromy v Ukraïni, 1914–1920: Vid shtuchnykh stereotypiv do hirkoï pravdy, prykhovuvanoï v radians´kykh arkhivakh* (Kyiv: O. Telihy,

1998); and William W. Hagen, *Anti-Jewish Violence in Poland, 1914–1920* (Cambridge: Cambridge University Press, 2018).

4. Today, the parts of the Polish Second Republic that Seff was referring to are also within Ukraine. "Ukrainian Jews Aim to Stop Pogroms," *New York Times*, September 8, 1919.

5. "Report by Head of Information Branch, Committee of Russian Red Cross Society for the Relief of Pogrom Sufferers," p. 34, JDC Archives, Records of the New York Office of the American Jewish Joint Distribution Committee, 1919–1921, folder 256.2.

6. Emma Goldman, *My Further Disillusionment in Russia* (New York: Doubleday, Page, 1924), 11.

7. D. S. Pasmanik, *Russkaia revoliutsiia i evreistvo* (Berlin: Feilchenfeld, 1923), 188.

8. Dietrich Beyrau, "Brutalization Revisited: The Case of Russia," *Journal of Contemporary History* 50, no. 1 (2015): 15–37; and Stefan Plaggenborg, "Weltkrieg, Bürgerkrieg, Klassenkrieg. Mentalitätsgeschichtliche Versuche über die Gewalt in Sowjetrussland 1917–1930," *Historische Anthropologie* 3 (1995): 493–505.

9. For some excellent recent attempts to explain the Holocaust along these lines see Alon Confino, *A World Without Jews: The Nazi Imagination from Persecution to Genocide* (New Haven, CT: Yale University Press, 2014); Peter Hayes, *Why? Explaining the Holocaust* (New York: W. W. Norton, 2018); Timothy Snyder, *Bloodlands: Europe Between Hitler and Stalin* (New York: Basic Books, 2010); and Timothy Snyder, *Black Earth: The Holocaust as History and Warning* (New York: Tim Duggan Books, 2015).

10. Paul Hanebrink, *A Specter Haunting Europe: The Myth of Judeo-Bolshevism* (Cambridge, MA: Belknap Press of Harvard University Press, 2018).

11. Christopher R. Browning, *Ordinary Men: Reserve Police Battalion 101 and the Final Solution in Poland* (New York: HarperCollins, 1992); Jan T. Gross, *Neighbors: The Destruction of the Jewish Community in Jedwabne, Poland* (Princeton, NJ: Princeton University Press, 2001), 7. See also Harald Welzer, *Täter: Wie aus ganz normalen Menschen Massenmörder werden* (Frankfurt am Main: S. Fischer, 2005); Charles King, "Can There Be a Political Science of the Holocaust?," *Perspectives on Politics* 10, no. 2 (June 2012): 323–41; Timothy Snyder, "The Causes of the Holocaust," *Contemporary European History* 21, no. 2 (May 2012): 149–68; Father Patrick Desbois, *The Holocaust by Bullets: A Priest's Journey to Uncover the Truth Behind the Murder of 1.5 Million Jews* (New York: St. Martin's Press, 2009); Ray Brandon and Wendy Lower, eds., *The Shoah in Ukraine: History, Testimony, Memorialization* (Bloomington: Indiana University Press, 2008); Jeffrey Burds, *Holocaust in Rovno: A Massacre in Ukraine, November 1941* (New York: Palgrave Macmillan, 2013); Kai Struve, *Deutsche Herrschaft, ukrainischer Nationalismus, antijüdische Gewalt: Der Sommer 1941 in der Westukraine* (Berlin/Boston: De Gruyter Oldenbourg, 2015); Michael David-Fox, Peter Holquist,

and Alexander M. Martin, eds., *The Holocaust in the East: Local Perpetrators and Soviet Responses* (Pittsburgh: University of Pittsburgh Press, 2014); Wendy Lower, "Pogroms, Mob Violence and Genocide in Western Ukraine, Summer 1941: Varied Histories, Explanations and Comparisons," *Journal of Genocide Research* 13, no. 3 (2011): 238; Piotr Wróbel, "The Seeds of Violence: The Brutalization of an Eastern European Region, 1917–1921," *Journal of Modern European History* 1, no. 1 (2003): 125–49; and Waitman Wade Beorn, *Marching into Darkness: The Wehrmacht and the Holocaust in Belarus* (Cambridge, MA: Harvard University Press, 2014).

12. For some recent works that demonstrate continuities between the world wars in East Central Europe see George O. Liber, *Total Wars and the Making of Modern Ukraine, 1914–1954* (Toronto: University of Toronto Press, 2016); Omer Bartov and Eric D. Weitz, eds., *Shatterzone of Empires: Coexistence and Violence in the German, Habsburg, Russian, and Ottoman Borderlands* (Bloomington: Indiana University Press, 2013); Götz Aly, *Europe Against the Jews, 1880–1945*, trans. Jefferson Chase (New York: Metropolitan Books, 2020); Alexander V. Prusin, *The Lands Between: Conflict in the East European Borderlands, 1870–1992* (Oxford: Oxford University Press, 2010); Omer Bartov, *Anatomy of a Genocide: The Life and Death of a Town Called Buczacz* (New York: Simon & Schuster, 2018); Shimon Redlich, *Together and Apart in Brzezany: Poles, Jews, and Ukrainians, 1919–1945* (Bloomington and Indianapolis: Indiana University Press, 2002); Jeffrey S. Kopstein and Jason Wittenberg, *Intimate Violence: Anti-Jewish Pogroms on the Eve of the Holocaust* (Ithaca, NY: Cornell University Press, 2018); Cathie Carmichael, *Genocide Before the Holocaust* (New Haven, CT: Yale University Press, 2009); and Donald Bloxham and Robert Gerwarth, eds., *Political Violence in Twentieth-Century Europe* (Cambridge: Cambridge University Press, 2011).

13. Jacob Lestschinsky, "The Anti-Jewish Program: Tsarist Russia, the Third Reich and Independent Poland," *Jewish Social Studies* 3, no. 2 (April 1941): 147.

14. https://www.cbsnews.com/news/text-of-clintons-rwanda-speech/.

15. The Jewish Statistical Society has estimated the 1917 Jewish population of the provinces of Volhynia, Katerynoslav, Kyiv, Podilia, Taurida, Kharkiv, Kherson, and Chernyhiv to be 2.14 million. See Evreiskoe Statisticheskoe Obshchestvo, *Evreiskoe naselenie Rossii po dannym perepisi 1897 g i po noveishim istochnikam* (Petrograd: Kadima, 1917), ix and 68. The Jewish population of Eastern Galicia was about 660,000.

16. For statistics on the Russian provinces see N. A. Trointskii, ed., *Pervaia vseobshchaia perepis' naseleniia Rossiiskoi Imperii, 1897 g* (St. Petersburg: Tsentral'nyi statisticheskii komitet MVD, 1899–1907). For statistics on Galicia see John-Paul Himka, "Dimensions of a Triangle: Polish-Ukrainian-Jewish Relations in Austrian Galicia," *Polin: Studies in Polish Jewry* 12 (1999): 26–28.

17. Paul Robert Magocsi and Yohanan Petrovsky-Shtern, *Jews and Ukrainians: A Millennium of Co-Existence* (Toronto: University of Toronto Press, 2016).

18. Olga Belova and V. Petrukhin, *Evreiskii mif v slavianskoi kul'ture* (Moscow: Mosty Kul'tury, 2008); George G. Grabowicz, "The Jewish Theme in Nineteenth- and Early Twentieth-Century Ukrainian Literature," in Howard Aster and Peter J. Potichnyj, eds., *Ukrainian-Jewish Relations in Historical Perspective*, 327–42 (Edmonton: Canadian Institute of Ukrainian Studies, 1990); Amelia M. Glaser, *Jews and Ukrainians in Russia's Literary Borderlands: From the Shtetl Fair to the Petersburg Bookshop* (Evanston, IL: Northwestern University Press, 2012); and Myroslav Shkandrij, *Jews in Ukrainian Literature: Representation and Identity* (New Haven, CT: Yale University Press, 2009).

19. Translation from Hillel Halkin's translation of Sholem Aleichem, *Tevye the Dairyman and the Railroad Stories* (New York: Schocken Books, 1987), 72.

20. Sholem Aleichem, "Drite klas," in *Ale verk fun Sholem Aleykhem*, vol. 5, bk. 5 (New York: Forverts, 1942), 299.

21. Sholem Aleichem, *Fun'm yarid*, vol. 2 (New York: Varhayt, 1917), 63–64. On Jewish-Christian relations in nineteenth-century Ukraine see Yohanan Petrovsky-Shtern, *The Golden-Age Shtetl: A New History of Jewish Life in East Europe* (Princeton, NJ: Princeton University Press, 2014); Magocsi and Petrovsky-Shtern, *Jews and Ukrainians*; and Aster and Potichnyj, *Ukrainian-Jewish Relations in Historical Perspective*. For Galicia, see Himka, "Dimensions of a Triangle," 25–48; and C. M. Hann and Paul R. Magocsi, eds., *Galicia: A Multicultural Land* (Toronto and Buffalo: University of Toronto Press, 2005).

22. *Russia: Its Industries and Trade* (Glasgow: Hay Nisbet, 1901), 160–61.

23. For recent work on the civil wars that followed the Russian revolutions, see Jochen Böhler, *Civil War in Central Europe, 1918–1921: The Reconstruction of Poland* (Oxford: Oxford University Press, 2018); Laura Engelstein, *Russia in Flames: War, Revolution, Civil War, 1914–1921* (New York: Oxford University Press, 2018); Orlando Figes, *A People's Tragedy: A History of the Russian Revolution* (New York: Viking, 1997); Robert Gerwarth, *The Vanquished: Why the First World War Failed to End* (New York: Farrar, Straus and Giroux, 2016); and Jonathan D. Smele, *The 'Russian' Civil Wars, 1916–1926: Ten Years That Shook the World* (London: Hurst, 2015).

24. Beyrau, "Brutalization Revisited," 15–37.

25. Liber, *Total Wars and the Making of Modern Ukraine, 1914–1954*. See also Elissa Bemporad and Thomas Chopard, "Introduction," in Bemporad and Chopard, "The Pogroms of the Russian Civil War at 100."

26. Snyder, *Bloodlands*; Bartov and Weitz, *Shatterzone of Empires*; Prusin, *The Lands Between*; and Kate Brown, *A Biography of No Place: From Ethnic Borderland to Soviet Heartland* (Cambridge, MA: Harvard University Press, 2005).

27. For scholarship on civil wars and ethnic violence that inform this book

see Donald L. Horowitz, *The Deadly Ethnic Riot* (Berkeley: University of California Press, 2001); Stathis N. Kalyvas, "The Ontology of 'Political Violence': Action and Identity in Civil Wars," *Perspectives on Politics* 1, no. 3 (2003): 475–94; Stathis N. Kalyvas, *The Logic of Violence in Civil War* (Cambridge: Cambridge University Press, 2006); Benjamin Valentino, Paul Huth, and Dylan Balch-Lindsay, "'Draining the Sea': Mass Killing and Guerrilla Warfare," *International Organization* 58, no. 2 (2004): 375–407; Stanley Jeyaraja Tambiah, *Leveling Crowds: Ethnonationalist Conflicts and Collective Violence in South Asia* (Berkeley: University of California Press, 1996); and Christian Gerlach, *Extremely Violent Societies: Mass Violence in the Twentieth-Century World* (Cambridge: Cambridge University Press, 2010).

A NOTE ON SOURCES, NUMBERS, DATES, AND PLACE-NAMES

1. Elias Tsherikover, *Di ukrayner pogromen in yor 1919* (New York: YIVO, 1966), 333–34.
2. Steven J. Zipperstein, "The Politics of Relief: The Transformation of Russian-Jewish Communal Life During the First World War," in Jonathan Frankel, ed., *Studies in Contemporary Jewry: The Jews and the European Crisis, 1914–21* (New York: Oxford University Press, 1988), 22–40; Mikhail Beizer, *Relief in Time of Need: Russian Jewry and the Joint, 1914–24* (Bloomington, IN: Slavica Publishers, 2015); "Proekt Ustava Tsentral'nago evreiskago obshchestva pomoshchi zhertvam voiny," DAKO 445/1/362/1; and "Ustav tsentral'nago evreiskago komiteta pomoshchi postradavshim ot pogromov," TsDAVO 3299/1/1.
3. Beizer, *Relief in Time of Need*, 21.
4. Elijah Gumener, *A kapitl Ukrayne (2 yor in Podolie)* (Vilna: Sh. Shreberk, 1921), 76.
5. "Tsu di kehiles," YIVO 80/202/17849.
6. For more on Tsherikover see Joshua M. Karlip, "Between Martyrology and Historiography: Elias Tcherikower and the Making of a Pogrom Historian," *East European Jewish Affairs* 38, no. 3 (December 1, 2008): 257–80. For Lestschinsky see Gur Alroey, "Demographers in the Service of the Nation: Liebmann Hersch, Jacob Lestschinsky, and the Early Study of Jewish Migration," *Jewish History* 20, no. 3/4 (2006): 265–82. On Jewish aid work during the civil war see Polly Zavadivker, "Contending with Horror: Jewish Aid Work in the Russian Civil War Pogroms," in Elissa Bemporad and Thomas Chopard, eds., "The Pogroms of the Russian Civil War at 100: New Trends, New Sources," *Quest. Issues in Contemporary Jewish History*, no. 15 (August 2019).
7. See, for instance, "Anketa: Nimkovskyi," DAKO R-3050/1/244/30.
8. "Di reshime fun gehergete in uvrutsher pogrom," DAKO R-3050/1/268/6.

9. The first of the planned book series, Tsherikover's *Antisemitism and Pogroms in Ukraine, 1917–1918*, was published in Yiddish and Russian editions in Berlin in 1923 as Elias Tsherikover, *Antisemitizm un pogromen in Ukrayne 1917–1918* (Berlin: Mizrekh-yidishn historishn arkhiv, 1923), and *Antisemitizm i pogromy na Ukraine, 1917–1918 gg* (Berlin: Ostjüdisches Historisches Archiv, 1923). In the 1930s, Tsherikover wrote a second volume on the pogroms of 1919, which would only be published posthumously in Yiddish in New York in 1965 as Elias Tsherikover, *Di ukrayner pogromen in yor 1919* (New York: YIVO, 1966). The third volume in the series was written by the former parliamentarian and refugee activist Joseph Schechtman, and was published in Russian in Berlin as *Pogromy dobrovol'cheskoi armii na Ukraine* (Berlin: Ostjüdisches Historisches Archiv, 1932). None of the remaining volumes were completed, although Shtif did succeed in publishing a different book as Nokhem Shtif, *Pogromen in Ukrayne: Di tsayt fun der frayviliger armey* (Berlin: Vostok, 1923). See also Elias Heifetz, *Pogrom geshikhte (1919–1920)* (New York: Workmen's Circle, 1921), translated into English as *The Slaughter of the Jews in the Ukraine in 1919* (New York: Thomas Seltzer, 1921). For some other near-contemporary works on the pogroms see Bernard Lecache, *Quand Israël meurt* (Paris: Editions du *Progrès civique*, 1927); Committee of the Jewish Delegations, *The Pogroms in the Ukraine Under the Ukrainian Governments (1917–1920): Historical Survey with Documents and Photographs* (London: J. Bale & Danielsson, 1927); *Jewish Pogroms in South Russia: Report by the Kieff Pogrom Relief Committee* (London: Central Committee of the Zionist Organization in Russia, 1920); Sergei Ivanovich Gusev-Orenburgskii, *Bagrovaia kniga: pogrom 1919–1920 gg. na Ukraine* (Harbin, China: Dekopo, 1922); and Federation of Ukrainian Jews, *The Ukraine Terror and the Jewish Peril* (London: Federation of Ukrainian Jews, 1921).

10. For more on the history of YIVO see Cecile Esther Kuznitz, *YIVO and the Making of Modern Jewish Culture: Scholarship for the Yiddish Nation* (Cambridge: Cambridge University Press, 2017).

11. Efim Melamed, "'Immortalizing the Crime in History . . .': The Activities of the Ostjüdisches Historisches Archiv (Kiev—Berlin—Paris, 1920–1940)," in Jörg Schulte, Olga Tabachnikova, and Peter Wagstaff, eds., *The Russian Jewish Diaspora and European Culture, 1917–1937* (Leiden: Brill, 2012), 387–416.

12. See, for instance, Itsik Kipnis, *Khadoshim un teg: a khronik* (Kyiv: Kultur-Lige, 1926); Rukhl Faygnberg, *A pinkes fun a toyter shtot: hurbn-Dubove* (Warsaw: Ahisefer, 1926); M. Sadikov, *In yene teg: zikhroynes vegen der Rusisher revolutsie un di Ukrayner pogromen* (New York: 1926); Shmuel Rubinshteyn, *Tsvishn fayer un shverd: bletlakh zikhroynes vegn birger-krig in Ukrayne, 1918–1920* (Warsaw: Emes, 1924); Eliezer David Rosenthal, ed., *Tetiever khurbn* (New York: Idgezkom, 1922); *Yizkor dem ondeynken*

fun di Zshitomirer kdoshim (New York: Zshitomirer fareynigten relif komi, 1921); and Elijah Gumener, *A kapitl Ukrayne (2 yor in Podolie)* (Vilna: Sh. Shreberk, 1921).

13. Eliezer David Rosental, *Megilat ha-tevaḥ: ḥomer le-divre yeme ha-pera'ot veha-tevaḥ ba-Yehudim ba-Ukra'inah, be-Rusyah ha-Gedolah uve-Rusyah ha-levanah* (Jerusalem: Ḥavurah, 1927–1931).

14. The Jewish Public Committee, or *Evreiskii Obshchestvennyi Komitet*, is known by its Russian contraction Evobshchestkom. I consulted microfilmed versions of the Kyiv branch of the Public Committee's materials at the University of Michigan's Hatcher Graduate Library, and digitized versions of additional materials from the archives of both the Public Committee and the Central Committee held at the United States Holocaust Memorial Museum in Washington, DC.

15. Zalman Solomonovich Ostrovskii, *Evreiskie pogromy 1918–1921* (Moscow: Obshchestvo shkola i kniga, 1926), 74.

16. Jacob Lestschinsky, *Crisis, Catastrophe and Survival: A Jewish Balance Sheet, 1914–1948* (New York: Institute of Jewish Affairs of the World Jewish Congress, 1948), 11–12.

17. N. Gergel, "The Pogroms in the Ukraine in 1918–21," *YIVO Annual of Jewish Social Science* 6 (1951): 237–52.

18. "Svedeniia o pogromakh na territorii Ukrainy v 1918–1921 gg.," TsDAVO 2497/3/188/4 and 6.

19. Miliakova, *Kniga pogromov*, xiii–xiv.

20. Amelia M. Glaser, ed., *Stories of Khmelnytsky: Competing Literary Legacies of the 1648 Ukrainian Cossack Uprising* (Stanford, CA: Stanford University Press, 2015).

CHAPTER 1: THE LAST YEARS OF THE RUSSIAN EMPIRE

1. "The Russo-Jewish Question," *Times* (London), March 17, 1882. For some of the problems defining pogroms see John D. Klier, "The Pogrom Paradigm in Russian History," in John D. Klier and Shlomo Lambroza, eds., *Pogroms: Anti-Jewish Violence in Modern Russian History*, 13–38 (New York: Cambridge University Press, 1992); David Engel, "What's in a Pogrom? European Jews in the Age of Violence," in Jonathan Dekel-Chen et al., eds., *Anti-Jewish Violence: Rethinking the Pogrom in East European History* (Bloomington: Indiana University Press, 2011), 19–37; and Eugene M. Avrutin, "Pogroms in Russian History," *Kritika* 14, no. 3 (2013): 585–98.

2. For Jewish involvement in the revolutionary movement and specifically the assassination of Alexander II see Erich E. Haberer, *Jews and Revolution in Nineteenth-Century Russia* (Cambridge: Cambridge University Press, 1995), 186–205.

3. Evgenii Petrovich Semenoff, *The Russian Government and the Massacres: A Page of the Russian Counter-Revolution* (London: John Murray, 1907), xi.

4. Irwin Michael Aronson, *Troubled Waters: The Origins of the 1881 Anti-Jewish Pogroms in Russia* (Pittsburgh: University of Pittsburgh Press, 1990); Eliyahu Feldman, *Yehude Rusyah bi-yeme ha-mahpekhah ha-rishonah veha-pogromim* (Jerusalem: Magnes, 1999); John Klier, *Russians, Jews, and the Pogroms of 1881–1882* (New York: Cambridge University Press, 2011); and Aleksandr Mindlin, *Antievreiskie pogromy na territorii Rossiiskogo gosudarstva* (St. Petersburg: Aleteiia, 2018).

5. Steven J. Zipperstein, *Pogrom: Kishinev and the Tilt of History* (New York: Liveright, 2018).

6. Shlomo Lambroza, "The Pogroms of 1903–1906," in Klier and Lambroza, *Pogroms*, 195–247.

7. For more on Jewish political parties in Ukraine and the Russian Empire see Henry Abramson, *A Prayer for the Government: Ukrainians and Jews in Revolutionary Times, 1917–1920* (Cambridge, MA: Harvard University Press, 1999); Jonathan Frankel, *Prophecy and Politics: Socialism, Nationalism, and the Russian Jews, 1862–1917* (Cambridge: Cambridge University Press, 1981); Christoph Gassenschmidt, *Jewish Liberal Politics in Tsarist Russia, 1900–1914: The Modernization of Russian Jewry* (New York: New York University Press, 1995); and Simon Rabinovitch, *Jewish Rights, National Rites: Nationalism and Autonomy in Late Imperial and Revolutionary Russia* (Stanford, CA: Stanford University Press, 2014).

8. Isaac Deutscher, *The Non-Jewish Jew and Other Essays* (London: Oxford University Press, 1968), 26–27.

9. Hans Rogger, *Jewish Policies and Right-Wing Politics in Imperial Russia* (Berkeley: University of California Press, 1986).

10. For studies of the Zhytomyr pogroms see Kommission zür Untersuchung der Pogrome, *Die Judenpogrome in Russland*, vol. 2 (Köln and Leipzig: Jüdischer Verlag, 1910), 44–58; Stefan Wiese, *Pogrome im Zarenreich* (Hamburg: Hamburg Edition, 2016); and Stefan Wiese, "Jewish Self-Defense and Black Hundreds in Zhitomir: A Case Study on the Pogroms of 1905 in Tsarist Russia," *Quest. Issues in Contemporary Jewish History*, no. 3 (July 2012). For works on other pogroms of the era see Artur Markowski, *Przemoc antyżydowska i wyobrażenia społeczne. Pogrom Białostocki 1906 roku* (Warsaw: University of Warsaw Press, 2018); and Robert Weinberg, *The Revolution of 1905 in Odessa: Blood on the Steps* (Bloomington: Indiana University Press, 1993). See also the two-volume *Pogromy v Rossii* (Berlin: J. Ladyschniko, 1908).

11. B. Prushinskii, *Plan goroda Zhytomyra* (Zhytomyr: M. Deneman, 1898).

12. Cited in Wiese, "Jewish Self-Defense and Black Hundreds in Zhitomir."

13. See *Yizkor dem ondeynken fun di Zshitomirer kdoshim* (New York: Zshitomirer fareynigten relif komi, 1921), 14–22.

14. See *Yizkor dem ondeynken fun di Zshitomirer kdoyshim*, 23–29.

15. *Die Judenpogrome in Russland*; Lambroza, "The Pogroms of 1903–1906."

16. On the 1905 Odesa pogrom see Weinberg, *The Revolution of 1905 in Odessa*; and Caroline Humphrey, "Odessa: Pogroms in a Cosmopolitan City," *Ab Imperio* 2010, no. 4 (2010): 27–79. For pogroms during this period in Lithuania see Darius Staliūnas, *Enemies for a Day: Antisemitism and Anti-Jewish Violence in Lithuania Under the Tsars* (Budapest: CEU Press, 2015).

17. For more on the flourishing of cultural life after the 1905 revolution see Jeffrey Veidlinger, *Jewish Public Culture in the Late Russian Empire* (Bloomington: Indiana University Press, 2009).

18. For a contemporary analysis of the legal situation of Jews in Russia see Lucien Wolf, *The Legal Sufferings of the Jews in Russia: A Survey of Their Present Situation, and a Summary of Laws* (London: T. F. Unwin, 1912).

19. For recent work on the *Protocols* see Cesare G. De Michelis, *The Non-Existent Manuscript: A Study of the Protocols of the Sages of Zion* (Lincoln: University of Nebraska Press, 2004).

20. Robert Weinberg, *Blood Libel in Late Imperial Russia: The Ritual Murder Trial of Mendel Beilis* (Bloomington: Indiana University Press, 2014).

21. Sean McMeekin, *The Russian Origins of the First World War* (Cambridge, MA: Belknap Press of Harvard University Press, 2011). For more on Russia in World War I see Peter Holquist, *Making War, Forging Revolution: Russia's Continuum of Crisis, 1914–1921* (Cambridge, MA: Harvard University Press, 2002).

22. Cited in Semion Goldin, *Russkaia armia i evrei. 1914–1917* (Moscow: Mosty Kul'tury/Gesharim, 2018), 108. For more on Jews in the Russian army during the war see Yohanan Petrovsky-Shtern, *Jews in the Russian Army, 1827–1917: Drafted into Modernity* (Cambridge: Cambridge University Press, 2009), 248–68. For Jews in the military more generally see Derek J. Penslar, *Jews and the Military: A History* (Princeton, NJ: Princeton University Press, 2013).

23. Cited in Goldin, *Russkaia armia i evrei*, 111.

24. S. An-sky, *Gezamelte shriftn*, vol. 4 (Warsaw: Farlag "An-sky," 1928), 6; and S. An-sky, *The Enemy at His Pleasure: A Journey Through the Jewish Pale of Settlement During World War I*, trans. and ed. Joachim Neugroschel, (New York: Metropolitan Books, 2002), 3. See also Marc Caplan, "A Disenchanted Elijah: Folklore, Conspiracy Theories, and Allegory in S. An-sky's *Destruction of Galicia*," *Polin: Studies in Polish Jewry* 34 (forthcoming).

25. *Khurbn Proskurov: Tsum ondenken fun di heylige neshomes, vos zaynen umgekumen in der shreklikher shkhite* (New York: Levant Press, 1923 or 1924), 7.

26. "Der khurbn fun'm hornosteypoler hoyf," YIVO 80/51/4136.

27. N. P. Poletika, *Vidennoe i perezhitoe (iz vospominanii)* (Jerusalem: Bibioteka-Aliia, 1982).

28. An-sky, *The Enemy at His Pleasure*, 78; and Goldin, *Russkaia armia i evrei*, 286–88. See also Peter Holquist, "The Role of Personality in the First

(1914–1915) Russian Occupation of Galicia and Bukovina," in Dekel-Chen et al., *Anti-Jewish Violence*, 52–73.

29. Cited in Holquist, "The Role of Personality," 54.

30. An-sky, *The Enemy at His Pleasure*, 91.

31. See Goldin, *Russkaia armia i evrei*; Semion Goldin, "'Ia srazu opoznal v nem zhida': evrei v dokumentakh russkoi armeiskoi kontrrazvedki i voennykh sudov v gody Pervoi mirovoi voiny," *Jews and Slavs* 19, (2008): 132–45; Semion Goldin, "Deportations of Jews by the Russian Military Command, 1914–1915," *Jews in Eastern Europe* 41, no. 1 (2000): 40–72; Vladimir Kosovsky, *Der idisher khurbn in Rusland* (New York: Tsentral Farband fun Bund in Amerike, 1915); G. Ioffe, "Vyselenie evreev iz prifrontovoi polosy v 1915 g," *Voprosy istorii*, no. 9 (September, 2001): 85–97; Eric Lohr, "The Russian Army and the Jews: Mass Deportation, Hostages, and Violence During World War I," *Russian Review* 60, no. 3 (July 2001): 404–19; Eric Lohr, *Nationalizing the Russian Empire: The Campaign Against Enemy Aliens During World War I* (Cambridge, MA: Harvard University Press, 2003); Mindlin, *Antievreiskie pogromy*, 350–78; Joshua A. Sanborn, "Unsettling the Empire: Violent Migrations and Social Disaster in Russia During World War I," *Journal of Modern History* 77, no. 2 (June 2005): 290–324; D. A. Zaslavsky, "Iz 'Chernoi knigi' rossiiskago evreistva. Materialy dlia istorii voiny 1914–1915 g," *Evreiskaia starina* 10, (1918): 195–296; and Konrad Zieliński, *Stosunki polsko-żydowskie na ziemiach Królestwa Polskiego w czasie pierwszej wojny światowej* (Lublin: Wydawnictwo Uniwersytetu Marii Curie-Skłodowskiej, 2005).

32. Zaslavsky, "Iz 'Chernoi knigi,'" 223.

33. Holquist, "The Role of Personality," 68.

34. "Vserossiiskomu s gorodskomu soizu pomoshchi bol'nym i ranenym voinam," DAKO 445/1/374/l.

35. Zaslavsky, "Iz 'Chernoi knigi,'" 240.

36. "Dokladnaia zapiska KOPE k glavnoupolnomochennomu pravitel'stvennoi organizatsii po ustroistvu bezhentsev Iugo-Zapadnago fronta, Kniaziu Urusovu," DAKO 445/1/356/3.

37. Cited in Goldin, *Russkaia armia i evrei*, 117. Also see "Dokladnaia zapiska KOPE," DAKO 445/1/356/3–6.

38. "Russia's Expulsion of Jews," *New York Times*, August 15, 1915.

CHAPTER 2: THE REVOLUTIONS OF 1917

1. Arnold Margolin, *Ukraina i politika Antanty zapiski evreia i grazhdanina* (Berlin: Izdatel'stvo S. Efron, 1922), 48.

2. Margolin, *Ukraina i politika Antanty*, 42.

3. See Roy Tomlin, "Celebrating the Romanov Tercentenary with Fabergé Imperial Presentation Gifts: A Review," http://www.fabergeresearch.com/downloads/fabfall2012featurestory.pdf.

4. Cecil L'Estrange Malone, *The Russian Republic* (New York: Harcourt, Brace and Howe, 1920), 15.

5. Margolin, *Ukraina i politika Antanty*, 42.

6. Orlando Figes, "'Down with the Jew Kerensky!,'" *Jewish Quarterly* 45, no. 2 (January 1, 1998): 5–11. Notably the *Dearborn Independent*'s "International Jew," published in the United States under Henry Ford's direction, also repeated the canard that Kerensky was Jewish. *The International Jew, the World's Foremost Problem, Being a Reprint of a Series of Articles Appearing in The "Dearborn Independent" from May 22 to October 2, 1920*, vol. 1 (Dearborn, MI: Dearborn Publishing Company, 1920), 214.

7. Margolin, *Ukraina i politika Antanty*, 13.

8. Victoria Khiterer, "Arnold Davidovich Margolin: Ukrainian-Jewish Jurist, Statesman and Diplomat," *Revolutionary Russia* 18, no. 2 (December 1, 2005): 145–67.

9. Margolin, *Ukraina i politika Antanty*, 128.

10. Rosa Luxemburg, *The Russian Revolution and Leninism or Marxism?* (Ann Arbor: University of Michigan Press, 1961), 54.

11. Serhii Plokhy, *The Gates of Europe: A History of Ukraine* (New York: Basic Books, 2015), 201–7.

12. Abraham Revusky, *In di shvere teg oyf Ukrayne: zikhroynes fun a Yidishn minister* (Berlin: Yidisher literarisher farlag, 1924), 43.

13. Shmuel Rubinshteyn, *Tsivshn fayer un shverd: bletlekh zikhroynes vegn birger-krig in Ukrayne, 1918–1920* (Warsaw: Emes, 1924), 31.

14. "A la cour d'assises," YIVO 80/432/37257.

15. Revutsky, *In di shvere teg oyf Ukrayne*, 281.

16. "Petlura and the Poles," *Times* (London), October 14, 1919.

17. For more on Petliura see Sergei Shumov, *Petliurovshchina* (Moscow: Eksmo, 2005); and M. Popovicha and V. Mironenko, eds., *Glavnyi ataman: v plenu nesbytochnyx nadezhd* (Moscow and St. Petersburg: Letnii sad, 2008). On his treatment of the Jews see Volodymyr Serhiychuk, *Symon Petliura and the Jewry* (Kyiv: Iunivers, 2000); Taras Hunczak, *Symon Petliura and the Jews: A Reappraisal*, updated and rev. ed. (Lviv: Ukrainian Historical Association, 2008); Zosa Szajkowski, "'A Reappraisal of Symon Petliura and Ukrainian-Jewish Relations, 1917–1921': A Rebuttal," *Jewish Social Studies* 31, no. 3 (1969): 184–213; Serhii Iekelchyk, "Trahichna storinka Ukraïns'koï revoliutsii: Symon Petliura ta Ievreis'ki pogrom v Ukraini (1917–1920)," in Vasyl Mykhal'chuk, ed., *Symon Petliura ta ukraïns'ka natsional'na revoliutsiia* (Kyiv: Rada, 1995), 165–217; Christopher Gilley, "Beyond Petliura: The Ukrainian National Movement and the 1919 Pogroms," *East European Jewish Affairs* 47, no. 1 (2017): 45–61; and Christopher Gilley, "Beat the Jews, Save . . . Ukraine: Antisemitic Violence and Ukrainian State-Building Projects, 1918–1920," in Elissa Bemporad and Thomas Chopard, eds., "The Pogroms of the Russian Civil War at 100:

New Trends, New Sources," *Quest. Issues in Contemporary Jewish History*, no. 15 (August 2019).

18. "A la cour d'assises," YIVO 80/432/37258.

19. Oleksander Udovychenko, *Ukraina u viini za derzhavnist': istoriia orhanizatsii i boiovykh dii Ukkrains'kykh zbroinykh syl, 1917–1921* (Winnipeg: D. Mykytiuk, 1954).

20. Mikhail Bulgakov, *White Guard*, trans. Marian Schwartz (New Haven, CT: Yale University Press, 2008), 77.

21. Leon Trotsky, *History of the Russian Revolution*, trans. Max Eastman, vol. 3 (London: Sphere Books, 1967), 45.

22. Cited in Solomon Goldelman, *Jewish National Autonomy in Ukraine, 1917–1920* (Chicago: Ukrainian Research and Information Institute, 1968), 29; originally in Volodymyr Vynnychenko, *Vidrodzhennia natsii,* vol. 1 (Kyiv: Dzvin, 1920), 295. See also Vynnychenko's speech of December 16, 1917, in the Rada as recorded in "O natsional'nykh men'shinstvakh," CAHJP P10a/3/S1/3.

23. Revutsky, *In di shvere teg oyf Ukrayne,* 15.

24. There is significant variation in estimates for the number of displaced people during the war. See Peter Gatrell, *A Whole Empire Walking: Refugees in Russia During World War I* (Bloomington: Indiana University Press, 1999), 211–15; and Irina Berlova, *Vynuzhdennye migranty: bezhentsy i voennoplennye Pervoi mirovoi voiny v Rossii, 1914–1925* (Moscow: Airo, 2014), 39–47.

25. "Khroniki revoliutsionnykh sobytii na Volyne za 1917–1921," DAZhO 1/1/118/32b.

26. A. E. Shiller, "An Officer's Experience with Bolshevism," *Current History* 10, no. 2 (September 1, 1919): 514.

27. "Khroniki revoliutsionnykh sobytii na Volyne za 1917–1921," DAZhO 1/1/118/20–35.

28. Ronald Grigor Suny, "Toward a Social History of the October Revolution," *American Historical Review* 88, no. 1 (February 1983): 31–52; Laura Engelstein, *Russia in Flames: War, Revolution, Civil War, 1914–1921* (Oxford: Oxford University Press, 2018), 177–97; and Alexander Rabinowitch, *The Bolsheviks Come to Power: The Revolution of 1917 in Petrograd*, 1st ed. (New York: W. W. Norton, 1976).

29. Taras Hunczak, *The Ukraine, 1917–1921: A Study in Revolution* (Cambridge, MA: Harvard University Press, 1927), 387–91; and Paul Robert Magosci, *A History of Ukraine: The Land and Its Peoples*, 2nd ed. (Toronto: University of Toronto Press, 2010), 509–10.

30. I. Stalin, "Chto takoe ukrainskaia rada," in *Sochineniia*, vol. 4 (Stanford, CA: Hoover Institution on War, Revolution, and Peace, Stanford University, 1967). Originally published in *Pravda*, December 15, 1917.

31. There is dispute over the exact number of delegates that appeared for the

assembly and which parties they represented. For more on results of the elections see Oliver H. Radkey, *Russia Goes to the Polls: The Election to the All-Russian Constituent Assembly, 1917* (Ithaca: Cornell University Press, 1990), 23; and O. N. Znamenskii, *Vserossiiskoe uchreditel'noe sobranie* (Leningrad: Nauka, 1976), 338–39.

32. Arnold Margolin, *From a Political Diary: Russia, the Ukraine, and America, 1905–1945* (New York: Columbia University Press, 1946), 18.
33. Leon Trotsky, *Lenin: Notes for a Biographer* (New York: Capricorn Books, 1971), 113.
34. Vynnychenko, *Vidrodzhennia natsii*, vol. 2, 137–38.

CHAPTER 3: THE CENTRAL RADA OF UKRAINE

1. Arnold Margolin, *From a Political Diary: Russia, the Ukraine, and America, 1905–1945* (New York: Columbia University Press, 1946), 29.
2. Margolin, *From a Political Diary*, 31.
3. Henry Abramson, *A Prayer for the Government: Ukrainians and Jews in Revolutionary Times, 1917–1920* (Cambridge, MA: Harvard University Press, 1999).
4. "The first interpellation concerning pogroms," YIVO 80/440/37597.
5. Taras Vintskovs'kyi and V. M. Khmars'kyi, *Chornomors'ka khvyia Ukraïns'koï revoliutsii: providnyky natsional'noho rukhu v Odesi u 1917–1920 rr.* (Odesa: Odes'kyi natsional'nyi universytet imeni I.I. Mechnykova, 2011).
6. Lidia B. Miliakova, ed., *Kniga pogromov: Pogromy na Ukraine, v Belorussii i evropeiskoi chasti Rossii v period grazhdanskoi voiny, 1918–1922 gg. Sbornik dokumentov* (Moscow: Rosspen, 2007), 5–6.
7. "Prikaz No. 5 o 1-mu Evreiskomu Pekhotnomu Batal'onu," February 17, 1918, TsDAVO 1688/1/1/6.
8. "Idishe oytonomie in Rusland," *Der tog*, December 5, 1917.
9. *Evreiskaia nedelia*, no. 1–2 (January 18, 1918), 23–25.
10. Volodymyr Vynnychenko, *Vidrodzhennia natsii*, vol. 1 (Kyiv: Dzvin, 1920), 297.
11. Cited in Elias Tsherikover, *Antisemitizm un pogromen in Ukrayne 1917–1918* (Berlin: Mizrekh-yidishn historishn arkhiv, 1923), 67.
12. Ottokar Theobald Otto Maria Czernin von und zu Chudenitz, *In the World War* (New York: Cassell, 1919), 226. For more on the negotiations see Włodzimierz Mędrzecki, "Germany and Ukraine Between the Start of the Brest-Litovsk Peace Talks and Hetman Skoropads'kyi's Coup," *Harvard Ukrainian Studies* 23, no. 1/2 (June 1999): 47–71.
13. Czernin, *In the World War*, 216.
14. Czernin, *In the World War*, 220.
15. Czernin, *In the World War*, 221.
16. William Hard, *Raymond Robins' Own Story* (New York: Harper & Brothers, 1920), 125.

17. Andrei Lobanov-Rostovsky, *The Grinding Mill: Reminiscences of War and Revolution in Russia, 1913–1920* (New York: Macmillan, 1935), 323.

18. Czernin, *In the World War*, 231.

19. Czernin, *In the World War*, 231–32.

20. Leon Trotsky, *My Life: An Attempt at an Autobiography* (New York: C. Scribner's Sons, 1930), 365.

21. Czernin, *In the World War*, 234–35.

22. "Zasedanie maloi rady," *Kievskaia Mysl'*, April 18, 1918.

23. Committee of the Jewish Delegations, *The Pogroms in the Ukraine Under the Ukrainian Governments (1917–1920): Historical Survey with Documents and Photographs* (London: John Bale, Sons & Danielsson, 1927), 126.

24. Committee of the Jewish Delegations, *The Pogroms in the Ukraine*, 126.

25. Elias Tsherikover, *Di ukrayner pogromen in yor 1919* (New York: YIVO, 1966), 116. See also Miliakova, *Kniga pogromov*, 119–54.

26. "Bolshevistskie pogromi," YIVO 80/195/16921; and Tsherikover, *Antisemitizm un pogromen*, 275–91.

27. "Bolshevistskie pogromi," YIVO 80/195/16922, "Dokladnaia zapiska Soveta Kievskoi evreiskoi obshchiny k ministru vnutrennykh del Ukrainskoi derzhavy," YIVO 80/32/2881–2881. For more on the Hlukhiv events and the presence of antisemitism within the Bolshevik military ranks see Brendan McGeever, *Antisemitism and the Russian Revolution* (Cambridge: Cambridge University Press, 2019).

28. McGeever, *Antisemitism and the Russian Revolution*, 53–87.

29. Tsherikover, *Antisemitizm un pogromen*, 74–75.

30. V. Savchenko, *Dvenadtsat' voin za Ukrainu* (Kharkiv: Folio, 2005), 55.

31. Victoria Khiterer, *Jewish Pogroms in Kiev During the Russian Civil War, 1918–1920* (Lewiston, NY: Edwin Mellen Press, 2015), 17–18; and "Les pogroms antijuifs en Ukraine en 1917–1920 et le role de Petlioura," CAHJP P10a/1-S1-2, 3.

32. A. E. Shiller, "An Officer's Experience with Bolshevism," *Current History* 10, no. 2 (September 1, 1919): 515.

33. *Proceedings of the Brest-Litovsk Peace Conference: The Peace Negotiations Between Russia and the Central Powers* (Wilmington, DE: Scholarly Resources, 1974), 136.

34. *Proceedings of the Brest-Litovsk Peace Conference*, 138–39.

35. *Proceedings of the Brest-Litovsk Peace Conference*, 158.

36. Cited in Mędrzecki, "Germany and Ukraine," 50.

37. Cited in Mędrzecki, "Germany and Ukraine," 52.

38. Cited in Mędrzecki, "Germany and Ukraine," 51. See also Xenia Joukoff Eudin, "The German Occupation of the Ukraine in 1918," *Russian Review* 1, no. 1 (1941): 90–105; and Henry Cord Meyer, "Germans in the Ukraine, 1918: Excerpts from Unpublished Letters," *American Slavic and East European Review* 9, no. 2 (1950): 105–15. For more on the German occupation see Frank Grelka, *Die Ukrainische Nationalbewegung unter deutscher*

Besatzungsherrschaft 1918 und 1941/1942 (Wiesbaden: Harrassowitz Verlag, 2005).

39. Trotsky, *My Life*, 377.
40. Trotsky, *My Life*, 390. For the details of the treaty see Borislav Chernev, *Twilight of Empire: The Brest-Litovsk Conference and the Remaking of East-Central Europe, 1917–1918* (Toronto: University of Toronto Press, 2017), 212–20; and Irina Mikhutina, *Ukrainskii Brestskii mir* (Moscow: Evropa, 2017).

CHAPTER 4: FROM THE HETMANATE TO THE DIRECTORY

1. "Russian Sugar Notes," *International Sugar Journal* 15 (April 1913): 159–60; "The Sugar Situation in Europe," *Sugar* 18 (1916): 256–59; and "Russia," *Sugar* 18 (1916): 526.
2. Larysa Bilous, "Jews in Wartime Urban Space: Ethnic Mobilization and the Formation of a New Community in Kyiv, 1914–1918" (PhD diss., University of Alberta, 2018), 136.
3. James Bunyan, *Intervention, Civil War, and Communism in Russia, April–December, 1918: Documents and Materials* (Baltimore: Johns Hopkins Press, 1936), 7–8.
4. Cited in Włodzimierz Mędrzecki, "Germany and Ukraine Between the Start of the Brest-Litovsk Peace Talks and Hetman Skoropads'kyi's Coup," *Harvard Ukrainian Studies* 23, no. 1/2 (June 1999): 53.
5. Mędrzecki, "Germany and Ukraine," 9–13.
6. Pavlo Petrovych Skoropads'kyj, *Erinnerungen: 1917 bis 1918* (Stuttgart: F. Steiner, 1999), 168.
7. Skoropads'kyj, *Erinnerungen*, 168.
8. Skoropads'kyj, *Erinnerungen*, 85.
9. Translation adapted from Bunyan, *Intervention, Civil War, and Communism in Russia*, 16–17.
10. Cited in Henry Cord Meyer, "Germans in the Ukraine, 1918: Excerpts from Unpublished Letters," *American Slavic and East European Review* 9, no. 2 (1950): 108.
11. Elias Tsherikover, *Antisemitizm un pogromen in Ukrayne 1917–1918* (Berlin: Mizrekh-yidishn historishn arkhiv, 1923), 160; notice issued by German District Commander Colonel Nickisch von Roseneck, July 18, 1918, translation from CAHJP P10a/1/S2/8.
12. Command of the Imperial and Royal Cavalry Brigade, "Influence of Jewry on the Men," August 25, 1918. Translation from CAHJP P10a/1/S2/9.
13. Tsherikover, *Antisemitizm un pogromen*, 163.
14. George Katkov," The Assassination of Count Mirbach," in David Footman, ed., *Soviet Affairs*, vol. 3 (London: Chatto & Windus, 1962), 53–93; Lutz Hafner, "The Assassination of Count Mirbach and the 'July Uprising' of the Left Socialist Revolutionaries in Moscow, 1918," *Russian Review*

50, no. 3 (July 1991): 328–44; and Yuri Felshtinsky, *Lenin and His Comrades: The Bolsheviks Take Over Russia, 1917–1924* (New York: Enigma Books, 2010), 105–8.

15. "Protokol Eliasberg, Efim," June 20, 1919, YIVO 80/199/17516; and "Zakliuchenie sledstvennoi kommissii po delu o pervom i vtorom pogromakh v gorode Zhitomire," YIVO 80/200/17689. See also "Khroniki revoliutsionnykh sobytii na Volyne za 1917–1921," DAZhO 1/1/118/42.

16. Tsherikover, *Antisemitizm un pogromen*, 275–77.

17. The Cheka was originally created as the Extraordinary Commission for Combating Counterrevolution and Sabotage, but its name was changed in 1918.

18. Cited in Bunyan, *Intervention, Civil War, and Communism in Russia*, 227.

19. Cited in Bunyan, *Intervention, Civil War, and Communism in Russia*, 238.

20. Martyn Latsis quoted in Bunyan, *Intervention, Civil War, and Communism in Russia*, 261.

21. Sergey Petrovich Melgounov, *The Red Terror in Russia* (London: J. M. Dent & Sons, 1925), 77. See also I. S. Ratkovskii, *Krasnyi terror i deiatel'nost' V'CHK v 1918 godu* (St. Petersburg: St. Petersburg University Press, 2006); A. S. Velidov, *Krasnaia kniga VChK* (Moscow: Politicheskaia literatura, 1989); and James Ryan, "The Sacralization of Violence: Bolshevik Justifications for Violence and Terror During the Civil War," *Slavic Review* 74, no. 4 (2015): 808–31.

22. Orlando Figes, *A People's Tragedy: A History of the Russian Revolution* (New York: Viking, 1996), 534.

23. Christy Jean Story, "In a Court of Law: The Revolutionary Tribunals in the Russian Civil War, 1917–1921" (PhD diss., University of California–Santa Cruz, 1998), 145; Matthew Rendle, "Revolutionary Tribunals and the Origins of Terror in Early Soviet Russia," *Historical Research* 84, no. 226 (November 2011): 693–721; Matthew Rendle, "The Battle for Spaces and Places in Russia's Civil War: Revolutionary Tribunals and State Power, 1917–1922," *Historical Research* 90, no. 247 (February 2017): 101–16; and Matthew Rendle, "Quantifying Counter-Revolution: Legal Statistics and Revolutionary Justice During Russia's Civil War, 1917–1922," *Europe-Asia Studies* 68, no. 10 (December 2016): 1672–92.

24. Rendle, "Quantifying Counter-Revolution," 1683.

25. Joseph Schechtman, *Pogromy dobrovol'cheskoi armii na Ukraine* (Berlin: Ostjüdisches historisches archiv, 1932), 282–83.

26. John Ernest Hodgson, *With Denikin's Armies: Being a Description of the Cossack Counter-Revolution in South Russia, 1918–1920* (London: Temple Bar Publishing, 1932), 55.

27. Solomon Goldelman, *Jewish National Autonomy in Ukraine, 1917–1920* (Chicago: Ukrainian Research and Information Institute, 1968), 33.

28. *American Jewish Chronicle*, September 21, 1917, 522.

29. "Mirovaia revoliutsiia nachalas'!" *Pravda*, November 1, 1918.

30. "Vsia severnaia Germaniia—v rukakh vosstavshikh rabochikh, matrosov

i soldat. Vo vsekh gorodakh—Sovety rabochikh soldatskikh deputatov. Korona Vil'gel'ma upala v griaz'. Eto—chetvertaia po schetu!" *Pravda*, November 10, 1918.

31. Adolf Hitler, *Mein Kampf*, trans. Ralph Manheim (Boston: Houghton Mifflin, 1943), 202–3. For a recent analysis questioning this narrative see Thomas Weber, *Becoming Hitler: The Making of a Nazi* (New York: Basic Books, 2017).

32. Joseph V. Fuller, ed., *Papers Relating to the Foreign Relations of the United States, the Paris Peace Conference, 1919*, vol. 2 (Washington, DC: Government Printing Office, 1944), 136.

33. Mikhail Bulgakov, *Notes on the Cuff and Other Stories*, trans. Alison Rice (Ann Arbor, MI: Ardis, 1991), 209.

34. John S. Reshetar Jr., *The Ukrainian Revolution, 1917–1920: A Study in Nationalism* (Princeton, NJ: Princeton University Press, 1952), 147. See also Skoropads'kyj, *Erinnerungen*, 356–57.

35. Markian Prokopovych, *Habsburg Lemberg: Architecture, Public Space, and Politics in the Galician Capital, 1772–1914* (West Lafayette, IN: Purdue University Press, 2009); and Christoph Mick, *Lemberg, Lwów, L'viv, 1914–1947: Violence and Ethnicity in a Contested City* (West Lafayette, IN: Purdue University Press, 2015), 1–16.

36. Cited in Mick, *Lemberg, Lwów, L'viv*, 144–45.

37. Mission of the United States to Poland, S. Doc. No. 177, at 5 (1920).

38. For more details on the events in the city see Mick, *Lemberg, Lwów, Lviv*, 137–74; William W. Hagen, *Anti-Jewish Violence in Poland, 1914–1920* (New York: Cambridge University Press, 2018), 148–72; Zbigniew Zaporowski, "Ofiary rozruchów i rabunków we Lwowie 22–24 listopada 1918 roku w świetle ustaleń Lwowskiej Dyrekcji Policji," *Pamięć i sprawiedliwość* 1, no. 31 (2018): 465–70; and Zbigniew Zaporowski, "Wokół wydarzen we Lwowie 22–24 listopada 1918 roku," *Pamięć i sprawiedliwość* 1, no. 33 (2019): 270–81.

39. Israel Cohen, *A Report on the Pogroms in Poland* (London: Central Office of the Zionist Organization, 1919), 27.

40. Cited in Hagen, *Anti-Jewish Violence in Poland*, 161. See also Leonid Kondratiuk, "The Ukrainian-Galician Army in the Ukrainian-Polish War, 1918–1919" (master's thesis, Kansas State University, 1979).

41. Cited in Mick, *Lemberg, Lwów, L'viv*, 160.

42. Cited in Hagen, *Anti-Jewish Violence in Poland*, 166.

43. "A Record of Pogroms in Poland," *New York Times*, June 1, 1919; "Di pogrom shkhites in Lemberg geshildert fun eydes far der idisher kamisie fun Varshoy," *Di varhayt*, February 15, 1919. See also David Engel, "Lwów, 1918: The Transmutation of a Symbol and Its Legacy in the Holocaust," in Joshua D. Zimmerman, ed., *Contested Memories: Poles and Jews During the Holocaust and Its Aftermath* (New Brunswick: Rutgers University Press, 2002) 32–44. The Morgenthau report cited a death toll of sixty-four Jews.

44. Cited in Mick, *Lemberg, Lwów, L'viv*, 162.
45. Cited in Mick, *Lemberg, Lwów, L'viv*, 159.
46. Cohen, *Pogroms in Poland*, 33.
47. Hagen, *Anti-Jewish Violence in Poland*, 124.
48. *Neue jüdische Monatshefte* 3, no. 3–5 (1918–1919), 111.
49. Joseph V. Fuller, *Foreign Relations of the United States, Paris Peace Conference*, vol. 2, 121.
50. Joseph V. Fuller, *Foreign Relations of the United States, Paris Peace Conference*, vol. 2, 413.
51. Joseph V. Fuller, *Foreign Relations of the United States, Paris Peace Conference*, vol. 2, 419.
52. Mikhail Bulgakov, *White Guard*, trans. Marian Schwartz (New Haven, CT: Yale University Press, 2008), 76.
53. Stephen Velychenko, *State Building in Revolutionary Ukraine: A Comparative Study of Governments and Bureaucrats, 1917–1922* (Toronto: University of Toronto Press, 2011), 147.
54. Ilya Ehrenburg, *First Years of Revolution, 1918–1921* (London: MacGibbon & Kee, 1962), 80.
55. "Tsu der direktorie fun der ukrayner folksrepublik," December 19, 1918, YIVO 80/453/38180.
56. "Fun ministerium far idishe inyonim," *Naye tsayt*, January 29, 1919, in TsDAVO 3304/1/7/18.
57. Arnold Margolin, *From a Political Diary: Russia, the Ukraine, and America, 1905–1945* (New York: Columbia University Press, 1946), 34–35.
58. Margolin, *From a Political Diary*, 36.

CHAPTER 5: THE OVRUCH POGROM

1. William E. Gill, "The Russian-American Hide and Leather Trade," *Russia: A Journal of Russian-American Trade* 1, no. 4 (August 1916): 11–18.
2. Pavlo Shandruk, *Arms of Valor* (New York: R. Speller, 1959), 63.
3. Interview with Veniamin Leybovich Feldman, May 24, 2003, Ovruch, Ukraine, AHEYM, MDV 624.
4. For a list of the names of fifty-eight victims see "Di reshime fun gehargete in ovrutsher pogrom," DAKO FR-R-3050/1/268/6. Hillerson's report cites eighty victims. Hillerson's report on the Ovruch pogrom is available as "Doklad upolnomochennago A. I. Gillersona," R-3050/ 1/225/1–9 and YIVO 80/177/15295–15303. A published version is also available in Lidia B. Miliakova, ed., *Kniga pogromov: Pogromy na Ukraine, v Belorussii i evropeiskoi chasti Rossii v period grazhdanskoi voiny, 1918–1922 gg. Sbornik dokumentov* (Moscow: Rosspen, 2007), 32–44; and an English translation can be found in Elias Heifetz, *The Slaughter of the Jews in the Ukraine in 1919* (New York: Thomas Seltzer, 1921). Subsequent citations are from the YIVO copy.

5. N. Gergel, "The Pogroms in the Ukraine in 1918–21," *YIVO Annual of Jewish Social Science* 6 (1951): 240.

6. Evreiskoe Statisticheskoe Obshchestvo, *Evreiskoe naselenie Rossii po dannym perepisi 1897 g i po noveishim istochnikam* (Petrograd: Kadima, 1917), 17.

7. John Martin Crawford, ed., *The Industries of Russia: Manufactures and Trade*, vol. 1 (St. Petersburg: Department of Agriculture Ministry of Crown Domains, 1893), 80–104.

8. N. A. Trointskii, ed., *Pervaia vseobshchaia perepis' naseleniia Rossiiskoi Imperii, 1897 g*, vol. 8 (St. Petersburg: Tsentral'nyi statisticheskii komitet MVD, 1899–1907), 83–84. Jews represented less than 10 percent of the rural population at the turn of the century.

9. "Doklad upolnomochennago S. S. Kagana. Ovruch-Korosten," YIVO 80/177/15306.

10. "Doklad upolnomochennago S. S. Kagana," YIVO 80/177/15307.

11. "Doklad upolnomochennago S. S. Kagana," YIVO 80/177/15308.

12. "Panu golovi direktorii ukrainskoi narodnoi respubliki," TsDAVO 1429/1/21/2.

13. For more on Kozyr-Zirka see Iaroslav Tynchenko, *Ofitsers'kyi korpus armii Ukrains'koi Narodnoi Respubliky, 1917–1921* (Kyiv: Tempora, 2007), 206–7.

14. "Doklad upolnomochennago A. I. Gillersona," YIVO 80/177/15296.

15. "Kozyr Zirka," TsDAVO 4011/2/5/44–45.

16. "Doklad upolnomochennago S. S. Kagana," YIVO 80/177/15307.

17. "Doklad upolnomochennago A. I. Gillersona," YIVO 80/177/15296.

18. "Tsu di geshehenishn in Ovrutsh," YIVO 80/177/15316.

19. "Doklad upolnomochennago A. I. Gillersona," YIVO 80/177/15296.

20. "Doklad upolnomochennago S. S. Kagana," YIVO 80/177/15307–15309.

21. This detail of the railway track comes from the Red Cross report at JDC Archives, Records of the New York Office of the American Jewish Joint Distribution Committee, 1919–1921, folder 256.2.

22. "Doklad upolnomochennago A. I. Gillersona," YIVO 80/177/15297.

23. "Toyzende iden oysgekoylet in Ukrayne," *Der morgen zhurnal*, April 7, 1919.

24. "Obrashcheniia vseukrainskogo tsentral'nogo komitet pomoshchi evreis-komu naseleniiu," DAKO 445/4/8/13–14.

25. For a study of rape during the pogroms see Irina Astashkevich, *Gendered Violence: Jewish Women in the Pogroms of 1917 to 1921* (Boston: Academic Studies Press, 2018).

26. "Doklad upolnomochennago A. I. Gillersona," YIVO 80/177/15298.

27. "Doklad upolnomochennago A. I. Gillersona," YIVO 80/177/15299.

28. "Sobitiia v Ovruche," YIVO 80/177/15319; and "Ovruch," YIVO 80/177/15310.

29. "Obrashcheniia vseukrainskogo tsentral'nogo komitet," DAKO 445/4/8/13–14.

30. "Donesenie evreiskoi obshchina o pogrome v Ovruche," TsDAVO 3301/2/84/2.

31. See Chone Shmeruk, "*Mayufes*: A Window on Polish-Jewish Relations," *Polin: Studies in Polish Jewry* 10 (1997): 273–86; and Bret Werb, "Mayufes: A Vestige of Jewish Traditional Song in Polish Popular Entertainments," *Polish Music Journal* 6, no. 1 (Summer 2003), https://polishmusic.usc.edu /research/publications/polish-music-journal/vol6no1/majufes/.

32. Donald L. Horowitz, *The Deadly Ethnic Riot* (Berkeley: University of California Press, 2001), 114–15.

33. "Donesenie evreiskoi obshchina," TsDAVO 3301/ 2/ 84/2; and Meir Grosman, "Di masen-shkhites oyf iden in Ukraine," *Der morgen zhurnal*, October 5, 1919.

34. "Doklad upolnomochennago S. S. Kagana," YIVO 80/177/15309. See also "Donesenie evreiskoi obshchina," TsDAVO 3301/2/84/2, which counts twenty-seven killed.

35. Abraham Revusky, *In di shvere teg oyf Ukrayne: zikhroynes fun a Yidishn minister* (Berlin: Yidisher literarisher farlag, 1924), 137–38.

36. Arnold Margolin, *Ukraina i politika Antanty zapiski evreia i grazhdanina* (Berlin: Izdatel'stvo S. Efron, 1922), 125.

37. Mikhail Bulgakov, *White Guard*, trans. Marian Schwartz (New Haven, CT: Yale University Press, 2008), 58 (translation adapted).

38. "Doklad upolnomochennago A. I. Gillersona," YIVO 80/177/15302.

CHAPTER 6: THE ZHYTOMYR POGROM

1. "K pervomu pogromu v Zhitomire (material sledstvennoi komissii)," DAKO R-3050/1/127/25. For more on the situation in the city see G. L. Makhorin, *Ukrain'ska natsional'na revoliutsiia 1917–1922 rr. Ta ii perebih na Zhytomyrshchyni* (Zhytomyr: Evenok, 2017).

2. "K pervomu pogromu," DAKO R-3050/1/127/33.

3. "Khroniki revoliutsionnykh sobytii na Volyne za 1917–1921," DAZhO 1/1/118/50–51.

4. "K 1-mu zhitomirskomu pogromu," YIVO 80/199/17471.

5. "Doklad glavnokomanduiushchemu voiskom iugo-zapadnogo raiona," February 20, 1919, YIVO 80/45/3749.

6. "K pervomu pogromu," DAKO R-3050/1/127/39.

7. "K pervomu pogromu," DAKO R-3050/1/127/40.

8. "K pervomu pogromu," DAKO R-3050/1/127/41.

9. "K pervomu pogromu," DAKO R-3050/1/127/39b.

10. "K pervomu pogromu," DAKO R-3050/1/127/39 and "Khroniki revoliutsionnykh sobytii," DAZhO 1/1/118/53–54.

11. There were nine or possibly ten Jews among the forty-nine delegates who comprised the council.

12. "Khroniki revoliutsionnykh sobytii," DAZhO 1/1/118/54–54b.

13. "Protokol Bezymensky, Noyakh," February 14, 1919, YIVO 80/197/17081.

14. "Protokol Bregman, Avraam," February 14, 1919, YIVO 80/197/17082.

15. "Protokol Stakhovskii, Shlem," February 12, 1919, YIVO 80/197/17077b; and "Protokol Bregman," YIVO 80/197/17082.
16. "Protokol Bezymensky," YIVO 80/197/17081.
17. "Protokol Brusilovsky, Duvid," February 14, 1919, YIVO 80/197/17088.
18. "Protokol Bezymensky," YIVO 80/197/17081.
19. "Protokol Bregman," YIVO 80/197/17082.
20. "Protokol Bezymensky," YIVO 80/197/17081. See also "Protokol Brusilovsky," YIVO 80/19717088; "Protokol Bregman," YIVO 80/197/17082; and "Protokol Vaynshteyn, Shmul," February 16, 1919, YIVO 80/197/17094.
21. "Protokol Bregman," YIVO 80/197/17082.
22. "Protokol Brusilovsky," YIVO 80/197/17088.
23. "Protokol Brusilovsky," YIVO 80/197/17088; "Protokol Bezymensky," YIVO 80/197/17081; and "Protokol Bregman," YIVO 80/197/17082.
24. "K pervomu pogromu," DAKO R-3050/1/127/33–33b.
25. "K pervomu pogromu," DAKO R-3050/1/127/33b.
26. "Protokol Eliasberg, Efim," June 20, 1919, YIVO 80/199/17519.
27. "Zakliuchenie sledstvennoi komissii po delu o pervom i vtorom pogromakh v gorode Zhitomire," YIVO 80/200/17700.
28. "K pervomu pogromu," DAKO R-3050/1/127/30.
29. "K pervomu pogromu," DAKO R-3050/1/127/30–31.
30. "K pervomu pogromu," DAKO R-3050/1/127/13.
31. "K pervomu pogromu," DAKO R-3050/1/127/25b.
32. Committee of the Jewish Delegations, *The Pogroms in the Ukraine Under the Ukrainian Governments (1917–1920): Historical Survey with Documents and Photographs* (London: John Bale, Sons & Danielsson, 1927), 171–72.
33. "K pervomu pogromu," DAKO R-3050/1/127/42.
34. "K pervomu pogromu," DAKO R-3050/1/127/30–31.
35. Lidia B. Miliakova, ed., *Kniga pogromov: Pogromy na Ukraine, v Belorussii i evropeiskoi chasti Rossii v period grazhdanskoi voiny, 1918–1922 gg. Sbornik dokumentov* (Moscow: Rosspen, 2007), 29.
36. "Protokol Eliasberg," YIVO 80/199/17520.
37. "K pervomu pogromu," DAKO R-R-3050/1/127/34.
38. "Protokol Eliasberg," YIVO 80/200/17767.
39. "Protokol Shulkhin, Yulii," February 14, 1919, YIVO 80/197/17087.
40. "Protokol Gorlovsky, Zelman," February 9, 1919, YIVO 80/197/17058.
41. For example, "Protokol Shulkhin, Yulii," February 14, 1919, YIVO 80/197/17087.
42. "Protokol Taran, Pavel," July 1, 1919, YIVO 80/199/17515.
43. "N485 In alukraynishn idishn hilfs-komitet," YIVO 80/200/17770.
44. "Protokol R," February 11, 1919, YIVO 80/197/17068.
45. "K pervomu pogromu," DAKO R-R-3050/1/127/31b.
46. "Protokol Zamd, Elia-Aron," March 10, 1919, YIVO 80/198/17358; "Protokol Segal, Pesia," March 7, 1919, RU 80/198/17334; "Protokol Nudel,

Shama," March 10, 1919, YIVO 80/198/17359; and "Protokol Gaetsky, Hirsh," February 18, 1919, YIVO 80/199/17116.

47. "Protokol Nudel," YIVO 80/198/17359.
48. "Zakliuchenie sledstvennoi komissii," YIVO 80/200/17702.
49. "Protokol Eliasberg," YIVO 80/200/17767.
50. "Protokol Azhorskii, Kive-Khayim," February 17, 1919, YIVO 80/197/17128.
51. "The Dvórnik," *Russia: A Journal of Russian-American Trade* 1, no. 4 (August 1916): 31.
52. "Protokol Filtser, Shlem-Avrum," February 6, 1919, YIVO 80/197/17039.
53. "Protokol Melamed, Itskhok," February 4, 1919, YIVO 80/197/17033.
54. "Protokol Pressman, Shlem Pressman," February 6, 1919, YIVO 80/197/17038. See also "Protokol Kovalskii, Evsei Kovalskii," February 6, 1919, YIVO 80/197/17041.
55. "Protokol Vinkur, Moisei," February 10, 1919, YIVO 80/197/17071.
56. "K pervomu pogromu," DAKO R-3050/1/127/36–37b.
57. "Zakliuchenie o dal'neishem napravlenii dela Kharitiny Shumskoi," DAZhO 1820/5/128.
58. "Protokol Slepak, Elia-Itskhok," February 7, 1919, YIVO 80/197/17048.
59. "Zakliuchenie sledstvennoi komissii," YIVO 80/200/17750.
60. "Zakliuchenie o dal'neishem napravlenii dela po obvineniiu Georgeiia Pazdernika, Agafii Ivashchenko, Gustava Fezera i Idy Fezer," DAZhO 1820/5/136/2b.
61. "Zakliuchenie o dal'neishem napravlenii," DAZhO 1820/5/136/2b.
62. "Zakliuchenie o dal'neishem napravlenii," DAZhO 1820/5/136/2b.
63. "Zakliuchenie o dal'neishem napravlenii," DAZhO 1820/5/136/3.
64. "Zakliuchenie o dal'neishem napravlenii," DAZhO 1820/5/136/3b.
65. "Zakliuchenie o dal'neishem napravlenii," DAZhO 1820/5/136/3.
66. "Protokol Frenkel, Meyer," February 12, 1919, YIVO 80/197/17072.
67. "Protokol Feldman, Khana," March 7, 1919, YIVO 80/198/17335.
68. "Protokol Makaron, Avrum," February 10, 1919, YIVO 80/197/17063.
69. "Protokol Pressman," YIVO 80/197/17038; "Protokol Menamer, Borukh," February 11, 1919, YIVO 80/197/17066; and "Protokol Hirman, Pinkhus," February 12, 1919, YIVO 80/197/17076.
70. "Protokol Kovalsky, Evsey; Kovalsky, Alexander; and Kogan, Mikhail," February 6–8, 1919, YIVO 80/197/17042.
71. "Protokol Stakhovsky, Shlem; Stakhovsky Alexander; and Bobr, Fyodor," February 12, 1919, YIVO 80/197/17077–17078.
72. "Zakliuchenie sledstvennoi komissii," YIVO 80/200/17708.
73. "Protokol Vainshtein, Moisei," February 10, 1919, YIVO 80/197/17060; "Protokol Prokh, Mishlem-Zus," February 2, 1919, YIVO 80/197/17073; "Protokol Poliak, Dr. Gersh," February 10, 1919, YIVO 80/197/17062; "Protokol Feldman, Perets," February 11, 1919, YIVO 80/197/17070; "Protokol Lyubarsky, Nakhman," February 7, 1919, YIVO 80/197/17050.
74. "Protokol Lyubarsky," YIVO 80/197/17050.

75. "Protokol Lyubarsky," YIVO 80/197/17050b.

76. "Protokol Vaynshteyn," YIVO 80/197/17060b.

77. "Protokol Vaynshteyn," YIVO 80/197/17060; "Protokol Lerman, Pinkhos," February 10, 1919, YIVO 80/197/17064; "Protokol Korol, Aron," February 10, 1919, YIVO 80/197/17061; "Protokol Polyak, Dr. Hersh," February 10, 1919, YIVO 80/197/17062; "Protokol Feldman, Perets," February 11, 1919, YIVO 80/197/17070; "Protokol Prokh, Avrum," February 11, 1919, YIVO 80/197/17069; "Protokol Prokh, Mishlem," February 11, 1919, YIVO 80/197/17073; "Protokol Vaynshtayn, Pen," February n.d., 1919, YIVO 80/197/17075; "Protokol Tartakovsky, Grigory," February 13, 1919, YIVO 80/197/17079; and "Protokol Lyubarsky," YIVO 80/197/17050.

78. "Protokol Kashuk, Shmul," February 10, 1919, YIVO 80/197/17059.

79. "Khroniki revoliutsionnykh sobytii na Volyne za 1917–1921," DAZhO 1/1/118/113–114.

80. The official report by the committee of inquiry counted fifty-three fatalities. The provincial governor, however, estimated the death toll at ninety and Eliasberg at eighty. The Zhytomyr Memorial Book names forty-eight victims, while foreign news claimed as many as two hundred. Elias Tsherikover, *Di ukrayner pogromen in yor 1919* (New York: YIVO, 1966), 85; Abraham Revusky, *In di shvere teg oyf Ukrayne: zikhroynes fun a Yidishn minister* (Berlin: Yidisher literarisher farlag, 1924), 152; "Zakliuchenie sledstvennoi komissii," YIVO 80/200/17769; *Yizkor dem ondeynken fun di Zshitomirer kdoshim* (New York: Zshitomirer fareynigten relif komi, 1921), 37–38; and "Shreklikhe shkhite oyf iden in Zshitomir," *Der morgen zhurnal*, February 11, 1919.

81. "Zakliuchenie sledstvennoi komissii," YIVO 80/200/17725–6.

82. Committee of the Jewish Delegations, *The Pogroms in the Ukraine*, 171.

83. See "How Palienko Was Punished," CAHJP P10a/1/S2/18.

84. Ilya Ehrenburg, *First Years of Revolution, 1918–1921* (London: MacGibbon & Kee, 1962), 81.

85. "In alukraynishn idishn hilfs-komitet," YIVO 80/200/17770–17774.

86. "Zhytomyr protokoly iuridicheskago biuro," YIVO 80/197–200/17030–17359.

87. "Protokol Reznik, Shulim," February 20, 1919, YIVO 80/198/17136.

88. "Protokol Vinokur, Moisei," February 10, 1919, YIVO 80/197/17071.

89. Miliakova, *Kniga pogromov*, 87.

90. "Protokol Bromshteyn, Idko," February 16, 1919, YIVO 80/197/17103b; "Zakliuchenie sledstvennoi komissii," YIVO 80/200/17711; and "Protokol Volyansky, Berko," February 10, 1919, YIVO 80/197/17048b.

91. See "Dokladnaia zapiska," YIVO 80/200/17757–17763.

92. "Protokol Moishe Toybenshlak," February 17, 1919, YIVO 80/197/17109b.

93. "Protokol Zelman Fayner," February 9, 1919, YIVO 80/197/17055.

94. Giterman statement. Also "Zakliuchenie sledstvennoi komissii," YIVO 80/200/17723.

95. "K pervomu pogromu," DAKO R-3050/1/127/26.

96. "Zakliuchenie sledstvennoi komissii," YIVO 80/200/17711–17712.

97. "Zakliuchenie sledstvennoi komissii," YIVO 80/200/17727–9. See also Revusky, *In di shvere teg oyf Ukrayne*, 270–72; I. Giterman, "Istoriia odnogo soveshchania o pogrome," CAHJP P10a/3/S1/6; and Committee of the Jewish Delegations, *The Pogroms in the Ukraine*, 172–76.

98. Gustave Le Bon, *The Crowd: A Study of the Popular Mind* (London: T. F. Unwin, 1926), 29–30.

99. Sigmund Freud, *Group Psychology and the Analysis of the Ego* (New York: Boni & Liveright, 1922), 10.

100. Mark Granovetter, "Threshold Models of Collective Behavior," *American Journal of Sociology* 83, no. 6 (May 1978): 1422.

101. Donald L. Horowitz, *The Deadly Ethnic Riot* (Berkeley: University of California Press, 2001), 58.

102. Revutsky, *In di shvere teg oyf Ukrayne*, 150.

CHAPTER 7: THE PROSKURIV POGROM

1. For more on the Proskuriv pogrom see the Hillerson report in Lidia B. Miliakova, ed., *Kniga pogromov: Pogromy na Ukraine, v Belorussii i evropeiskoi chasti Rossii v period grazhdanskoi voiny, 1918–1922 gg. Sbornik dokumentov* (Moscow: Rosspen, 2007), 47–65; and in English translation in Elias Heifetz, *The Slaughter of the Jews in the Ukraine in 1919* (New York: Thomas Seltzer, 1921), 202–27; Zvi Zektser (Hirsch Zekcer), "Mertvyi gorod," YIVO 80/34342–34389; and *Khurbn Proskurov: tsum ondenken fun di heylige neshomes, vos zaynen umgekumen in der shreklikher shkhite* (New York: Levant, 1923 or 1924). See also the analysis in Elias Tsherikover, *Di ukrayner pogromen in yor 1919* (New York: YIVO, 1966), 114–64.

2. V. Lukin, ed., *100 evreiskikh mestechek Ukrainy*, vol. 1 (Jerusalem: Èzro, 1998), 181.

3. Serhii Iesiunin, *Mista Podilia u druhii polovyni XIX-na pochatku XX st* (Khmelnytskyi: FOP Mel'nyk A.A., 2015), 152–54; and Leonid Zapadenko, "Gorod nachinaetsia s vokzala," http://www.sandronic.ru/e/3170626-gorod -nachinaetsya-s-vokzala.

4. Iesiunin, *Mista Podilia*, 50.

5. For some background on the city and its Jewish population, see "Report on Proskurov, Podolsk Gubernia," JDC Archives, Records of the New York Office of the American Jewish Joint Distribution Committee, 1919–1921, folder 502.

6. Zektser, "Mertvyi gorod," YIVO 80/381/34349.

7. Zektser, "Mertvyi gorod," YIVO 80/381/34350.

8. Bernard Lecache, *Quand Israël meurt* (Paris: Editions du *Progrès civique*, 1927), 220.

9. Pavlo Shandruk, *Arms of Valor* (New York: R. Speller, 1959), 69.

10. "Protokol Semosenko-Shidlovskaya, Anna," October 27, 1927, YIVO 80/404/35272–35273b.

11. *Khurbn Proskurov*, 17.

12. "Protokol No. 8 Shenkman, Lev Moiseevich," DAKO R-3050/1/237/22–23.

13. Ivan Alekseev, *Iz vospominanii levogo esera: podpol'naia rabota na Ukraine* (Moscow: Glavpolitprosvet, 1922), 32. The Zhmerynka station was actually so important that the Left SRs originally assigned their top agent, Yakov Bliumkin, to the task. But Bliumkin, who had assassinated German ambassador Wilhelm von Mirbach in 1918 and was now working under the nom de guerre Vishnevsky, was unwilling to collaborate with the Bolsheviks this time. So the party turned to Alekseev and entrusted him to replace Bliumkin and to establish a Military Revolutionary Committee.

14. See the February 9, 1919, report TsDAVO 1429/05/0018/2.

15. Alekseev, *Iz vospominanii*, 33.

16. For more details on the planning see Zektser, "Mertvyi gorod," YIVO 80/381/34359; and "Kto v deistvitel'nosti ustroil bol'shevistkoe vozstanie v proskurov nakanun pogroma," YIVO 80/381/34338–34341.

17. "Protokol No. 5 Vasserman, Simkha Abramovich," DAKO R-3050/1/237/19b.

18. "Protokol No. 18 Ioffe, Il'ia Izrailevich," DAKO R-3050/1/237/36–36b.

19. "Protokol No. 18 Ioffe," DAKO R-3050/1/237/35–37b.

20. "Protokol No. 18 Ioffe," DAKO R-3050/1/237/37b.

21. "Protokol No. 8 Shenkman," DAKO R-3050/1/237/22b.

22. "Protokol No. 8 Shenkman," DAKO R-3050/1/237/22b.

23. "Protokol No. 8 Shenkman," DAKO R-3050/1/237/22b.

24. Alekseev, *Iz vospominanii*, 34.

25. "Protokol No. 5 Vasserman, Simkha Abramovich," DAKO R-3050/1/237/20.

26. "Protokol No. 5 Vasserman," DAKO R-3050/1/237/20.

27. "Protokol No. 13 Verkhola, Trofim Fedorovich," DAKO R-3050/1/237/27–27b.

28. "Protokol No. 13 Verkhola," DAKO R-3050/1/237/27b. See also Zektser, "Mertvyi gorod," YIVO 80/381/34360–34361.

29. "Protokol No. 15 Stavinsky, Marian Ivanovich," DAKO R-3050/1/237/33–34.

30. "Akt N70 Stambulchik, Moshke," YIVO 80/366/33195.

31. "Protokol No. 16 Shpigel', Iosif Moiseevich," DAKO R-3050/1/237/34b-35.

32. "Protokol No. 13 Verkhola," DAKO R-3050/1/237/26b-28. See also Zektser, "Mertvyi gorod," YIVO 80/381/34369.

33. "Akt N 40 Nemichenitser," YIVO/80/366/33160. See also "Ochevidtsa Petliurovskikh pogromov v gor Proskurove Nemchintser Anny," YIVO 80/358/32695.

34. "Protokol No. 31 L. Baliner," DAKO R-3050/1/237/44b. See also Zektser,

"Mertvyi gorod," YIVO 80/381/34366. For a discussion of oaths and rituals before a riot see Donald L. Horowitz, *The Deadly Ethnic Riot* (Berkeley: University of California Press, 2001), 94–102.

35. "Protokol No. 8 Shenkman, Lev Moiseevich," DAKO R-3050/1/237/23b. See also Zektser, "Mertvyi gorod," YIVO 80/381/34360.

36. "Akt N43 Shapiro, Lazar Abramovich," YIVO /80/366/33163.

37. "Akt N63 Akselbandt, Muka," YIVO 80/366/33183.

38. "Akt N66 Kibrik, Shlem Shmuelevich Kibrik," YIVO 80/366/33187–33189.

39. "Akt N66 Kibrik," YIVO 80/366/33187–33188.

40. "Akt N42 Greshgorin, Sofia," YIVO 80/366/33162.

41. "Protokol No 30 E. Zemel'man," DAKO R-3050/1/237/44.

42. "Akt N78 Kozovy, Leyb Davidovich," YIVO 80/366/33208–33209. See also "Protokol No 22 Leyb Faner," DAKO R-3050/1/237/42.

43. "Akt N86 Dayter, Dayter," YIVO 80/366/33220.

44. "Akt N76 Zaydman, Iakov Pertsovich," YIVO 80/366/33206.

45. "Akt N77 Zemel'man, Gitl Davidovna," YIVO 80/366/33207.

46. "Akt N71 Baran, Khaim Iakovlevich," YIVO 80/366/33197–33198.

47. "Akt N50 Brukhis, Volf Lazarovich," YIVO 80/366/33179.

48. "Akt N64 Tenenboym, Khaim Peysakhovich," YIVO 80/366/33184.

49. "Protokol No. 1 Dom Balagura," DAKO R-3050/1/237/40.

50. "Protokol No. 39 Dom Einbinder," DAKO R-3050/1/237/46b.

51. "Protokol No. 44 Dom Kitsis," DAKO R-3050/1/237/47–47b.

52. Zektser, "Mertvyi gorod," YIVO 80/381/34367.

53. "Akt N68 Plotkin, Moyshe," YIVO 80/358/32727.

54. "Akt N79 Preysayzen, Zel'man Mordkhovich," YIVO 80/366/33210–33211.

55. "Akt N58 Kaczerowski, Appolinaria Kazimirovna," YIVO 80/381/34283.

56. For some examples see "Protokol No. 7 Dom Kupershliaka, kv Borukha Breslera," DAKO R-3050/1/237/40b; "Protokol No. 12 Dom Gershona Raizmana," DAKO R-3050/1/237/41; "Protokol No. 18 Dom Gitmana Shragi, kv Gitl Gel'fand," DAKO R-3050/1/237/41b; "Protokol No. 29 Dom Gorenshteina," DAKO R-3050/1/237/45; and "Protokol No. 28 Dom F. Berenshteina," DAKO R-3050/1/237/44–45.

57. Zektser, "Mertvyi gorod," YIVO 80/381/34378–34379.

58. "Iz materialov datskago Krasnago Kresta," DAKO R-3050/1/237/55b; and Committee of the Jewish Delegations, *The Pogroms in the Ukraine Under the Ukrainian Governments (1917–1920): Historical Survey with Documents and Photographs* (London: J. Bale & Danielsson, 1927), 190. In 1923, Boris Bogen, the director of the JDC in Moscow, was claiming that 3,500 Jews were murdered and over 800 were wounded. J. M. Kowalsky, the JDC representative for the Kyiv district, gave the figures of 2,625 men and 875 women killed and 800 men and 200 women wounded. "Report on Proskurov, Podolsk Gubernia," JDC Archives, Records of the New York Office of the American Jewish Joint Distribution Committee, 1921–1932, folder 502. Another typed list of "the murdered in Proskurov" includes

917 names (YIVO 325/30321–30351). In 1926, the rabbi of Proskurov compiled a list of 877 names. "Spisok ubitykh-pavshikh evreev vo vremia pogroma-petliurovskoi reznia," YIVO 80/398/35048–35062.

59. Abram de Swaan, *The Killing Compartments: The Mentality of Mass Murder* (New Haven, CT: Yale University Press, 2015).

60. Cited in Heifetz, *Slaughter of the Jews*, 227.

61. "Protokol No. 13 Verkhola," DAKO R-3050/1/ 237/28b.

62. Zektser, "Mertvyi gorod," YIVO 80/381/34374.

63. "Protokol No. 13 Verkhola," DAKO R-3050/1/239/28b-29.

64. "Protokol No. 13 Verkhola," DAKO R-3050/1/239/29.

65. "Protokol No. 13 Verkhola," DAKO R-3050/1/239/29b.

66. Committee of the Jewish Delegations, *The Pogroms in the Ukraine*, 188.

67. Cited in "The Lurid Trial of Petlura's Slayer," *Literary Digest*, November 19, 1927, 40–41.

68. "Protokol No. 1 'Finkel', Srul Shulimovich," DAKO R-3050/1/237/17.

69. "Kratkii svedeniia o pogromakh v Balte, Volkovitsakh, Proskurove, o polozhenii v Zhmerinke," YIVO 80/381/34381.

70. "Protokol No. 12 Salitirinik," DAKO R-3050/1/237/26b; and "Zaiavelnie Dr. Silitrinika, Avraama Iakovlevicha," YIVO 80/381/34273–34274. See also "Kratkii svedeniia o pogromakh," YIVO 80/381/34381.

71. "Qu'est devenu le complice de Semosenko dans l'organisation du pogrome de Proskourov, le Colonel J. Kivertchouk?" CAHJP P10a/4/S4/18.

72. Elias Tsherikover, ed., *In der tkufe fun revolutsie: memuarn, material, dokumentn* (Berlin: Yidisher literarisher farlag, 1924), 263.

CHAPTER 8: THE SECOND ZHYTOMYR POGROM

1. "K 1-mu zhitomirskomu pogromu: dokladnaia zapiska (proekt), sostavliennaia zaveduishchim okhranoi g. Zhitomira Abariusom dlia predstavleniia Direkotrii," YIVO 80/199/17480.

2. "Khroniki revoliutsionnykh sobytii na Volyne za 1917–1921," DAZhO 1/1/118/61–61b.

3. "Doklad holovno komanduiuchomu viis'kom pivdeno-zakhidnoho raionu," YIVO 80/199/17466b.

4. "Doklad holovno komanduiuchomu viis'kom pivdeno-zakhidnoho raionu," YIVO 80/199/17466b.

5. "Khroniki revoliutsionnykh," DAZhO 1/1/118/62.

6. "Zakliuchenie sledstvennoi komissii po delu o pervom i vtorom pogromakh v gorode Zhitomire," YIVO 80/200/17742.

7. "Zakliuchenie sledstvennoi komissii," YIVO 80/200/17745.

8. "Khroniki revoliutsionnykh," DAZhO 1/1/118/63b.

9. "Zakliuchenie sledstvennoi komissii," YIVO 80/200/17733.

10. "Zakliuchenie sledstvennoi komissii," YIVO 80/200/17733; and "Protokol Mikhail Skokovsky," July 3, 1919, DAKO R-3050/1/127/43b.

11. Committee of the Jewish Delegations, *The Pogroms in the Ukraine Under the Ukrainian Governments (1917–1920): Historical Survey with Documents and Photographs* (London: J. Bale & Danielsson, 1927), 201; and "Zakliuchenie sledstvennoi komissii," YIVO 80/200/17723.

12. "Khroniki revoliutsionnykh," DAZhO 1/1/118/65.

13. "Protokol Khasis, Duvid," April 27, 1919, YIVO 80/198/17409.

14. "Zakliuchenie sledstvennoi komissii," YIVO 80/200/17734–17735; and Lidia B. Miliakova, ed., *Kniga pogromov: Pogromy na Ukraine, v Belorussii i evropeiskoi chasti Rossii v period grazhdanskoi voiny, 1918–1922 gg. Sbornik dokumentov* (Moscow: Rosspen, 2007), 90.

15. "Zakliuchenie sledstvennoi komissii," YIVO/80/200/17735.

16. "Protokol Kaminsky, Israel," April 27, 1919, YIVO 80/198/17414. See also "Protokol Shvartsman, Yosef," April 25, 1919, YIVO 80/198/17392.

17. "K vtoromu pogromu v Zhitomire," DAKO R-3050/1/127/44.

18. "Protokol Volkis, Mikhlya," April 23, 1919, YIVO 80/198/17382.

19. "Protokol Leibman, Nekhama," April 25, 1919, YIVO 80/198/17399. See also "Protokol Lerman, Khaya," April 25, 1919, YIVO 80/198/17397.

20. "Protokol Braverman, Rivka," April 27, 1919, YIVO 80/198/17408.

21. "Protokol Goldfeld, Blyuma," April 24, 1919, YIVO 80/198/17385.

22. "Protokol Shats, Shakhno," April 27, 1919, YIVO 80/198/17418.

23. "Protokol Tsybulevskaya, Riva," April 27, 1919, YIVO 80/198/17410.

24. "Protokol Reibel, Shlomo," April 27, 1919, YIVO 80/198/17405.

25. "Telegramma golovnogo atamana UNR S. Petliury"; Miliakova, *Kniga pogromov*, 85.

26. "K vtoromu pogromu v Zhitomire," DAKO R-3050/1/127/45b.

27. "K vtoromu pogromu v Zhitomire," DAKO R-3050/1/127/44b-45.

28. Committee of the Jewish Delegations, *The Pogroms in the Ukraine*, 206; and "Zakliuchenie sledstvennoi komissii," YIVO 80/200/17740. Another list of murdered Jews in Zhytomyr between March 23 and March 26, 1919, includes the names of 305 people: "Spisok ubitykh evreev," DAKO R-3050/1/127/88–89.

29. "Zakliuchenie sledstvennoi komissii," YIVO 80/200/17750.

30. "Zakliuchenie sledstvennoi komissii," YIVO 80/200/17739.

31. "Protokol Voronitsyn, Ivan," July 1, 1919, YIVO 80/198/17489.

32. "Protokol Lyubarskii, Nakhman," February 7, 1919, YIVO 80/198/17050.

33. "K pervomu pogromu v Zhitomire," DAKO R-3050/1/127/26.

CHAPTER 9: THE ENTENTE

1. "An Interview with Dr. Arnold Margolin in 1919," TsDAVO 5235/01/0623/90.

2. "The Situation in Ukraine," The National Archives, CAB 24/73/92.

3. A. G. Shlikhter, *Chernaia kniga: sbornik statei i materialov ob interventsii antanty na Ukraine* (Ekaterynoslav: Gos. izd-vo Ukrainy, 1925), 77; Viktor

Faitel'berg-Blank, *Odessa v epokhu voin i revoliutsii: 1914–1920* (Odesa: Optimum, 2008); and P. E. Shchegolev, ed., *Frantsuzy v Odesse: iz belykh memuarov* (Leningrad: Krasnaia gazeta, 1928).

4. M. N. Ivlev, *Diktator Odessy: Zigzagi sud'by belogo generala* (Moscow: Veche, 2013), 152.

5. George A. Hill, *Dreaded Hour* (London: Cassell, 1936), 62.

6. Robin Bruce Lockhart, *Ace of Spies* (New York: Stein & Day, 1968).

7. Hill, *Dreaded Hour*, 9.

8. Andrei Lobanov-Rostovsky, *The Grinding Mill: Reminiscences of War and Revolution in Russia, 1913–1920* (New York: Macmillan, 1935), 330–31.

9. Arnold Margolin, *Ukraina i politika Antanty zapiski evreia i grazhdanina* (Berlin: Izdatel'stvo S. Efron, 1922), 168–84. See also Leonid Utesov, *Spasibo, serdtse! Vospominaniia. Vstrechi. Razdum'ia* (Moscow: VTO, 1976).

10. Laura Spinney, *Pale Rider: The Spanish Flu of 1918 and How It Changed the World* (New York: PublicAffairs, 2017), 126–35.

11. Shlikhter, *Chernaia kniga*, 120.

12. Shlikhter, *Chernaia kniga*, 125.

13. Shlikhter, *Chernaia kniga*, 355.

14. Shlikhter, *Chernaia kniga*, 358.

15. Shlikhter, *Chernaia kniga*, 362.

16. M. Kuban, cited in Elias Tsherikover, *Di ukrayner pogromen in yor 1919* (New York: YIVO, 1966), 293.

17. Cited in William Henry Chamberlin, *The Russian Revolution*, vol. 2 (New York: Macmillan, 1935), 214.

18. Lobanov-Rostovsky, *The Grinding Mill*, 333.

19. Lobanov-Rostovsky, *The Grinding Mill*, 334.

20. Ivan Alekseevich Bunin, *Cursed Days: A Diary of Revolution*, trans., intro., and notes by Thomas Gaiton Marullo (Chicago: Ivan R. Dee, 1998), 84.

21. Shlikhter, *Chernaia kniga*, 190.

22. Faitel'berg-Blank, *Odessa v epokhu voin i revoliutsii*, 164–65. See also Shlikhter, *Chernaia kniga*, 189.

23. Shlikhter, *Chernaia kniga*, 191.

24. Viktor Savchenko, *Avantiuristy grazhdanskoi voiny* (Kharkiv: Folio, 2000), 178. Iaroslav Tynchenko puts his birthplace in Verbliuzhka, Kherson Province, in Iaroslav Tynchenko, *Ofitsers'kyi korpus armii Ukrains'koi Narodnoi Respubliky, 1917–1921* (Kyiv: Tempora, 2007), 122.

25. Savchenko, *Avantiuristy grazhdanskoi voiny*, 179.

26. V. Antonov-Ovseenko, *Zapiski o grazhdanskoi voine*, vol. 3 (Moscow: gosudarstvennoe voennoe izdatel'stvo, 1932), 218–20; and Savchenko, *Avantiuristy grazhdanskoi voiny*, 181.

27. Arthur E. Adams, *Bolsheviks in the Ukraine: The Second Campaign, 1918–1919* (New Haven, CT: Yale University Press, 1963), 150, 183; and Christopher Gilley, "Fighters for Ukrainian Independence? Imposture and Identity

Among Ukrainian Warlords, 1917–22," *Historical Research* 90, no. 247 (February 1, 2017): 172–90.

28. Adams, *Bolsheviks in the Ukraine*, 158; Antonov-Ovseenko, *Zapiski o grazhdanskoi voine*, vol. 3, 218–21.

29. V. P. Butt et al., *The Russian Civil War: Documents from the Soviet Archives* (New York: St. Martin's Press, 1996), 84–85.

30. Adams, *Bolsheviks in the Ukraine*, 168–69; and Antonov-Ovseenko, *Zapiski o grazhdanskoi voine*, vol. 3, 225–29.

31. Adams, *Bolsheviks in the Ukraine*, 169.

32. Antonov-Ovseenko, *Zapiski o grazhdanskoi voine*, vol. 4, 131.

33. Adams, *Bolsheviks in the Ukraine*, 182–83.

34. Vladimir N. Brovkin, ed. and trans., *Dear Comrades: Menshevik Reports on the Bolshevik Revolution and the Civil War* (Stanford, CA: Hoover Institution Press, 1991), 168.

35. Bunin, *Cursed Days*, 91.

36. Faitel'berg-Blank, *Odessa v epokhu voin i revoliutsii*, 181.

37. Bunin, *Cursed Days*, 102–3.

38. Sergey Petrovich Melgounov, *The Red Terror in Russia* (London: J. M. Dent & Sons, 1925), 221–22.

39. Bunin, *Cursed Days*, 139.

40. Cited in Margolin, *Ukraina i politika Antanty*, 272.

41. "Die Lage Der Juden in Ukraine," TsDAVO 5235/01/624/67–91.

42. Margaret MacMillan, *Paris 1919: Six Months That Changed the World* (New York: Random House, 2001). For Jewish minority rights and international diplomacy see Carole Fink, *Defending the Rights of Others: The Great Powers, the Jews, and International Minority Protection, 1878–1938* (Cambridge: Cambridge University Press, 2004).

43. Arnold Margolin, *From a Political Diary: Russia, the Ukraine, and America, 1905–1945* (New York: Columbia University Press, 1946), 41–42.

44. *The Peace Conference, Paris, 1919: Report of the Delegation of the Jews of the British Empire on the Treaties of Versailles, Saint-German-en-Laye and Neuilly and the Annexed Minority Treaties* (London: Joint Foreign Committee of the Board of Deputies of British Jews and the Anglo-Jewish Association, 1920), 80.

45. *The Peace Conference, Paris, 1919*, 80.

46. *The Peace Conference, Paris, 1919*, 72–76.

47. Reported in "Direct News of Pogroms," *B'nai B'rith Messenger*, July 18, 1919; "84,000 iden oysgekoylet in Ukrayne in tsvey monaten," *Der morgen zhurnal*, June 10, 1919. See, for example, "Shoyderlikhe fakten vegen dem pogrom in Proskurov," *Der morgen zhurnal*, June 27, 1919.

48. "Calls Bolsheviki Enemies of Jews," *New York Times*, August 2, 1919.

49. For more on Jewish lobbying in Paris see Mark Levene, *War, Jews, and the New Europe: The Diplomacy of Lucien Wolf, 1914–1919* (Portland, OR: Littman Library of Jewish Civilization, 1992).

50. For more on Wolf see Eugene C. Black, "Lucien Wolf and the Making of Poland: Paris 1919," *Polin: Studies in Polish Jewry* 2 (1987): 5–36.

51. Jerzy Tomaszewski, "Pińsk, Saturday 5 April 1919," *Polin: Studies in Polish Jewry* 1 (1986): 227–51; Józef Lewandowski, "History and Myth: Pińsk, April 1919," *Polin: Studies in Polish Jewry* 2 (1987): 50–72; and William W. Hagen, *Anti-Jewish Violence in Poland, 1914–1920* (Cambridge: Cambridge University Press, 2018), 320–54. Accounts differ on the exact number of men executed, ranging from thirty-three to thirty-five.

52. Tomaszewski, "Pińsk, Saturday 5 April 1919," 240.

53. James Wycliffe Headlam, *A Memoir of the Paris Peace Conference, 1919*, ed. Agnes Headlam-Morley, Russell Bryant, and Anna Cienciala (London: Methuen, 1972), 85.

54. David Engel, "Lwów, 1918: The Transmutation of a Symbol and Its Legacy in the Holocaust," in Joshua D. Zimmerman, ed., *Contested Memories: Poles and Jews During the Holocaust and Its Aftermath* (New Brunswick: Rutgers University Press, 2002), 32–44.

55. Brian Porter, *When Nationalism Began to Hate: Imagining Modern Politics in Nineteenth-Century Poland* (New York: Oxford University Press, 2000); and Robert Blobaum, *Boycott! The Politics of Anti-Semitism in Poland, 1912–1914* (Washington, DC: National Council for Eurasians and East European Research, 1988).

56. David A. Taylor, "Paderewski's Piano," *Smithsonian Magazine*, March 1999, https://www.smithsonianmag.com/arts-culture/paderewskis-piano -164445847/.

57. David Hunter Miller, *My Diary at the Conference of Paris, with Documents*, vol. 1 (New York: Appeal, 1924), 270.

58. Miller, *My Diary at the Conference of Paris, with Documents*, vol. 1, 286.

59. George J. Lerski, "Dmowski, Paderewski and American Jews (A Documentary Compilation)," *Polin: Studies in Polish Jewry* 2 (1987): 112.

60. Lerski, "Dmowski, Paderewski and American Jews," 95–116.

61. "Paderewski Asks American Inquiry," *New York Times*, June 2, 1919.

62. Joseph V. Fuller, ed., *Papers Relating to the Foreign Relations of the United States, the Paris Peace Conference, 1919*, vol. 6 (Washington, DC: Government Printing Office, 1944), 536.

63. *Foreign Relations of the United States, Paris Peace Conference*, vol. 5, 393–94.

64. Mark Levene, "Britain, a British Jew, and Jewish Relations with the New Poland: The Making of the Polish Minorities Treaty of 1919," *Polin: Studies in Polish Jewry* 8 (2004): 14–41.

65. "Call on Nations to Protect Jews," *New York Times*, May 22, 1919.

66. Cited in telegram to Leo Motzkin, December 1, 1919, CAHJP P10a/1/S5/2.

67. Cited in Andrzej Kapiszewski, "Controversial Reports on the Situation of Jews in Poland in the Aftermath of World War I: The Conflict Between the US Ambassador in Warsaw Hugh Gibson and American Jewish Leaders,"

Studia Judaica: Biuletyn Polskiego Towarzystwa Studiów Żydowskich 7, no. 14 (2004): 276.

CHAPTER 10: WARLORDS

1. Volodymyr Vynnychenko, *Vidrodzhennia natsii*, vol. 3 (Kyiv: Dzvin, 1920), 293.

2. Arnold Margolin, *Ukraina i politika Antanty zapiski evreia i grazhdanina* (Berlin: Izdatel'stvo S. Efron, 1922), 125. See also B. Martos, "S. Petliura i zhydivski pogroma na Ukraini," TsDAVO 3890/1/10.

3. Margolin, *Ukraina i politika Antanty*, 186.

4. Mikhail Akulov, "War Without Fronts: Atamans and Commissars in Ukraine, 1917–1919" (PhD diss., Harvard University, 2013); Christopher Gilley, "'Otamanshchyna'? The Self-Formation of Ukrainian and Russian Warlords at the Beginning of the Twentieth and Twenty-First Centuries," *Ab Imperio* 2015, no. 3 (2015): 73–95; Christopher Gilley, "The Ukrainian Anti-Bolshevik Risings of Spring and Summer 1919: Intellectual History in a Space of Violence," *Revolutionary Russia* 27, no. 2 (2014): 109–31; and Joshua Sanborn, "The Genesis of Russian Warlordism: Violence and Governance During the First World War and the Civil War," *Contemporary European History* 19, no. 13 (August 2010): 195–213. See also the anonymous essay "Petliura et les partisans," YIVO 80/456/38282–38294, which argues that the warlord partisans were closely related to Petliura and the army of the Directory.

5. N. Gergel, "The Pogroms in the Ukraine in 1918–21," *YIVO Annual of Jewish Social Science* 6 (1951): 240.

6. From V. Antonov-Ovseenko, *Zapiski o grazhdanskoi voine*, vol. 3 (Moscow: gosudarstvennoe voennoe izdatel'stvo, 1932), 223.

7. Cited in Arthur E. Adams, *Bolsheviks in the Ukraine: The Second Campaign, 1918–1919* (New Haven, CT: Yale University Press, 1963), 291–96.

8. Trotsky to CC, May 17, 1919, in Jan M. Meijer, ed., *The Trotsky Papers,* vol.1 (The Hague: Mouton, 1964), 431.

9. *The Trotsky Papers*, 409–11; and Martin McCauley, ed., *The Russian Revolution and the Soviet State 1917–1921: Documents* (London: Macmillan, 1975), 158.

10. "Universal," YIVO 80/74/5848. For an analysis of this proclamation see Gilley, "The Ukrainian Anti-Bolshevik Risings."

11. "Universal," YIVO 80/74/5849; Viktor Savchenko, *Avantiuristy grazhdanskoi voiny* (Kharkiv: Folio, 2000), 205; and Antonov-Ovseenko, *Zapiski o grazhdanskoi voine*, vol. 4, 131.

12. See the reports in DAKO R-3050/1/162. See also Brendan McGeever, *Antisemitism and the Russian Revolution* (Cambridge: Cambridge University Press, 2019); and "Sobytiia v Elisavetgrade," CAHJP P10a/2/S1/20.

13. B. Vest, "Far'n pogrom in Tsherkas," YIVO 80/191/16556–16557.

14. B. Vest, "Far'n pogrom in Tsherkas," YIVO 80/191/16556.

15. A. Ephrussi, "Krovavyia sobytiia v Cherkassakh," YIVO 80/191/16557.

16. A. Ephrussi, "Krovavyia sobytiia v Cherkassakh," YIVO 80/191/16557b.
    See also Antonov-Ovseenko, *Zapiski o grazhdanskoi voine*, vol. 4, 227–35.

17. "Pokazaniia odnogo iz uchastnikov levago flanga," YIVO 80/191/16574. See
    also Elias Heifetz, *The Slaughter of the Jews in the Ukraine in 1919* (New
    York: Thomas Seltzer, 1921), 268; Lidia B. Miliakova, ed., *Kniga pogromov:
    Pogromy na Ukraine, v Belorussii i evropeiskoi chasti Rossii v period grazh-
    danskoi voiny, 1918–1922 gg. Sbornik dokumentov* (Moscow: Rosspen,
    2007), 140–41.

18. A. Ephrussi, "Krovavyia sobytiia v Cherkassakh," YIVO 80/191/16558.

19. A. Ephrussi, "Krovavyia sobytiia v Cherkassakh," YIVO 80/191/16558.

20. "Pokazaniia odnogo iz uchastnikov," YIVO 80/191/16574b; Heifetz, *Slaugh-
    ter of the Jews*, 268–69; and Miliakova, *Kniga pogromov*, 141.

21. "Pokazaniia odnogo iz uchastnikov," YIVO 80/191/16574b; Heifetz, *Slaugh-
    ter of the Jews*, 269; Miliakova, *Kniga pogromov*, 141–42; I. Tsifrinovich,
    "Cherkassi. Pogrom 16–20 Maia 1919. K sobrannomu materialu predislovie
    upolnomochennago krasnago kresta," July 15, 1919, YIVO 80/191/16562
    and R-3050/1/54/97–111; and I. Vernik, "Cherkasskii raion. Doklad upolo-
    mochennago tsentral'noi sektsii," YIVO 80/191/16590.

22. A. Ephrussi, "Krovavyia sobytiia v Cherkassakh," YIVO 80/191/16558b.

23. "Protokol Dubnikova, Mariam," YIVO 80/191/16567–16567b. See also
    Miliukova, *Kniga pogromov*, 146.

24. Heifetz, *Slaughter of the Jews*, 267; and "Pokazanie M. Ukrainskoi," YIVO
    80/191/16573.

25. Heifetz, *Slaughter of the Jews*, 262; and "Pokazaniia Avrama Shenderova,"
    YIVO 80/191/16569b.

26. Heifetz, *Slaughter of the Jews*, 160; and "Pokazaniia Rotmistrovskago
    Gedz'," 80/191/16568.

27. Heifetz *Slaughter of the Jews*, 159–63; and "Pokazaniia Rotmistrovskago
    Gedz'," YIVO 80/191/16568–16568b.

28. Heifetz, *Slaughter of the Jews*, 259–60; Miliakova, *Kniga pogromov*, 146;
    and "Pokazanie Mar'iam' Dubnikovoi," YIVO 80/191/16567–16567b.

29. Heifetz, *Slaughter of the Jews*, 260; and "Pokazanie Mar'iam' Dubnikovoi,"
    "Pokazanie M. Ukrainskoi," YIVO 80/191/16567–16567b.

30. "Pokazanie V. Petrova," YIVO 80/191/16564; and Heifetz, *Slaughter of the
    Jews*, 253.

31. Heifetz, *Slaughter of the Jews*, 267; "Pokazanie M. Ukrainskoi," YIVO
    80/191/16573b.

32. Elias Tsherikover, *Di ukrayner pogromen in yor 1919* (New York: YIVO,
    1966), 312–13.

33. A. Ephrussi, "Krovavyia sobytiia v Cherkassakh," YIVO 80/191/16559b.

34. "Spisok evreev ubitykh vo vremia Grigor'evskogo pogroma 16–20 Maia
    1919 g," R-3050/1/54/154–160. Another list prepared by the Joint found
    621 names, CAHJP P10a/1/S8/9.

35. Lenin to Rakovsky, May 26, 1919, in *The Trotsky Papers*, 471.

36. Leon Trotsky, "Ukrainskie uroki," *Izvestiia*, May 24, 1919.

37. Ilia Vardin, "Protiv Evreia-za tsaria," *Pravda*, May 14, 1919. See also Brendan McGeever, "Revolution and Antisemitism: the Bolsheviks in 1917," *Patterns of Prejudice* 51, no. 3–4 (2017): 235–52.

38. Ilia Vardin, "Pogromnaia 'Demokratiia,'" *Pravda*, June 12, 1919.

39. McGeever, *Antisemitism and the Russian Revolution*, 140–82.

40. M. Rafes, *Dva goda revoliutsii na Ukraine* (Moscow: Gosudarstvennoe izdatel'stvo, 1920), 162–68.

41. E. I. Melamed and G. Estraikh, "O pogrome v Berdicheve," *Arkhiv everiskoi istorii* 8 (2016): 156–76.

42. Cited in Zvi Gitelman, *Jewish Nationality and Soviet Politics: The Jewish Sections of the CPSU, 1917–1930* (Princeton, NJ: Princeton University Press, 1972), 166.

43. Cited in Gitelman, *Jewish Nationality and Soviet Politics*, 166–67.

44. Peter Arshinov, *History of the Makhnovist Movement, 1918–1921* (Detroit: Black & Red, 1974).

45. Isaac Babel, *The Complete Works of Isaac Babel*, ed. Nathalie Babel, trans. Peter Constantine (New York: W. W. Norton, 2002), 240.

46. "Pogromy Makhno," YIVO 80/29/2634–2637. See also Sean Patterson, "The Eichenfeld Massacre: Recontextualizing Mennonite and Makhnovist Narratives," *Journal of Mennonite Studies* 32 (2014): 151–74.

47. Arshinov, *History of the Makhnovist Movement*, 136.

48. "Ubiistvo Grigoreva," DAKO R-3050/2/1/1. See also Heifetz, *Slaughter of the Jews*, 72.

49. Yakov Kotliar, "Di memshole fun di brider Sokolovski," February 17, 1921, YIVO 80/31/2822.

50. Kotliar, "Di memshole," YIVO 80/31/2826.

51. "Bezhentsy iz Radomyslia," June 30, 1919 DAKO R-3050/1/50/55. For other earlier figures see Evreiskoe Statisticheskoe Obshchestvo, *Evreiskoe naselenie Rossii* (Petrograd: Kadima, 1917), 32. According to Berta Ayzengart, "Pogrom in Radomisl," YIVO 80/237/22023, there were twelve thousand Jews and eight thousand Christians, which puts the Jews at about 60 percent of the population. See also N. A. Trointskii, ed., *Pervaia vseobshchaia perepis' naseleniia Rossiiskoi Imperii, 1897 g* (St. Petersburg: Tsentral'nyi statisticheskii komitet MVD, 1899–1907), vol. 16, 85–87.

52. *Ves Iugo-zapadnyi krai 1913* (Kyiv: Iugo-Zapadnomu otdeleniiu Rossiiskoi Eksportnoi palaty, 1913), 559–64.

53. Viktor Savchenko, *Atamany kazach'ego voiska* (Moscow: Eksmo, 2006), 194, on background; and Stepan Rudnytskyi, *Ukraine: The Land and Its People: An Introduction to Its Geography* (New York: Rand McNally, 1918), 285.

54. "Protokol Avram Rafailovich Eitenzon," DAKO R-3050/1/50/52.

55. Tsherikover, *Ukrayner pogromen*, 89–90.

56. Kotliar, "Di memshole," YIVO 80/31/2822.

57. "Sokolovski, Dmitri," YIVO 80/31/2828.
58. "Radomysl'," DAKO R-3050/1/50/59b.
59. Kotliar, "Di memshole," YIVO 80/31/2823.
60. "Radomysl'," DAKO R-3050/1/50/57–59.
61. Kotliar, "Di memshole," YIVO 80/31/2823.
62. "M. Feshchenko-Chopivskyi," TsDAVO 4011/2/5/83.
63. Kotliar, "Di memshole," YIVO 80/31/2823.
64. Savchenko, *Atamany kazach'ego voiska*, 195. See also Antonov-Ovseenko, *Zapiski o grazhdanskoi voine*, vol. 3, 280.
65. "Protokol Avram Rafailovich Eitenzon," R-3050/1/50/52.
66. Ayzengart, "Pogrom in Radomisl," YIVO 80/237/22023, provides the figure of fifteen; "Khurbn bays Radomisl," YIVO 80/51/4132, claims thirty; "Sokolovski, Dmitri," YIVO 80/31/2828–2829, gives the figure of sixty; YIVO 80/248/23721–23723 gives separate lists of thirty-one, seven, and six. See also B. Kagan and B. Rabinovich, "Perepiska iz doklada o polozhenii v Radomyslskiom raione za vse vremia," R-3050/1/50/50.
67. Antonov-Ovseenko, *Zapiski o grazhdanskoi voine*, vol. 3, 276–81; "Sokolovski, Dmitri," YIVO 80/31/2830.
68. "M. Feshchenko-Chopivskyi," TsDAVO 4011/2/5/77. For more on Ungern-Sternberg's murder, see Aleksandr Pirogov, "Dvorianskoe sobranie v uezdnom gorode Radomysle," *Polissia Today*, October 12, 2017.
69. "M. Feshchenko-Chopivskyi," TsDAVO 4011/2/5/77.
70. "Khurbn bays Radomisl," YIVO 80/51/4133.
71. Estimates range from 300 (YIVO 80/237/22023), to 400 ("Svedeniia o pogromakh na territorii Ukrainy v 1918–1921 gg," TsDAVO 2497/3/188/4), to more than 500 (YIVO 80/51/4134) and even 1,100 ("Sokolovski, Dmitri," YIVO 80/31/2831). We have the names of 44 victims (YIVO 80/248/23721–23723).
72. "Khurbn bays Radomisl," YIVO 80/51/4134.
73. "Khurbn bays Radomisl," YIVO 80/51/4134.
74. "Radomisl, dertseylt fun Sheyndl Vaynshteyn," DAKO R-3050/1/50/62.
75. Kagan and Rabinovich, "Perepiska iz doklada," DAKO R-3050/1/50/50.
76. "Sokolovski, Dmitri," YIVO 80/31/2831; and Tsherikover, *Ukrayner pogromen*, 221.
77. "Sokolovski, Dmitri," YIVO 80/31/2833.
78. "Victims of the Anti-Jewish Pogromistic Wave in Ukrainia," CAHJP P10a/3/S1/16.
79. Tsherikover, *Ukrayner pogromen*, 221–22. See also Kotliar, "Di memshole," YIVO 80/31/2824.
80. Savchenko, *Atamany kazach'ego voiska*, 196; and Kotliar, "Di memshole," YIVO 80/31/2824.
81. Kotliar, "Di memshole," YIVO 80/31/2824.
82. Kotliar, "Di memshole," YIVO 80/31/2824–2825. Also see "Svedeniia o pogromakh," TsDAVO 2497/3/188/4.

83. Savchenko, *Atamany kazach'ego voiska*, 196; and Kotliar, "Di memshole," YIVO 80/31/2825.

84. Savchenko, *Atamany kazach'ego voiska*, 196.

85. *Ves Iugo-zapadnyi krai 1913*, 573–74. Population figures from Lev Zinger, *Evreiskoe naseleie SSSR* (Moscow: gosudarstvennoe sotsial'no-ekonomicheskoe izdatel'stvo, 1932), 22.

86. For more on Nat Pinkerton see Louise McReynolds, *Murder Most Russian: True Crime and Punishment in Late Imperial Russia* (Ithaca, NY: Cornell University Press, 2012), 205–30.

87. I. Braudo, "Ataman I. Struk," YIVO 80/31/2842. See also "Pol'kovnik Struk," TsDAVO 4011/2/5/65–67.

88. Savchenko, *Atamany kazach'ego voiska*, 204.

89. Braudo, "Ataman I. Struk," YIVO 80/31/2843b.

90. Heifetz, *Slaughter of the Jews*, 239.

91. Braudo, "Ataman I. Struk," YIVO 80/31/2844.

92. On Struk's photography see Anne Brennan, "Ataman Struk Has His Photograph Taken: Testimony and Portraiture in the Russian Civil War Period," in Johannes Schlegel and Brita Hansen, eds., *Challenging Evil: Time, Society and Changing Concepts of the Meaning of Evil* (Oxford: Brill, 2010), 141–47.

93. "Protokol Braginski, Lev," YIVO 80/65/5252.

94. Steven G. Marks, "The Russian Experience of Money, 1914–1924," in Murray Frame et al., eds., *Russian Culture in War and Revolution, 1914–22*, vol. 2 (Bloomington IN: Slavica Publishers, 2014), 121–48.

95. "Komendantu Podola," YIVO 80/65/5248.

96. "Ukrainskie i Russkie liudi," YIVO 80/380/34243.

97. "Malorossiiskie partizany," YIVO 80/85/6625. See also Gilley, "The Ukrainian Anti-Bolshevik Risings," 109–13.

98. Udovychenko to Struk, August 16, 1918, YIVO 80/377/34120.

99. Udovychenko to Dragomirov, August 21, 1919, YIVO 80/377/34123.

100. "Pol'kovnik Struk," TsDAVO 4011/2/5/65–67.

101. "O Struke (nekotoryia svedeniia)," YIVO 80/31/2851.

102. I. Braudo, "Ataman I. Struk," YIVO 80/31/2844; Savchenko, *Atamany kazach'ego voiska*, 205.

103. "Seliane," YIVO 80/343/31814.

104. "Seliane," YIVO 80/343/31814.

105. List of murdered Jews in pogroms, YIVO 80/245/23295–23297. See also "Vidozva do hromadian chornobyl'skoho povitu," February 10, 1919, YIVO 80/343/31811.

106. "Universal No. 1," YIVO 80/343/31826. See also copies of the other declarations in this file.

107. Heifetz, *Slaughter of the Jews*, 149–50; also Miliakova, *Kniga pogromov*, 94–95.

108. Heifetz, *Slaughter of the Jews*, 154.

109. "Victims of the Anti-Jewish Pogromistic Wave in Ukrainia," CAHJP P10a/3/ S1/16.

110. Joseph Schechtman, *Pogromy dobrovol'cheskoi armii na Ukraine* (Berlin: Ostjüdisches Historisches Archiv, 1932), 181.

111. Schechtman, *Pogromy dobrovol'cheskoi armii na Ukraine*, 182.

112. *Ves Iugo-zapadnyi krai 1913*, 467.

113. Margolin, *Ukraina i politika Antanty*, 74–95. For more on Zelenyi and Trypillya see E. Portnoy, ed., *Tripolie: Zamlbukh gevidmet dem ondeynk fun di yunge komunarn velkhe zaynen gefaln hinter Tripolie in yuni 1919-tn yor* (Kyiv: Melukhe farlag fun Ukrayne, 1925).

114. "Pro Otamana Zelennogo," YIVO 80/31/2772.

115. Savchenko, *Atamany kazach'ego voiska*, 33.

116. Savchenko, *Atamany kazach'ego voiska*, 33.

117. Savchenko, *Atamany kazach'ego voiska*, 58.

118. Cited in Tsherikover, *Ukrayner pogromen*, 257.

119. V. Fastovsky, "Di blutike shkhite hinter Tripolie," in *Tripolie: Zamlbukh*, 18.

120. Evreiskoe Statisticheskoe Obshchestvo, *Evreiskoe naselenie Rossii* (Petrograd: Kadima, 1917), 34. See also *Pervaia*, vol. 16, 110–11.

121. Leo Miller and Diana F. Miller, eds., *Sokolievka/Justingrad: A Century of Struggle and Suffering in a Ukrainian Shtetl* (New York: Loewenthal Press, 1983).

122. Miller and Miller, *Sokolievka/Justingrad*, 54.

123. "Der pogrom in Uman. Dertseylt fun inzshener Eliezer Lipovetski un Asher Koralnik," YIVO 80/188/16408.

CHAPTER 11: MONTHS AND DAYS

1. Itsik Kipnis, *Khadoshim un teg: a khronik* (Kyiv: Kooperataiver farlag kultur-lige, 1926). For more on the work see Mikhail Krutikov, "Rediscovering the Shtetl as a New Reality: David Bergelson and Itsik Kipnis," in Steven T. Katz, ed., *The Shtetl: New Evaluations* (New York: New York University Press, 2007), 211–32; Harriet Murav, "Archive of Violence: Neighbors, Strangers, and Creatures in Itsik Kipnis's 'Months and Days,'" in Elissa Bemporad and Thomas Chopard, eds., "The Pogroms of the Russian Civil War at 100: New Trends, New Sources," in *Quest. Issues in Contemporary Jewish History*, no. 15 (August 2019); and David G. Roskies, *Against the Apocalypse: Responses to Catastrophe in Modern Jewish Culture* (Syracuse, NY: Syracuse University Press, 1984), 183–85. An English translation of parts of the work can be found in David G. Roskies, ed., *The Literature of Destruction: Jewish Responses to Catastrophe* (Philadelphia: Jewish Publication Society, 1988), 323–55.

2. Kipnis, *Khadoshim un teg*, 42. In Itsik Kipnis, *Mayn shtetl Sloveshno*, vol. 1 (Tel Aviv: Farlag I. L. Perets, 1971), 205, Kipnis gives the name as Marko Lutan rather than Lukhtan. According to the testimony of Itsko

Pashkovsky, in "Pokazanie Itsko Pashkovskogo," YIVO 80/184/16028b, Lukhtan was a nickname, and the real last name was Detskii.

3. *Ves Iugo-zapadnyi krai 1913* (Kyiv: Iugo-Zapadnomu otdeleniiu Rossiiskoi Eksportnoi palaty, 1913), 839.

4. Lidia B. Miliakova, ed., *Kniga pogromov: Pogromy na Ukraine, v Belorussii i evropeiskoi chasti Rossii v period grazhdanskoi voiny, 1918–1922 gg. Sbornik dokumentov* (Moscow: Rosspen, 2007), 172.

5. Kipnis, *Mayn shtetl Sloveshno*, vol. 1, 117.

6. Miliakova, *Kniga pogromov*, 172–76; and Elias Heifetz, *The Slaughter of the Jews in the Ukraine in 1919* (New York: Thomas Seltzer, 1921), 372–77. Documents in DAKO R-3050/1/225 and YIVO 80/184.

7. "Bandit Kosenko," DAKO R-3050/1/225/19.

8. Kipnis, *Khadoshim un teg*, 72.

9. "Pokazanie Ia. M. Melameda," YIVO 80/184/16016b. See also Heifetz, *Slaughter of the Jews*, 373; and Miliakova, *Kniga pogromov*, 175. Melamed actually gives an incorrect date, but must have been referring to July 12.

10. "Wohlnnian [*sic*] J.D.C. Report, Oct. 1919–July 1920," p. 41, JDC Archives, Records of the New York Office of the American Jewish Joint Distribution Committee, 1919–1921, folder 233.

11. "Wohlnnian [*sic*] J.D.C. Report," 41.

12. Kipnis, *Khadoshim un teg*, 88; "Isaak Gol'dberg," DAKO R-3050/1/225/11–13.

13. "Pokazanie Ia. M. Melameda," YIVO 80/184/16016–16018; and "Pokazanie Khany Avrum-Berovoi Gozman," YIVO 80/184/16020b-16022. See also Heifetz, *Slaughter of the Jews*, 377–80.

14. Shoah Foundation VHA, interview with Roza Zaks. She also wrote unpublished memoirs, which I have consulted from the collection of the Herbert D. Katz Center for Advanced Judaic Studies at the University of Pennsylvania.

15. Kipnis, *Khadoshim un teg*, 89.

16. Kipnis, *Khadoshim un teg*, 89–90.

17. Kipnis, *Khadoshim un teg*, 91.

18. According to Melamed's Warsaw testimony, the bodies were those of Gedaliah Wassman, Mordecai Eliezer, and two Minsk merchants both named Gechman. "Wohlnnian [*sic*] J.D.C. Report," 42. For a summary of the violence that notes twelve people killed in Narodychi see "Narodichi," DAKO R-3050/1/225/10.

19. "Begun," DAKO FR-R-3050/1/225/75–76.

20. Kipnis, *Khadoshim un teg*, 107.

21. "Pokazanie Itsko Pashkovskogo," July 30, 1919, YIVO 80/184/16028.

22. Kipnis, *Khadoshim un teg*, 113.

23. Kipnis, *Khadoshim un teg*, 114.

24. Kipnis, *Khadoshim un teg*, 114.

25. "Wohlnnian [*sic*] J.D.C. Report," 44.

26. "Wohlnnian [*sic*] J.D.C. Report," 44.

27. "Pokazanie Khany Avrum-Berovoi Gozman," YIVO 80/184/16021. See also Heifetz, *Slaughter of the Jews*, 378.

28. "Pokazanie Srul'-Ber' Bergera," YIVO 80/184/16026. See also Heifetz, *Slaughter of the Jews*, 381.

29. "Pokazanie Srul'-Ber' Bergera," YIVO 80/184/16026–16026b. See also Heifetz, *Slaughter of the Jews*, 381.

30. "Pokazanie Srul'-Ber' Bergera," YIVO 80/184/16026b. See also Heifetz, *Slaughter of the Jews*, 382.

31. "Pokazanie Ia. M. Melameda, " YIVO 80/184/16016–16018.

32. "Pokazanie Motl Kaplan," YIVO 80/184/16022b-16023.

33. Kipnis, *Khadoshim un teg*, 135–36.

34. "Pokazanie Khany Avrum-Berovoi Gozman," YIVO 80/184/16020b-16022. See also Heifetz, *Slaughter of the Jews*, 379.

35. "Pokazanie Khany Avrum-Berovoi Gozman," YIVO 80/184/16022.

36. Roza Zaks, "Memoirs" (unpublished manuscript, 1991), 8.

37. "Pokazanie Moishe Fel'dmana," YIVO 80/184/16024b-16025; and Heifetz, *Slaughter of the Jews*, 383.

38. Miliakova, *Kniga pogromov*, 174.

39. "Pokazanie Moishe Fel'dmana," YIVO 80/184/16024b-16025.

40. "Pokazanie Ari Tereshko," YIVO 80/184/16023b-16024.

41. "Wohlnnian [*sic*] J.D.C. Report," 45.

42. Kipnis, *Khadoshim un teg*, 148–49.

43. Kipnis, *Khadoshim un teg*, 147.

44. Kipnis, *Khadoshim un teg*, 143.

45. "Slavoshir," YIVO 80/205/18168. This report refers to the town as Slavoshir, but the details of the report suggest that it was actually Slovechno.

46. "Obvinitel'nyi akt," DAKO R-3050/1/225/21.

47. "Obvinitel'nyi akt," DAKO R-3050/1/225/21.

48. "Prigovor, " DAKO 3050/1/225/22/98. See also Miliakova, *Kniga pogromov*, 482–83.

49. "Opredelenie," DAKO 3050/1/225/24. See also P. S. Romashkin, *Amnistiia i pomilovanie v SSSR* (Moscow: Gos. izd-vo iuridicheskoi lit-ry, 1959), 139.

50. See Christopher Gilley, *The "Change of Signposts" in the Ukrainian Emigration: A Contribution to the History of Sovietophilism in the 1920s* (Stuttgart: Ibidem-Verlag, 2009), 232–42. See also Matthew Rendle, "Mercy amid Terror? The Role of Amnesties During Russia's Civil War," *Slavonic and East European Review* 92, no. 3 (July 1, 2014): 449–78.

51. Kipnis, *Khadoshim un teg*, 150.

CHAPTER 12: POLAND AND UKRAINE ON THE WORLD STAGE

1. James Wycliffe Headlam, *A Memoir of the Paris Peace Conference, 1919*, ed. Agnes Headlam-Morley, Russell Bryant, and Anna Cienciala (London: Methuen, 1972), 178.

2. "Celebrators Fill Streets of Paris," *New York Times*, June 30, 1919. Other details from "Treaty Ceremony Went with Speed," *New York Times*, June 30, 1919; Headlam, *A Memoir of the Paris Peace Conference*, 178–79; and Margaret MacMillan, *Paris 1919: Six Months That Changed the World* (New York: Random House, 2001), 474–78.

3. Cited in Donald I. Buzinkai, "The Bolsheviks, the League of Nations and the Paris Peace Conference, 1919," *Soviet Studies* 19, no. 2 (October 1967): 261.

4. Carole Fink, *Defending the Rights of Others: The Great Powers, the Jews, and International Minority Protection, 1878–1938* (New York: Cambridge University Press, 2004), 247–64.

5. "Vider debaten in seym vegen pogromen," *Haynt*, June 29, 1919.

6. *The Jews in Poland: Official Reports of the American and British Investigating Missions* (Chicago: National Polish Committee of America, 1920), 4.

7. "Protest to Wilson Against Zionist State," *New York Times*, March 5, 1919.

8. Henry Morgenthau, *All in a Life-Time* (Garden City, NY: Doubleday, Page, 1923), 385.

9. Morgenthau, *All in a Life-Time*, 384.

10. Morgenthau, *All in a Life-Time*, 357–58.

11. Morgenthau, *All in a Life-Time*, 361.

12. Morgenthau, *All in a Life-Time*, 362.

13. Morgenthau, *All in a Life-Time*, 376.

14. Morgenthau, *All in a Life-Time*, 377.

15. Morgenthau, *All in a Life-Time*, 415. See also "Fixes Blame for Polish Pogroms," *New York Times*, January 19, 1920.

16. Morgenthau, *All in a Life-Time*, 415.

17. Morgenthau, *All in a Life-Time*, 415.

18. Morgenthau, *All in a Life-Time*, 418.

19. Morgenthau, *All in a Life-Time*, 382.

20. "Podil's'ka osoblyva slidcha komisiia dlia rozsliduvannia protyevreis'kykh pohromykh," 1123/1/36; and "Law Establishing an Extraordinary Commission for Investigation of anti-Jewish Pogroms," TsDAVO 5235/1/624/156–160. For more on the commission see L. V. Hrynevych, "'Provesty naishyrshe v svidomist' mas, shcho zdiiani zlochyny ne zalyshat'sia bez kary': pro stvorennia i diial'nist' Osoblyvoi slidchoi komisii dlia rozsliduvannia protyevreis'kikh pohromnykh dii pry Radi narodnykh ministriv UNR," *Storinky Istorii* 46 (2018): 54–73.

21. "Do Ukrains'ko-evreiskikh vidnosyn v rokakh revoliutsii," TsDAVO 5235/1/623/40.

22. "Do Ukrains'ko-evreiskikh vidnosyn v rokakh revoliutsii," TsDAVO 5235/1/623/70. For an English translation see *Material Concerning Ukrainian-Jewish Relations During the Years of the Revolution (1917–1921)* (Munich: Ukrainian Information Bureau, 1956), 66–67.

23. "Do Ukrains'ko-evreiskikh vidnosyn v rokakh revoliutsii," TsDAVO

5235/1/623/76 and 5235/1/623/42. For an English translation see *Material Concerning Ukrainian-Jewish Relations During the Years of the Revolution (1917–1921)*, 68–69.

24. "Do Ukrains'ko-evreiskikh vidnosyn v rokakh revoliutsii," TsDAVO 5235 /1/623/76.

25. Joseph V. Fuller, ed., *Papers Relating to the Foreign Relations of the United States, the Paris Peace Conference, 1919* (Washington, DC: Government Printing Office, 1944), vol. 5, 795.

26. The Inter-Allied Commission for the Negotiation of an Armistice Between Poland and the Ukraine met between April 26 and May 15. Their minutes are in David Hunter Miller, *My Diary at the Conference of Paris, with Documents*, vol. 1 (New York: Appeal, 1924), 319–488. See also Sam Johnson, *Pogroms, Peasants, Jews: Britain and Eastern Europe's 'Jewish Question,' 1867–1925* (London: Palgrave Macmillan, 2011), 166–81.

27. CIA Report, T-452, *The Problem of Eastern Galicia, 1919–1923*, March 4, 1944.

28. See, for instance, "Shkhite in Pereiaslav," *Yidishes tageblat*, August 29, 1919; and "450 Iden toyt in Zshmerinka pogrom," *Yidishes tageblat*, August 17, 1919.

29. "Halb million pogrom karbanos in Ukrayne," *Der morgen zhurnal*, September 2, 1919.

30. "Ukrainian Jews Aim to Stop Pogroms," *New York Times*, September 8, 1919.

31. "Jews Slain in Ukraine," *New York Times*, September 14, 1919; "35,000 Jews Killed in Savage Pogroms," *New York Times*, October 11, 1919; "40,000 Jews Slain in Ukraine, He Says," *New York Times*, December 8, 1919; "29,000 Jews Slain in Ukraine Pogroms," *New York Times*, January 13, 1920; and "Tells of Killing of Jews: Russian Leader Asserts 138,000 Were Slain," *New York Times*, August 8, 1920.

32. "Appel à l'Humanité," CAHJP P10a/1/S5/3/46; "Prominente frantsoyzen opeliren far iden," *Der morgen zhurnal*, September 30, 1919; and *The Ukraine Terror and the Jewish Peril* (London: Federation of Ukrainian Jews, 1921), 16.

33. "Half Million Jews in Pogrom Protest; Procession of 25,000 Marks 'Day of Sorrow' at Conditions in Ukraine. Mass Meeting at Night. Speakers Appeal to the Conscience of the World to Right Wrongs of Their Race. Veterans in Parade," *New York Times*, November 25, 1919.

34. "Canadian Jewish Congress Resolution," YIVO 80/35/3381.

35. Julian Batchinsky et al., *The Jewish Pogroms in Ukraine: Authoritative Statements on the Question of Responsibility for Recent Outbreaks Against the Jews in Ukraine* (Washington, DC: Friends of Ukraine, 1919), 23.

36. Arnold Margolin, *Ukraina i politika Antanty zapiski evreia i grazhdanina* (Berlin: Izdatel'stvo S. Efron, 1922), 251.

37. For more examples see David Engel, ed., *The Assassination of Symon Petliura*

and the Trial of Scholem Schwarzbard, 1926–1927: A Selection of Documents (Göttingen: Vandenhoeck & Ruprecht, 2016), 131–40.

38. Engel, *The Assassination of Symon Petliura and the Trial of Scholem Schwarzbard*, 20.

CHAPTER 13: THE VOLUNTEER ARMY

1. Christopher Lazarski, "White Propaganda Efforts in the South During the Russian Civil War, 1918–19 (The Alekseev-Denikin Period)," *Slavonic and East European Review* 70, no. 4 (October 1992): 688–707.

2. Nokhem Shtif, *Pogromen in Ukrayne* (Berlin: Wostok, 1923), 43.

3. N. Gergel, "The Pogroms in the Ukraine in 1918–21," *YIVO Annual of Jewish Social Science* 6 (1951): 249. Tsherikover estimated the death toll from Denikin's pogroms at closer to 8,000. See his introduction to Joseph Schechtman, *Pogromy dobrovol'cheskoi armii na Ukraine* (Berlin: Ostjüdisches Historisches Archiv, 1932), 25–26.

4. Shmuel Rubinshteyn, *Tsivshn fayer un shverd: bletlekh zikhroynes vegn birger-krig in Ukrayne, 1918–1920* (Warsaw: Emes, 1924), 61.

5. Anton Ivanovich Denikin, *The Russian Turmoil: Memoirs: Military, Social, and Political* (London: Hutchinson, 1922), 326.

6. Denikin, *The Russian Turmoil*, 31.

7. Denikin, *The Russian Turmoil*, 91.

8. John Ernest Hodgson, *With Denikin's Armies: Being a Description of the Cossack Counter-Revolution in South Russia, 1918–1920* (London: Temple Bar, 1932), 54–55.

9. "Chto dal narodu sotsializm i bols'sheviki?," YIVO 80/85/6644.

10. *Rassvet*, October 6, 1917, no. 9.

11. "Selianam pro mobilizatsiiu," YIVO 80/85/6634. For more on White propaganda against the Jews see Oleg Budnitskii, *Russian Jews Between the Reds and the Whites, 1917–1920*, trans. Timothy J. Portice (Philadelphia: University of Pennsylvania Press, 2012).

12. Arkady Borman, "My Meetings with White Russian Generals," *Russian Review* 27, no. 2 (April 1968): 215.

13. Shtif, *Pogromen in Ukrayne*, 49.

14. Ilya Ehrenburg, *First Years of Revolution, 1918–1921* (London: MacGibbon & Kee, 1962), 94.

15. On the Cossacks during the civil war, see Brent Mueggenberg, *The Cossack Struggle Against Communism, 1917–1945* (Jefferson, NC: McFarland, 2019), 120–29.

16. Peter Wrangel, *Always with Honour: Memoirs of General Wrangel* (New York: R. Speller, 1963), 87.

17. Cecil L'Estrange Malone, *The Russian Republic* (New York: Harcourt, Brace and Howe, 1920), 125.

18. See Mark Robert Baker, "Peasants, Power and Revolution in the Village:

A Social History of Kharkiv Province, 1914–1921" (PhD diss., Harvard University, 2001).

19. "Pogromy v Kremenchugskoi gubernii," TsDAVO 2497/3/147/45.

20. *Fifth Supplement to the London Gazette*, April 20, 1920, https://www.thegazette.co.uk/London/issue/31875/supplement/4693; and Hodgson, *With Denikin's Armies*, 52–53.

21. Bela Bodo, "The White Terror in Hungary, 1919–1921: The Social Worlds of Paramilitary Groups," *Austrian History Yearbook* 42 (April 2011): 133–63.

22. "Prikaz No. 1 po garnizonu gor. Cherkassy," YIVO 80/85/6554.

23. On White ideology and the Jews see Oleg Budnitskii, "Jews, Pogroms, and the White Movement: A Historiographical Critique," *Kritika: Explorations in Russian and Eurasian History* 2, no. 4 (Fall 2001): 751–72; Peter Kenez, *Civil War in South Russia, 1918: The First Year of the Volunteer Army* (Berkeley: University of California Press, 1971); Peter Kenez, *Civil War in South Russia, 1919–1920: The Defeat of the Whites* (Berkeley: University of California Press, 1977); and Peter Kenez, "Pogroms and White Ideology in the Russian Civil War," in John D. Klier and Shlomo Lambroza, eds., *Pogroms: Anti-Jewish Violence in Modern Russian History* (New York: Cambridge University Press, 1992), 293–313. See also Aleksei L'vovich Litvin, "Krasnyi i belyi terror v Rossii, 1917–1922," *Otechestvennaia istoriia*, no. 6 (1993): 46–62; and E. I. Dostovalov, "O belykh i belom terrore," *Rossiiskii arkhiv* 6 (1995): 637–97.

24. Sergey Petrovich Melgounov, *The Red Terror in Russia* (London: J. M. Dent & Sons, 1925), 179–80.

25. Hodgson, *With Denikin's Armies*, 75.

26. Hodgson, *With Denikin's Armies*, 75.

27. Hodgson, *With Denikin's Armies*, 63.

28. Richard Pipes, *The Russian Revolution* (New York: Vintage, 1991), 824–25.

29. Vadim Abramov, *Evrei v KGB* (Moscow: Iauza, Eksmo, 2005), 291.

30. Leonard Schapiro, "The Rôle of the Jews in the Russian Revolutionary Movement," *Slavonic and East European Review* 40, no. 94 (1961): 165.

31. Rubinshteyn, *Tsivshn fayer un shverd*, 40.

32. Budnitskii, *Russian Jews Between the Reds and the Whites*, 150–55.

33. A. I. Denikin, *Ocherki russkoi smuty*, vol. 5 (Berlin: Mednyi Vsadnik, 1926), 146.

34. Malone, *The Russian Republic*, 125–26.

35. "Pogromy v kremenchugskoi gubernii," TsDAVO 2497/3/147/42–45.

36. "Dokladnaia zapiska soiuza vozrozhdeniia Rossii," YIVO 80/82/6054.

37. Brendan McGeever, *Antisemitism and the Russian Revolution* (Cambridge: Cambridge University Press, 2019).

38. "Fastov," TsDAVO 3299/1/48/40.

39. "Perezhivaniia evreev v Fastove," YIVO 80/210/18924.

40. "Perezhivaniia evreev v Fastove," YIVO 80/210/18925.

41. On Kraus see Lidia B. Miliakova, ed., *Kniga pogromov: Pogromy na Ukraine, v Belorussii i evropeiskoi chasti Rossii v period grazhdanskoi voiny, 1918–1922 gg. Sbornik dokumentov* (Moscow: Rosspen, 2007), 857. See also TsDAVO 3299/1/48/40.

42. "K sobytiiam v Fastove," YIVO 80/210/18857.

43. "Perezhivaniia evreev v Fastove," YIVO 80/210/18926b.

44. "K sobytiiam v Fastove," YIVO 80/210/18854.

45. Isaac Berliand, "The Slaughter of Fastoff," YIVO 80/210/18902.

46. "Fastov," TsDAVO 3299/1/48/41; and "Sobytiia v Fastove," TsDAVO 3299/1/48/43.

47. "K sobytiiam v Fastove," YIVO 80/210/18857.

48. "K sobytiiam v Fastove," YIVO 80/210/18853.

49. "Fastov," TsDAVO 3299/1/48/40.

50. "Fastov," TsDAVO 3299/1/48/41.

51. "K sobytiiam v Fastove," YIVO 80/210/18854.

52. "Fastov," TsDAVO 3299/1/48/40.

53. "K sobytiiam v Fastove," YIVO 80/210/18855. Also in Miliakova, *Kniga Pogromov*, 251–52.

54. "K sobytiiam v Fastove," YIVO 80/210/18861–18861b.

55. "K sobytiiam v Fastove," YIVO 80/210/18861b.

56. "K sobytiiam v Fastove," YIVO 80/210/18861b. See also "The Slaughter of Fastoff," YIVO 80/210/18907.

57. "K sobytiiam v Fastove," YIVO 80/210/18855–57b. Derevensky gives the OS date of September 9, September 22 according to the new calendar, in Ivan Derevensky, "Sobytiia v Fastove," YIVO 80/210/18871–18873.

58. Schechtman, *Pogromy dobrovol'cheskoi armii na Ukraine*, 103; and "K sobytiiam v Fastove," YIVO 80/210/18862.

59. Kh. Goffman, "Sobytiia v Fastove," YIVO 80/210/18890b.

60. Derevensky, "Sobytiia v Fastove," YIVO 80/210/18871b.

61. Derevensky, "Sobytiia v Fastove," YIVO 80/210/18873.

62. Derevensky, "Sobytiia v Fastove," YIVO 80/210/18871.

63. Isaac Berliand, "The Slaughter of Fastoff," YIVO 80/210/18905–18906.

64. "Perezhivaniia evreev v Fastiv," YIVO 80/210/18926b.

65. Cited in Schechtman, *Pogromy dobrovol'cheskoi armii na Ukraine*, 118.

66. "Kharkov," YIVO 80/135/10438.

67. Testimony of Leyb Yakhnis, YIVO 80/237/21987–21988. For more on rape during the pogroms see Irina Astashkevich, *Gendered Violence: Jewish Women in the Pogroms of 1917 to 1921* (Boston: Academic Studies Press, 2018).

68. Report of I. O. Zaved with the help of the Fastiv region and Bila Tserkva of A. A. Krizinsky, December 28, 1919, YIVO 80/210/18921–18921b. See also United States Department of State, and United States President,

Conditions in the Ukraine Respecting Treatment of Jews (Washington, DC: Government Printing Office, 1920).

69. "Soobshchenie sdelal' Timofei Aleksandrovich Sadnikov," TsDAVO 3299/1 /48/27.
70. On the use of fire in ethnic riots, see Donald L. Horowitz, *The Deadly Ethnic Riot* (Berkeley: University of California Press, 2001), 113–14.
71. "Sobytiia v Fastove," YIVO 80/210/18865.
72. A. O. Nikolaidi, "K sobytiiami v Fastove," YIVO 80/210/18867b.
73. Berliand, "The Slaughter of Fastoff," YIVO 80/210/18904.
74. Shechtman, *Pogromy dobrovol'cheskoi armii na Ukraine*, 149.
75. "Fastiv: po svedeniiam gazet," YIVO 80/210/18894b.
76. Nikolaidi, "K sobytiiami v Fastove," YIVO 80/210/18868b.
77. Kh. Hoffman, "Sobytiia v Fastove," YIVO 80/210/18892b. See also Miliakova, *Kniga pogromov*, 250.
78. Nikolaidi, "K sobytiiami v Fastove," YIVO 80/210/18868–18868b.
79. Cited in Shechtman, *Pogromy dobrovol'cheskoi armii na Ukraine*, 109.
80. "Fastoff: Extract of the Evidence of Different Witnesses," JDC Archives, Records of the New York Office of the American Jewish Joint Distribution Committee, 1919–1921, folder 260.
81. "Pogromy v Kievskoi gubernii," TsDAVO 2497/3/188/3.
82. Isaac Berliand, "K polozheniiu pogromlennykh v Fastiv," YIVO 80/210/18920; and "Fastovskii pogrom," YIVO 80/210/18922b. See also Miliakova, *Kniga pogromov*, 253–55.
83. G. I. Rabinovich "Pogrom v Fastove 8-go sentiabria 1919 g," YIVO 80/210/18928b.
84. Statement on medical conditions in Fastiv, September 1919, TsDAVO 3299/1/48/38. For an alternative view on the number of casualties based on published works see A. A. Nemirovskii, "K voprosu o chisle zhertv evreiskikh pogromov v Fastove i v Kieve (Osen' 1919 g.)," *Novyi istoricheskii vestnik* 14, no. 1 (2006).
85. Ilya Ehrenburg, *First Years of Revolution, 1918–1921* (London: MacGibbon & Kee, 1962), 84.
86. Ehrenburg, *First Years of Revolution*, 90.
87. "Fall of Kieff," *Times* (London), September 4, 1919.
88. "Rezoliutsiia, priniataia v pervom zasedanii soveta po vozstanovleniiu kievskoi evreiskoi obshchiny 4-go sentiabria 1919 g," YIVO 80/82/5958.
89. *Arkhiv russkoi revoliutsii* 15 (Berlin, 1924), 229.
90. Ehrenburg, *First Years of Revolution*, 78.
91. "Kieff Under the Terror" *Times* (London), September 23, 1919.
92. "Kieff Under the Terror," *Times*.
93. "The Red Terror in Kiev," *Current History: A Monthly Magazine of the New York Times* 11, no. 3 (December 1919), 492.
94. "Kazachiy dvor' na delovoi ulitse," TsDAVO 3299/1/49/17.

95. Thomas Chopard, *Le martyre de Kiev: 1919: l'Ukraine en révolution entre terreur soviétique, nationalisme et antisémitisme* (Paris: Vendémiaire, 2015), 192–202.

96. "Telegramma gen. Denikina," YIVO 80/ 85/6642.

97. On the Kyiv pogrom see Chopard, *Le martyre de Kiev*; Victoria Khiterer, *Jewish Pogroms in Kiev During the Russian Civil War, 1918–1920* (Lewiston, NY: Edwin Mellen Press, 2015), 53–76; Mark Shekhtman, "Shul'gin Ehrenburg i drugie o kievskikh pogromakh 1917–1921 godov," *Novosti nedeli*, October 14, 2010; and Raisa Lert, "Evreiskii pogrom v Kieve v 1919 gody," *Vestnik evreiskogo universiteta Moskve* 1, no. 14 (1997).

98. Charles Jacobovitz, "Impressions sur le pogrom de Kiev," YIVO 80/84/6389-6390b.

99. "Pogrom v Kieve," YIVO 80/211/19078–19093.

100. "Sobytiia v Kieve," YIVO 80/211/19112; Khiterer, *Pogroms in Kiev During the Russian Civil War*, 55; and Viktor Savchenko, *Atamany kazach'ego voiska* (Moscow: Eksmo, 2006), 246–48.

101. Shmuil Gankin, October 10, 1919 (OS), TsDAVO 3299/1/49/20.

102. A. Teitel'baum, "K sobytiiam v Kieve," YIVO 80/211/19122–19123. See also Miliakova, *Kniga pogromov*, 309.

103. "Zaiavlenie," Mel'tser, Samuil Abramovich, YIVO 80/332/30979.

104. *Arkhiv russkoi revoliutsii* 15 (Berlin, 1924), 235. See also "Zaiavlenie," Anopolskaia, Eva Markova. YIVO 80/332/30966.

105. "Zaiavlenie," Burakovskaia, Polina, YIVO 80/332/30969.

106. Jacobovitz, "Impressions sur le pogrom de Kiev," YIVO 80/84/6391.

107. Rubinshteyn, *Tsivshn fayer un shverd*, 61.

108. Rubinshteyn, *Tsivshn fayer un shverd*, 61.

109. Ehrenburg, *First Years of Revolution*, 78.

110. Cited in Schechtman, *Pogromy dobrovol'cheskoi armii na Ukraine*, 182; and "Zhenshchiny," YIVO 80/85/6630.

111. *Arkhiv russkoi revoliutsii* 15 (Berlin, 1924), 232.

112. "1–4 Oktiabre v Kieve," *Kievlianin*, October 19, 1919, no. 35. Copy of article in CAHJP P10a/3/S2/8.

113. V. V. Shulgin, "Pytka strakhom," *Kievlianin*, October 8, 1919.

114. "Kievskii sovet rabochix professional' nikh soiuzov," YIVO 80/85/6636.

115. Chopard, *Le martyre de Kiev*, 210; and "Grazhdane!," YIVO 80/85/6639.

116. "Kiev," TsDAVO 3299/1/49/28.

117. "Zaiavleniia evreev, postradavshikh ot pogromov i grabezhei v 1919," TsDAVO 3299/1/73–81.

118. YIVO 80/249/23836 lists 134 names. "Karbones fun Kiever pogrom," *Der morgen zhurnal*, January 18, 1920; and Zalman Solomonovich Ostrovsky, *Evreiskie pogrom, 1918–1921* (Moscow: Obshchestvo shkola i kniga, 1926), 50–51.

119. *Arkhiv russkoi revoliutsii* 15 (Berlin, 1924), 235.

CHAPTER 14: THE TETIIV POGROM

1. *Arkhiv russkoi revoliutsii* 15 (Berlin, 1924), 237.
2. Berta Kashtelian, "Tetiev in yor 1919," YIVO 80/186/16188. See also Eliezer David Rosenthal, *Tetiever khurbn* (New York: Idgezkom, 1922).
3. "Tetiev, Kiever gub.," YIVO 80/186/16210.
4. Kashtelian, "Tetiev in yor 1919," YIVO 80/186/16195.
5. Aron Sery, "Sobytiia v Tetieve," YIVO 80/209/18837.
6. Kashtelian, "Tetiev in yor 1919," YIVO 80/186/16196.
7. Kashtelian, "Tetiev in yor 1919," YIVO 80/186/16197; "Tetiev, Kiever gub.," YIVO 80/186/16213.
8. Efraim Ispo, "Der pogrom in Tetiev," YIVO 80/186/16219; "Tetiev, Kiever gub.," YIVO 80/209/18836; and "Tetiev, Kiever gub.," YIVO 80/186/16213.
9. "Krivo-Ozerskii pogrom," TsDAVO 2497/3/157/8.
10. "Doklad Komissii po okazaniiu pomoshchi naselenniiu, postradavshemu ot pogroma v m. Krivoe-Ozero," 3050/1/226/20.
11. "Doklad Komissii," 3050/1/226/15–29.
12. *Tetiever khurbn* refers to Vynnychenko as Danchenko.
13. "Tetiev, Kiever gub.," YIVO 80/186/16214.
14. "Tetiever pogrom," YIVO 80/186/16228.
15. Sonia Lev, "Protokol N1," YIVO 80/186/16230b.
16. "Tetiever pogrom," YIVO 80/186/16228.
17. "Belotserkovskomu uezdvoenkomu," YIVO 80/67/5411.
18. "Belotserkovskomu uezdvoenkomu," YIVO 80/67/5411–5412.
19. "Tetiev, Kiever gub.," YIVO 80/186/16214.
20. "Pogrom v Tetieve," YIVO 80/186/16243.
21. Rosenthal, *Tetiever khurbn*, 29.
22. Ispo, "Der pogrom in Tetiev," YIVO 80/186/16219. The surname "Ispo" is likely a typographic error, as a result of which I have rendered the name as "Joffe" in the text, but have retained "Ispo" in the notes.
23. Ispo, "Der pogrom in Tetiev," YIVO 80/186/16219. Another testimony claims it was more like ten men: YIVO 80/186/16228.
24. Ispo, "Der pogrom in Tetiev," YIVO 80/186/16220.
25. Rosenthal, *Tetiever khurbn*, 30–31.
26. http://tetiy.at.ua/publ/istorija_tymoshni/istorija_tetieva/velikodni_zhniva_tetijivskikh_gajdamakiv/3-1-0-13.
27. "Tetiever pogrom," YIVO 80/186/16228b. The Tetiev memorial book identified the person who threw the bomb as Ostrovsky. See Rosenthal, *Tetiever khurbn*, 38.
28. "Tetiever pogrom," YIVO 80/186/16229.
29. Ispo, "Der pogrom in Tetiev," YIVO 80/186/16220.
30. Sh. Kupershmid, "Pogrom Tetiev," YIVO 80/186/16243.
31. Kupershmid, "Pogrom Tetiev," YIVO 80/186/16243.
32. Teme Novofastovskaia, "Protokol N6," YIVO 80/186/16238b.

33. Hinde Feldman, "Protokol N7," YIVO 80/186/16240.

34. Chaya Goldenberg "Protokol N3," YIVO 80/186/16235.

35. Ispo, "Der pogrom in Tetiev," YIVO 80/186/16221.

36. Goldenberg "Protokol N3," YIVO 80/187/16235.

37. Feldman, "Protokol N7," YIVO 80/186/16240.

38. "Pogrom Tetiev," YIVO 80/186/16243.

39. "Tetiev, Kiever gub.," YIVO 80/186/16215.

40. Lev, "Protokol N1," YIVO 80/186/16230b.

41. Ispo, "Der pogrom in Tetiev," YIVO 80/186/16222.

42. "Tetiev, Kiever gub.," YIVO 80/186/16215.

43. Ispo, "Der pogrom in Tetiev," YIVO 80/186/16222.

44. Ispo, "Der pogrom in Tetiev," YIVO 80/186/16223.

45. Ispo, "Der pogrom in Tetiev," YIVO 80/186/16224, 16241b.

46. "Tetiev, Kiever gub.," YIVO 80/186/16216.

47. Ispo, "Der pogrom in Tetiev," YIVO 80/186/16225.

48. Ispo, "Der pogrom in Tetiev," YIVO 80/186/16226.

49. Aniute Glatskaia, "Protokol N4," YIVO 80/186/16237–8.

50. Lev, "Protokol N1," YIVO 80/186/16232b.

51. A list of names of victims of the pogrom has 631 names: YIVO 80/234/21665.

52. Tsherikover, "Les Pogromes antijuifs en Ukraine en 1917–1920 et le rôle de Petlioura," CAHJP P10a/1/S1/2, 46.

53. Lidia B. Miliakova, ed., *Kniga pogromov: Pogromy na Ukraine, v Belorussii i evropeiskoi chasti Rossii v period grazhdanskoi voiny, 1918–1922 gg. Sbornik dokumentov* (Moscow: Rosspen, 2007), 358.

54. Miliakova, *Kniga pogromov*, originally from GARF 1339/2/18/59–59a.

55. "Protokol doprosa," YIVO 80/67/5415.

56. Committee of the Jewish Delegations, *The Pogroms in the Ukraine Under the Ukrainian Governments (1917–1920): Historical Survey with Documents and Photographs* (London: John Bale, Sons & Danielsson, 1927), 241.

57. "Protokol," YIVO 80/67/5468.

58. "Vypiska iz protokola no. 4, zasedaniia Kollegii Kievskoi Gubern. Chrez. Komissii," YIVO 80/67/5474.

CHAPTER 15: THE POLISH-SOVIET WAR

1. Edgar Vincent D'Abernon, *The Eighteenth Decisive Battle of the World: Warsaw, 1920* (London: Hodder and Stoughton, 1931); Norman Davies, *White Eagle, Red Star: The Polish-Soviet War 1919–1920 and "the Miracle on the Vistula"* (London: Pimlico, 2003); and Michael Palij, *The Ukrainian-Polish Defensive Alliance, 1919–1921* (Edmonton: Canadian Institute of Ukrainian Studies Press, 1995).

2. Cited in *The Year 1920: The War Between Poland and Bolshevik Russia* (Warsaw: KARTA Centre, 2005), 19.

3. Cited in *The Year 1920*, 28.
4. "Pol'skiie dni v Zhitomire," YIVO 80/86/6807.
5. Cited in *The Year 1920*, 28.
6. "Pol'skiie dni v Zhitomire," YIVO 80/86/6809.
7. "Pol'skiie dni v Zhitomire," YIVO 80/86/6810.
8. Cited in *The Year 1920*, 49.
9. Cited in *The Year 1920*, 46.
10. Lidia B. Miliakova, ed., *Kniga pogromov: Pogromy na Ukraine, v Belorussii i evropeiskoi chasti Rossii v period grazhdanskoi voiny, 1918–1922 gg. Sbornik dokumentov* (Moscow: Rosspen, 2007), 363. See also "Protocol 8: statement of Borukh Shvartsman," YIVO 80/88/7240.
11. "Protocol 8: statement of Borukh Shvartsman," YIVO 80/88/7240b.
12. "Protocol 8: statement of Borukh Ostrovsky," YIVO 80/88/7240b.
13. "Protokol 5: statement of Nuty Kigsman," YIVO 80/88/7239–7240.
14. "Dokladnaia zapiska," cover letter on statements to Kyiv Jewish Community, YIVO 80/88/7250.
15. "Poliaki v Kieve: V komitet pomoshchi postradavshim," YIVO 80/88/7252–7253.
16. "Poliaki i evrei na Ukraine," YIVO 80/86/6834.
17. "Poliaki i evrei na Ukraine," YIVO 80/86/6834.
18. Israel Joshua Singer, "Bakhmatsch Station," trans. Anita Norich, in Ezra Glinter, ed., *Have I Got a Story for You: More Than a Century of Fiction from The Forward* (New York: W. W. Norton, 2017), 235.
19. Stephen Brown, "Communists and the Red Cavalry: The Political Education of the Konarmiia in the Russian Civil War, 1918–1920," *Slavonic and East European Review* 73, no. 1 (1995): 82–99.
20. Singer, "Bakhmatsh Station," 238.
21. "Pol'skie dni v Zhitomire," YIVO 80/86/6815. See also "Ustroennyi pol'skimi belogvardeitsami," YIVO 80/89/7371; "Evreiskii pogrom v Zhitomire," YIVO 80/89/7372–7374; "Pol'skii pogrom v Zhitomire," YIVO 80/90/7416–7425; and Miliakova, *Kniga pogromov*, 362–65 and 382–90.
22. Cited in *The Year 1920*, 75.
23. Vincent, *The Eighteenth Decisive Battle of the World*, 108.
24. Vincent, *The Eighteenth Decisive Battle of the World*, 120.
25. M. N. Tukhachevskii, "March Beyond the Vistula," in *Year 1920* (London: Piłsudski Institute of London, 1972), 244.
26. Oleg Budnitskii, *Russian Jews Between the Reds and the Whites* 1917–1920, trans. Timothy J. Portice (Philadelphia: University of Pennsylvania Press, 2012), 356–405.
27. Isaac Babel, *The Complete Works of Isaac Babel*, ed. Nathalie Babel, trans. Peter Constantine (New York: W. W. Norton, 2002), 457.
28. Babel, *The Complete Works of Isaac Babel*, 387.
29. Cited in *The Year 1920*, 196–97.

30. Babel, *The Complete Works of Isaac Babel*, 454.
31. Babel, *The Complete Works of Isaac Babel*, 411.
32. Babel, *The Complete Works of Isaac Babel*, 260.
33. Miliakova, *Kniga pogromov*, 400.
34. Babel, *The Complete Works of Isaac Babel*, 271.
35. Babel, *The Complete Works of Isaac Babel*, 367–68.
36. Babel, *The Complete Works of Isaac Babel*, 372.
37. "Prikaz," YIVO 80/42/3587.
38. "O Bulak-Balakhovich," YIVO 80/96/7907.
39. Cited in *The Year 1920*, 126.
40. Cited in *The Year 1920*, 189.
41. "Zakliuchenie o predanii sudu," YIVO 80/96/7898–7899.
42. Miliakova, *Kniga pogromov*, 619–20.
43. "Zakliuchenie o predanii sudu," YIVO 80/96/7898–7905.
44. "Balakhovitshes bandes in mazirer raion," YIVO 80/96/7912.
45. Miliakova, *Kniga pogromov*, 613
46. "Balakhovitshes bandes in mazirer raion," YIVO 80/96/7911.
47. Miliakova, *Kniga pogromov*, 619.
48. "Balakhovitshes bandes in mazirer raion," YIVO 80/96/7910–7911.
49. "Balakhovitshes bandes in mazirer raion," YIVO 80/96/7913–7914.
50. "Balakhovitshes bandes in mazirer raion," YIVO 80/96/7912.
51. Miliakova, *Kniga pogromov*, 636.
52. "Yurevitshi, Retshitster uyezd," YIVO 80/96/7889–7890.
53. "Yurevitshi, Retshitster uyezd," YIVO 80/96/7889–7890.
54. Stanisław Dąbrowski, "The Peace Treaty of Riga," *Polish Review* 5, no. 1 (Winter 1960): 3–34. For the implementation of the treaty and its impact on refugees, see Jerzy Borzęcki, *The Soviet-Polish Peace of 1921 and the Creation of Interwar Europe* (New Haven, CT: Yale University Press, 2008), 230–74.

CHAPTER 16: REFUGEES

1. Anne Applebaum, *Red Famine: Stalin's War on Ukraine* (New York: Doubleday, 2017), 67; and Kazuo Nakai, "Soviet Agricultural Policies in the Ukraine and the 1921–1922 Famine," *Harvard Ukrainian Studies* 6, no. 1 (March 1982): 43–61.
2. "Odessa. Polozhenie bezhentsev," YIVO 80/298/28378–28380.
3. Lev Singer, *Evreiskoe naselenie SSSR* (Moscow: ORT, 1927), 13–17; and Tsentral'noe statisticheskoe upravlenie, *Vsesoiuznaia perepis' naseleniia 1926 goda* vol. 46 (Moscow: TsSU Souiza SSR, 1928–1933), 24–53.
4. *Vsesoiuznaia perepis'*, vol. 45, 113–43; and vol. 46, 340–45.
5. Ilya Ehrenburg, *First Years of Revolution, 1918–1921* (London: MacGibbon & Kee, 1962), 77.

6. For more on the murder of Friedlaender and Cantor see Michael Beizer, "Who Murdered Professor Israel Friedlaender and Rabbi Bernard Cantor: The Truth Rediscovered," *American Jewish Archives Journal* 55, no. 1 (2003): 63–114. See also Michael Miller, "The Ukraine Commission of the Joint Distribution Committee, 1920, with Insight from the Judge Harry Fisher Papers," *Jewish Social Studies* 49, no. 1 (1987): 53–60; Jaclyn Granick, "The First American Organization in Soviet Russia: JDC and Relief in the Ukraine, 1920–1923," in Avinoam Patt et al., *The JDC at 100: A Century of Humanitarianism*, (Detroit: Wayne State University Press, 2019) 61–93; Jacob Kohn, "Israel Friedlaender: A Biographical Sketch," *American Jewish Year Book* 23 (October 3, 1921, to September 22, 1922): 65–79; and JDC Archives, Records of the New York Office of the American Jewish Joint Distribution Committee, 1919–1921, folder 247.3, Subcommittee on Ukraine to JDC, November 13, 1919.

7. Louis Marshall to Secretary of State, August 11, 1920, JDC Archives, Records of the New York Office of the American Jewish Joint Distribution Committee, 1919–1921, folder 27.3.

8. Charter of All Ukrainian Jewish Public Committee for Relief of Victims of Pogroms, TsDAVO 2497/1/2/3.

9. Zosa Szajkowski, "'Reconstruction' vs. 'Palliative Relief' in American Jewish Overseas Work (1919–1939)," *Jewish Social Studies* 32, no. 1 (January 1970): 14–42.

10. "Jewish Delegations at State Department," CAHJP P10a/1/S5/8; and Mark Vishnitzer to N. Sokolov, November 17, 1919, CAHJP P10a/1/S8/1.

11. "Jewish Delegations at State Department," YIVO 80/46/3788–3789. Also "U.S. Can't Aid Jews in Ukraine Yet," *New York Times*, December 11, 1919.

12. "The State Department Has Advised the Joint Distribution Committee," October 6, 1920, JDC Archives, Records of the New York Office of the American Jewish Joint Distribution Committee, 1919–1921, folder 248.

13. Z. Litvakova, "O polozhenii v Kievskoi gub k kontsu 1920 goda," YIVO 80/45/3691–3702.

14. "Dr. Bogen's First Impressions of Ukraina," JDC Archives, Records of the New York Office of the American Jewish Joint Distribution Committee, 1921–1932, folder 453.

15. *The Ukraine Terror and the Jewish Peril* (London: Federation of Ukrainian Jews, 1921), 2.

16. Boris David Bogen, *Born a Jew* (New York: Macmillan, 1930), 282.

17. In 1917, about 2.3 million Jews lived in the provinces of Katerynoslav, Kyiv, Podilia, Poltava, Taurida, Kherson, Chernihiv, and the unoccupied parts of Volhynia, according to the Jewish Statistical Society. The Jewish population of Soviet Ukraine was 1.47 million in 1923. See Evreiskoe Statisticheskoe Obshchestvo, *Evreiskoe naselenie Rossii* (Petrograd: Kadima, 1917), ix; and Singer, *Evreiskoe naselenie SSSR*, 8 and 38–39.

18. Yuri Slezkine, *The Jewish Century* (Princeton, NJ: Princeton University Press, 2004), especially 151–53 and 223.

19. League of Nations, *Réfugiés russes. Rapport de la Cinquième commission*, Geneva, 1922. For more on the European refugee situation see John Hope Simpson, "The Refugee Problem," *International Affairs* 17, no. 5 (September–October 1938): 612; Martyn Housden, "White Russians Crossing the Black Sea: Fridtjof Nansen, Constantinople, and the First Modern Repatriation of Refugees Displaced by Civil Conflict, 1922–23," *Slavonic and East European Review* 88, no. 3 (July 2010): 495–524; Irina Berlova, *Vynuzhdennye migranty: bezhentsy i voennoplennye pervoi mirovoi voiny v Rossii, 1914–1925* (Moscow: Airo, 2014); and Tara Zahra, *The Great Departure: Mass Migration from Eastern Europe and the Making of the Free World* (New York: W. W. Norton, 2016). Totals for the estimated number of Russian refugees in Europe range from 1.9 million provided by the Red Cross to 635,000 provided by the Russian archives in Prague. For more see Eugene Kulischer, *Europe on the Move: War and Population Changes, 1914–1947* (New York: Columbia University Press, 1948), 54; Eli Lederhendler, "The Interrupted Chain: Traditional Receiver Countries, Migration Regimes, and the East European Jewish Diaspora, 1918–39," *East European Jewish Affairs* 44, no. 2–3 (2014): 171–86; and Arieh Tartakower and Kurt R. Grossmann, *The Jewish Refugee* (New York: Institute of Jewish Affairs of the American Jewish Congress and World Jewish Congress, 1944).

20. "General Remarks on the Activity of the Refugee and Repatriate Department," JDC Archives, Records of the New York Office of the American Jewish Joint Distribution Committee, 1921–1932, folder 162; "Activities of Refugee Department American Joint Distribution Committee in Europe During the Years 1921, 1922, 1923," JDC Archives, Records of the New York Office of the American Jewish Joint Distribution Committee, folder 164; Piotr Wróbel, "Migracje Żydów polskich. Próba syntezy," Biuletyn Żydowskiego Instytutu Historycznego, 185–86 (1998): 3–30; and Jerzy Borzęcki, *The Soviet-Polish Peace of 1921 and the Creation of Interwar Europe* (New Haven, CT: Yale University Press, 2008), 241–42.

21. J. M. Kowalsky to European Executive Council, February 1, 1921, JDC Archives, Records of the New York Office of the American Jewish Joint Distribution Committee, 1919–1921, folder 141.2.

22. Borzęcki, *The Soviet-Polish Peace of 1921*, 241–42.

23. Borzęcki, *The Soviet-Polish Peace of 1921*, 242.

24. H. Breckler to J. Schweitzer, January 15, 1922, JDC Archives, Records of the New York Office of the American Jewish Joint Distribution Committee, 1921–1932, folder 161.

25. Joseph Hyman to James Rosenberg, January 18, 1922, JDC Archives, Records of the New York Office of the American Jewish Joint Distribution Committee, 1921–1932, folder 161.

26. "Activities of Refugee Department American Joint Distribution Committee in Europe," pp. 40–44, JDC Archives, Records of the New York Office of the American Jewish Joint Distribution Committee, 1921–1932, folder 164.

27. Tartakower and Grossmann, *The Jewish Refugee*, 25.

28. "40,000 idishe flikhtlinge in besarabien," *Forverts*, July 12, 1921.

29. "Heymloze," R-3050/1/ 272/6–7; and "Eynige statistishe yedies," R-3050 /1/272/39–40.

30. "To the Joint Distribution Committee of the American Funds for Jewish War and Pogrom Victims," May 28, 1921, p. 12, JDC Archives, Records of the New York Office of the American Jewish Joint Distribution Committee, 1919–1921, folder 247.1.

31. "Activities of Refugee Department American Joint Distribution Committee in Europe," p. 61, JDC Archives, Records of the New York Office of the American Jewish Joint Distribution Committee, 1921–1932, folder 164.

32. Joint Distribution Committee, Bucharest, to Dr. Kahn, June 1, 1921, JDC Archives, Records of the New York Office of the American Jewish Joint Distribution Committee, 1919–1921, folder 245.1. Also Joint Distribution Committee, Paris, to Morris Lewis, June 15, 1921, JDC Archives, Records of the New York Office of the American Jewish Joint Distribution Committee, 1919–1921, folder 245.1.

33. "To the Joint Distribution Committee of the American Funds for Jewish War and Pogrom Victims," May 28, 1921, JDC Archives, Records of the New York Office of the American Jewish Joint Distribution Committee, 1919–1921, folder 247.1.

34. "Report on Refugees Bessarabian Section," JDC Archives, Records of the New York Office of the American Jewish Joint Distribution Committee, 1919–1921, folder 245.1.

35. "Activities of Refugee Department American Joint Distribution Committee in Europe," p. 62, JDC Archives, Records of the New York Office of the American Jewish Joint Distribution Committee, 1921–1932, folder 164.

36. Paul Hanebrink, *A Specter Haunting Europe: The Myth of Judeo-Bolshevism* (Cambridge, MA: Belknap Press of Harvard University Press, 2018), 63–67; and Diana Dumitru, *The State, Antisemitism, and Collaboration in the Holocaust: The Borderlands of Romania and the Soviet Union* (Cambridge: Cambridge University Press, 2016), 55–68.

37. Isaac Unterman, *Fun di shkhite shtet* (Jersey City, NJ: Hudson Jewish News, 1925), 130. See also "Correspondence, reports (English, Hungarian) on refugees, aid, reconstruction in Hungary," JDC Archives, Records of the New York Office of the American Jewish Joint Distribution Committee, 1919–1921, folder 148.1.

38. "Report of Joseph Marcus," June 5, 1921, JDC Archives, Records of the

New York Office of the American Jewish Joint Distribution Committee, 1919–1921, folder 151.4.

39. "Activities of the Joint Distribution Committee in Czechoslovakia June 24, 1921," p. 17, JDC Archives, Records of the New York Office of the American Jewish Joint Distribution Committee, 1919–1921, folder 127.3. These figures include seventy-five hundred refugees aided by the Joint and seven thousand student refugees, who are calculated separately.

40. "Activities of the Joint Distribution Committee in Czechoslovakia June 24, 1921," p. 25, JDC Archives, Records of the New York Office of the American Jewish Joint Distribution Committee, 1919–1921, folder 127.3.

41. See "Flikhtlinge muzen farlozen Romenie biz'n 1ten oktober," *Forverts*, June 20, 1923; "Der ershter oktober vet zayn a tragisher tog far di ukrayner flikhtlinge," *Forverts*, September 27, 1923; "Finds Refuge for 40,000," *New York Times*, December 27, 1921; "Rumenishe regierung erloybt komisie tsu helfen flikhtlinge," *Der morgen zhurnal*, December 7, 1921; and Mark Wischnitzer, *To Dwell in Safety; the Story of Jewish Migration Since 1800* (Philadelphia: Jewish Publication Society of America, 1948), 153.

42. "Activities of Refugee Department American Joint Distribution Committee in Europe," p. 92, JDC Archives, Records of the New York Office of the American Jewish Joint Distribution Committee, 1921–1932, folder 164. See also Simpson, "The Refugee Problem," 362.

43. Bernard Kahn estimated that about sixty thousand Jews had arrived in Germany between October 1918 and November 1920: "Report Presented by Dr. Kahn at the Vienna Conference," JDC Archives, Records of the New York Office of the American Jewish Joint Distribution Committee, 1919–1921, folder 143.2. Robert C. Williams writes that seventy-five thousand eastern Europeans arrived in Germany after the revolution. See Robert Chadwell Williams, *Culture in Exile: Russian Emigrés in Germany, 1881–1941* (Ithaca, NY: Cornell University Press, 1972), 154. For more on Russian Jewish immigration to Germany see S. Adler-Rudel, *Ostjuden in Deutschland, 1880–1940: Zurgliech eine Geschichte der Organisationen, die sie Betreuten* (Tübingen: Mohr, 1959); Trude Maurer, *Ostjuden in Deutschland 1918–1933* (Hamburg: Hans Christians Verlag, 1986); and Karl Schlögel, ed., *Russische Emigration in Deutschland 1918 bis 1941: Leben im europäischen Bürgerkrieg* (Berlin: Akademie Verlag, 1995).

44. "The situation of the Jews from Poland and other parts of Eastern Europe in Germany," p. 1, JDC Archives, Records of the New York Office of the American Jewish Joint Distribution Committee, 1919–1921, folder 145.2.

45. Joseph Roth, *What I Saw: Reports from Berlin 1920–1933* (New York: W. W. Norton, 2003), 37.

46. Israel Joshua Singer, *The Family Carnovsky* (New York: Vanguard Press, 1969), 161.

47. Arnold Margolin, *From a Political Diary: Russia, the Ukraine, and America, 1905–1945* (New York: Columbia University Press, 1946), 65.

48. Arnold Margolin, *Ukraina i politika Antanty zapiski evreia i grazhdanina* (Berlin: Izdatel'stvo S. Efron, 1922), 246.

49. Cited in Verena Dohm and Gertrud Pickhan, eds., *Transit und Transformation: Osteuropäisch-jüdische Migranten in Berlin 1918–1939* (Göttingen: Wallstein, 2010), 87.

50. Ilya Ehrenburg, *Memoirs: 1921–1941* (Cleveland, OH: World Publishing Co., 1963), 9.

51. Ehrenburg, *Memoirs: 1921–1941*, 13.

52. Cited in Shachar Pinsker, *A Rich Brew: How Cafés Created Modern Jewish Culture* (New York: New York University Press, 2018), 181. For more on Jewish immigrants in interwar Berlin and Germany see Michael Brenner, *The Renaissance of Jewish Culture in Weimar Germany* (New Haven, CT: Yale University Press, 1998); Oleg Budnitskii and Aleksandra Polian, *Russko-evreiskii Berlin, 1920–1941* (Moscow: Novoe literaturnoe obozrenie, 2013); Gennady Estraikh and Mikhail Krutikov, eds., *Yiddish in Weimar Berlin: At the Crossroads of Diaspora Politics and Culture* (London: Modern Humanities Research Association, 2010); Reiner Pommerin, "Die Ausweisung von 'Ostjuden' aus Bayern 1923. Ein Beitrag zum Krisenjahr der Weimarer Republik," *Vierteljahrshefte für Zeitgeschichte* 34, no. 3 (1986): 311–40; and Rachel Seelig, *Strangers in Berlin: Modern Jewish Literature Between East and West, 1919–1933* (Ann Arbor: University of Michigan Press, 2016). On the Russian cultural scene in Berlin see Fritz Mierau, ed., *Russen in Berlin, 1918–1933* (Leipzig: Quadriga Verlag, 1988); Marc Raeff, *Russia Abroad: A Cultural History of the Russian Emigration, 1919–1939* (Oxford: Oxford University Press, 1990); and Karl Schlögel, *Der grosse Exodus: Die russische Emigration und ihre Zentren 1917 bis 1941* (Munich: C. H. Beck, 1994).

53. On Revutsky's career after leaving Ukraine, see Simon Rabinovitch, "Jewish-Ukrainian-Soviet Relations During the Civil War and the Second Thoughts of a Minister for Jewish Affairs," *Studies in Ethnicity and Nationalism* 17, no. 3 (2017): 339–53.

54. Annemarie Sammartino, *The Impossible Border: Germany and the East, 1914–1922* (Ithaca, NY: Cornell University Press, 2010), 123; Adler-Rudel, *Ostjuden in Deutschland*, 165; "Telegram from Goldman to Jointdisco, New York," March 10, 1920, JDC Archives, Records of the New York Office of the American Jewish Joint Distribution Committee, 1919–1921, folder 143.1; and Maurer, *Ostjuden in Deutschland 1918–1933*, 72–81.

55. Dovid Bergelson, *The Shadows of Berlin: The Berlin Stories of Dovid Bergelson*, trans. Joachim Neugroschel (San Francisco: City Lights Books, 2005), 38.

56. Vic Satzewich, *The Ukrainian Diaspora* (New York: Routledge, 2003), 57.

57. Michael Kellogg, *The Russian Roots of Nazism: White Émigrés and the Making of National Socialism 1917–1945* (Cambridge: Cambridge

University Press, 2004), 52–54, 190–91, and 255–59; Williams, *Culture in Exile*, 97; Pavlo Petrovych Skoropads'kyj, *Erinnerungen: 1917 bis 1918* (Stuttgart: F. Steiner, 1999), 85–87; and *Völkischer Beobachter* of April 7, May 17, and August 29, 1923.

58. Andrii Bolianovs'kyi, "Cooperation Between the German Military of the Weimar Republic and the Ukrainian Military Organization, 1923–1928," *Harvard Ukrainian Studies* 23, no. 1/2 (June 1999): 73–84.

59. Pavel Sudoplatov et al., *Special Tasks: The Memoirs of an Unwanted Witness, a Soviet Spymaster* (Boston: Little, Brown, 1995), 23–28.

60. Cited in Maurer, *Ostjuden in Deutschland, 1918–1933*, 186.

61. "The Situation of the Jews from Poland and Other Parts of Eastern Europe in Germany," JDC Archives, Records of the New York Office of the American Jewish Joint Distribution Committee, 1919–1921, folder 145.2.

62. "Telegram from Goldman to Jointdisco, New York," March 10, 1920, JDC Archives, Records of the New York Office of the American Jewish Joint Distribution Committee, 1919–1921, folder 143.1.

63. "Translated Letter from Dr. Horvits to Mr. Speyor," JDC Archives, Records of the New York Office of the American Jewish Joint Distribution Committee, 1919–1921, folder 145.2.

64. Maurer, *Ostjuden in Deutschland, 1918–1933*, 109–23. See also Jack Wertheimer, *Unwelcome Strangers: East European Jews in Imperial Germany* (Oxford: Oxford University Press, 1987); and Williams, *Culture in Exile*.

65. Cited in Maurer, *Ostjuden in Deutschland, 1918–1933*, 123.

66. "Gegen die Ostjuden," *Völkischer Beobachter*, March 6, 1920. See also Dr. Sieghart, "Deutschland den Ostjuden," *Völkischer Beobachter*, January 21, 1920.

67. "Macht ganze Arbeit mit den Juden," *Völkischer Beobachter*, March 10, 1920.

68. Maurer, *Ostjuden in Deutschland, 1918–1933*, 123; and Franz Haiser, "Sombart und die Juden," *Deutschlands Erneuerung*, July 1922, 424.

69. Sammartino, *The Impossible Border*, 128–30; and "Abstract of a Report of the Labor Welfare Department of the Jewish Organizations in Germany," JDC Archives, Records of the New York Office of the American Jewish Joint Distribution Committee, 1919–1921, file 145.2.

70. Albert Einstein, "How I Became a Zionist," in *The Collected Papers of Albert Einstein*, vol. 7 (Princeton, NJ: Princeton University Press, 2002), 352.

71. See Steven E. Aschheim, *Brothers and Strangers: The East European Jew in German and German Jewish Consciousness, 1800–1923* (Madison: University of Wisconsin Press, 1982), 233. For some examples see "Das jüdische Sowjetparadies," *Völkischer Beobachter*, January 27, 1921; and "Die jüdische Diktatur in Rußland," *Völkischer Beobachter*, September 16/17, 1923. See also Hanebrink, *A Specter Haunting Europe*.

72. See *Pravda*, January 5, 1919, for instance.
73. Cited in Robert Gerwarth, *The Vanquished: Why the First World War Failed to End, 1917–1923* (London: Allen Lane, 2016), 129. For more on Judeo-Bolshevism in Germany see Hanebrink, *A Specter Haunting Europe*, 83–93.
74. Alfred Rosenberg, "Die Russisch-jüdische Revolution," *Auf gut Deutsch* 8 (February 21, 1919): 120–24.
75. Alfred Rosenberg, "Russe und Deutscher," *Auf gut Deutsch* 11 and 12 (April 4, 1919): 187–88.
76. Alfred Rosenberg, "Judenheit und Politik," *Auf gut Deutsch* 17 and 18 (June 13, 1919): 272.
77. Alfred Rosenberg, "Jüdische Zeitfragen," *Auf gut Deutsch* 34 and 35 (October 23, 1919): 535.
78. *Foreign Relations of the United States, Paris Peace Conference*, vol. 5, 909.
79. Cited in Michael Brenner, *Der Lange Schatten der Revolution: Juden und Antisemiten in Hitlers München, 1918–1923* (Berlin: Jüdischer Verlag, 2019), 201.
80. Cited in Yitzhak Arad, Yisrael Gutman, and Abraham Margaliot, eds., *Documents on the Holocaust: Selected Sources on the Destruction of the Jews of Germany and Austria, Poland, and the Soviet Union* (Jerusalem: Yad Vashem, 1981), 20 (modified translation).
81. Adolf Hitler, *Mein Kampf*, trans. Ralph Manheim (New York: Houghton Mifflin, 1943), 325–26.
82. Hitler, *Mein Kampf*, 623.
83. Pommerin, "Die Ausweisung von 'Ostjuden' aus Bayern 1923"; and Józef Adelson, "The Expulsion of Jews with Polish Citizenship from Bavaria in 1923," *Polin: Studies in Polish Jewry* 5 (1990): 57–73.
84. Cited in Hanebrink, *A Specter Haunting Europe*, 98.
85. Margolin, *Ukraina i politika Antanty*, 355.
86. John Haycraft, *Disturbances in May 1921. Reports of the Commission of Inquiry with Correspondence Relating Thereto* (London: H. M. Stationery Office, 1921); "Les troubles de Palestine," *Paix et Droit*, May 1, 1921; and "Unruhen in Yafo beneyt," *Yidishes tageblat*, May 4, 1921.
87. Haycraft, *Disturbances in May 1921*, 43.
88. See for instance, "Eyntselheyten fun Yafo pogrom," *Yidishes tageblat*, May 6, 1921; "Pogrom in Yafo," *Yidishes tageblat*, May 3, 1921; and "20 Iden toyt, 150 farvundet in a pogrom," *Forverts*, May 3, 1921.
89. Anita Shapira, *Land and Power: The Zionist Resort to Force, 1881–1948* (Stanford, CA: Stanford University Press, 1999), 111–13.
90. See, for instance, "Dokladnaia zapiska. V odeskii evobshchestkom," TsDAVO 2497/3/182/4–7.
91. *Bolshevik Propaganda: Hearings Before a Subcommittee of the Committee on the Judiciary* (Washington, DC: Government Printing Office, 1919), 114–15.

92. *Bolshevik Propaganda*, 134–36.
93. "Senators Tell What Bolshevism in America Means," *New York Times*, June 15, 1919.
94. Cited in Evans Clark, *Facts and Fabrications About Soviet Russia* (New York: Rand School of Social Science, 1920), 18.
95. Joseph W. Bendersky, *The "Jewish Threat": Anti-Semitic Politics of the U.S. Army* (New York: Basic Books, 2000), 71.
96. *The International Jew, the World's Foremost Problem, Being a Reprint of a Series of Articles Appearing in The Dearborn Independent from May 22 to October 2, 1920*, vol. 1 (Dearborn, MI: Dearborn Publishing Company, 1920), 229.
97. *The International Jew*, vol. 2, 234.
98. *The International Jew*, vol. 2, 227.
99. Madison Grant, *The Passing of the Great Race; or, The Racial Basis of European History* (New York: C. Scribner's Sons, 1916), 81.
100. "Activities of Refugee Department American Joint Distribution Committee in Europe," p. 103, JDC Archives, Records of the New York Office of the American Jewish Joint Distribution Committee, 1921–1932, folder 164.
101. "Activities of Refugee Department American Joint Distribution Committee in Europe," p. 33, JDC Archives, Records of the New York Office of the American Jewish Joint Distribution Committee, 1921–1932, folder 164.
102. *Restriction of Immigration. Hearings Before the Committee on Immigration and Naturalization, House of Representatives, Sixty-Eighth Congress, First Session, on H.R.5, H.R.101, H.R.561 [H.R.6540] (1924)*, 389–90.
103. *Restriction of Immigration*, 20.

CHAPTER 17: THE SCHWARZBARD TRIAL

1. "Slayer of Petlura Stirs Paris Court," *New York Times*, October 19, 1927, 9. For more on the assassination of Petliura see David Engel, ed., *The Assassination of Symon Petliura and the Trial of Scholem Schwarzbard, 1926–1927: A Selection of Documents* (Göttingen: Vandenhoeck & Ruprecht, 2016); Saul S. Friedman, *Pogromchik: The Assassination of Simon Petlura* (New York: Hart, 1976); Meir Kotik, *Mishpat Shvartsbard* (Tel Aviv: Ḥadera, 1972); Anna Schur, "Shades of Justice: The Trial of Sholom Schwartzbard and Dovid Bergelson's *Among Refugees*," *Law and Literature* 19, no. 1 (2007): 15–43; Laura Engelstein, *The Resistible Rise of Antisemitism: Exemplary Cases from Russia, Ukraine, and Poland* (Waltham, MA: Brandeis University Press, 2020), 77–122; and Monique Slodzian, *L'Ukraine depuis le procès Schwartzbard Petlioura (1927)* (Paris: Politique Éditions de la Différence, 2014).
2. Cited in "The Lurid Trial of Petlura's Slayer," *Literary Digest*, November 19, 1927.

3. Cited in Engel, *The Assassination of Symon Petliura and the Trial of Scholem Schwarzbard*, 171.

4. Cited in Engel, *The Assassination of Symon Petliura and the Trial of Scholem Schwarzbard*, 177.

5. Sholem Ash, "Ver iz der 'merder'?," *Haynt*, June 7, 1926.

6. Statement of Dmytro Andriievskyi cited in Engel, *The Assassination of Symon Petliura and the Trial of Scholem Schwarzbard*, 30.

7. "Ukrainian Leaders Fear Alleged 'Jewish Terror,'" *Jewish Telegraphic Agency*, October 3, 1926.

8. Levko Chykalenko, "Sionisti i 'Sionisti,'" *Tryzub*, September 26, 1926. Translation adopted from Engel, *The Assassination of Symon Petliura and the Trial of Scholem Schwarzbard*, 232.

9. Cited in Engel, *The Assassination of Symon Petliura and the Trial of Scholem Schwarzbard*, 155.

10. For more speculation on Schwarzbard's connection with the Bolsheviks see Pavlo Shandruk, *Arms of Valor* (New York: R. Speller, 1959), 144; and "Confrontation Kossenko-Schwartzbard," YIVO 80/451/38071–38073.

11. Leo Motzkin, "An erklerung bnuge tsum shvartsbard-protsess," P10a/4/S1/5/7.

12. Engel, *The Assassination of Symon Petliura and the Trial of Scholem Schwarzbard*, 218–19.

13. "Semion Petlura League Is Formed in Lemberg," *Jewish Telegraphic Agency*, October 8, 1926.

14. Engel, *The Assassination of Symon Petliura and the Trial of Scholem Schwarzbard*, 261. See Margolin's letters to Lev Efimovich, July 6, 1926 (YIVO 80/478/39224–39225), August 3, 1926 (YIVO 80/478/39225–39228), and July 12, 1926 (YIVO 80/478/39229–39231).

15. Joseph Schechtman, "The Jabotinsky-Slavinsky Agreement: A Chapter in Ukrainian-Jewish Relations," *Jewish Social Studies* 17, no. 4 (1955): 289–306. For background see Olga Andriewsky, "Medved' iz berlogi: Vladimir Jabotinsky and the Ukrainian Question, 1904–1914," *Harvard Ukrainian Studies* 14 no. 3/4 (1990): 249–67.

16. Zeev Jabotinsky, "Torres," CAHJP P10a/1/S4/2.

17. Cited in Friedman, *Pogromchik*, 314.

18. "A la cour d'assises," YIVO 80/432/37245.

19. "A la cour d'assises," YIVO 80/432/37247.

20. "A la cour d'assises," YIVO 80/432/37247–37248.

21. "S. Petliura i zhydivski pohromy," DAKO 3890/1/10/12.

22. "S. Petliura i zhydivski pohromy," DAKO 3890/1/10/13.

23. "Pochatky dial'nosty S. V. Petliury nad vidrozhdeniiam Ukrains'kogo Viys'ka," TsDAVO 4011/2/5/54–58.

24. "M. Feshchenko-Chopivskyi," TsDAVO 4011/2/5/75–85.

25. Tsherikover, "Otvet na zapisku A. Shul'gina," YIVO 80/458/38412.

26. Tsherikover, "Otvet na zapisku A. Shul'gina," YIVO 80/458/38437.

27. Tsherikover, "Otvet na zapisku A. Shul'gina," YIVO 80/458/38444.

28. http://www.jta.org/1926/07/22/archive/50000-jews-killed-in-petlura
    -pogroms-paris-court-hears.

29. Friedman, *Pogromchik*, 85.

30. "A mes frères et soeurs Schwarzbard," YIVO 80/472/39073–39074.

31. Friedman, *Pogromchik*, 337.

32. Cited in "The Lurid Trial of Petlura's Slayer," 40.

33. Engel, *The Assassination of Symon Petliura and the Trial of Scholem Schwarzbard*, 357.

34. "Confrontation Procopovitch-Goldstein-Schwartzbard," YIVO 80/427/37057.

35. Friedman, *Pogromchik*, 191.

36. "Spectators Fight at Petlura Trial," *New York Times*, October 22, 1927, p. 6.

37. "Lawyers in Brawl at Petlura Trial," *New York Times*, October 23, 1927, p. 9.

38. Cited in "The Lurid Trial of Petlura's Slayer," 40.

39. Cited in "The Lurid Trial of Petlura's Slayer," 41.

40. Engel, *The Assassination of Symon Petliura and the Trial of Scholem Schwarzbard*, 426.

CHAPTER 18: THE INTERWAR IN UKRAINE

1. For more on the Soviet response to pogroms and the Schwarzbard trial, see Elissa Bemporad, *Legacy of Blood: Jews, Pogroms, and Ritual Murder in the Land of the Soviets* (New York: Oxford University Press, 2019), 66–69.

2. Z. S. Ostrovsky, *Evreiskie pogrom, 1918–1921* (Moscow, 1926).

3. Jeffrey Veidlinger, *In the Shadow of the Shtetl: Small-Town Jewish Life in Soviet Ukraine* (Bloomington: Indiana University Press, 2013). For the Soviet Union more broadly see also Elissa Bemporad, *Becoming Soviet Jews: The Bolshevik Experiment in Minsk* (Bloomington: Indiana University Press, 2013); Gennady Estraikh, *In Harness: Yiddish Writers' Romance with Communism* (Syracuse, NY: Syracuse University Press, 2005); Zvi Gitelman, *Jewish Nationality and Soviet Politics: The Jewish Sections of the CPSU, 1917–1930* (Princeton, NJ: Princeton University Press, 1972); David Shneer, *Yiddish and the Creation of Soviet Jewish Culture, 1918–1930* (Cambridge: Cambridge University Press, 2004); Anna Shternshis, *Soviet and Kosher: Jewish Popular Culture in the Soviet Union, 1923–1939* (Bloomington: Indiana University Press, 2006); Andrew Sloin, *The Jewish Revolution in Belorussia: Economy, Race, and Bolshevik Power* (Bloomington: Indiana University Press, 2017); and Arkadii Zel'tser, *Evrei sovetskoi provintsii: Vitebsk i mestechki, 1917–1941* (Moscow: Rosspen, 2006).

4. See, for instance, "Protsess ubitsy Petliury," *Pravda*, October 19, 1927; and

S. Iavorskii, "Petliurovshchina na skam'e podsudimikh," *Pravda*, October 22, 1927.

5. See "Vypiski iz gazety *Krasnaia gazeta*," in R-3050/1/37/84–100; and "*Krasnaia armiia*" R-3050/1/37/101–4.

6. Vadim Abramov, *Evrei v KGB* (Moscow: Eksmo, 2005), 32.

7. L(ev). Krichevskii, "Evrei v apparate VchK-OGPU v 20-e gody," in Oleg Budnitskii, ed., *Evrei i russkaia revoliutsiia: Materialy i issledovaniia* (Moscow: Gesharim, 1999), 333–34.

8. Iurii Shapoval and Vadim Zolotarov, "Evrei v kerivnytsvi orhaniv DPU-NKVC USSR," *Z arkhiviv VUChK-GPU-NKVD-KGB* 1, no. 34 (2010): 56.

9. Lynne Viola, *Stalinist Perpetrators on Trial: Scenes from the Great Terror in Soviet Ukraine* (New York: Oxford University Press, 2017), 32.

10. For more see Mikhail Tumshis and Vadim Zolotarev, *Evrei v NKVD, 1936–1938 gg. Opyt biograficheskogo slovaria* (Moscow: Universitet Dmitriia Pozharskogo, 2017).

11. Gershon Shapiro, *Di yidishe kolonye friling: zikhroynes fun a forzitser fun a yidishn kalkhaz* (Tel Aviv: Hmol, 1991); and Lev Kopelev, *The Education of a True Believer*, trans. Gary Kern, (New York: Harper & Row, 1980), 18–20. See also Anne Applebaum, *Red Famine: Stalin's War on Ukraine* (New York: Doubleday, 2017), 116; and Bernard Wasserstein, *On the Eve: The Jews of Europe Before the Second World War* (New York: Simon & Schuster, 2012), 346–50.

12. Miron Dolot, *Execution by Hunger: The Hidden Holocaust* (New York: W. W. Norton, 1985), 5.

13. Dolot, *Execution by Hunger*, 5.

14. Applebaum, *Red Famine*, 139–58; Lynne Viola, *Peasant Rebels Under Stalin: Collectivization and the Culture of Peasant Resistance* (New York: Oxford University Press, 1996); and Sheila Fitzpatrick, *Stalin's Peasants: Resistance and Survival in the Russian Village After Collectivization* (New York: Oxford University Press, 1994).

15. Kopelev, *The Education of a True Believer*, 234.

16. Cited in Kris Dietrich, *Taboo Genocide: Holodomor 1933 & the Extermination of Ukraine*, vol. 2 (Bloomington, IN: Xlibris, 2015), 117–20.

17. Applebaum, *Red Famine*, 280.

18. Applebaum, *Red Famine*, 262–77; and David R. Marples, "Ethnic Issues in the Famine of 1932–1933 in Ukraine," *Europe-Asia Studies* 61, no. 3 (May 2009): 505–18.

19. Frank A. Spragg, "Red Rock Wheat and Rosen Rye," *Agronomy Journal* 10 (1918): 167–71; and Frank A. Spragg, "The Spread of Rosen Rye," *Journal of Heredity* 11, no. 1 (January 1920): 42–45.

20. "John D. Rockefeller Jr. $500,000 Subscription for Jewish Farms Created Stir in Moscow," JDC Archives, Records of the New York Office of the American Jewish Joint Distribution Committee, 1921–1932, folder 530.

21. Jonathan L. Dekel-Chen, *Farming the Red Land: Jewish Agricultural Colonization and Local Soviet Power, 1924–1941* (New Haven, CT: Yale University Press, 2008), 99.

22. "Dr. Margolin, Ukraynisher idisher fihrer, zeht sakone in plan vegen idishe republik in Kriem," *Forverts*, February 21, 1924.

23. V. Bur, "Nova Palestyna," *Tryzub*, December 19, 1926; I. L-iy, "Navkruhy novoi Palestyny na Ukraini," *Tryzub*, March 7, 1926; L. L., "Istorychni pidstavy zhydivs'koi kolonizatsii v Krymu," *Tryzub*, March 14, 1926; and I. Repetenko, "Pro zhydivs'ki kolonii na Ukraini," *Tryzub*, September 18, 1927. For a critique of the paper prepared for the Schwarzbard trial see "Der 'Trizub' zetst fort zayn antisemitishe kampanie," CAHJP P10a/4/S1/31.

24. Bur, "Nova Palestyna."

25. I. Repetenko, "Pro zhydivs'ki kolonii na Ukraini," *Tryzub*, September 18, 1927.

26. Dekel-Chen, *Farming the Red Land*, 127.

27. "Many Jews in Ukraine Were Killed in Peasant Attack," JDC Archives, Records of the New York Office of the American Jewish Joint Distribution Committee, 1921–1932, folder 530.

28. On interwar Eastern Galicia see Shimon Redlich, *Together and Apart in Brzezany: Poles, Jews, and Ukrainians, 1919–1945* (Bloomington: Indiana University Press, 2002), 3; and Omer Bartov, *Anatomy of a Genocide: The Life and Death of a Town Called Buczacz* (New York: Simon & Schuster, 2018), 82–128.

29. USC Shoah Foundation Visual History Archive, Simon Feldman, interviewed April 13, 1997, 28387.

30. Jan T. Gross, *Revolution from Abroad: The Soviet Conquest of Poland's Western Ukraine and Western Belorussia*, 2nd ed. (Princeton, NJ: Princeton University Press, 2002); Grzegorz Hryciuk, "Victims 1939–1941: The Soviet Repressions in Eastern Poland," in Elazar Barkan, Elizabeth A. Cole, and Kai Struve, eds., *Shared History—Divided Memory: Jews and Others in Soviet-Occupied Poland, 1939–1941* (Leipzig: Leipziger Universitätsverlag, 2007), 173–200; and Timothy Snyder, *Black Earth: The Holocaust as History and Warning* (New York: Tim Duggan Books, 2015), 117–43.

31. Christoph Mick, *Lemberg, Lwów, L'viv, 1914–1947: Violence and Ethnicity in a Contested City* (West Lafayette, IN: Purdue University Press, 2015), 267.

32. USC Shoah Foundation Visual History Archive, Edward Spicer, interviewed March 3, 1996, 12729.

33. Dieter Pohl, *Nationalsozialistische Judenverfolgung in Ostgalizien 1941–1944: Organisation und Durchführung eines staatlichen Massenverbrechens* (Munich: Oldenbourg, 1996), 43–44.

34. Cited, with modified translation, from Joanna B. Michlic, "Anti-Polish and Pro-Soviet? Stereotyping of the Jew in Polish Historiography," in Barkan, Cole, and Struve, *Shared History—Divided Memory*, 77.

35. Citation from Christopher Mick, "Incompatible Experiences: Poles, Ukrainians and Jews in Lviv Under Soviet and German Occupation, 1939–1944," *Journal of Contemporary History* 46, no. 2 (April 2011): 344; and Mick, *Lemberg, Lwów, Lviv*, 259–78. See also Marco Carynnyk, "Foes of our Rebirth: Ukrainian Nationalist Discussions About Jews, 1929–1947," *Nationalities Papers* 39, no. 3 (May 2011): 315–52; Gross, *Revolution from Abroad*; and Alexander V. Prusin, *The Lands Between: Conflict in the East European Borderlands, 1870–1992* (Oxford: Oxford University Press, 2010), 124–48.

36. Both quotes are cited by John-Paul Himka in "The Lviv Pogrom of 1941: The Germans, Ukrainian Nationalists, and the Carnival Crowd," *Canadian Slavonic Papers/Revue canadienne des slavistes* 53, no. 2–4 (2011): 225. See also Karel Berkhoff and Marco Carynnyk, "The Organization of Ukrainian Nationalists and Its Attitude Toward Germans and Jews: Iaroslav Stets'ko's 1941 *Zhyttiepys*," *Harvard Ukrainian Studies* 23, no. 3–4 (1999): 149–84.

CHAPTER 19: THE ONSET OF THE HOLOCAUST

1. A version of Heydrich's instructions were delivered orally on June 17 before being delivered in written form on June 29. See Peter Klein, ed., *Die Einsatzgruppen in der besetzten Sowjetunion, 1941/42: die Tätigkeits-und Lageberichte des Chefs der Sicherheitspolizei und des SD* (Berlin: Edition Hentrich, 1997), 319; and Kai Struve, *Deutsche Herrschaft, ukrainischer Nationalismus, antijüdische Gewalt. Der Sommer 1941 in der Westukraine* (Oldenbourg: De Gruyter, 2015), 130–33. Rosenberg's words were recorded by Georg Leibbrandt and are cited in Christoph Dieckmann, "Lithuania in Summer 1941: The German Invasion and the Kaunas Pogrom," in Elazar Barkan, Elizabeth A. Cole, and Kai Struve, eds., *Shared History—Divided Memory: Jews and Others in Soviet-Occupied Poland, 1939–1941* (Leipzig: Leipziger Universitätsverlag, 2007), 366.

2. Marco Carynnyk, "Foes of our Rebirth: Ukrainian Nationalist Discussions about Jews, 1929–1947," *Nationalities Papers* 39, no. 3 (May 2011): 328–44.

3. Cited in Christoph Mick, *Lemberg, Lwów, L'viv, 1914–1947: Violence and Ethnicity in a Contested City* (West Lafayette, IN: Purdue University Press, 2015), 289.

4. Cited in Tarik Cyril Amar, *The Paradox of Ukrainian Lviv: A Borderland City Between Stalinists, Nazis, and Nationalists* (Ithaca: Cornell University Press, 2015), 100.

5. See Karel Berkhoff and Marco Carynnyk, "The Organization of Ukrainian Nationalists and Its Attitude Toward Germans and Jews: Iaroslav Stets'ko's 1941 *Zhyttiepys*," *Harvard Ukrainian Studies* 23, no. 3–4 (1999):152.

6. Mick, *Lemberg, Lwów, L'viv*, 291.

7. John-Paul Himka in "The Lviv Pogrom of 1941: The Germans, Ukrainian Nationalists, and the Carnival Crowd," *Canadian Slavonic Papers/Revue canadienne des slavistes* 53, no. 2–4 (2011): 209–243. See also Eliakhu Iones, *Evrei L'vova v gody vtoroi mirovoi voiny i katastrofy evropeiskogo evreistva* (Moscow: Rossiiskaia biblioteka kholokosta, 1999).

8. Mick, *Lemberg, Lwów, L'viv*, 292.

9. Kai Struve, "Komanda osobogo naznacheniia 'L'vov', ukrainskaia militsiia i 'Dni Petliury' 25 i 26 iulia 1941 g," *Probelmy istorii holokostu* 6 (2013): 102–24.

10. Cited in Mick, *Lemberg, Lwów, L'viv*, 291.

11. USC Shoah Foundation Visual History Archive, Edward Spicer, interviewed March 3, 1996, 12729. See also Himka, "The Lviv Pogrom of 1941," 220.

12. *Encyclopedia of Camps and Ghettos*, vol. 2, part A, 802. Although the Einsatzgruppen had been deployed against civilians in German-occupied Poland since 1939, their role was vastly expanded with the invasion of the Soviet Union. For the Einsatzgruppen in Poland see Jürgen Matthäus, Jochen Böhler, and Klaus-Michael Mallmann, *War, Pacification, and Mass Murder, 1939: The Einsatzgruppen in Poland* (Lanham, MD: Rowman & Littlefield, 2014).

13. David Kahane, *Lvov Ghetto Diary* (Amherst: University of Massachusetts Press, 1990), 12–13.

14. Struve, "Komanda," 102–24.

15. Kahane, *Lvov Ghetto Diary*, 26.

16. Kahane, *Lvov Ghetto Diary*, 37.

17. Kahane, *Lvov Ghetto Diary*, 36.

18. Amar, *The Paradox of Ukrainian Lviv*, 99.

19. Cited in Stanislovas Stasiulis, "The Holocaust in Lithuania: The Key Characteristics of Its History, and the Key Issues in Historiography and Cultural Memory," *East European Politics and Societies and Cultures* 34, no. 1 (February 2020): 266. See also Christoph Dieckmann, "Lithuania in Summer 1941: The German Invasion and the Kaunas Pogrom," in Barkan, Cole, and Struve, eds., *Shared History—Divided Memory* 355–85; and Christoph Dieckmann, *Deutsche Besatzungspolitik in Litauen 1941–1944* (Göttingen: Wallstein, 2011).

20. See, for instance, anonymous members of the Kovno Jewish Ghetto Police, *The Clandestine History of the Kovno Jewish Ghetto Police*, trans. and ed. Samuel Schalkowsky (Bloomington: Indiana University Press, 2014), 65–70.

21. Jan T. Gross, *Neighbors: The Destruction of the Jewish Community in Jedwabne, Poland* (Princeton, NJ: Princeton University Press, 2001).
22. Andrzej Żbikowski, "Pogroms in Northeastern Poland—Spontaneous Reactions and German Instigations," in Barkan, Cole, and Struve, eds., *Shared History—Divided Memory*, 315–54; Jeffrey S. Kopstein and Jason Wittenberg, *Intimate Violence: Anti-Jewish Pogroms on the Eve of the Holocaust* (Ithaca: Cornell University Press, 2015), 57–83; and Leopold Rein, "Local Collaboration in the Execution of the 'Final Solution' in Nazi-Occupied Belorussia," *Holocaust and Genocide Studies* 20, no. 3 (Winter 2006): 381–409.
23. Wendy Lower, "Pogroms, Mob Violence and Genocide in Western Ukraine, Summer 1941: Varied Histories, Explanations and Comparison," *Journal of Genocide Research* 13, no. 3 (2011): 217–46; Kopstein and Wittenberg, *Intimate Violence*, 84–113; Dieter Pohl, "Anti-Jewish Pogroms in Western Ukraine: A Research Agenda," in Barkan, Cole, and Struve, eds., *Shared History—Divided Memory*, 305–13; Dieter Pohl, *Die Herrschaft der Wehrmacht: Deutsche Militärbesatzung und einheimische Bevölkerung in der Sowjetunion 1941–1944* (Munich: Oldenbourg, 2008); Dieter Pohl, *Nationalsozialistische Judenverfolgung in Ostgalizien 1941–1944: Organisation und Durchführung eines staatlichen Massenverbrechens* (Munich: Oldenbourg, 1996), 54–74; and Struve, *Deutsche Herrschaft, ukrainischer Nationalismus, antijüdische Gewalt*.Estimates of the total Jewish death toll in Eastern Galicia and Volhynia during the first weeks of the war range between 12,000 and 35,000. See Kai Struve, "Rites of Violence? The Pogroms of Summer 1941," in *Polin: Studies in Polish Jewry* 24 (2012): 257–74. The United States Holocaust Memorial Museum's *Encyclopedia of Camps and Ghettos* concludes that "more than 20,000 Jews were murdered" in Eastern Galicia throughout the summer. See vol. 2, part A, 744.
24. Wendy Lower, *The Diary of Samuel Golfard and the Holocaust in Galicia* (Lanham, MD: AltaMira Press, 2011), 42.
25. Omer Bartov, *Anatomy of a Genocide: The Life and Death of a Town Called Buczacz* (New York: Simon & Schuster, 2018), 160–67.
26. Kopstein and Wittenberg, *Intimate Violence*, 102–3; and *Encyclopedia of Camps and Ghettos*, vol. 2, part A, 849–50.
27. Lower, "Pogroms, Mob Violence and Genocide in Western Ukraine, Summer 1941," 222; Struve, *Deutsche Herrschaft*, 465–71.
28. Operational Situation Report 13, July 5, 1941, Klaus-Michael Mallmann et al., eds., *Die "Ereignismeldungen UdSSR" 1941* (Darmstadt: WBG, 2011), 82.
29. Operational Situation Report 24, July 16, 1941, Mallmann et al., *Die "Ereignismeldungen UdSSR" 1941*, 132.
30. USC Shoah Foundation Visual History Archive, Simon Feldman, interviewed April 13, 1997, 28387.
31. Lower, "Pogroms, Mob Violence and Genocide in Western Ukraine, Summer 1941," 226.

32. Gabriel N. Finder and Alexander V. Prusin, "Collaboration in Eastern Galicia: The Ukrainian Police and the Holocaust," *East European Jewish Affairs* 34 (Winter 2004): 95–118; Martin Dean, "The German *Gendarmerie*, the Ukrainian *Schutzmannschaft* and the 'Second Wave' of Jewish Killings in Occupied Ukraine: German Policing at the Local Level in the Zhitomir Region, 1941–1944," *German History* 14, no. 2 (1996): 168–92; Martin Dean, *Collaboration in the Holocaust: Crimes of the Local Police in Belorussia and Ukraine, 1941–44* (New York: St. Martin's Press, 2000); and Yuri Radchenko, "'We Emptied Our Magazines into Them': The Ukrainian Auxiliary Police and the Holocaust in Generalbezirk Charkow, 1941–1943," *Yad Vashem Studies* 41 (2013): 63–98.

33. Testimony of Sergei Stepanovich Sukov, Lutsk, December 4, 1945, DA, CBU case N 23017, vol. 28, 68. See also Jared McBride, "'A Sea of Blood and Tears': Ethnic Diversity and Mass Violence in Nazi-Occupied Volhynia, Ukraine, 1941–1944" (PhD diss., University of California–Los Angeles, 2014), 217–18.

34. "Lyashchenko, Fedir Kyrylovych," DA, CBU, case N 26693, vol. 1, 122.

35. "Tomasevich, Mikhail Vasil'evich," DA, CBU, case N 26693, vol. 1, 132.

36. "Terpilo, Andry Saveliovych," DA, CBU, case N 59681.

37. "Grabar, Stepan Karlovich," DA, CBU, case N 1910 (1296).

38. McBride, "'A Sea of Blood and Tears,'" 220–40.

39. USC Shoah Foundation Visual History Archive, Liusia Blekhman, interviewed May 17, 1998, 44315.

40. USC Shoah Foundation Visual History Archive, David Bershtin, interviewed December 20, 1996, 25286.

41. Operational Situation Report 37, July 29, 1941, Mallmann et al., *Die "Ereignismeldungen UdSSR" 1941*, 201.

42. Operational Situation Report 40, August 1, 1941, Mallmann et al., *Die "Ereignismeldungen UdSSR" 1941*, 218.

43. *Encyclopedia of Camps and Ghettos*, vol. 2, part B, 1579.

44. *Encyclopedia of Camps and Ghettos*, vol. 2, part B, 1538.

45. USC Shoah Foundation Visual History Archive, Boris Kazak, interviewed August 5, 1996, 18181.

46. *Encyclopedia of Camps and Ghettos*, vol. 2, part B, 1593–94.

47. Amar, *The Paradox of Ukrainian Lviv*, 95; Himka, "The Lviv Pogrom of 1941," 209–43; and Christopher Mick, "Incompatible Experiences: Poles, Ukrainians and Jews in Lviv Under Soviet and German Occupation, 1939–1944," *Journal of Contemporary History* 46, no. 2 (April 2011): 336–63.

48. Waitman Wade Beorn, *Marching into Darkness: The Wehrmacht and the Holocaust in Belarus* (Cambridge, MA: Harvard University Press, 2014), 99; and Christopher R. Browning and Jürgen Matthäus, *The Origins of the Final Solution: The Evolution of Nazi Jewish Policy,*

September 1939–March 1942 (Lincoln: University of Nebraska Press, 2004), 310–14.

49. Cited in Yitzhak Arad, *The Holocaust in the Soviet Union* (Lincoln: University of Nebraska Press, 2009), 133.

50. *"The Good Old Days": The Holocaust as Seen by Its Perpetrators and Bystanders,* 113–15. The incident is also described in Operation Situation Report 47, August 9, 1941, and Operation Situation Report 58, August 20, 1941, Mallmann et al., *Die "Ereignismeldungen UdSSR" 1941,* 265–66 and 319–22.

51. Ernst Klee, Willi Dressen, Volker Riess, eds., *"The Good Old Days": The Holocaust as Seen by Its Perpetrators and Bystanders,* trans. Deborah Burnstone (Old Saybrook, CT: Konecky & Konecky, 1991), 114. For more on the Nazi occupation of Zhytomyr see Wendy Lower, *Nazi Empire-Building and the Holocaust in Ukraine* (Chapel Hill: University of North Carolina Press, 2005).

52. *Encyclopedia of Camps and Ghettos,* vol. 2, part B, 1563.

53. *Encyclopedia of Camps and Ghettos,* vol. 2, part B, 1553–1554. On Ovruch see Yahad in Unum, https://yahadmap.org/#village/ovruch-owrucz-ovrutch-owrutsch-zhytomyr-ukraine.760.

54. https://yahadmap.org/#village/slovechne-slovechno-slaveshna-claweczno-zhytomyr-ukraine.758.

55. *"The Good Old Days",* 139–40.

56. *"The Good Old Days",* 142.

57. *"The Good Old Days",* 154.

58. "Yatsenko, Ivan Aleksandrovich," DA, CBU, case N 26693, vol. 1, 136.

59. "Tomasevich, Mikhail Vasil'evich," DA, CBU, case N 26693, vol. 1, 132.

60. Figures from Alexander Kruglov, "Jewish Losses in Ukraine, 1941–1944," in Ray Brandon and Wendy Lower, eds., *The Shoah in Ukraine: History, Testimony, Memorialization,* (Bloomington: Indiana University Press, 2008), 292–90.

61. USC Shoah Foundation Visual History Archive, Liusia Blekhman, interviewed May 17, 1998, 44315.

62. *Encyclopedia of Camps and Ghettos,* vol. 2, part B, 1563.

63. *Encyclopedia of Camps and Ghettos,* vol. 2, part B, 1580; and Operational Situation Report 106, October 7, 1941, Mallmann et al., *Die "Ereignismeldungen UdSSR" 1941,* 642–43.

64. *Encyclopedia of Camps and Ghettos,* vol. 2, part B, 1539; and https://yahadmap.org/#village/korostyshiv-korostyshev-zhytomyr-ukraine.131.

65. "Protokol isledovanie," GARF 7021/60/310/76.

66. USC Shoah Foundation Visual History Archive, Liusia Blekhman, interviewed May 17, 1998, 44315. The timing is unclear in the interview, but she seems to be referring to the November 4 massacre.

67. Cited in Vladyslav Hrynevych and Paul Robert Magocsi, *Babyn Yar: History and Memory* (Kyiv: Dukh i litera, 2016), 83.
68. Cited in Hrynevych and Magocsi, *Babyn Yar: History and Memory*, 85.
69. Operation Situation Report 106, October 7, 1941, Mallmann et al., *Die "Ereignismeldungen UdSSR" 1941*, 640–43.

ACKNOWLEDGMENTS

The idea for this book began when I was a researcher with the Archives of Historical and Ethnographic Yiddish Memories (AHEYM), which conducted oral history and linguistic interviews with elderly Yiddish speakers in Ukraine. I was struck at the time by the cataclysmic impact the pogroms of 1918–1921 had in shaping many of their lives, and by the similarities in how they spoke about the pogroms and how they remembered the beginnings of the Holocaust. That project launched in 2002, about twenty years ago. It is the same amount of time that elapsed between the pogroms and the Holocaust, driving home for me the close proximity between those two events and the many ways in which they are related. It was in 2007 that I met Naum Gaiviker, who was a boy of six when his father was taken away during a pogrom in Proskuriv. Two years later, I met ninety-one-year-old Nisen Yurkovetsky, who showed me the scar where, during the pogroms of 1919, the bullet that killed his mother had grazed him as she held him in her arms. The infant Yurkovetsky was rescued when a Polish priest noticed some movement in the mass grave that held the rest of his family. I am grateful to all those who shared with me the stories that gave the impetus for this book, and to my colleague Dov-Ber Kerler and the rest of our research team in Ukraine, Lithuania, Poland, Israel, and Germany.

I started writing this book as a fellow at the Frankel Institute for Advanced Judaic Studies at the University of Michigan, where, thanks to the leadership of Deborah Dash Moore and Misha Krutikov, I was able to benefit from the invaluable advice of a stellar cohort of fellows. I was subsequently appointed director of the institute myself, and gained immeasurable knowledge from the sixty-three fellows who have been in residence during my six-year tenure as director. At the University of Michigan, I have also had the honor to work with a group of scholars who inspire me every day. In addition to Deborah and Misha, I have particularly drawn upon the support and expertise of Joshua Cole, Geoff Eley, Todd Endelman, Zvi Gitelman, Karla Goldman, Val Kivelson, Julian Levinson, Olga Maiorova, Devi Mays, Anita Norich, Doug Northrop, Shachar Pinsker, Scott Spector, Ron Suny, and Geneviève Zubrzycki.

I worked with several research assistants throughout this project, and thank them for all their help. Michael Martin has worked with me from the beginning and contributed in many important ways. J. D. Arden, Charles Bonds, Maria Eitinguina, Liliya Kulik, Anna Moshkovich, Ilya Slavutskyi, and Sophie Wunderlich also helped at various stages. As always, I am grateful to the staff of the Frankel Center and the Department of History at the University of Michigan for all their assistance on a daily basis.

Over the years, I had the opportunity to present my work in several academic workshops and conferences, where I have been offered sound advice and constructive critique. I thank the organizers and participants of these events at Yale University, Harvard University, Georgetown University, Taras Shevchenko University, the University of Michigan, the Kennan Institute, the YIVO Institute, the Ukrainian Jewish Encounter, the Association for Jewish Studies, the Center for Jewish History, and the Association for Slavic, East European, and Eurasian Studies.

Maya Balakirsky Katz, Elissa Bemporad, Michael Brenner, Zvi Gitelman, Misha Krutikov, Hiroaki Kuromiya, Natalya Lazar, Harriet Murav, Serhii Plokhii, Anna Reid, Timothy Snyder, Ron Suny, and Serhy Yekelchyk all read either complete drafts of the manuscript or substantial portions of it and offered useful advice. Other colleagues and friends who have been helpful along the way include Irina Astashkevich, Eugene Avrutin, Matt Chosid, John Efron, David Fishman, Sarah Garibova, Matthias Lehmann, James Loeffler, Brendan McGeever, Matt Pauly, Simon Rabinovitch, Mark Roseman, Andrii Rukkas, Joshua Shanes, and Anna Shternshis. In addition, at the United States Holocaust Memorial Museum's Mandel Center for Advanced Holocaust Studies, where I am a member of the Academic Advisory Committee, Vadim Altskan, Elana Jakel, Emil Kerenji, Natalya Lazar, and Jürgen Matthäus helped me access documents and provided advice and support.

Don Fehr helped shape the book proposal and brought me to Metropolitan Books. There I have had the privilege to work with Sara Bershtel, who always asks the most difficult and probing questions and has greatly improved my writing. I am thankful as well to Grigory Tovbis and everybody else at Metropolitan. Jonathan Wyss and Kelly Sandefer at Beehive Mapping were patient and responsive in working with me on designing the maps. The National Endowment for the Humanities' Public Scholars Program provided valuable support.

Finally, I would like to thank my family for their love and support: Rebecca, Naomi, and Mae; my parents, Otto and Marilyn; my siblings, Daniel and Shira; and all my aunts, uncles, cousins, nieces, nephews, and in-laws. I dedicate this book to the memory of my uncle, Louis Greenspan, whose humor and love of intellectual exchange had a way of bringing out the best in everyone.

INDEX

Entries in italics refer to maps and illustrations.

ABOUT THE AUTHOR

JEFFREY VEIDLINGER is a professor of history and Judaic studies at the University of Michigan. His books, which include *The Moscow State Yiddish Theater* and *In the Shadow of the Shtetl*, have won a National Jewish Book Award, the Barnard Hewitt Award for Outstanding Research in Theatre History, two Canadian Jewish Book Awards, and the J. I. Segal Award. He lives in Ann Arbor, Michigan.